T0224844

Pro Spring MVC with WebFlux

Web Development in Spring Framework 5 and Spring Boot 2

Second Edition

Marten Deinum
Iuliana Cosmina

Apress®

Pro Spring MVC with WebFlux: Web Development in Spring Framework 5 and Spring Boot 2

Marten Deinum
MEPPEL, Drenthe, The Netherlands

Iuliana Cosmina
EDINBURGH, UK

ISBN-13 (pbk): 978-1-4842-5665-7
https://doi.org/10.1007/978-1-4842-5666-4

ISBN-13 (electronic): 978-1-4842-5666-4

Managing Director, Apress Media LLC: Welmoed Spahr
Acquisitions Editor: Steve Anglin
Development Editor: Matthew Moodie
Coordinating Editor: Mark Powers

Cover designed by eStudioCalamar

Cover image by rawpixel (www.rawpixel.com)

Distributed to the book trade worldwide by Apress Media, LLC, 1 New York Plaza, New York, NY 10004, U.S.A. Phone 1-800-SPRINGER, fax (201) 348-4505, e-mail orders-ny@springer-sbm.com, or visit www. springeronline.com. Apress Media, LLC is a California LLC and the sole member (owner) is Springer Science + Business Media Finance Inc (SSBM Finance Inc). SSBM Finance Inc is a **Delaware** corporation.

For information on translations, please e-mail booktranslations@springernature.com; for reprint, paperback, or audio rights, please email bookpermissions@springernature.com.

Apress titles may be purchased in bulk for academic, corporate, or promotional use. eBook versions and licenses are also available for most titles. For more information, reference our Print and eBook Bulk Sales web page at http://www.apress.com/bulk-sales.

Any source code or other supplementary material referenced by the author in this book is available to readers on GitHub via the book's product page, located at www.apress.com/9781484256657. For more detailed information, please visit http://www.apress.com/source-code.

Printed on acid-free paper

*To all of you that have bought other books that I worked on,
this book is dedicated to you.*

Thank you for trusting me.

— Iuliana Cosmina

Table of Contents

About the Authors

Marten Deinum is a submitter on the open source Spring Framework project. He is also a Java/software consultant working for Conspect. He has developed and architected software, primarily in Java, for small and large companies. He is an enthusiastic open source user and a longtime fan, user, and advocate of the Spring Framework. His work experience includes being a software engineer, development lead, coach, and a Java and Spring trainer. When not working on software, he can be found near or in the water scuba diving or teaching scuba diving.

Iuliana Cosmina is currently a software engineer for Cloudsoft in Edinburgh, Scotland. She has been writing Java code since 2002. She has contributed to various types of applications, including experimental search engines, ERPs, track and trace, and banking. During her career, she has been a teacher, a team leader, a software architect, a DevOps professional, and a software manager. She is a Spring Certified Professional, as defined by Pivotal, the makers of Spring Framework, Boot, and other tools, and considers Spring the best Java framework to work with.

When she is not programming, she spends her time reading, blogging, learning to play piano, traveling, hiking, or biking.

About the Technical Reviewer

Manuel Jordan Elera is an autodidactic developer and researcher who enjoys learning new technologies for his own experiments and creating new integrations. Manuel won the Springy Award—Community Champion and Spring Champion 2013. In his free time, he reads the Bible and composes music on his guitar. Manuel is known as dr_pompeii. He has tech-reviewed numerous books for Apress, including *Pro Spring Boot 2* (2019), *Rapid Java Persistence and Microservices* (2019), *Java Language Features* (2018), *Spring Boot 2 Recipes* (2018), and *Java APIs, Extensions, and Libraries* (2018). You can read his 13 detailed tutorials about Spring technologies, or contact him, through his blog at www.manueljordanelera.blogspot.com, and follow him on his Twitter account, @dr_pompeii.

Acknowledgments

I would like to say thank you to Mark Powers. He has been with me since the time I began collaborating with Apress, and I consider him my project manager at Apress. When writing a book, he is the one that I agree schedules and deadlines with and then say sorry to when I am unable to deliver as agreed. He has been supportive and understanding and one of the people I respect the most. Most of my books, including this one, happened because he was there to make sure I didn't postpone the work too long because of writer's block or my imposter syndrome.

Additionally, a special thanks to Manuel Jordan, the reviewer for all my books but one—and I missed him a lot when working on that one. I missed his patience, his attention to detail, and his suggestions on what else should be in a book to be more valuable. I was happy when I was told he would be joining the team for this book as a reviewer.

A very heartfelt thanks to Mihaela Filipiuc, who has been my most supportive remote friend, even while she was going through a tough time. She has provided the motivational words that I needed to keep my spirits up and push through sleepless nights to make this book happen.

Another heartfelt thanks to my dear friend Mihai Fat for all the inspiring technical chats.

An additional thanks to my team at Cloudsoft for being patient with me when I was working while sleep deprived and for all the moral support during these tough times. Having a full-time job and writing a book during a pandemic that has kept me away from my friends and family would have been way more difficult without them. Thank *you* for being the best environment in which I can continue to learn and grow as a software developer.

— Iuliana Cosmina

CHAPTER 1

Setting up a Local Development Environment

Released in October 2002 as an open source framework and inversion of control (IoC) container developed using Java, Spring was built for the Java platform. It has transformed from a small collection of libraries into a huge collection of full-blown projects designed to simplify development even when the solution is complex.

This book journeys from a classic web application packaged as a jar and deployed to an application server to an application composed of a set of microservices that are easily deployed in a cloud environment, each of them on its own VM or container.

It all starts with a set of tools that need to be installed before the developer can write and run code.

🛈 If you know how to use SDKMAN,[1] you can skip the next two sections that explain how to install the Java SDK and Gradle. If you do not know how to use SDKMAN or never knew it existed, give it a try; it is a tool for managing parallel versions of multiple SDKs. If you have other projects using different versions of Java and Gradle locally, this tool helps you switch between them without a fuss.

---

[1] https://sdkman.io/

© Marten Deinum and Iuliana Cosmina 2021
M. Deinum and I. Cosmina, *Pro Spring MVC with WebFlux*, https://doi.org/10.1007/978-1-4842-5666-4_1

Install the Java SDK

Since Spring is a Java framework to write and run Spring applications, you need to install the Java SDK. This project was written and built with **JDK 14**. To install JDK 14, download the JDK matching your operating system from www.oracle.com/java/ and install it. So, if you are building an application and intend to use it for financial gain, you might want to look at Oracle licensing or use an open source JDK.[2]

Figure 1-1. *The Java logo[3]*

 We recommend that you set the JAVA_HOME environment variable to point to the directory where Java 14 was installed (the directory in which the JDK was unpacked) and add $JAVA_HOME/bin (%JAVA_HOME%\bin for Windows users) to the general path of the system. The reason behind this is to ensure any other development application written in Java use this version of Java and prevent strange incompatibility errors during development. If you want to run the build from a terminal, you are certain that the expected version of Java is used.

Restart the terminal and verify that the version of Java the operating system sees is the one that you installed by opening a terminal (the Command prompt in Windows or any type of terminal installed on macOS and Linux) and type the following.

```
> java -version  # to check the runtime
```

And then the following.

```
> javac -version # to check the compiler
```

---

[2]https://adoptopenjdk.net/
[3]Image source: https://www.programmableweb.com

You should see an output similar to the following.

```
>  java -version
java version "14.0.2" 2020-07-14
Java(TM) SE Runtime Environment (build 14.0.2+12-46)
Java HotSpot(TM) 64-Bit Server VM (build 14.0.2+12-46, mixed mode, sharing)

>  javac -version
javac 14.0.2
```

Install Gradle

Gradle is an open source build automation tool designed to be flexible enough to build almost any type of software. It uses Groovy in its configuration files, which makes it customizable. The project attached to this book was successfully built with **Gradle 6.x**.

Figure 1-2. *The Gradle logo[4]*

The sources attached to this book can be compiled and executed using the Gradle Wrapper, which is a batch script on Windows and a shell script on other operating systems.

When you start a Gradle build via the wrapper, Gradle is automatically downloaded inside your project to run the build; thus, you do not need to explicitly install it on your system. The recommended editor for development introduced next knows how to build code using Gradle Wrapper. Instructions on how to use the Gradle Wrapper are available in the public documentation at `www.gradle.org/docs/current/userguide/gradle_wrapper.html`.

A recommended practice is to keep the code and build tools separately. If you decide to install Gradle on your system, you can download the binaries from `www.gradle.org`, unpack it and copy the contents to the hard drive. (Or, if you are curious, you can download the full package containing binaries, sources, and documentation.) Create a `GRADLE_HOME`

---

[4]Image source: `https://www.gradle.org`

environment variable and point it to the location where you unpacked Gradle. Also, add $GRADLE_HOME/bin (%GRADLE_HOME%\bin for Windows users) to the system's general path so that you can build the project in a terminal.

Gradle was chosen as a build tool for this book's sources because of the easy setup, small configuration files, flexibility in defining execution tasks, and the Spring team currently uses it to build all Spring projects.

To verify that the operating system sees the Gradle version that you just installed, open a terminal (the Command prompt in Windows, and any type of terminal installed on macOS and Linux) and type

```
gradle -version
```

You should see something similar to the following.

```
gradle -version

------------------------------------------------------------
Gradle 6.7
------------------------------------------------------------

Build time:   2020-08-04 22:01:06 UTC
Revision:     00a2948da9ea69c523b6b094331593e6be6d92bc

Kotlin:       1.3.72
Groovy:       2.5.12
Ant:          Apache Ant(TM) version 1.10.8 compiled on May 10 2020
JVM:          14.0.2 (Oracle Corporation 14.0.2+12-46)
OS:           Mac OS X 10.15.6 x86_64
```

Running this command also verifies that Gradle is using the intended JDK version.

Install Apache Tomcat

Web applications are meant to be hosted by an application server unless they are built using Spring Boot, in which case it is more practical to rely on an embedded server. Apache Tomcat[5] is an open source implementation of the Java Servlet, JavaServer Pages, Java Expression Language, and WebSocket technologies.

Figure 1-3. *The Apache Tomcat logo[6]*

The Spring MVC projects of this book were tested in Apache Tomcat 9.x. To install Apache Tomcat, go to the official site and get the version matching your operating system. Unpack it in a familiar location. On Unix-based systems, you might be able to install it using a package manager. If you install it manually, remember to go to the `bin` directory and make all files executable.

---

[5]`https://tomcat.apache.org/`
[6]Image source: `https://tomcat.apache.org`

Recommended IDE

The IDE that we recommend you use with the code in this book is IntelliJ IDEA. It is the most intelligent Java IDE.

Figure 1-4. *The IntelliJ IDEA logo[7]*

IntelliJ IDEA offers outstanding framework-specific coding assistance and productivity-boosting features for Java EE and Spring also includes very good support for Gradle. It is the perfect choice to help you focus on learning Spring (and not how to use an IDE). It can be downloaded from the JetBrains official site (`www.jetbrains.com/idea/`). It is also light on your operating system and easy to use.

IntelliJ IDEA also integrates well with Apache Tomcat, which allows you to deploy your projects to start and stop the server from the editor.

And now that the tools have been discussed, let's talk about the project.

The Bookstore Project

The project containing the sources for this book is organized as a multi-module Gradle Project. Each chapter has one or more corresponding projects that you can easily recognize because they are prefixed with the chapter number. Table 1-1 lists these projects and provides a short description for each.

---

[7]Image source: `https://www.jetbrains.com/idea/`

Table 1-1. *Bookstore Project Modules*

Chapter	Project Name	Description
–	bookstore-mvc-shared	Entity and utility classes used by Spring MVC projects
–	bookstore-shared	Entity and utility classes used by Spring Boot projects
1	chapter1-bookstore	A simple Spring Boot Web MVC project with typical web structure (static resources in the `webapp` directory)
1	chapter1-mvc-bookstore	A simple Spring MVC project.
2	chapter2-bookstore	A simple Spring Boot Web MVC project with typical Boot structure (static resources in the `resources/static` directory)
2	chapter2-sample	A simple project with non-web samples for Chapter 2
5	chapter5-bookstore	The Bookstore Spring Boot MVC project, using Thymeleaf views
6	chapter6-bookstore	The Bookstore Spring Boot MVC project, using Apache Tiles views
7	chapter7-bookstore	The Bookstore Spring Boot MVC project with support for upload files
8	chapter8-bookstore	The Bookstore Spring Boot MVC project with support for various view types
9	chapter9-1-bookstore-no-boot	The Bookstore Spring WebFlux project deployed on Apache Tomcat (uses reactive controllers)
9	chapter9-2-bookstore	The Bookstore Spring Boot WebFlux project (uses reactive controllers)
9	chapter9-3-bookstore	The Bookstore Spring Boot WebFlux project (uses functional endpoints)
10	chapter10-1-bookstore	The Bookstore Spring Boot WebFlux project supporting case-insensitive URIs and internationalization via a web filter (the most elegant solution)
10	chapter10-2-bookstore	The Bookstore Spring Boot WebFlux project supporting validation

(*continued*)

Table 1-1. (*continued*)

Chapter	Project Name	Description
10	chapter10-3-bookstore	The Bookstore Spring Boot WebFlux project supporting case-insensitive URIs and internationalization via `LocaleContextResolver`
11	chapter11-1-bookstore	The Bookstore Spring Boot MVC project with WebSocket chat
11	chapter11-2-bookstore	The Bookstore Spring Boot WebFlux project with Tech News emitted by a reactive stream over WebSocket
11	chapter11-3-client-bookstore	RSocket client project
11	chapter11-3-server-bookstore	RSocket server project
11	chapter11-4-server-bookstore	The Bookstore Spring Boot WebFlux project using reactive security
12	chapter12-bookstore	The Bookstore Spring Boot MVC project using Spring Security
12	chapter12-mvc-bookstore	The Bookstore Spring MVC project using Spring Security
13	chapter13-account-service	Microservice providing the Reactive Account API
13	chapter13-book-service	Microservice providing the Reactive Book API
13	chapter13-discovery-service	Microservice discovering and registering the other microservices
13	chapter13-newreleases-service	Microservice providing a single reactive endpoint emitting random `Book` instances
13	chapter13-presentation-service	Microservice with a Thymeleaf web interface interacting with the other interface
13	chapter13-technews-service	Microservice providing a single reactive endpoint emitting random `String` instances representing tech news

Projects with names that contain -mvc- and chapter9-1-bookstore-no-boot are compiled and packed as a *.war can be run in Apache Tomcat. Except for chapter2-sample, all the other projects are built using Spring Boot and can be run by executing their main class. The chapter2-sample project has multiple main classes that you can run to test a specific scenario.

Building the Project

Once you've installed the recommended tools, the next step is getting the project sources from GitHub.

ⓘ   The GitHub project page is at https://github.com/Apress/spring-mvc-and-webflux.

You can download the repo page sources, clone the project using IntelliJ IDEA, or clone it using Git in the terminal. You can use HTTPS or Git protocol—whatever feels familiar and easy.

You can build the project using IntelliJ IDEA, but if you are opening it for the first time, it takes a while to figure out the project structure and index the files. We recommend that you open a terminal and build the project by executing the command in Listing 1-1. The output should be similar to that one, and it must certainly contain BUILD SUCCESSFUL.

Listing 1-1. Building the Project for This Book

```
> gradle clean build
...
BUILD SUCCESSFUL in 3m 1s
150 actionable tasks: 148 executed, 2 up-to-date
```

Once the project builds in the terminal, you can verify that you have the right project and the right tools. It is now time to open it in IntelliJ IDEA.

The first thing you notice is that IntelliJ IDEA is trying to decide the Gradle and the JDK versions. And it doesn't always work, especially if you have multiple versions of each on your system. In the right corner, you might see notifications like the one in Figure 1-5.

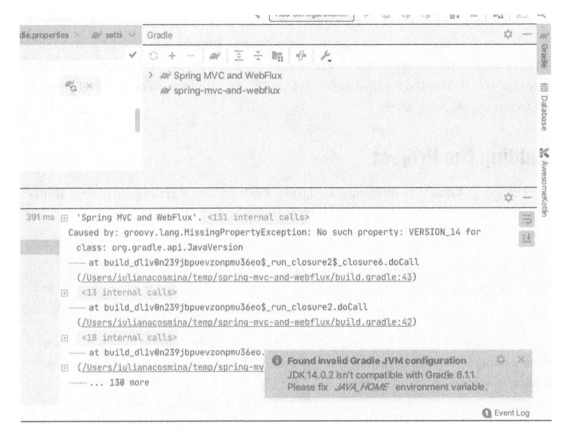

Figure 1-5. *IntelliJ IDEA trying to infer Gradle and JDK version*

To fix that, you must do the following.

1. First, if you want to use Gradle Wrapper, skip this step. Otherwise, go to the Gradle view, click the little wrench button (the one labeled Build Tool Settings), and a window appears to allow you to choose the Gradle version. If you have Gradle installed on your system, and the GRADLE_HOME environment variable is set up, IntelliJ IDEA finds it. Still, it does not use it if the project contains a Gradle Wrapper configuration. To use Gradle on your system, choose **Specified location** in the section of the window marked in Figure 1-6.

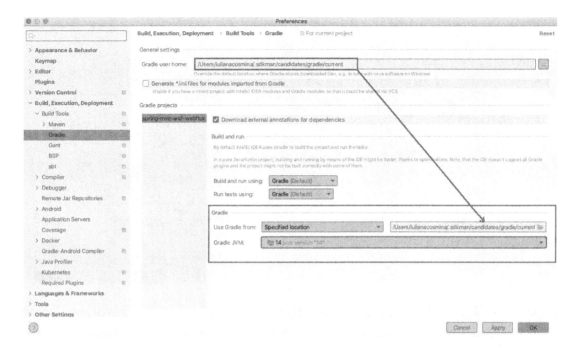

Figure 1-6. *IntelliJ IDEA Gradle and Gradle JVM setup*

And, while you're at it, make sure the Gradle JVM is set to JDK 14 as well.

2. In the IntelliJ IDEA main menu, select **File > Project structure…**
    . The Project Structure window allows you to configure the project
    SDK and the project language level. Make sure it is JDK 14 for
    both, as depicted in Figure 1-7.

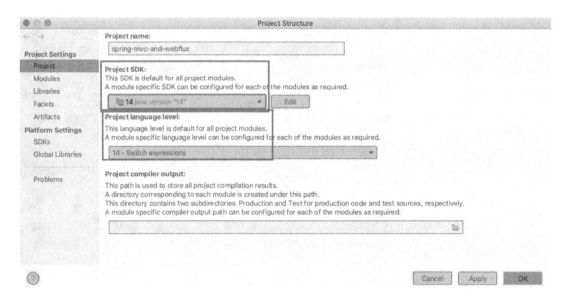

Figure 1-7. *IntelliJ IDEA Project JDK setup*

If all goes well, IntelliJ IDEA uses Gradle and JDK to build your project and execute tests. If you want to build your project in IntelliJ IDEA, use the Gradle View. When the project is loaded correctly, all modules should be listed together with a set of Gradle tasks grouped by their purpose. Under the **build** group, a task named **build** is the equivalent of the Gradle command in Listing 1-1. Figure 1-8 shows a successful Gradle build run in IntelliJ IDEA.

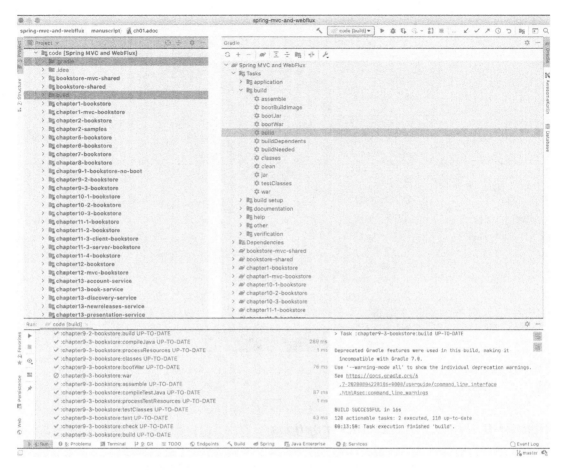

Figure 1-8. *IntelliJ IDEA successful Gradle build*

Running the Projects

The projects that are not built using Spring Boot need to be deployed to an Apache
Tomcat server. After a successful Gradle build, the artifacts should be already generated
for all projects. To deploy your project on your local Apache server, you must do the
following.

1. Click the list of project launchers in the upper-right corner.

2. Select **Edit Configurations…**.

3. In the Edit Configurations window, select the type of launcher that
   you want to create.

4. In the upper-left corner, click the **+** button. In the list of launcher
   types, select **Tomcat Server > Local** (see Figure 1-9).

13

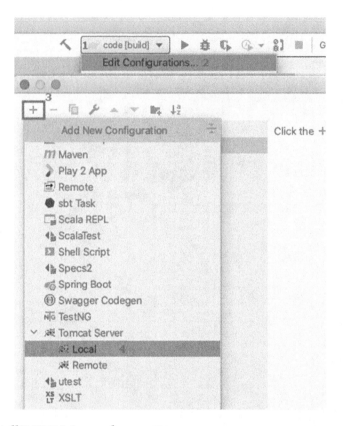

Figure 1-9. *IntelliJ IDEA Launcher options*

5. In the Run/Debug Configurations window, a form needs to be
    populated with the location of the Apache server and the project
    to deploy. First, name the configuration. Choose a name related to
    your project.

6. Click the **Configure** button.

7. Select your Apache Tomcat server directory.

8. Click the **OK** button.

9. Click the **Fix** button. You are warned that you must select
    something to deploy (see Figure 1-10).

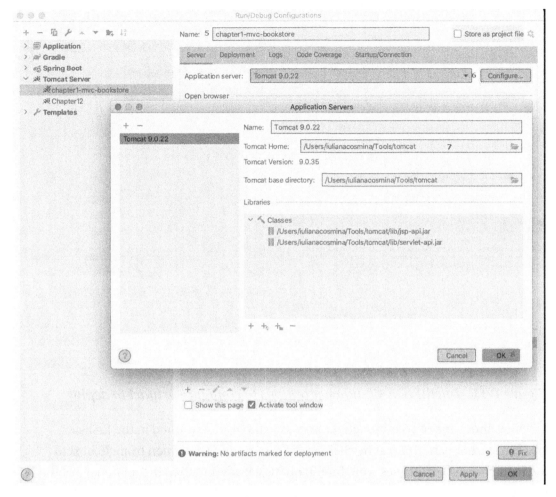

Figure 1-10. *IntelliJ IDEA Launcher options for configuring Apache Tomcat server and artifact to deploy*

10.   In the list, select the project that you want to deploy.

11.   Next, in the Deployment tab, you can edit the context path because the autogenerated one is weird.

12.   Click the **OK** button, and you are done (see Figure 1-11).

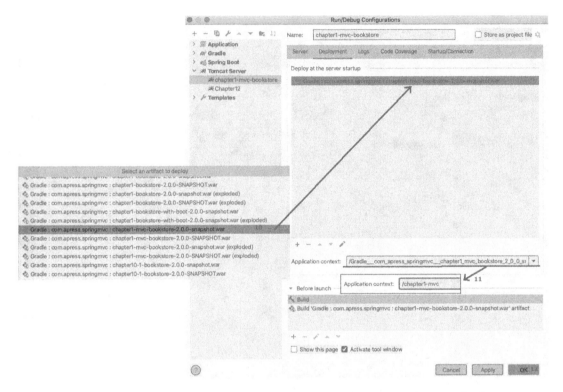

Figure 1-11. *IntelliJ IDEA Launcher options to configure artifact to deploy*

Now, the name of your launcher appears in the list mentioned in the first step. You can start Apache Tomcat by clicking the Run button (the green triangle next to the Launcher list). If all goes well, IntelliJ opens a browser tab to the main page of the project.

The log console of the Apache Tomcat in IntelliJ IDEA can give you more information in case the deployment failed. Figure 1-12 shows the page for the chapter1-mvc-bookstore project (after it has been successfully deployed) and the Apache Tomcat log console.

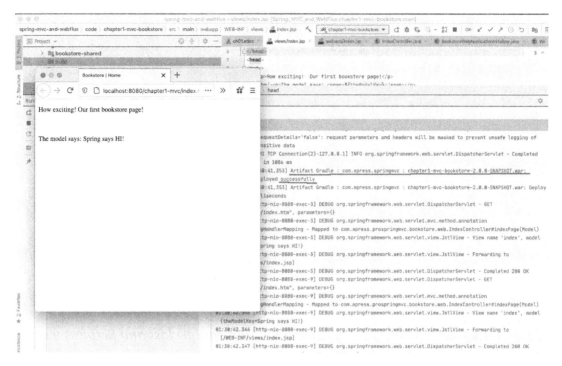

Figure 1-12. *IntelliJ IDEA Apache Tomcat log console*

Running the Spring Boot projects is even easier. Find the main class, right-click it, and choose **Run**. If the project was built successfully, the application should start and should appear in the Services view, as depicted in Figure 1-13.

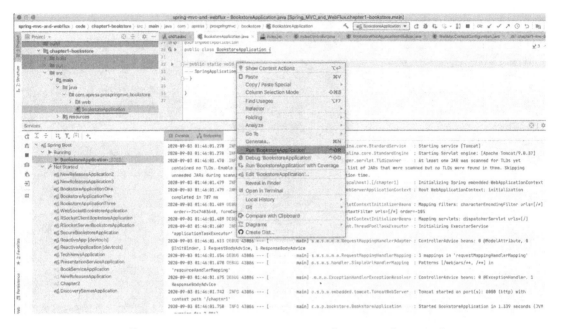

Figure 1-13. *IntelliJ IDEA Spring Boot main application class and Services view*

It seems IntelliJ IDEA has some difficulties with Gradle multi-module project because, for Spring Boot Web applications, it cannot detect the working directory, which means it cannot build an application context correctly. To fix this, open the project launcher generated for the Spring Boot application and select the directory of the project you want to run as a value for the **Working directory** option, as depicted in Figure 1-14.

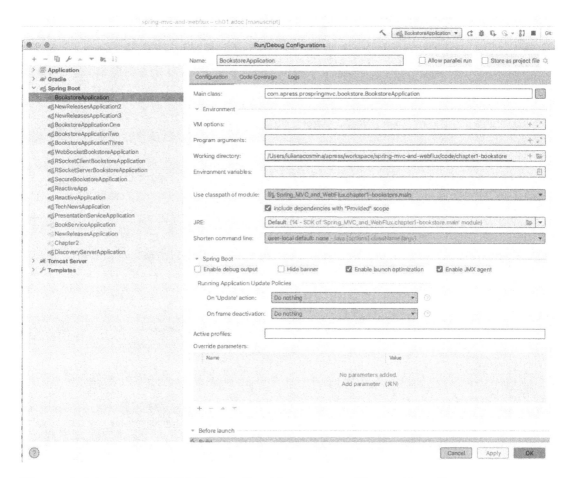

Figure 1-14. *IntelliJ IDEA Spring Boot Launcher with working directory populated explicitly*

Summary

Hopefully, the instructions in this chapter are enough to help you get started. If anything is missing or unclear, feel free to first ask Google. If that does not work, create an issue on GitHub.

Happy coding!

CHAPTER 2

Spring Framework Fundamentals

The Spring Framework evolved from the code written for *Expert One-on-One J2EE Design and Development* by Rod Johnson (Wrox, 2002).[1] The framework combines best practices for Java Enterprise Edition (JEE) development from the industry and integration with the best-of-breed third-party frameworks. It also provides easy extension points to write your own integration if you need one that doesn't exist yet. The framework was designed with developer productivity in mind, and it makes it easier to work with the existing, sometimes cumbersome Java and JEE APIs.

Spring Boot was released in April 2014 to simplify application development for the cloud era. Spring Boot makes it easy to create stand-alone, production-grade Spring-based applications. The applications "just run" either stand-alone or deployed to a traditional Servlet container or JEE server.

Spring Boot takes an opinionated view of the Spring platform as a whole and supported third-party libraries. It gets you started with little effort but gets out of your way if you want more complex configurations or make configuration easier for you.

Before starting our journey into Spring MVC and Spring WebFlux, we provide a quick refresher on Spring (also known as the **Spring Framework**). Spring is the de facto standard for Java enterprise software development. It introduced *dependency injection*, *aspect-oriented programming* (AOP), and programming with *plain-old-Java-objects* (POJOs).

---

[1]https://www.amazon.com/Expert-One-One-Design-Development/dp/0764543857

21

© Marten Deinum and Iuliana Cosmina 2021
M. Deinum and I. Cosmina, *Pro Spring MVC with WebFlux*, https://doi.org/10.1007/978-1-4842-5666-4_2

In this chapter, we cover dependency injection and AOP. Specifically, we cover how Spring helps us implement dependency injection and how to use programming to our advantage. To do the things mentioned here, we explore the Inversion of Control (IoC) container; the *application context*.

We only touch on the necessary basics of the Spring Framework here. If you want more in-depth information about it, we suggest the excellent Spring Framework documentation[2] or books such as *Pro Spring 5* (Apress, 2017)[3] or *Spring 5 Recipes, 4th Edition* (Apress, 2017)[4].

Next to the Spring Framework refresher, we also touch on the basics of Spring Boot. For more in-depth information on Spring Boot, we suggest the excellent *Spring Boot Reference Guide*[5] or *Spring Boot 2 Recipes* (Apress, 2018)[6].

Let's begin by taking a quick look at the Spring Framework and the modules that comprise it.

ℹ️   You can find the sample code for this chapter in the chapter2-samples project. Different parts of the sample contain a class with a `main` method, which you can run to execute the code.

The Spring Framework

In the introduction, we mentioned that the Spring Framework evolved from code written for the book *Expert One-on-One J2EE Design and Development* by Rod Johnson. This book was written to explain some of the complexities in JEE and how to overcome them. And while many of the complexities and problems in JEE have been solved in the newer JEE specifications (especially since JEE 6), Spring has become very popular due to its simple (not simplistic!) approach to building applications. It also offers a consistent programming model for different technologies, be they for data access or messaging infrastructure. The framework allows developers to target discrete problems and build solutions specifically for them.

---

[2]https://docs.spring.io/spring/docs/current/spring-framework-reference/index.html
[3]https://www.apress.com/gp/book/9781484228074
[4]https://www.apress.com/gp/book/9781484227893
[5]https://docs.spring.io/spring-boot/docs/current/reference/html/index.html
[6]https://www.apress.com/gp/book/9781484239629

The framework consists of several modules (see Figure 2-1) that work together and build on each other. We can pretty much cherry-pick the modules we want to use.

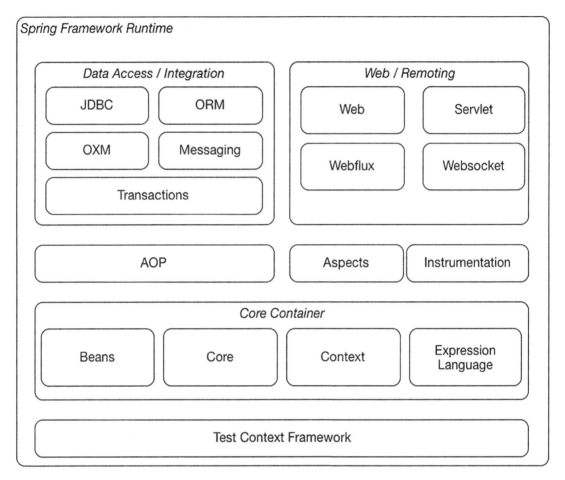

Figure 2-1. *Overview of the Spring Framework*

All the modules from Figure 2-1 represent jar files that we can include in the classpath if we need a specific technology. Table 2-1 lists all the modules that comes with Spring 5.2 and includes a brief description of each module's content and any artifact names used for dependency management. The name of the actual jar file might differ, depending on how you obtain the module.

Table 2-1. *The Spring Framework Module Overview*

Module	Artifact	Description
AOP	spring-aop	The proxy-based AOP framework for Spring
Aspects	spring-aspects	AspectJ-based aspects for Spring
Beans	spring-beans	Spring's core bean factory support
Context	spring-context	Application context runtime implementations; also contains scheduling and remoting support classes
Context	spring-context-indexer	Support for providing a static index of beans used in the application; improves startup performance
Context	spring-context-support	Support classes for integrating third-party libraries with Spring
Core	spring-core	Core utilities
Expression Language	spring-expression	Classes for the Spring Expression Language (SpEL)
Instrumentation	spring-instrument	Instrumentation classes to be used with a Java agent
JCL	spring-jcl	Spring specific replacement for commons-logging
JDBC	spring-jdbc	JDBC support package that includes datasource setup classes and JDBC access support
JMS	spring-jms	JMS support package that includes synchronous JMS access and message listener containers
ORM	spring-orm	ORM support package that includes support for Hibernate 5+ and JPA
Messaging	spring-messaging	Spring messaging abstraction; used by JMS and WebSocket
OXM	spring-oxm	XML support package that includes support for object-to-XML mapping; also includes support for JAXB, JiBX, XStream, and Castor
Test	spring-test	Testing support classes
Transactions	spring-tx	Transaction infrastructure classes; includes JCA integration and DAO support classes
Web	spring-web	Core web package for use in any web environment

(continued)

Table 2-1. (*continued*)

Module	Artifact	Description
WebFlux	spring-webflux	Spring WebFlux support package Includes support for several reactive runtimes like Netty and Undertow
Servlet	spring-webmvc	Spring MVC support package for use in a Servlet environment Includes support for common view technologies
WebSocket	spring-websocket	Spring WebSocket support package Includes support for communication over the WebSocket protocol

Most of the modules have a dependency on some other module in the Spring Framework. The core module is an exception to this rule. Figure 2-2 gives an overview of the commonly used modules and their dependencies on other modules. Notice that the instrumentation, aspect, and test modules are missing from the figure; this is because their dependencies depend on the project and what other modules are used. The other dependencies differ based on the needs of the project.

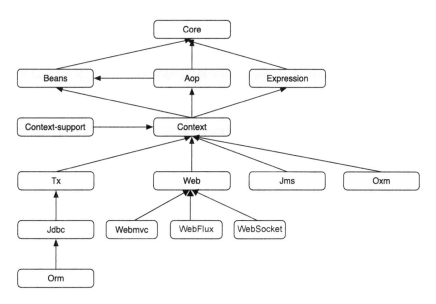

Figure 2-2. *The Spring Framework module dependencies*

Dependency Injection

In dependency injection (DI), objects are given their dependencies at construction time. It is a Spring Framework foundation. You have probably heard of *Inversion of Control* (IoC).[7] IoC is a broader, more general concept that can be addressed in different ways. IoC lets developers decouple and focus on what is important for a given part of an enterprise application, but without thinking about what other parts of the system do. Programming to interfaces is one way to think about decoupling.

Almost every enterprise application consists of multiple components that need to work together. In the early days of Java enterprise development, we simply put all the logic of constructing those objects (and the objects they needed) in the constructor (see Listing 2-1). At first sight, there is nothing wrong with that approach; however, as time progresses, object construction became slow, and objects had a lot of knowledge they shouldn't have had (see the single-responsibility principle).[8] Those classes became hard to maintain, and they were also hard to the unit and/or integration test.

Listing 2-1. A MoneyTransferService Implementation with Hardcoded Dependencies

```
package com.apress.prospringmvc.moneytransfer.simple;

import java.math.BigDecimal;
import com.apress.prospringmvc.moneytransfer.domain.Account;
import com.apress.prospringmvc.moneytransfer.domain.
MoneyTransferTransaction;
import com.apress.prospringmvc.moneytransfer.domain.Transaction;
import com.apress.prospringmvc.moneytransfer.repository.AccountRepository;
import com.apress.prospringmvc.moneytransfer.repository.
MapBasedAccountRepository;
import com.apress.prospringmvc.moneytransfer.repository.
MapBasedTransactionRepository;
import com.apress.prospringmvc.moneytransfer.repository.
TransactionRepository;
import com.apress.prospringmvc.moneytransfer.service.MoneyTransferService;
```

---

[7]http://www.martinfowler.com/articles/injection.html

[8]https://www.oodesign.com/single-responsibility-principle.html

```java
public class SimpleMoneyTransferServiceImpl implements MoneyTransferService
{

  private AccountRepository accountRepository = new
  MapBasedAccountRepository();

  private TransactionRepository transactionRepository = new
  MapBasedTransactionRepository();

  @Override
  public Transaction transfer(String source, String target, BigDecimal amount)
  {
    Account src = this.accountRepository.find(source);
    Account dst = this.accountRepository.find(target);
    src.credit(amount);
    dst.debit(amount);

    MoneyTransferTransaction transaction =
    new MoneyTransferTransaction(src, dst, amount);
    this.transactionRepository.store(transaction);
    return transaction;
  }
}
```

The class from Listing 2-1 programs to interfaces, but it still needs to know about the concrete implementation of an interface simply to do object construction. Applying IoC by decoupling the construction logic (collaborating objects) makes the application easier to maintain and increases testability. There are seven ways to decouple this dependency construction logic.

- Factory pattern

- Service locator pattern

- Dependency injection

  - Constructor based

  - Setter based

  - Field based

- Contextualized lookup

When using the factory pattern, service locator pattern, or contextualized lookup, the class that needs the dependencies still has some knowledge about obtaining the dependencies. This can make things easier to maintain, but it can still be hard to test. Listing 2-2 shows a contextualized lookup from JNDI (Java Naming and Directory Interface). The constructor code would need to know how to do the lookup and handle exceptions.

Listing 2-2. MoneyTransferService Implementation with Contextualized Lookup

```
package com.apress.prospringmvc.moneytransfer.jndi;

import javax.naming.InitialContext;
import javax.naming.NamingException;

//other import statements omitted.

public class JndiMoneyTransferServiceImpl implements MoneyTransferService {
  private AccountRepository accountRepository;
  private TransactionRepository transactionRepository;

  public JndiMoneyTransferServiceImpl() {

    try {
      InitialContext context = new InitialContext();
      this.accountRepository = (AccountRepository) context.
      lookup("accountRepository");
      this.transactionRepository = (TransactionRepository) context.lookup("
      transactionRepository");
    } catch (NamingException e) {
      throw new IllegalStateException(e);
    }
  }

//transfer method omitted, same as listing 2-1

}
```

The immediately preceding code isn't particularly clean; for example, imagine multiple dependencies from different contexts. The code would quickly become messy and increasingly hard, if not impossible, to unit test.

To solve the construction/lookup logic in the constructor of an object, we can use dependency injection. We simply pass the object the dependencies it needs to do its work. This makes our code clean, decoupled, and easy to test (see Listing 2-3). Dependency injection is a process where objects specify the dependencies they work with. The IoC container uses that specification; when it constructs an object, it also injects its dependencies. This way, our code is cleaner, and we no longer burden our class with construction logic. It is easier to maintain and easier to do the unit and/or integration test. Testing is easier because we could inject a stub or mock object to verify the behavior of our object.

Listing 2-3. A MoneyTransferService Implementation with Constructor-Based Dependency Injection

```
package com.apress.prospringmvc.moneytransfer.constructor;

// import statements ommitted

public class MoneyTransferServiceImpl implements MoneyTransferService {

  private final AccountRepository accountRepository;
  private final TransactionRepository transactionRepository;

  public MoneyTransferServiceImpl(AccountRepository accountRepo,
                                  TransactionRepository transactionRepo) {
    this.accountRepository = accountRepo;
    this.transactionRepository = transactionRepo;
  }

//transfer method omitted, same as listing 2-1


}
```

As the name implies, constructor-based dependency injection uses the constructor to inject the dependencies in the object. Listing 2-3 uses constructor-based dependency injection. It has a constructor that takes two objects as arguments: `com.apress.prospringmvc.moneytransfer.repository.AccountRepository` and `com.apress.prospringmvc.moneytransfer.repository.TransactionRepository`. When we construct an instance of `com.apress.prospringmvc.moneytransfer.constructor.MoneyTransferServiceImpl`, we need to hand it the needed dependencies.

Setter-based dependency injection uses a *setter* method to inject the dependency. The JavaBeans specification defines both setter and getter methods. If we have a method named `setAccountService`, we set a property with the name `accountService`. The property name is created using the name of the method, minus the "set" and with the first letter lowercased (the full specification is in the JavaBeans specification)[9]. Listing 2-4 shows an example of setter-based dependency injection. It isn't mandatory to have both a getter and setter for a property. A property can be read-only (only a *getter* method is defined) or write-only (only a *setter* method is defined). Listing 2-4 only shows the setter method because we only need to write the property; internally, we can directly reference the field.

Listing 2-4. A `MoneyTransferService` Implementation with Setter-Based Dependency Injection

```java
package com.apress.prospringmvc.moneytransfer.setter;

// imports ommitted

public class MoneyTransferServiceImpl implements MoneyTransferService {

  private AccountRepository accountRepository;
  private TransactionRepository transactionRepository;

  public void setAccountRepository(AccountRepository accountRepository) {
    this.accountRepository = accountRepository;
  }
```

[9] http://download.oracle.com/otn-pub/jcp/7224-javabeans-1.01-fr-spec-oth-JSpec/beans.101.pdf

```java
public void setTransactionRepository(TransactionRepository
transactionRepo) {
  this.transactionRepository = transactionRepository;
}
```

```
//transfer method omitted, same as listing 2-1
```

```
}
```

Finally, there is field-based dependency injection using annotations (see Listing 2-5). We do not need to specify a constructor argument or a setter method to set the dependencies for this to work. We begin by defining a class-level field that can hold the dependency. Next, we put an annotation on that field to express our intent to have that dependency injected into our object. Spring accepts several different annotations: @Autowired, @Resource, and @Inject. All these annotations more or less work in the same way. It isn't within the scope of this book to explain the differences among these annotations in depth, so we suggest the *Spring Boot Reference Guide* or *Pro Spring 5* (Apress, 2017) if you want to learn more. The main difference is that the @Autowired annotation is from the Spring Framework, whereas @Resource and @Inject are Java standard annotations.

Listing 2-5. A MoneyTransferService Implementation with Field-Based Dependency Injection

```java
package com.apress.prospringmvc.moneytransfer.annotation;

import org.springframework.beans.factory.annotation.Autowired;

//other imports omitted

public class MoneyTransferServiceImpl implements MoneyTransferService {

  @Autowired
  private AccountRepository accountRepository;

  @Autowired
  private TransactionRepository transactionRepository;

//transfer method omitted, same as listing 2.1

}
```

> **ⓘ**   *@Autowired and @Inject can be placed on methods and constructors to express dependency injection configuration, even when there are multiple arguments! When there is only a single constructor for the object, you can omit the annotations.*

To sum things up, we want to use dependency injection for the following reasons.

- Cleaner code

- Decoupled code

- Easier code testing

The first two reasons make our code easier to maintain. The fact that the code is easier to test should allow us to write unit tests to verify the behavior of our objects—and thus, our application.

ApplicationContexts

To do dependency injection in Spring, you need an *application context*. In Spring, this is an instance of the org.springframework.context.ApplicationContext interface. The application context is responsible for managing the beans defined in it. It also enables more elaborate things like applying AOP to the beans defined in it.

Spring provides several different ApplicationContext implementations (see Figure 2-3). Each of these implementations provides the same features but differs in how it loads the application context configuration. Figure 2-3 also shows us the org.springframework.web.context.WebApplicationContext interface, which is a specialized version of the ApplicationContext interface used in web environments.

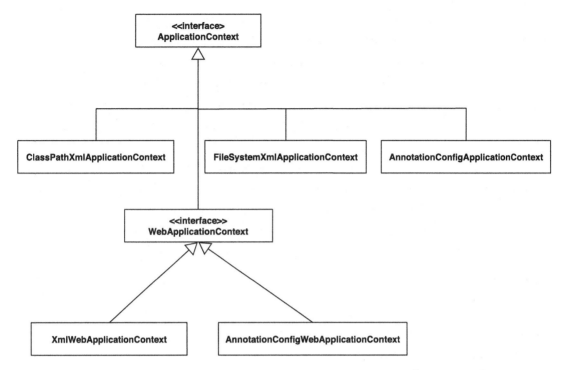

Figure 2-3. *Various* `ApplicationContext` *implementations (simplified)*

As mentioned previously, the different implementations have different configuration mechanisms (i.e., XML or Java). Table 2-2 shows the default configuration options and indicates the resource loading location.

Table 2-2. *An ApplicationContext Overview*

Implementation	Location	File type
ClassPathXmlApplicationContext	Classpath	XML
FileSystemXmlApplicationContext	File system	XML
AnnotationConfigApplicationContext	Classpath	Java
XmlWebApplicationContext	Web Application Root	XML
AnnotationConfigWebApplicationContext	Web Application Classpath	Java

Let's look at a Java-based configuration file—the com.apress.prospringmvc.
moneytransfer.annotation.ApplicationContextConfiguration class (see Listing 2-6).
There are two annotations used in the class: org.springframework.context.annotation.
Configuration and org.springframework.context.annotation.Bean. The first
stereotypes our class as a configuration file, while the second indicates that the method's
result is used as a factory to create a bean. The name of the bean is the method name by
default.

In Listing 2-6, there are three beans. They are named accountRepository,
transactionRepository, and moneyTransferService. We could also explicitly specify a
bean name by setting the name attribute on the @Bean annotation.

Listing 2-6. The ApplicationContextConfiguration Configuration File

```
package com.apress.prospringmvc.moneytransfer.annotation;

import com.apress.prospringmvc.moneytransfer.repository.AccountRepository;
import com.apress.prospringmvc.moneytransfer.repository.
MapBasedAccountRepository;
import com.apress.prospringmvc.moneytransfer.repository.
MapBasedTransactionRepository;
import com.apress.prospringmvc.moneytransfer.repository.
TransactionRepository;
import com.apress.prospringmvc.moneytransfer.service.MoneyTransferService;
import org.springframework.context.annotation.Bean;
import org.springframework.context.annotation.Configuration;
@Configuration
public class ApplicationContextConfiguration {

  @Bean
  public AccountRepository accountRepository() {
    return new MapBasedAccountRepository();
  }

  @Bean
  public TransactionRepository transactionRepository() {
    return new MapBasedTransactionRepository();
  }
```

```
@Bean
public MoneyTransferService moneyTransferService() {
    return new MoneyTransferServiceImpl();
  }
}
```

Configuration classes can be `abstract`; however, they cannot be `final`. To parse the class, Spring might create a dynamic subclass of the configuration class.

Having a class with only the @Configuration annotation isn't enough. We also need something to bootstrap our application context. We use this to launch our application. In the sample project, this is the responsibility of the MoneyTransferSpring class (see Listing 2-7). This class bootstraps our configuration by creating an instance of org. springframework.context.annotation.AnnotationConfigApplicationContext and passes it the class containing our configuration (see Listing 2-6).

Listing 2-7. The MoneyTransferSpring Class

```
package com.apress.prospringmvc.moneytransfer.annotation;

import com.apress.prospringmvc.ApplicationContextLogger;
import com.apress.prospringmvc.moneytransfer.domain.Transaction;
import com.apress.prospringmvc.moneytransfer.service.MoneyTransferService;
import org.slf4j.Logger;
import org.slf4j.LoggerFactory;
import org.springframework.context.ApplicationContext;
import org.springframework.context.annotation.
AnnotationConfigApplicationContext;

import java.math.BigDecimal;

public class MoneyTransferSpring {
```

```java
private static final Logger logger =
  LoggerFactory.getLogger(MoneyTransferSpring.class);

/**
 * @param args
 */
public static void main(String[] args) {

  ApplicationContext ctx =
    new AnnotationConfigApplicationContext(ApplicationContext
    Configuration.class);
  transfer(ctx);
  ApplicationContextLogger.log(ctx);
}

private static void transfer(ApplicationContext ctx) {
  MoneyTransferService service =
    ctx.getBean("moneyTransferService", MoneyTransferService.class);
  Transaction transaction = service.transfer("123456", "654321", new
  BigDecimal("250.00"));
  logger.info("Money Transfered: {}", transaction);
  }
}
```

Finally, note that application contexts can be in a hierarchy. We can have an application context that serves as a parent for another context (see Figure 2-4). An application context can only have a single parent, but it can have multiple children. Child contexts can access beans defined in the parent context; however, parent beans cannot access beans in the child contexts. For example, if we enable transactions in the parent context, this won't apply to child contexts (see the "Enabling Features" section later in this chapter).

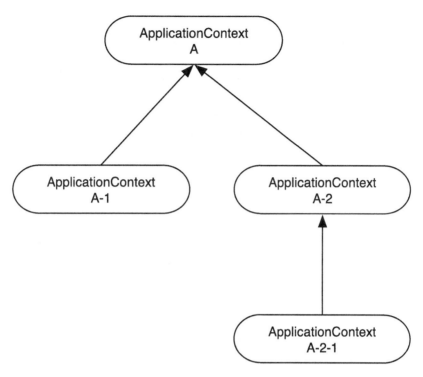

Figure 2-4. *The ApplicationContext Hierarchy*

This feature allows us to separate our application beans (e.g., services, repositories, and infrastructure) from our web beans (e.g., request handlers and views). It can be useful to have this separation. For example, assume that multiple servlets need to reuse the same application beans. Instead of recreating them for each servlet, we can simply reuse the already existing instances. This can be when there is one servlet handling the web UI and another that is handling the web services.

Resource Loading

Table 2-2 provided an overview of the different `ApplicationContext` implementations and the default resource loading mechanisms. However, this doesn't mean that you are restricted to loading resources only from the default locations. You can also load resources from specific locations by including the proper prefix (see Table 2-3).

Table 2-3. *A Prefixes Overview*

Prefix	Location
classpath:	The root of the classpath
file:	File system
http:	Web application root

Besides being able to specify where to load files from, you can also use ant-style regular expressions to specify which files to load. An ant-style regular expression is a resource location containing ** and/or * characters. A * character indicates "on the current level" or "a single level," whereas multiple * characters indicate "this and all sublevels."

Table 2-4 shows some examples. This technique only works when dealing with file resources on the classpath or file system; it does not work for web resources or package names.

Table 2-4. *Ant-Style Regular Expressions*

Expression	Description
classpath:/META-INF/spring/*.xml	Loads all files with the XML file extensions from the classpath in the META-INF/spring directory
file:/var/conf/*/.properties	Loads all files with the properties file extension from the /var/conf directory and all subdirectories

Component Scanning

Spring also has something called **component scanning**. In short, this feature enables Spring to scan your classpath for classes that are annotated with org.springframework. stereotype.Component (or one of the specialized annotations like @Service, @Repository, @Controller, or org.springframework.context.annotation. Configuration). If we want to enable component scanning, we need to instruct the application context to do so. The org.springframework.context.annotation. ComponentScan annotation enables us to accomplish that. This annotation needs to be put on our configuration class to enable component scanning. Listing 2-8 shows the modified configuration class.

Listing 2-8. Implementing Component Scanning with
ApplicationContextConfiguration

```
package com.apress.prospringmvc.moneytransfer.scanning;

import org.springframework.context.annotation.ComponentScan;
import org.springframework.context.annotation.Configuration;

/**
 * @author Marten Deinum
 */
@Configuration
@ComponentScan(basePackages = {
    "com.apress.prospringmvc.moneytransfer.scanning",
    "com.apress.prospringmvc.moneytransfer.repository" })
public class ApplicationContextConfiguration {}
```

A look at Listing 2-8 reveals that the class has no more content. There are only two annotations. One annotation indicates that this class is used for configuration, while the other enables component scanning. The component-scan annotation is configured with a package to scan.

It is considered bad practice to scan the whole classpath by not specifying a package or to use too broad a package (like `com.apress`). This can lead to scanning most or all classes, which severely impacts your application's startup time.

Scopes

By default, all beans in a Spring application context are *singletons*. As the name implies, there is a single instance of a bean, and it is used for the whole application. This doesn't typically present a problem because our services and repositories don't hold state; they simply execute a certain operation and (optionally) return a value.

However, a singleton would be problematic if we wanted to keep the state inside our bean. We are developing a web application that we hope attracts thousands of users. If there is a single instance of a bean, and all users operate in the same instance, the users see and modify each other's data or data from several users combined. This is not something we want. Fortunately, Spring provides several scopes for beans to use to our advantage (see Table 2-5).

Table 2-5. *An Overview of Scopes*

Prefix	Description
singleton	The default scope. A single instance of a bean is created and shared throughout the application.
prototype	Each time a certain bean is needed, a fresh instance of the bean is returned.
thread	The bean is created when needed and bound to the currently executing thread. If the thread dies, the bean is destroyed.
request	The bean is created when needed and bound to the lifetime of the incoming `javax.servlet.ServletRequest`. If the request is over, the bean instance is destroyed.
session	The bean is created when needed and stored in `javax.servlet.HttpSession`. When the session is destroyed, so is the bean instance.
globalSession	The bean is created when needed and stored in the globally available session (which is available in Portlet environments). If no such session is available, the scope reverts to the session scope functionality.
application	This scope is very similar to the singleton scope; however, beans with this scope are also registered in `javax.servlet.ServletContext`.

Profiles

Spring introduced profiles in version 3.1. Profiles make it easy to create different configurations of our application for different environments. For instance, we can create separate profiles for our local environment, testing, and our deployment to CloudFoundry. Each of these environments requires some environment-specific configuration or beans. You can think of database configuration, messaging solutions, and testing environments, stubs of certain beans.

To enable a profile, we need to tell the application context in which profiles are active. To activate certain profiles, we need to set a system property called `spring.profiles.active` (in a web environment, this can be a servlet initialization parameter or web context parameter). This is a comma-separated string containing the names of the active profiles. If we now add some (in this case static inner) classes (see Listing 2-9) with the `org.springframework.context.annotation.Configuration` and `org.springframework.context.annotation.Profile` annotations, then only the classes that match one of the active profiles are processed. All other classes are ignored.

Listing 2-9. ApplicationContextConfiguration with Profiles

```java
package com.apress.prospringmvc.moneytransfer.annotation.profiles;

import com.apress.prospringmvc.moneytransfer.annotation.
MoneyTransferServiceImpl;
import com.apress.prospringmvc.moneytransfer.repository.AccountRepository;
import com.apress.prospringmvc.moneytransfer.repository.
MapBasedAccountRepository;
import com.apress.prospringmvc.moneytransfer.repository.
MapBasedTransactionRepository;
import com.apress.prospringmvc.moneytransfer.repository.
TransactionRepository;
import com.apress.prospringmvc.moneytransfer.service.MoneyTransferService;
import org.springframework.context.annotation.Bean;
import org.springframework.context.annotation.Configuration;
import org.springframework.context.annotation.Profile;

@Configuration
public class ApplicationContextConfiguration {

  @Bean
  public AccountRepository accountRepository() {
    return new MapBasedAccountRepository();
  }

  @Bean
  public MoneyTransferService moneyTransferService() {
    return new MoneyTransferServiceImpl();
  }

  @Configuration
  @Profile(value = "test")
  public static class TestContextConfiguration {
    @Bean
    public TransactionRepository transactionRepository() {
      return new StubTransactionRepository();
    }
  }
}
```

```
@Configuration
@Profile(value = "local")
public static class LocalContextConfiguration {

  @Bean
  public TransactionRepository transactionRepository() {
    return new MapBasedTransactionRepository();
  }

}
}
```

Listing 2-10 shows some example bootstrap code. In general, we are not setting the active profiles from our bootstrap code. Instead, we set up our environment using a combination of system variables. This enables us to leave our application unchanged, but still have the flexibility to change our runtime configuration.

Listing 2-10. MoneyTransferSpring with Profiles

```
package com.apress.prospringmvc.moneytransfer.annotation.profiles;

import com.apress.prospringmvc.ApplicationContextLogger;
import com.apress.prospringmvc.moneytransfer.domain.Transaction;
import com.apress.prospringmvc.moneytransfer.service.MoneyTransferService;
import org.slf4j.Logger;
import org.slf4j.LoggerFactory;
import org.springframework.context.ApplicationContext;
import org.springframework.context.annotation.
AnnotationConfigApplicationContext;

import java.math.BigDecimal;

/**
 * @author Marten Deinum
 */
public class MoneyTransferSpring {

  private static final Logger logger = LoggerFactory.
  getLogger(MoneyTransferSpring.class);
```

```java
/**
 * @param args
 */
public static void main(String[] args) {

  System.setProperty("spring.profiles.active", "test");

  AnnotationConfigApplicationContext ctx1 =
    new AnnotationConfigApplicationContext(ApplicationContext
    Configuration.class);
  transfer(ctx1);
  ApplicationContextLogger.log(ctx1);

  System.setProperty("spring.profiles.active", "local");
  AnnotationConfigApplicationContext ctx2 =
    new AnnotationConfigApplicationContext(ApplicationContext
    Configuration.class);
  transfer(ctx2);
  ApplicationContextLogger.log(ctx2);
}

private static void transfer(ApplicationContext ctx) {
  MoneyTransferService service = ctx.getBean("moneyTransferService",
  MoneyTransferService.class);
  Transaction transaction = service.transfer("123456", "654321", new
  BigDecimal("250.00"));
  logger.info("Money Transfered: {}", transaction);
}
}
```

You might wonder why we should use profiles, anyway. One reason is that it allows flexible configurations. This means that our entire configuration is under version control and in the same source code, instead of being spread out over different servers, workstations, and so on. Of course, we can still load additional files containing some properties (like usernames and passwords). This can prove useful if a company's security policy doesn't allow us to put these properties into version control. We use profiles extensively when we cover testing and deploying to the cloud because the two tasks require different configurations for the datasource.

Enabling Features

The Spring Framework offers a lot more flexibility than dependency injection; it also provides many different features we can enable. We can enable these features using annotations (see Table 2-6). Note that we won't use all the annotations in Table 2-6; however, our sample application uses transactions, and we use some AOP. The largest part of this book is about the features provided by the `org.springframework.web.servlet.config.annotation.EnableWebMvc` and `org.springframework.web.reactive.config.EnableWebFlux` annotations.

Spring Boot automatically enables some of these features; it depends on the classes detected on the classpath.

Table 2-6. *An Overview of the Features Enabled by Annotations*

Annotation	Description	Detected by Spring Boot
`org.springframework.context.annotation.EnableAspectJAutoProxy`	Enables support for handling beans stereotyped as org.aspectj.lang.annotation. Aspect.	Yes
`org.springframework.scheduling.annotation.EnableAsync`	Enables support for handling bean methods with the `org.springframework.scheduling.annotation.Async` or `javax.ejb.Asynchronous` annotations.	No
`org.springframework.cache.annotation.EnableCaching`	Enables support for bean methods with the org.springframework.cache.annotation. Cacheable annotation.	Yes
`org.springframework.context.annotation.EnableLoadTimeWeaving`	Enables support for load-time weaving. By default, Spring uses a proxy-based approach to AOP; however, this annotation enables us to switch to load-time weaving. Some JPA providers require it.	No

(continued)

Table 2-6. (*continued*)

Annotation	Description	Detected by Spring Boot
org.springframework. scheduling.annotation. EnableScheduling	Enables support for annotation-driven scheduling, letting us parse bean methods annotated with the org.springframework. scheduling.annotation.Scheduled annotation.	No
org.springframework. beans.factory.aspectj. EnableSpringConfigured	Enables support for applying dependency injection to non-Spring managed beans. In general, such beans are annotated with the org.springframework.beans.factory. annotation.Configurable annotation. This feature requires load-time or compile-time weaving because it needs to modify class files.	No
org.springframework. transaction.annotation. EnableTransactionManagement	Enables annotation-driven transaction support, using org.springframework. transaction.annotation. Transactional or javax.ejb. TransactionAttribute to drive transactions.	Yes
org.springframework.web. servlet.config.annotation. EnableWebMvc	Enables support for the powerful and flexible annotation-driven controllers with request handling methods. This feature detects beans with the org.springframework. stereotype.Controller annotation and binds methods with the org. springframework.web.bind. annotation.RequestMapping annotations to URLs.	Yes
org.springframework.web. reactive.config.EnableWebFlux	Enables support for the powerful and flexible reactive web implementation using the well-known concepts from Spring Web MVC and, where possible, extend on them.	Yes

ℹ️   For more information on these features, we recommend that you examine the Java documentation for the different annotations and the dedicated reference guide chapters.

Aspect-Oriented Programming

To enable the features listed in Table 2-4, Spring uses aspect-oriented programming (AOP). AOP is another way of thinking about the structure of software. It enables you to modularize things like transaction management or performance logging, features that span multiple types and objects (cross-cutting concerns). In AOP, there are a few important concepts to keep in mind (see Table 2-7).

Table 2-7. *Core AOP Concepts*

Concept	Description
Aspect	The modularization of a cross-cutting concern. In general, this is a Java class with the `org.aspectj.lang.annotation.Aspect` annotation.
Join Point	A point during the execution of a program. This can be the execution of a method, the assignment of a field, or the handling of an exception. In Spring, a join point is always the execution of a method!
Advice	The specific action taken by an aspect at a particular join point. There are several types of advice: *before*, *after*, *after throwing*, *after returning*, and *around*. In Spring, an advice is called an **interceptor** because we are intercepting method invocations.
Pointcut	A predicate that matches join points. The advice is associated with a pointcut expression and runs at any join point matching the pointcut. Spring uses the AspectJ expression language by default. Join points can be written using the `org.aspectj.lang.annotation.Pointcut` annotation.

Now let's look at transaction management and how Spring uses AOP to apply transactions around methods. The transaction advice, or interceptor, is `org.springframework.transaction.interceptor.TransactionInterceptor`. This advice is placed around methods with the `org.springframework.transaction.annotation.Transactional` annotation. To do this, Spring creates a wrapper around the actual object, which is known as a **proxy** (see Figure 2-5). A proxy acts like an enclosing object, but it allows (dynamic) behavior to be added (in this case, the transactionality of the method).

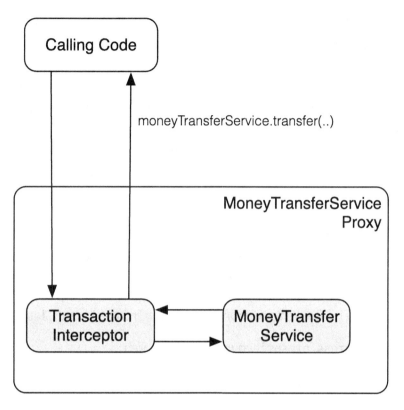

Figure 2-5. *A proxy method invocation*

The `org.springframework.transaction.annotation.`
`EnableTransactionManagement` annotation registers the beans containing the pointcut
(acting on the `org.springframework.transaction.annotation.Transactional`
annotation). At this point, the interceptor is ready to use. The other annotations for
enabling features work similarly; they register beans to enable the desired feature,
including AOP (and thus proxy creation) for most features.

Web Applications

So how does all that technology apply to a web application? For example, how do
application contexts play a role? And what about all the other things mentioned?

When developing a web application, there is actual business logic (e.g., services,
repositories, and infrastructure information), and there are web-based beans. These
things should be separated, so we need to have multiple application contexts and
relationships.

We also need code that bootstraps our application, or else nothing happens. In this chapter's examples, we used a `MoneyTransferSpring` class with a main method to start the application context. This is not something we can do in a web environment. Spring ships with two components that can bootstrap an application: `org.springframework.web.servlet.DispatcherServlet` and `org.springframework.web.context.ContextLoaderListener`. Both components bootstrap and configure an application context.

Let's look at the class that configures `DispatcherServlet`. This is the `com.apress.prospringmvc.bookstore.web.BookstoreWebApplicationInitializer` class (see Listing 2-11). Our Servlet 3.0+ container detects this class, and it initializes our application (see Chapter 3 for more information on this topic). We create the `DispatcherServlet` and pass it `org.springframework.web.context.support.AnnotationConfigWebApplicationContext`. Next, we map the servlet to everything (the "/") and tell it to load on startup.

Listing 2-11. The `BookstoreWebApplicationInitializer` Class

```
package com.apress.prospringmvc.bookstore.web;

import javax.servlet.ServletContext;
import javax.servlet.ServletException;
import javax.servlet.ServletRegistration;

import org.springframework.context.annotation.Configuration;
import org.springframework.web.WebApplicationInitializer;
import org.springframework.web.context.WebApplicationContext;
import org.springframework.web.context.support.
AnnotationConfigWebApplicationContext;
import org.springframework.web.servlet.DispatcherServlet;

import com.apress.prospringmvc.bookstore.web.config.
WebMvcContextConfiguration;

public class BookstoreWebApplicationInitializer implements
WebApplicationInitializer {

    @Override
```

```java
public void onStartup(final ServletContext servletContext) throws
ServletException {
    registerDispatcherServlet(servletContext);
}

private void registerDispatcherServlet(final ServletContext
servletContext) {
    WebApplicationContext dispatcherContext =
      createContext(WebMvcContextConfiguration.class);
    DispatcherServlet dispatcherServlet =
      new DispatcherServlet(dispatcherContext);
    ServletRegistration.Dynamic dispatcher =
      servletContext.addServlet("dispatcher", dispatcherServlet);
    dispatcher.setLoadOnStartup(1);
    dispatcher.addMapping("*.htm");
}

private WebApplicationContext createContext(final Class<?>...
annotatedClasses) {
    AnnotationConfigWebApplicationContext context =
      new AnnotationConfigWebApplicationContext();
    context.register(annotatedClasses);
    return context;
}
}
```

Let's make things a bit more interesting by adding a ContextLoaderListener
class so that we can have a parent context and a child context (see Listing 2-12).
The newly registered listener uses com.apress.prospringmvc.bookstore.config.
InfrastructureContextConfiguration (see Listing 2-13) to determine which beans to
load. The already configured DispatcherServlet automatically detects the application
context loaded by ContextLoaderListener.

Listing 2-12. The Modifcation for the BookstoreWebApplicationInitializer Class

```
package com.apress.prospringmvc.bookstore.web;

import org.springframework.web.context.ContextLoaderListener;

import com.apress.prospringmvc.bookstore.config.
InfrastructureContextConfiguration;

// other imports omitted, see listing 2-11

public class BookstoreWebApplicationInitializer implements
WebApplicationInitializer {

  @Override
  public void onStartup(final ServletContext servletContext) throws
  ServletException {

    registerListener(servletContext);
    registerDispatcherServlet(servletContext);
  }

// registerDispatcherServlet method ommitted see Listing 2-11
// createContext method omitted see Listing 2-11

  private void registerListener(final ServletContext servletContext) {

    AnnotationConfigWebApplicationContext rootContext =
      createContext(InfrastructureContextConfiguration.class);

    servletContext.addListener(new ContextLoaderListener(rootContext));

  }
}
```

Listing 2-13 is our main application context. It contains the configuration for our services and repositories. This listing also shows our JPA entity manager, including its annotation-based transaction support.

Listing 2-13. The InfrastructureContextConfiguration Source File

```
package com.apress.prospringmvc.bookstore.config;

import org.springframework.context.annotation.Bean;
import org.springframework.context.annotation.ComponentScan;
import org.springframework.context.annotation.Configuration;
import org.springframework.jdbc.datasource.embedded.
EmbeddedDatabaseBuilder;
import org.springframework.jdbc.datasource.embedded.EmbeddedDatabaseType;
import org.springframework.orm.jpa.JpaTransactionManager;
import org.springframework.orm.jpa.JpaVendorAdapter;
import org.springframework.orm.jpa.LocalContainerEntityManagerFactoryBean;
import org.springframework.orm.jpa.vendor.HibernateJpaVendorAdapter;
import org.springframework.transaction.PlatformTransactionManager;
import org.springframework.transaction.annotation.
EnableTransactionManagement;

import javax.persistence.EntityManagerFactory;
import javax.sql.DataSource;

@Configuration
@EnableTransactionManagement
@ComponentScan(basePackages = {
    "com.apress.prospringmvc.bookstore.service",
    "com.apress.prospringmvc.bookstore.repository"})
public class InfrastructureContextConfiguration {

  @Bean
  public LocalContainerEntityManagerFactoryBean
  entityManagerFactory(DataSource dataSource) {
    LocalContainerEntityManagerFactoryBean emfb = new
    LocalContainerEntityManagerFactoryBean();
    emfb.setDataSource(dataSource);
```

```
    emfb.setJpaVendorAdapter(jpaVendorAdapter());
    return emfb;
  }

  @Bean
  public JpaVendorAdapter jpaVendorAdapter() {
    return new HibernateJpaVendorAdapter();
  }

  @Bean
  public PlatformTransactionManager transactionManager(EntityManagerFactory
  emf) {
    return new JpaTransactionManager(emf);
  }

  @Bean
  public DataSource dataSource() {
    return new EmbeddedDatabaseBuilder().setType(EmbeddedDatabaseType.H2).
build();
  }
}
```

Spring Boot

All the things mentioned previously in this chapter also apply to Spring Boot. Spring
Boot builds upon and extends the features of the Spring Framework. It does make things
a lot easier, however. Spring Boot automatically configures the features it finds on the
classpath by default. When Spring Boot detects Spring MVC classes, it starts Spring
MVC. When it finds a DataSource implementation, it bootstraps it.

Customizations can be done by adding properties to the application.properties
or application.yml files. You can configure the datasource, view handling, and server
port, among others, through this. Another option is to configure things manually, as you
would do in a regular Spring application. When Spring Boot detects the preconfigured
parts of a feature, it typically refrains from autoconfiguring that feature.

The application from the previous sections can be reduced with Spring Boot (see
Listing 2-14 and Listing 2-15).

Listing 2-14. The BookstoreApplication

```java
package com.apress.prospringmvc.bookstore;

import org.springframework.boot.SpringApplication;
import org.springframework.boot.autoconfigure.SpringBootApplication;
import org.springframework.boot.builder.SpringApplicationBuilder;
import org.springframework.boot.web.servlet.support.
SpringBootServletInitializer;
import org.springframework.context.annotation.Configuration;
import org.springframework.web.servlet.DispatcherServlet;

@SpringBootApplication
public class BookstoreApplication extends SpringBootServletInitializer  {

  public static void main(String[] args) {
    SpringApplication.run(BookstoreApplication.class);
  }

  @Override
  protected SpringApplicationBuilder configure(SpringApplicationBuilder
  builder) {
    return builder.sources(BookstoreApplication.class);
  }
}
```

The BookstoreApplication class has @SpringBootApplication, which enables autoconfiguration of detected features and third-party libraries. In this case, it extends SpringBootServletInitializer because the application is packaged as a WAR and deployed onto a container. Instead of writing our own WebApplicationInitializer, Spring Boot provides one out-of-the-box. It enables most Spring Boot features in a classic container.

Configuration properties can be given in an application.properties or application.yml file (see Listing 2-15) to configure the features needed when the defaults wouldn't apply. For a list of the most common features, check Appendix A[10] of the *Spring Boot Reference Guide.*

---

[10]https://docs.spring.io/spring-boot/docs/current/reference/html/common-
application-properties.html

Listing 2-15. application.properties

```
server.port=8080 # 8080 is also the default servlet port
spring.application.name=bookstore
```

One of the nice features of Spring Boot is that when running on different environments, we can use profiles to load different/additional configuration files. For instance, when enabling the `local` profile, Spring Boot would also load an `application-local.properties` or `application-local.yml`. When running in a cloud-based situation, the properties could also be obtained from a Git repository or the Docker environment.

Summary

This chapter covered the bare basics of Spring Core. We reviewed dependency injection and briefly covered three different versions of dependency injection. We also covered constructor-based, setter-based, and annotation-based dependency injection.

Next, we stepped into the Spring world and examined `org.springframework.context.ApplicationContexts`, including the role they play in our application. We also explained the different application contexts (e.g., XML or Java-based) and the resource loading in each of them. In our web environment, we use a specialized version of an application context in an implementation of the `org.springframework.web.context.WebApplicationContext` interface. We also covered how beans in an application context are singleton scoped by default. Fortunately, Spring provides us with additional scopes, such as `request`, `session`, `globalSession`, `prototype`, `application`, and `thread`.

To use different configurations in different environments, Spring also includes profiles. We briefly explained both how to enable profiles and how to use them. We use profiles in our sample application when we test it and deploy it to Cloud Foundry.

We also delved into the way several enabling annotations are required for Spring to enable certain features. These annotations register additional beans in the application context that enable the desired feature. Most of these features rely on AOP to be enabled (e.g., declarative transaction management). Spring creates proxies to apply AOP to beans registered in our application contexts.

Finally, we took a quick look at Spring Boot and how that makes our lives as software developers easy. Spring Boot uses autoconfiguration to configure features detected on the classpath. It builds upon and extends the Spring Framework where needed.

The next chapter looks at the architecture of an MVC web application, the different layers, and their roles in our application.

CHAPTER 3

Web Application Architecture

Before we start our journey into the internals of Spring MVC, we first need to understand the different layers of a web application. And we'll begin that discussion with a brief introduction of the MVC pattern in general, including what it is and why we should use it. We also cover some of the interfaces and classes provided by the Spring Framework to express the different parts of the MVC pattern.

After reviewing the MVC Pattern, we go through the different layers in a web application and see what role each layer plays in the application. We also explore how the Spring Framework can help us in the different layers and use them to our advantage.

The MVC Pattern

The Model View Controller pattern (MVC pattern) was first described by Trygve Reenskaug when he was working on Smalltalk at Xerox. At that time, the pattern was aimed at desktop applications. This pattern divides the presentation layer into different kinds of components. Each component has its own responsibilities. The view uses the model to render itself. Based on a user action, the view triggers the controller, which in turn updates the model. The model then notifies the view to (re)render itself (see Figure 3-1).

© Marten Deinum and Iuliana Cosmina 2021
M. Deinum and I. Cosmina, *Pro Spring MVC with WebFlux*, https://doi.org/10.1007/978-1-4842-5666-4_3

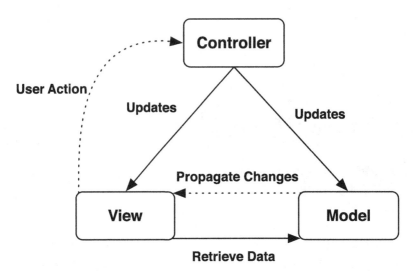

Figure 3-1. *The MVC pattern*

The MVC pattern is all about separation of concerns. Each component has its own role (see Table 3-1). Separation of concerns is important in the presentation layer because it helps us keep the different components clean. This way, we don't burden the actual view with business logic, navigation logic, and model data. Following this approach keeps everything nicely separated, which makes it easier to maintain and test our application.

Table 3-1. *MVC in Short*

Component	Description
Model	The model is the data needed by the view so that it can be rendered. It might be an order placed or a list of books requested by a user.
View	The view is the actual implementation, and it uses the model to render itself in a web application. This could be a JSP or JSF page, but it could also be a PDF, XML, or JSON representation of a resource.
Controller	The controller is the component that is responsible for responding to the action the user takes, such as form submission or clicking a link. The controller updates the model and takes other actions needed, such as invoking a service method to place an order.

The classic implementation of the MVC pattern (as shown in Figure 3-1) involves the user triggering an action. This prompts the controller to update the model, which pushes the changes back to the view. The view then updates itself with the updated data from the model. This is the ideal implementation of an MVC pattern, and it works very well in desktop applications based on Swing, for example. However, this approach is not feasible in a web environment due to the nature of the HTTP protocol. For a web application, the user typically initiates action by issuing a request. This prompts the app to update and render the view, which is sent back to the user. This means that we need a slightly different approach in a web environment. Instead of pushing the changes to the view, we need to pull the changes from the server.

This approach seems workable, but it isn't as straightforward to apply in a web application as one might think. The Web (or HTTP) is stateless by design, so keeping a model around can be difficult. For the Web, the MVC pattern is implemented as a Model 2 architecture (see Figure 3-2).[1] The difference between the original pattern (Model 1 is shown in Figure 3-1) and the modified pattern is that it incorporates a *front controller* that dispatches the incoming requests to other controllers. These controllers handle the incoming request, return the model, and select the view.

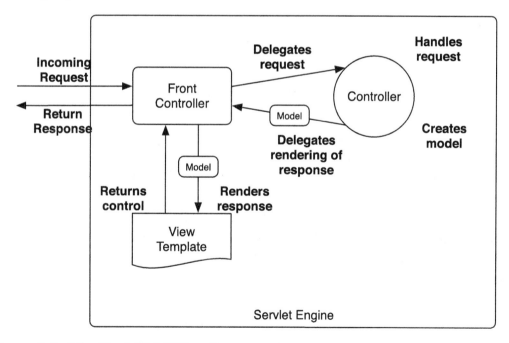

Figure 3-2. *The Model 2 MVC pattern*

[1]https://en.wikipedia.org/wiki/JSP_model_2_architecture1

The front controller is the component that handles the incoming requests. First, it delegates the request to a suitable controller. When that controller has finished processing and updating the model, the front controller determines which view to render based on the outcome. In most cases, this front controller is implemented as a `javax.servlet.Servlet` servlet (e.g., the `FacesServlet` in JSF). In Spring MVC, this front controller is `org.springframework.web.servlet.DispatcherServlet`.

Application Layering

In the introduction, we mentioned that an application consists of several layers (see Figure 3-3). We like to think of a layer as an area of concern for the application. Therefore, we also use layering to achieve separation of concerns. For example, the view shouldn't be burdened with business or data access logic because these are all different concerns and typically located in different layers.

Figure 3-3. *Typical application layering*

Layers should be thought of as conceptual boundaries, but they don't have to be physically isolated from each other (in another virtual machine). For a web application, the layers typically run inside the same virtual machine. Rod Johnson's book, *Expert One-on-One J2EE Design and Development* (Wrox, 2002), has a good discussion on application distribution and scaling.

Figure 3-3 is a highly generalized view of the layers of an application. The data access is at the bottom of the application, the presentation is on top, and the services (the actual business logic) are in the middle. This chapter looks at this architecture and how everything is organized. Table 3-2 provides a brief description of the different layers.

Table 3-2. *A Brief Overview of Layers*

Layer	Description
Presentation	This is most likely to be a web-based solution. The presentation layer should be as thin as possible. It should also be possible to provide alternative presentation layers like a web frontend or a web service façade. This should all operate on a well-designed service layer.
Service	The entry point to the actual system containing the business logic. It provides a coarse-grained interface that enables the use of the system. It is also the layer that should be the system's transactional boundary (and probably security, too). This layer shouldn't know anything (or as little as possible) about persistence or the view technology used.
Data Access	An interface-based layer provides access to the underlying data access technology without exposing it to the upper layers. This layer abstracts the actual persistence framework (e.g., JDBC, JPA, or something like MongoDB). Note that this layer should not contain business logic.

Communication between the layers is from top to bottom. The service layer can access the data access layer, but the data access layer cannot access the service layer. If you see these kinds of circular dependencies creep into your application, take a few steps back and reconsider your design. Circular dependencies (or bottom to top dependencies) are almost always signs of bad design and lead to increased complexity and a harder-to-maintain application.

Note   Sometimes, you encounter the term, *tier*. Many people use tier and layer interchangeably; however, separating them helps discuss the application architecture or its deployment. We like to use *layer* to indicate a conceptual layer in the application, whereas a *tier* indicates the physical separation of the layers on different machines at deployment time. Thinking in *layers* helps the software developer, whereas thinking in *tiers* helps the system administrator.

Although Figure 3-3 gives a general overview of the layers for a web application, we could break it down a little further. In a typical web application, we can identify five conceptual layers (see Figure 3-4). We can split the presentation layer into a web and user interface layer, but the application also includes a domain layer (see the "Spring MVC Application Layers" section later in this chapter). Typically, the domain layer cuts across all layers because it is used everywhere, from the data access layer to the user interface.

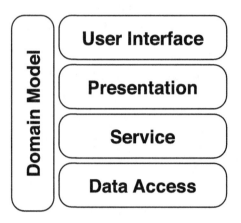

Figure 3-4. *Web MVC application layers*

Note   The layered architecture isn't the only application architecture out there; however, it is the most frequently encountered architecture for web applications.

If you look at the sample application, the architecture shown in Figure 3-4 is made explicit in the package structure. The packages can be found in the *bookstore-shared* project (see Figure 3-5). The main packages include the following.

- `com.apress.prospringmvc.bookstore.domain`: the domain layer

- `com.apress.prospringmvc.bookstore.service`: the service layer

- `com.apress.prospringmvc.bookstore.repository`: the data access layer

The other packages are supporting packages for the web layer, and the `com.apress. prospringmvc.bookstore.config` package contains the configuration classes for the root application context. The user interface and web layer we build over the course of this book, and these layers are in the `com.apress.prospringmvc.bookstore.web` package and in Thymeleaf [2] templates needed for the user interface.

---

[2]`https://www.thymeleaf.org`

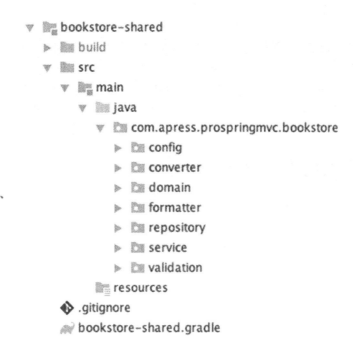

Figure 3-5. *The Bookstore packages overview*

Separation of Concerns

As mentioned in Chapter 2, it is important to have a clear separation of concerns. If you look at the architecture from Figure 3-4, the separation of concerns is present in the layers. Separating the concerns into different layers helps us achieve a clean design and a flexible and testable application.

Creating or detecting layers can be hard. A rule of thumb is that if a layer has too many dependencies on other layers, you might want to introduce another layer that incorporates all the dependencies. On the other hand, if you see a single layer throughout different layers, you might want to reconsider this layer and make it an aspect of the application. In this case, we can use the Spring Framework's AOP functionality to apply these aspects at runtime (see Chapter 2).

Coupling layers—for example, the service layer needs to talk to the data access layer—is done by defining clear interfaces. Defining interfaces and programming to interfaces reduces the actual coupling to concrete implementations. Reduced coupling and complexity results in an easier-to-test and easier-to-maintain application. Another benefit of using interfaces is that Spring can use JDK Dynamic Proxies[3] to create proxies and apply AOP. Spring can also apply AOP on class-based proxies using the Byte Code Generation Library (cglib), which ships in a repacked form with the Spring Framework.

The point is this: layering in an application leads to a more maintainable and testable application. A clear separation of concerns also leads to good application architecture.

Spring MVC Application Layers

You might wonder how all the layers fit into a Spring MVC application and how all the different layers help us build our Spring MVC application. This section looks at the five layers depicted in Figure 3-4. We pay particular attention to the roles the different layers play and what should be in each.

The Domain Layer

The domain is the most important layer in an application. It is the code representation of the business problem we are solving, and it contains the business rules of our domain. These rules might check whether we have sufficient funds to transfer money from our account or ensure that fields are unique (e.g., usernames in our system).

A popular technique to determine the domain model is to use the nouns in use case descriptions as domain objects (e.g., `Account` or `Transaction`). These objects contain both state (e.g., the username for the `Account`) and behavior (e.g., a `credit` method on the `Account`). These methods are typically more fine-grained than the methods in the service layer. For example, in the money transfer sample in Chapter 2, the `com.apress.prospringmvc.moneytransfer.domain.Account` object has a `debit` and `credit` method. The credit method contains some business logic for checking whether we have sufficient money in our account to transfer the money.

In Chapter 2, the implementations of the `com.apress.prospringmvc.moneytransfer.service.MoneyTransferService` used these supporting methods to implement a use case (in the sample, it transferred money from one account to another). This is not to be confused with an anemic domain model,[4] in which our domain objects only hold state and have no behavior.

---

[3]https://docs.oracle.com/javase/8/docs/technotes/guides/reflection/proxy.html
[4]https://martinfowler.com/bliki/AnemicDomainModel.html

In general, your domain model will not need dependencies injected; however, it is still possible to do this. For example, it's possible to use the Spring Framework and AspectJ to enable dependency injection in our domain objects. In that circumstance, we would give our domain classes the `org.springframework.beans.factory.annotation. Configurable` annotation. Next, we would need to set up load-time weaving or compile-time weaving and have our dependencies injected. For more information on the subject, please see the Spring Framework documentation.[5]

The User Interface Layer

The user interface layer presents the application to the user. This layer renders the response generated by the server into the type requested by the user's client. For instance, a web browser will probably request an HTML document, a web service may want an XML document, and another client could request a PDF or Excel document.

We separated the presentation layer into a user interface and web layer because, notwithstanding the wide range of different view technologies, we wanted to reuse as much code as possible. Our goal is to reimplement only the user interface. There are many different view technologies out there, including JSF, JSP(X), FreeMarker, and Thymeleaf, to name a few. In an ideal world, we would switch our user interface without changing our application's backend.

Spring MVC helps us in isolating the user interface from the rest of the system. In Spring, the view is represented by an interface: `org.springframework.web.servlet. View`. This interface is responsible for transforming the result of the action from the user (the model) into the type of response the user requested. The `View` interface is generic, and it has no dependencies on a particular view technology. There is an implementation provided either by the Spring Framework or by the view technologies for each supported view technology. Out of the box, Spring supports the following view technologies.

- JSP

- PDF

- Excel

- FreeMarker

---

[5]https://docs.spring.io/spring/docs/current/spring-framework-reference/core. html#aop-atconfigurable

- Thymeleaf

- Tiles 3

- XML (marshaling, XSLT, or plain)

- JSON (using Jackson or GSON)

- Groovy markup

- Script views (Handlebars, ERB, Kotlin Script templating)

In general, the user interface has a dependency on the domain layer. Sometimes, it is convenient to directly expose and render the domain model. This can be especially useful when we start to use forms in our application. For example, this would let us work directly with the domain objects instead of an additional layer of indirection. Some argue that this creates unnecessary or unwanted coupling between layers. However, the creation of another layer for the sole purpose of decoupling the domain from the view leads to unnecessary complexity and duplication. In any case, it is important to keep in mind that Spring MVC doesn't require us to directly expose the domain model to the view—whether we do so is entirely up to us.

The Web Layer

The web layer has two responsibilities. The first responsibility is to guide the user through the web application. The second is to be the integration layer between the service layer and HTTP.

Navigating the user through the website can be as simple as mapping a URL to views or a full-blown page flow solution like Spring Web Flow. The navigation is typically bound to the web layer only, and there isn't any navigation logic in the domain or service layer.

As an integration layer, the web layer should be as thin as possible. It should be the layer that converts the incoming HTTP request to something that can be handled by the service layer and then transforms the result (if any) from the server into a response for the user interface. The web layer should not contain any business logic—that is the sole purpose of the service layer.

The web layer also consists of cookies, HTTP headers, and possibly an HTTP session. It is the responsibility of the web layer to manage all these things consistently and transparently. The different HTTP elements should never creep into our service layer.

If they do, the whole service layer (and thus our application) becomes tied to the web environment. Doing this makes it harder to maintain and test the application. Keeping the service layer clean also allows us to reuse the same services for different channels. For example, it enables us to add a web service or JMS-driven solution. The web layer should be thought of as a client or proxy that connects to the service layer and exposes it to the end users.

In the early days of Java web development, servlets, or JavaServer Pages mainly implemented this layer. The servlets had the responsibility of processing and transforming the request into something the service layer could understand. More often than not, the servlets wrote the desired HTML directly back to the client. This kind of implementation quickly became hard to maintain and test. After a couple of years, the Model 2 MVC pattern emerged, and we finally had advanced MVC capabilities for the Web.

Frameworks like Spring MVC, Struts, JSF, and Tapestry provide different implementations for this pattern, and they all work differently. However, we can identify two main types of web layer implementations: request/response frameworks (e.g., struts and Spring MVC) and component-based frameworks (e.g., JSF and Tapestry). The request/response frameworks operate on `javax.servlet.ServletRequest` and `javax.servlet.ServletResponse` objects. Thus, the fact that they operate on the Servlet API isn't really hidden from the user. The component-based frameworks offer a completely different programming model. They try to hide the Servlet API from the programmer and offer a component-based programming model. Using a component-based framework feels a lot like working with a Swing desktop application.

Both approaches have their advantages and disadvantages. Spring MVC is powerful, and it strikes a good balance between the two. It can hide the fact that one works with the Servlet API; however, it is easy to access that API (among other things).

The web layer depends on the domain layer and the service layer. In most cases, you want to transform the incoming request into a domain object and call a method on the service layer to do something with that domain object (e.g., update a customer or create an order). Spring MVC makes it easy to map incoming requests to objects, and we can use dependency injection to access the service layer.

In Spring MVC, the web layer is represented by the `org.springframework.web.servlet.mvc.Controller` interface or classes with the `org.springframework.stereotype.Controller` annotation. The interface-based approach is historic, and it has been part of the Spring Framework since its inception; however, it is now considered outdated. Regardless, it remains useful for simple use cases, and Spring provides some convenient implementations out of the box. The new annotation-based approach is more powerful and flexible than the original interface-based approach. The focus in this book is on the annotation-based approach.

After executing a controller, the infrastructure (see Chapter 4 for more information on this topic) expects an instance of the `org.springframework.web.servlet.ModelAndView` class. This class incorporates the model (in the form of `org.springframework.ui.ModelMap`) and the view to render. This view can be an actual `org.springframework.web.servlet.View` implementation or the name of a view.

Caution   Don't use the `Controller` annotation on a class with the `Controller` interface. These are handled differently, and mixing both strategies can lead to surprising and unwanted results!

The Service Layer

The service layer is very important in the architecture of an application. It is considered the heart of our application because it exposes the system's functionality (the use cases) to the user. It does this by providing a coarse-grained API (as mentioned in Table 3-2). Listing 3-1 describes a coarse-grained service interface.

Listing 3-1. A Coarse-Grained Service Interface

```
package com.apress.prospringmvc.bookstore.service;

import com.apress.prospringmvc.bookstore.domain.Account;

public interface AccountService {

  Account save(Account account);

  Account login(String username, String password) throws
  AuthenticationException;

  Account getAccount(String username);

}
```

This listing is considered coarse-grained because it takes a simple method call from the client to complete a single use case. This contrasts with the code in Listing 3-2 (fine-grained service methods), which requires a couple of calls to perform a use case.

Listing 3-2. A Fine-Grained Service Interface

```
package com.apress.prospringmvc.bookstore.service;

import com.apress.prospringmvc.bookstore.domain.Account;

public interface AccountService {

  Account save(Account account);

  Account getAccount(String username);

  void checkPassword(Account account, String password);

  void updateLastLogin(Account account);

}
```

If possible, we should not call a sequence of methods to execute a system function. We should shield the user from data access and POJO interaction as much as possible. In an ideal world, a coarse-grained function should represent a single unit of work that either succeeds or fails. The user can use different clients (e.g., web application, web service, or desktop application); however, these clients should execute the same business logic. Hence, the service layer should be our single point of entry for the actual system (i.e., the business logic).

The added benefit of having a single point of entry and coarse-grained methods on the service layer is that we can simply apply transactions and security at this layer. We don't have to burden the different clients of our application with the security and transactional requirements. It is now part of the core of the system and is generally applied through AOP.

In a web-based environment, we probably have multiple users operating on the services at the same time. The service must be stateless, so it is a good practice to make the service a singleton. In the domain model, state should be kept as much as possible. Keeping the service layer stateless provides an additional benefit: it also makes the layer thread-safe.

Keeping the service layer to a single point of entry, keeping the layer stateless, and applying transactions and security on that layer enables other features of the Spring Framework to expose the service layer to different clients. For example, we could use configuration to easily expose our service layer over RMI or JMS. For more information on Spring Framework's remoting support, we suggest *Pro Spring 5* (Apress, 2017) or the online Spring Framework documentation.[6]

In our bookstore sample application, the `com.apress.prospringmvc.bookstore.` `service.BookstoreService` interface (see Listing 3-3) serves as the interface for our service layer (there are a couple of other interfaces, but this is the most important one). This interface contains several coarse-grained methods. In most cases, it takes a single method call to execute a single use case (e.g., createOrder).

Listing 3-3. The BookstoreService Interface

```
package com.apress.prospringmvc.bookstore.service;

import java.util.List;

import com.apress.prospringmvc.bookstore.domain.Account;
import com.apress.prospringmvc.bookstore.domain.Book;
import com.apress.prospringmvc.bookstore.domain.BookSearchCriteria;
import com.apress.prospringmvc.bookstore.domain.Cart;
import com.apress.prospringmvc.bookstore.domain.Category;
import com.apress.prospringmvc.bookstore.domain.Order;

public interface BookstoreService {

  List<Book> findBooksByCategory(Category category);

  Book findBook(long id);

  Order findOrder(long id);

  List<Book> findRandomBooks();

  List<Order> findOrdersForAccount(Account account);

  Order store(Order order);
```

---

[6]https://docs.spring.io/spring/docs/current/spring-framework-reference/index.html

```
List<Book> findBooks(BookSearchCriteria bookSearchCriteria);

Order createOrder(Cart cart, Account account);

List<Category> findAllCategories();
}
```

As Listing 3-3 demonstrates, the service layer depends on the domain layer to execute the business logic. However, it also depends on the data access layer to store and retrieve data from our underlying data store. The service layer can serve as the glue between one or more domain objects to execute a business function. The service layer should coordinate which domain objects it needs and how they interact together.

The Spring Framework has no interfaces that help us implement our service layer; however, this shouldn't come as a surprise. The service layer is what makes our application; in fact, it is specialized for our application. Nevertheless, the Spring Framework can help us with our architecture and programming model. We can use dependency injection and apply aspects to drive our transactions. All of this has a positive influence on our programming model.

The Data Access Layer

The data access layer is responsible for interfacing with the underlying persistence mechanism. This layer knows how to store and retrieve objects from the datastore. It does this in such a way that the service layer doesn't know which underlying datastore is used. (The datastore could be a database, but it could also consist of flat files on the file system.)

There are several reasons for creating a separate data access layer. First, we don't want to burden the service layer with knowledge of the kind of datastore (or datastores) we use; we want to transparently handle persistence. In our sample application, we use an in-memory database and JPA (Java Persistence API) to store our data. Now imagine that, instead of coming from the database, our com.apress.prospringmvc.bookstore. domain.Account comes from an Active Directory Service. We could simply create a new implementation of the interface that knows how to deal with Active Directory—all without changing our service layer. In theory, we could easily swap out implementations; for example, we could switch from JDBC to Hibernate without changing the service layer. It is unlikely that this will happen, but it is nice to have this ability.

The most important reason for this approach is that it simplifies testing our application. In general, data access is slow, so we must keep our tests running as fast as possible. A separate data access layer makes it easy to create a stub or mock implementation of our data access layer.

Spring has great support for data access layers. For example, it provides a consistent and transparent way to work with various data access frameworks (e.g., JDBC, JPA, and Hibernate). For each of these technologies, Spring provides extensive support for the following abilities.

- Transaction management

- Resource handling

- Exception translation

Transaction management is transparent in each technology it supports. A transaction manager handles the transactions, and it has support for JTA (Java Transaction API), which enables distributed or global transactions (a transaction that spans multiple resources like a database and JMS broker). This excellent transaction support means that the transaction manager can also manage the resources for you. We no longer have to worry that a database connection or file handle is closed; this is all handled for you. The supported implementations can be found in the `org.springframework.jdbc` and `org.springframework.orm` packages.

Tip   The Spring Data project[7] provides a deeper integration with several technologies. In several use cases, it eliminates the need to write our own implementation of a data access object (DAO) or repository.

The Spring Framework includes another powerful feature as part of its data access support: exception translation. Spring provides extensive exception translation support for all its supported technologies. This feature transforms technology-specific exceptions into a subclass of `org.springframework.dao.DataAccessException`. For database-driven technologies, it considers the database vendor, version, and error codes received from the database. The exception hierarchy extends from `java.lang.RuntimeException`; and as such, it doesn't have to be caught because it isn't a checked exception. For more

---

[7]https://spring.io/projects/spring-data

information on data access support, please see *Pro Spring 5* (Apress, 2017) or the online Spring Framework documentation.

Listing 3-4 shows how a data access object or repository might look. Note that the interface doesn't reference or mention any data access technology we use (we use JPA for the sample application). Also, the service layer doesn't care how or where the data is persisted; it simply wants to know how to store or retrieve it.

Listing 3-4. A Sample `AccountRepository` using Spring Data

```
package com.apress.prospringmvc.bookstore.repository;

import com.apress.prospringmvc.bookstore.domain.Account;

public interface AccountRepository extends CrudRepository<Account, Long> {

  Account findByUsername(String username);

}
```

More Roads to Rome

The architecture discussed here isn't the only application architecture out there. Which architecture is best for a given application depends on the size of the application, the experience of the development team, and the lifetime of the application. The larger the team or the longer an application lives, the more important a clean architecture with separate layers becomes.

A web application that starts with a single static page probably doesn't require any architecture. However, as the application grows, it becomes increasingly important that we don't try to put everything on that single page because that would make it very difficult to maintain or understand the app, let alone test it.

As an application's size and age increases, we need to refactor its design and keep in mind that each layer or component should have a single responsibility. If we detect some concern that should be in a different layer or touches multiple components, we should convert it into an aspect (cross-cutting concern) of the application and use AOP to apply it to the code.

When deciding how to structure our layers, we should try to identify a clear API (exposed through Java interfaces) for our system. Thinking of an API for our system makes us think about our design and a useful and useable API. In general, if an API is hard to use, it is also hard to test and maintain. Therefore, a clean API is important. In addition, using interfaces between the different layers allows the separate layers to be built and tested in isolation. This can be a great advantage in larger development teams (or teams consisting of multiple smaller teams). It allows us to focus on the function we're working with, not on the underlying or higher-level components.

When designing and building an application, it's also important to use good Object Oriented practices and patterns to solve problems. For example, we should use polymorphism and inheritance to our advantage, and we should use AOP to apply system-wide concerns. The Spring Framework can also help us wire our application together at runtime. Taken as a whole, the features and approaches described in this chapter can help us to keep our code clean and to achieve the best architecture for our applications.

Summary

In this chapter, we covered the MVC pattern, including its origins and what problems it solves. We also briefly discussed the three components of the MVC pattern: the model, view, and controller. Next, we touched on the Model 2 MVC pattern and how using a front controller distinguishes it from the Model 1 MVC pattern. In Spring MVC, this front controller is `org.springframework.web.servlet.DispatcherServlet`.

Next, we briefly covered web application architecture in general. We identified the five different layers generally available in a web application: domain, user interface, web, service, and data access. These layers play an important role in our application, and we discussed both what these roles are and how they fit together. We also covered how Spring can help us out in the different layers of an application.

The main take away from this chapter is that the various layers and components in the MVC pattern can separate the different concerns. Each layer should have a single responsibility, be it business logic or the glue between the HTTP world and the service layer. Separation of concerns helps us both achieve a clean architecture and create maintainable code. Finally, clean layering makes it easier to test our application.

The next chapter drills down on the Spring MVC. Specifically, it explores the `DispatcherServlet` servlet, including how it works and how to configure it. It also takes a closer look at how the different components described in this chapter work in a Spring MVC application.

CHAPTER 4

Spring MVC Architecture

This chapter dives into the internals of Spring MVC, taking a close look at `org.springframework.web.servlet.DispatcherServlet`. You begin by learning how the servlet handles an incoming request and identifying which components play a role in the request handling. After these components have been identified, we go deeper into their roles, functions, and implementations. You also learn how to configure `org.springframework.web.servlet.DispatcherServlet`, in part by examining the default configuration and extended configuration of Spring Boot.

DispatcherServlet Request Processing Workflow

In the previous chapter, you learned about the important role the front controller plays in a Model 2 MVC pattern. The front controller takes care of dispatching incoming requests to the correct handler and prepares the response to be rendered into something that the user would like to see. The role of the front controller in Spring MVC is played by `org.springframework.web.servlet.DispatcherServlet`. This servlet uses several components to fulfill its role. All these components are expressed as interfaces, for which one or more implementations are available. The next section explores the general role these components play in the request processing workflow. Another upcoming section covers the different implementations of the interfaces.

© Marten Deinum and Iuliana Cosmina 2021
M. Deinum and I. Cosmina, *Pro Spring MVC with WebFlux*, https://doi.org/10.1007/978-1-4842-5666-4_4

ⓘ   We purposely used the term **handler**. DispatcherServlet is very flexible and customizable, and it can handle more types of handlers than `org.springframework.web.servlet.mvc.Controller` implementations or `org.springframework.stereotype.Controller` annotated classes.

The Workflow

A high-level overview of the request processing workflow is illustrated in Figure 4-1.

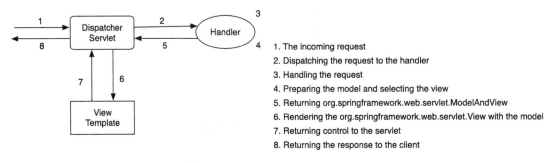

1. The incoming request
2. Dispatching the request to the handler
3. Handling the request
4. Preparing the model and selecting the view
5. Returning org.springframework.web.servlet.ModelAndView
6. Rendering the org.springframework.web.servlet.View with the model
7. Returning control to the servlet
8. Returning the response to the client

Figure 4-1. *The request processing workflow*

In the previous chapters, you learned about the importance of the separation of concerns. Within the Spring Framework, the same rules have been applied. A lot of supporting components have been designed as interfaces with extensibility and the separation of concerns in mind. Although the high-level overview in Figure 4-1 is correct, there is more happening behind the scenes. Figure 4-2 shows a complete view of the request processing workflow.

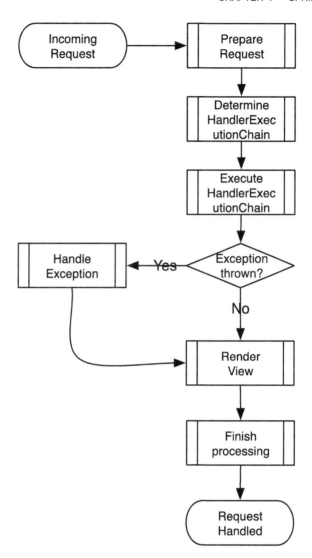

Figure 4-2. *The request processing workflow*

Figure 4-2 provides a global overview of the request processing workflow inside DispatcherServlet. The following sections zoom in on the different steps in this flow.

Prepare a Request

Before DispatcherServlet starts dispatching and handling the request, it prepares and preprocesses the request. The servlet starts by determining and exposing the current java.util.Locale for the current request using org.springframework.web. servlet.LocaleResolver. Next, it prepares and exposes the current request in org.

springframework.web.context.request.RequestContextHolder. This gives the framework code easy access to the current request, instead of passing it around.

Next, the servlet constructs the org.springframework.web.servlet.FlashMap implementation. It does this by calling org.springframework.web.servlet. FlashMapManager, which tries to resolve the input FlashMap. This map contains attributes that were explicitly stored in the previous request. In general, this is used when a redirect is made to go to the next page. This topic is discussed in depth in Chapter 5.

Next, the incoming request is checked to determine if it is a multipart HTTP request (this is used when doing file uploads). If so, the request is wrapped in org. springframework.web.multipart.MultipartHttpServletRequest by passing it through an org.springframework.web.multipart.MultipartResolver component. After this, the request is ready to be dispatched to the correct handler. Figure 4-3 shows a flow diagram of the first part of the request processing workflow.

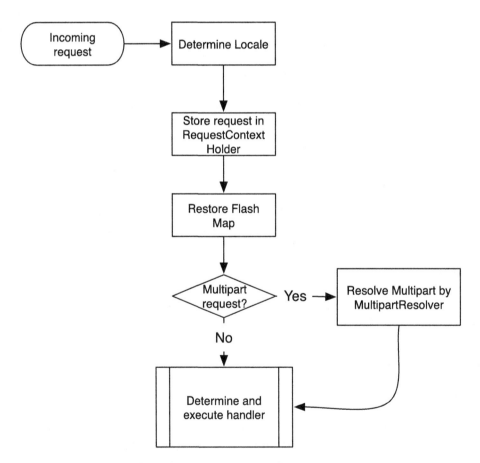

Figure 4-3. *The start of the request processing flow*

Determine the Handler Execution Chain

A couple of components are involved in dispatching the request (see Figure 4-4). When a request is ready for dispatch, DispatcherServlet consults one or more org. springframework.web.servlet.HandlerMapping implementations to determine which handler can handle the request. If no handler is found, an HTTP 404 response is sent back to the client. HandlerMapping returns org.springframework.web.servlet. HandlerExecutionChain (you learn more about this in the next section). When the handler has been determined, the servlet attempts to find org.springframework.web. servlet.HandlerAdapter to execute the found handler. If no suitable HandlerAdapter can be found, javax.servlet.ServletException is thrown.

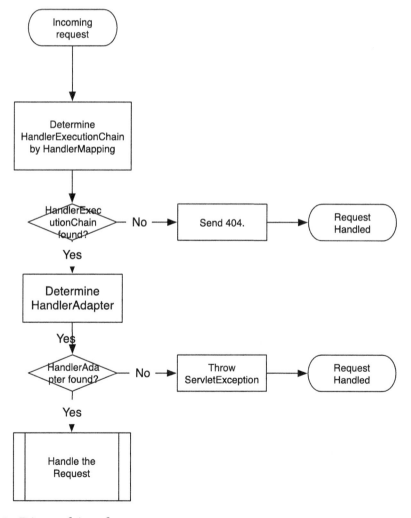

Figure 4-4. *Dispatching the request*

Execute the Handler Execution Chain

To handle the request, `DispatcherServlet` uses the `HandlerExecutionChain` class to determine what to execute. This class holds a reference to the actual handler that needs to be invoked; however, it also (optionally) references `org.springframework.web.servlet.HandlerInterceptor` implementations that are executed before (`preHandle` method) and after (`postHandle` method) the execution of the handler. These interceptors can apply crosscutting functionality (see Chapter 6 for more information about this topic). If the code executes successfully, the interceptors are called again in reverse order; and finally, when needed, the view is rendered (see Figure 4-5).

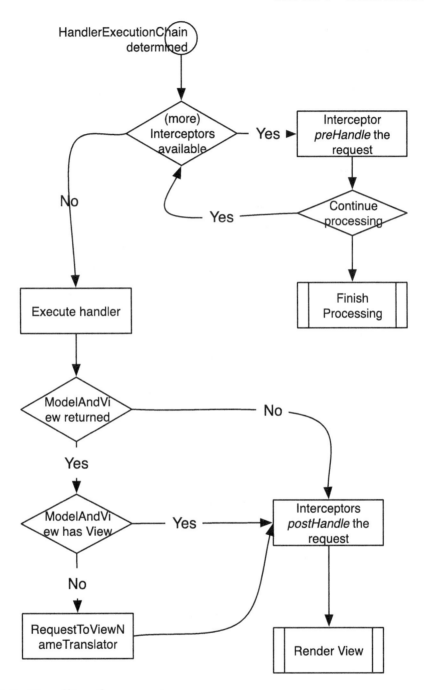

Figure 4-5. *Handling the request*

The execution of the handler is delegated to the selected HandlerAdapter that was determined in the previous step. It knows how to execute the selected handler and translate the response into org.springframework.web.servlet.ModelAndView.

If there is no view in the returned model and view, org.springframework.web. servlet.RequestToViewNameTranslator is consulted to generate a view name based on the incoming request.

Handler Exceptions

When an exception is thrown during the handling of the request, DispatcherServlet consults the configured org.springframework.web.servlet. HandlerExceptionResolver instances to handle the thrown exception. The resolver can translate the exception to a view to show the user. For instance, if there is an exception related to database errors, you could show a page indicating the database is down. If the exception isn't resolved, it is rethrown and handled by the servlet container, which generally results in an HTTP 500 response code (internal server error). Figure 4-6 shows this part of the request processing workflow.

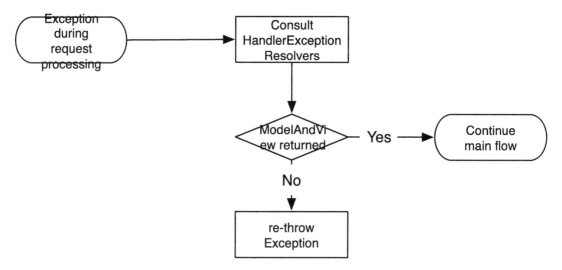

Figure 4-6. *Exception handling*

Render a View

If a view has been selected during the request processing workflow, `DispatcherServlet` first checks whether it is a view reference (this is the case if the view is `java.lang.String`). If so, the configured `org.springframework.web.servlet.ViewResolver` beans are consulted to resolve the view reference to an actual `org.springframework.web.servlet.View` implementation. If there is no view and one cannot be resolved, `javax.servlet.ServletException` is thrown. Figure 4-7 shows the view rendering process.

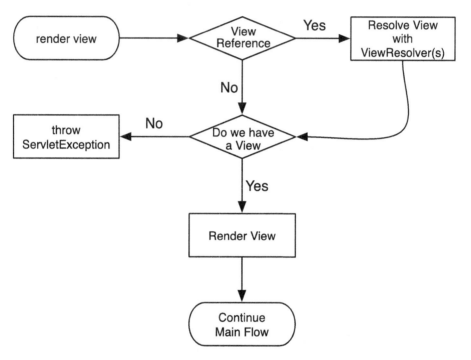

Figure 4-7. *The view rendering process*

Finish the Processing

Each incoming request passes through this step of the request processing flow, regardless of whether there are exceptions. If a `handler execution chain` is available, the `afterCompletion` method of the interceptors is called. Only the interceptors where the `preHandle` method was successfully invoked have their `afterCompletion` method is called. Next, these interceptors are executed in the reverse order that their `preHandle` method was called. This mimics the behavior seen in servlet filters, where the first filter called is also the last one to be called.

Finally, `DispatcherServlet` uses the event mechanism in the Spring Framework to fire `org.springframework.web.context.support.RequestHandledEvent` (see Figure 4-8). You could create and configure `org.springframework.context.ApplicationListener` to receive and log these events.

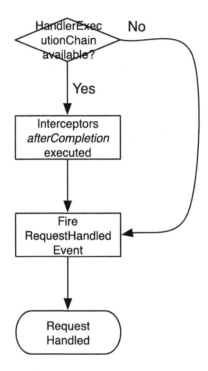

Figure 4-8. *Finish the processing*

The Request Processing Summary

`DispatcherServlet` is a key component in processing requests with Spring MVC. It is also highly flexible and configurable. This flexibility comes from the fact that the servlet uses many different components to fulfill its role, and these components are expressed as interfaces. Table 4-1 gives an overview of all the main component types involved in the request processing workflow.

Table 4-1. *The DispatcherServlet Components Used in Request Processing Workflow*

Component Type	Description
`org.springframework.web.multipart.` `MultipartResolver`	Strategy interface to handle multipart form processing
`org.springframework.web.servlet.` `LocaleResolver`	Strategy for locale resolution and modification
`org.springframework.web.servlet.` `ThemeResolver`	Strategy for theming resolution and modification
`org.springframework.web.servlet.` `HandlerMapping`	Strategy to map incoming requests to handler objects
`org.springframework.web.servlet.` `HandlerAdapter`	Strategy for the handler object type to execute the handler
`org.springframework.web.servlet.` `HandlerExceptionResolver`	Strategy to handle exceptions thrown during handler execution
`org.springframework.web.servlet.` `RequestToViewNameTranslator`	Strategy to determine a view name when the handler returns none
`org.springframework.web.servlet.` `ViewResolver`	Strategy to translate the view name to an actual view implementation
`org.springframework.web.servlet.` `FlashMapManager`	Strategy to simulate flash scope

In the upcoming sections, you see how to configure `DispatcherServlet`. You also take a closer look at different implementations of the various components.

DispatcherServlet

Like any servlet, `org.springframework.web.servlet.DispatcherServlet` needs to be configured so that the web container can bootstrap and map the servlet. This way, it can handle requests. Configuring `DispatcherServlet` is a two-way process. First, you need to tell the container to load a servlet and map it to one or more URL patterns.

After bootstrapping, the servlet uses the created `org.springframework.web.context.WebApplicationContext` to configure itself. The servlet tries to detect the needed components from this application context, and if not found, it uses a default (in most cases).

Bootstrapping DispatcherServlet

The servlet specification (as of version 3.0) has several options for configuring and registering a servlet.

- Option 1: Use a `web.xml` file (see Listing 4-1).

- Option 2: Use a `web-fragment.xml` file (see Listing 4-2).

- Option 3: Use `javax.servlet.ServletContainerInitializer` (see Listing 4-3).

- Option 4: The sample application uses Spring 5.2, so you can get a fourth option by implementing the `org.springframework.web.WebApplicationInitializer` interface.

- Option 5: Use Spring Boot to autoconfigure `DispatcherServlet`.

The dispatcher servlet needs a `web application context` that should contain all the beans that enable the dispatcher servlet to configure itself. By default, the dispatcher servlet creates `org.springframework.web.context.support.XmlWebApplicationContext`.

All samples in the upcoming sections load `org.springframework.web.servlet.DispatcherServlet` and map it to all incoming requests (`/`). All these configurations lead to the same runtime setup of the servlet. Only the mechanism by which you do that is different. The remainder of the book uses option 4 to configure the sample application.

ⓘ   `org.springframework.web.context.WebApplicationContext` is a specialized extension of `org.springframework.context.ApplicationContext` that is needed in web environments (see Chapter 2 for more information).

The sample application that you are building throughout the book uses option 5 as much as possible to configure the environment and application. Nevertheless, you learn the basic setup for all four options of configuring the servlet.

Using web.xml

The web.xml file has been around since the inception of the servlet specification. It is an XML file that contains all the configuration you need to bootstrap the servlet, listeners, and/or filters. Listing 4-1 shows the minimal web.xml configuration required to bootstrap DispatcherServlet. The web.xml file must be in the WEB-INF directory of the web application (this is dictated by the servlet specification).

Listing 4-1. The web.xml Configuration (Servlet 4.0)

```
<web-app xmlns="http://xmlns.jcp.org/xml/ns/javaee"
  xmlns:xsi="http://www.w3.org/2001/XMLSchema-instance"
  xsi:schemaLocation="http://xmlns.jcp.org/xml/ns/javaee
                      http://xmlns.jcp.org/xml/ns/javaee/web-app_4_0.xsd"
  version="4.0" metadata-complete="true">

  <servlet>
    <servlet-name>bookstore</servlet-name>
    <servlet-class>org.springframework.web.servlet.DispatcherServlet
    </servlet-class>
    <load-on-startup>1</load-on-startup>
  </servlet>

  <servlet-mapping>
    <servlet-name>bookstore</servlet-name>
    <url-pattern>/</url-pattern>
  </servlet-mapping>

</web-app>
```

> ℹ️ By default, the dispatcher servlet loads a file named [servletname]-servlet.xml from the WEB-INF directory.

The `metadata-complete` attribute in the web-app element instructs the servlet container to not scan the classpath for `javax.servlet.ServletContainerInitializer` implementations; neither it scan for `web-fragment.xml` files. Adding this attribute to your `web.xml` can considerably increase startup times because it scans the classpath, which takes time in a large application.

Using web-fragment.xml

The web-fragment.xml feature has been available since the 3.0 version of the servlet specification, and it allows a more modularized configuration of the web application. The `web-fragment.xml` has to be in the `META-INF` directory of a jar file. It isn't detected in the web application's `META-INF`; it must be in a jar file. `web-fragment.xml` can contain the same elements as `web.xml` (see Listing 4-2).

The benefit of this approach is that each module packaged as a jar file contributes to the configuration of the web application. This is also considered a drawback because now you have scattered your configuration over your code base, which could be troublesome in larger projects.

Listing 4-2. The `web-fragment.xml` Configuration (Servlet 4.0)

```xml
<web-fragment xmlns="http://java.sun.com/xml/ns/javaee"
              xmlns:xsi="http://www.w3.org/2001/XMLSchema-instance"
              xsi:schemaLocation="http://xmlns.jcp.org/xml/ns/javaee
              http://xmlns.jcp.org/xml/ns/javaee/web-fragment_4_0.xsd"
              version="4.0" metadata-complete="true">

  <servlet>
    <servlet-name>bookstore</servlet-name>
    <servlet-class>org.springframework.web.servlet.DispatcherServlet</servlet-class>
    <load-on-startup>1</load-on-startup>
  </servlet>

  <servlet-mapping>
    <servlet-name>bookstore</servlet-name>
    <url-pattern>/*</url-pattern>
  </servlet-mapping>

</web-fragment>
```

Using ServletContainerInitializer

The 3.0 version of the servlet specification introduced the option to use a Java-based approach to configuring your web environment (see Listing 4-3). A Servlet 3.0+ compatible container scan the classpath for classes that implement the `javax.servlet.ServletContainerInitializer` interface, and it invokes the `onStartup` method on those classes. By adding a `javax.servlet.annotation.HandlesTypes` annotation on these classes, you can also be handed classes that you need to further configure your web application (this is the mechanism that allows the fourth option to use `org.springframework.web.WebApplicationInitializer`).

Like web fragments, `ServletContainerInitializer` allows a modularized configuration of your web application, but now in a Java-based way. Using Java gives you all the added benefits of using the Java language instead of XML. At this point, you have strong typing, can influence the construction of your servlet, and have an easier way of configuring your servlets (in an XML file, this is done by adding init-param and/or context-param elements in the XML file).

Listing 4-3. A Java-based Configuration

```
package com.apress.prospringmvc.bookstore.web;

import java.util.Set;

// javax.servlet imports omitted.

import org.springframework.web.servlet.DispatcherServlet;

public class BookstoreServletContainerInitializer
  implements ServletContainerInitializer {

  @Override
  public void onStartup(Set<Class<?>> classes, ServletContext
  servletContext)
  throws ServletException {

    ServletRegistration.Dynamic registration;
    registration = servletContext.addServlet("ds", DispatcherServlet.
    class);
```

```
    registration.setLoadOnStartup(1);
    registration.addMapping("/");
  }
}
```

Using WebApplicationInitializer

Now it's time to look at option 4 for configuring your application while using Spring. Spring provides a ServletContainerInitializer implementation (org. springframework.web.SpringServletContainerInitializer) that makes life a little easier (see Listing 4-4). The implementation provided by the Spring Framework detects and instantiates all instances of org.springframework. web.WebApplicationInitializer and calls the onStartup method of those instances.

Listing 4-4. The WebApplicationInitializer Configuration

```
package com.apress.prospringmvc.bookstore.web;

// javax.servlet imports omitted

import org.springframework.web.WebApplicationInitializer;
import org.springframework.web.servlet.DispatcherServlet;

public class BookstoreWebApplicationInitializer
  implements WebApplicationInitializer {

  @Override
  public void onStartup(ServletContext servletContext)
  throws ServletException {

    ServletRegistration.Dynamic registration
    = servletContext.addServlet("dispatcher",
    DispatcherServlet.class);
    registration.addMapping("/");
    registration.setLoadOnStartup(1);
  }
}
```

> Using this feature can impact the startup time of your application! First, the servlet container needs to scan the classpath for all `javax.servlet.ServletContainerInitializer` implementations. Second, the classpath is scanned for `org.springframework.web.WebApplicationInitializer` implementations. This scanning can take some time in large applications.

Instead of directly implementing `WebApplicationInitializer`, use one of Spring's classes.

Using Spring Boot

When using Spring Boot, you don't need to configure `DispatcherServlet` manually. Spring Boot automatically configure based on the detected configuration. The properties mentioned in Table 4-2 are mostly configurable through properties in the `spring.mvc` namespace. See Listing 4-5 for a basic sample.

Listing 4-5. `BookstoreApplication` Using Spring Boot

```
package com.apress.prospringmvc.bookstore;

@SpringBootApplication
public class BookstoreApplication {

  public static void main(String[] args) {
    SpringApplication.run(BookstoreApplication.class, args);
  }
}
```

A specialized `WebApplicationInitializer` is needed when using Spring Boot in a classic WAR application. Spring Boot provides the `SpringBootServletInitializer` for this. See Listing 4-6 for a sample.

Listing 4-6. `BookstoreApplication` Using Spring Boot in a WAR

```
package com.apress.prospringmvc.bookstore;

@SpringBootApplication
public class BookstoreApplication extends SpringBootServletInitializer {
```

```
public static void main(String[] args) {
  SpringApplication.run(BookstoreApplication.class, args);
}

@Override
protected SpringApplicationBuilder configure(SpringApplicationBuilder
builder) {
    return builder.sources(BookstoreApplication.class);
  }
}
```

Configuring DispatcherServlet

Configuring org.springframework.web.servlet.DispatcherServlet is a two-step process. The first step is to configure the servlet's behavior by setting properties directly on the dispatcher servlet (the declaration). The second step is to configure the components in the application context (initialization).

The dispatcher servlet comes with a lot of default settings for components. This saves you from doing a lot of configuration for basic behavior, and you can override and extend the configuration however you want. In addition to the default configuration for the dispatcher servlet, there is also a default for Spring MVC. This can be enabled by using an org.springframework.web.servlet.config.annotation.EnableWebMvc annotation (see the "Enabling Features" section in Chapter 2).

When using Spring Boot, you don't need to add *@EnableWebMvc* because it is enabled by default when Spring Boot detects Spring MVC on the classpath.

DispatcherServlet Properties

The dispatcher servlet has several properties that can be set. All these properties have a setter method, and all can be either set programmatically or by including a servlet initialization parameter. Table 4-2 lists and describes the properties available on the dispatcher servlet.

Table 4-2. The DispatcherServlet's Properties

Property	Default	Description
cleanupAfterInclude	True	Indicates whether to clean up the request attributes after an include request. In general, the default suffices, and this property should only be set to false in special cases.
contextAttribute	Null	Stores the application context for this servlet. It is useful if the application context is created by some means other than the servlet itself.
contextClass	org.springframework.web.context.support.XmlWebApplicationContext	Configures the type of org.springframework.web.context.WebApplicationContext to be constructed by the servlet (it needs a default constructor). Configured using the given contextConfigLocation. It isn't needed if you pass in an application context by using the constructor.
contextConfigLocation	[servlet-name]-servlet.xml	Indicates the location of the configuration files for the specified application context class.
contextId	Null	Provides the application context ID. For example, this is used when the context is logged or sent to System.out.
contextInitializers contextInitializer Classes	Null	Use the optional org.springframework.context.ApplicationContextInitializer classes to do some initialization logic for the application context, such as activating a certain profile.

(continued)

91

Table 4-2. (*continued*)

Property	Default	Description
detectAllHandlerAdapters	True	Detects all org.springframework.web.servlet. HandlerAdapter instances from the application context. When set to false, a single one is detected by using the special name, handlerAdapter.
detectAllHandler ExceptionResolvers	True	Detects all org.springframework.web.servlet. HandlerExceptionResolver instances from the application context. When set to false, a single one is detected by using the special name, handlerExceptionResolver.
detectAllHandlerMappings	True	Detects all org.springframework.web.servlet. HandlerMapping beans from the application context. When set to false, a single one is detected by using the special name, handlerMapping.
detectAllViewResolvers	True	Detects all org.springframework.web.servlet.ViewResolver beans from the application context. When set to false, a single one is detected by using the special name, viewResolver.
dispatchOptionsRequest	False	Indicates whether to handle HTTP OPTIONS requests. The default is false; when set to true, you can also handle HTTP OPTIONS requests.

Property	Default	Description
dispatchTraceRequest	False	Indicates whether to handle HTTP TRACE requests. The default is false; when set to true, you can also handle HTTP TRACE requests.
environment	org.springframework. web.context.support. StandardServlet Environment	Configures org.springframework.core.env.Environment for this servlet. The environment specifies which profile is active and can hold properties specific to this environment.
namespace	[servletname]-servlet	Use this namespace to configure the application context.
publishContext	True	Indicates whether the servlet's application context is being published to the javax.servlet.ServletContext. For production, we recommend that you set this to false.
publishEvents	True	Indicates whether to fire after request processing org. springframework.web.context.support. ServletRequestHandledEvent. You can use org. springframework.context.ApplicationListener to receive these events.
threadContextInheritable	False	Indicates whether to expose the LocaleContext and RequestAttributes to child threads created from the request handling thread.

The Application Context

org.springframework.web.servlet.DispatcherServlet needs org.springframework.
web.context.WebApplicationContext to configure itself with the needed components.
You can either let the servlet construct one itself or use the constructor to pass an
application context. In an XML-based configuration file, the first option is used (because
there is no way to construct an application context). In a Java-based configuration, the
second option is used.

In the sample application, the com.apress.prospringmvc.bookstore.web.
BookstoreWebApplicationInitializer class bootstraps the application. To
enable Java-based configuration, you need to instruct the servlet to use a Java-
based application context (the default is an XML-based one) and pass it the
configuration classes. You use the org.springframework.web.context.support.
AnnotationConfigWebApplicationContext class to set up the application and to
configure the servlet. The changes are highlighted in bold in Listing 4-7.

Listing 4-7. The BookstoreWebApplicationInitializer with ApplicationContext

```
package com.apress.prospringmvc.bookstore.web;

// javax.servlet imports omitted.

import org.springframework.web.WebApplicationInitializer;
import org.springframework.web.context.WebApplicationContext;
import org.springframework.web.context.support.
AnnotationConfigWebApplicationContext;
import org.springframework.web.servlet.DispatcherServlet;
import com.apress.prospringmvc.bookstore.web.config.
WebMvcContextConfiguration;

public class BookstoreWebApplicationInitializer implements
WebApplicationInitializer {

  @Override
  public void onStartup(final ServletContext servletContext) throws
ServletException {
    registerDispatcherServlet(servletContext);
  }
```

```
private void registerDispatcherServlet(final ServletContext
servletContext) {
  WebApplicationContext dispatcherContext = createContext(WebMvcContextCo
  nfiguration.class);
  DispatcherServlet dispatcherServlet = new DispatcherServlet(dispatcherC
  ontext);
  ServletRegistration.Dynamic dispatcher;
  dispatcher = servletContext.addServlet("dispatcher",
  dispatcherServlet);

  dispatcher.setLoadOnStartup(1);
  dispatcher.addMapping("/");
}

private WebApplicationContext createContext(final Class<?>...
annotatedClasses) {

  AnnotationConfigWebApplicationContext
    context = new AnnotationConfigWebApplicationContext();
  context.register(annotatedClasses);
  return context;
  }
}
```

Listing 4-7 shows how to construct `org.springframework.web.servlet.`
`DispatcherServlet` and pass it an application context. This is the most basic way of
configuring the servlet.

Chapter 2 covered profiles. To select a profile, you could include a servlet-
initialization parameter (see Chapter 2); however, to be more dynamic, you could use
`org.springframework.context.ApplicationContextInitializer`. Such initializers
initialize an application context just before it loads all the beans.

This is useful in a web application when you want to configure or set the profile(s)
you want to use (again, see Chapter 2 for more information). For instance, you might
have a custom system property you need to set. Alternatively, you might detect the
profile by reading a certain file on the file system or selecting a profile based on the
operation system. You have an almost unlimited number of options.

Listing 4-8. The CloudApplicationContextInitializer

```
packag* org.cloudfoundry.reconfiguration.spring;

// Other imports omitted

import org.cloudfoundry.runtime.env.CloudEnvironment;
import org.springframework.context.ApplicationContextInitializer;
import org.springframework.context.ConfigurableApplicationContext;
import org.springframework.core.Ordered;
import org.springframework.core.env.ConfigurableEnvironment;
import org.springframework.core.env.EnumerablePropertySource;
import org.springframework.core.env.PropertiesPropertySource;
import org.springframework.core.env.PropertySource;

public final class CloudApplicationContextInitializer
implements ApplicationContextInitializer<ConfigurableApplicationContext>,
Ordered {

  private static final Log logger = LogFactory.getLog(CloudApplicationConte
  xtInitializer.class);

  private static final int DEFAULT_ORDER = 0;
  private ConfigurableEnvironment springEnvironment;
  private CloudEnvironment cloudFoundryEnvironment;

  public CloudApplicationContextInitializer() {
    cloudFoundryEnvironment = new CloudEnvironment();
  }

  @Override
  public void initialize(ConfigurableApplicationContext applicationContext)
{
```

```
  if (!cloudFoundryEnvironment.isCloudFoundry()) {
    logger.info("Not running on Cloud Foundry.");
    return;
  }

  try {
    logger.info("Initializing Spring Environment for Cloud Foundry");
    springEnvironment = applicationContext.getEnvironment();
    addPropertySource(buildPropertySource());
    addActiveProfile("cloud");
  } catch(Throwable t) {
    // be safe
    logger.error("Unexpected exception on initialization: " +
    t.getMessage**(), t);
  }
}

// Other methods omitted
}
```

Component Resolution

When the servlet is configured, it receives an initialization request from the servlet
container. When the servlet initializes, it uses logic to detect the components needed
(see Figure 4-9).

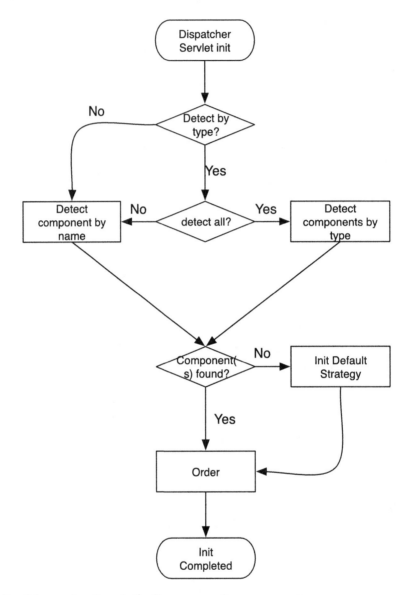

Figure 4-9. *DispatcherServlet's discovery of components*

Some components are detected by type, whereas others are detected by name. For the components detectable by type, you can specify (see Table 4-2) that you don't want to do this. In this case, the component is detected by a well-known name. Table 4-3 lists the different components involved in request processing and the bean name used to detect it. The table also indicates whether the dispatcher servlet detects multiple instances automatically (when yes can be disabled, then a single bean is detected by the name, as specified in the table).

Table 4-3. *Components and Their Names*

Component	Default Bean Name	Detect Multiple
org.springframework.web.multipart.MultipartResolver	multipartResolver	No
org.springframework.web.servlet.LocaleResolver	localeResolver	No
org.springframework.web.servlet.ThemeResolver	themeResolver	No
org.springframework.web.servlet.HandlerMapping	handlerMapping	Yes
org.springframework.web.servlet.HandlerAdapter	handlerAdapter	Yes
org.springframework.web.servlet.HandlerExceptionResolver	handlerExceptionResolver	Yes
org.springframework.web.servlet.RequestToViewNameTranslator	requestToViewNameTranslator	No
org.springframework.web.servlet.ViewResolver	viewResolver	Yes
org.springframework.web.servlet.FlashMapManager	flashMapManager	No

DispatcherServlet's Default Configuration

You might feel a bit overwhelmed by all the components involved in the handling of a request. You might even wonder if you need to configure all of them explicitly. Luckily, Spring MVC has some sensible defaults that, in a lot of cases, are enough—or at least enough to get started. As you can see in Table 4-4, the dispatcher servlet has a few default settings. You can find more information on the different implementations in the next section.

Table 4-4. *DispatcherServlet's Default Components*

Component	Default Implementation(s)
MultipartResolver	No default, explicit configuration is required
LocaleResolver	org.springframework.web.servlet.i18n. AcceptHeaderLocaleResolver
ThemeResolver	org.springframework.web.servlet.theme. FixedThemeResolver
HandlerMapping	org.springframework.web.servlet. handler.BeanNameUrlHandlerMapping, org. springframework.web.servlet.mvc.method. annotation.RequestMappingHandlerMapping, org. springframework.web.servlet.function.support. RouterFunctionMapping
HandlerAdapter	org.springframework.web.servlet. mvc.HttpRequestHandlerAdapter, org. springframework.web.servlet.mvc. SimpleControllerHandlerAdapter, org. springframework.web.servlet.mvc.method. annotation.RequestMappingHandlerAdapter, org. springframework.web.servlet.function.support. HandlerFunctionAdapter
HandlerExceptionResolver	org.springframework.web.servlet.mvc.method. annotation.ExceptionHandlerExceptionResolver, org.springframework.web.servlet.mvc. annotation.ResponseStatusExceptionResolver, org.springframework.web.servlet.mvc.support. DefaultHandlerExceptionResolver
RequestToViewNameTranslator	org.springframework.web.servlet.view. DefaultRequestToViewNameTranslator
ViewResolver	org.springframework.web.servlet.view. InternalResourceViewResolver
FlashMapManager	org.springframework.web.servlet.support. SessionFlashMapManager

The Spring Boot Defaults

Spring Boot inherits most of the default configuration mentioned in the previous section. It does differ in some parts, however.

Spring Boot enables `org.springframework.web.multipart.support.StandardServletMultipartResolver` by default. This can be disabled by declaring your own `MultipartResolver` or setting the `spring.servlet.multipart.enabled` property to `false`. Other properties in the `spring.servlet.multipart` namespace can configure file uploading.

Next to that, it adds two `ViewResolvers` to the list. It adds `org.springframework.web.servlet.view.BeanNameViewResolver` and `org.springframework.web.servlet.view.ContentNegotiatingViewResolver`. It still has the `InternalResourceViewResolver` which can be, partially, configured through using the `spring.mvc.view.prefix` and `spring.mvc.view.suffix` properties.

The Spring MVC Components

In the previous sections, you learned about the request processing workflow and the components used in it. You also learned how to configure `org.springframework.web.servlet.DispatcherServlet`. In this section, you take a closer look at all the components involved in the request processing workflow. For example, you explore the different components' APIs and see which implementations ship with the Spring Framework.

HandlerMapping

`Handler mapping` determines which handler to dispatch the incoming request to. A criterion that you could use to map the incoming request is the URL; however, implementations (see Figure 4-10) are free to choose what criteria to use to determine the mapping.

The API for `org.springframework.web.servlet.HandlerMapping` consists of a single method (see Listing 4-9). This method is called by `DispatcherServlet` to determine `org.springframework.web.servlet.HandlerExecutionChain`. It is possible to have more than one handler mapping configured. The servlet calls the different handler mappings in sequence until one of them doesn't return null.

Listing 4-9. The HandlerMapping API

```
package org.springframework.web.servlet;

import javax.servlet.http.HttpServletRequest;

public interface HandlerMapping {

    HandlerExecutionChain getHandler(HttpServletRequest request)
    throws Exception;

}
```

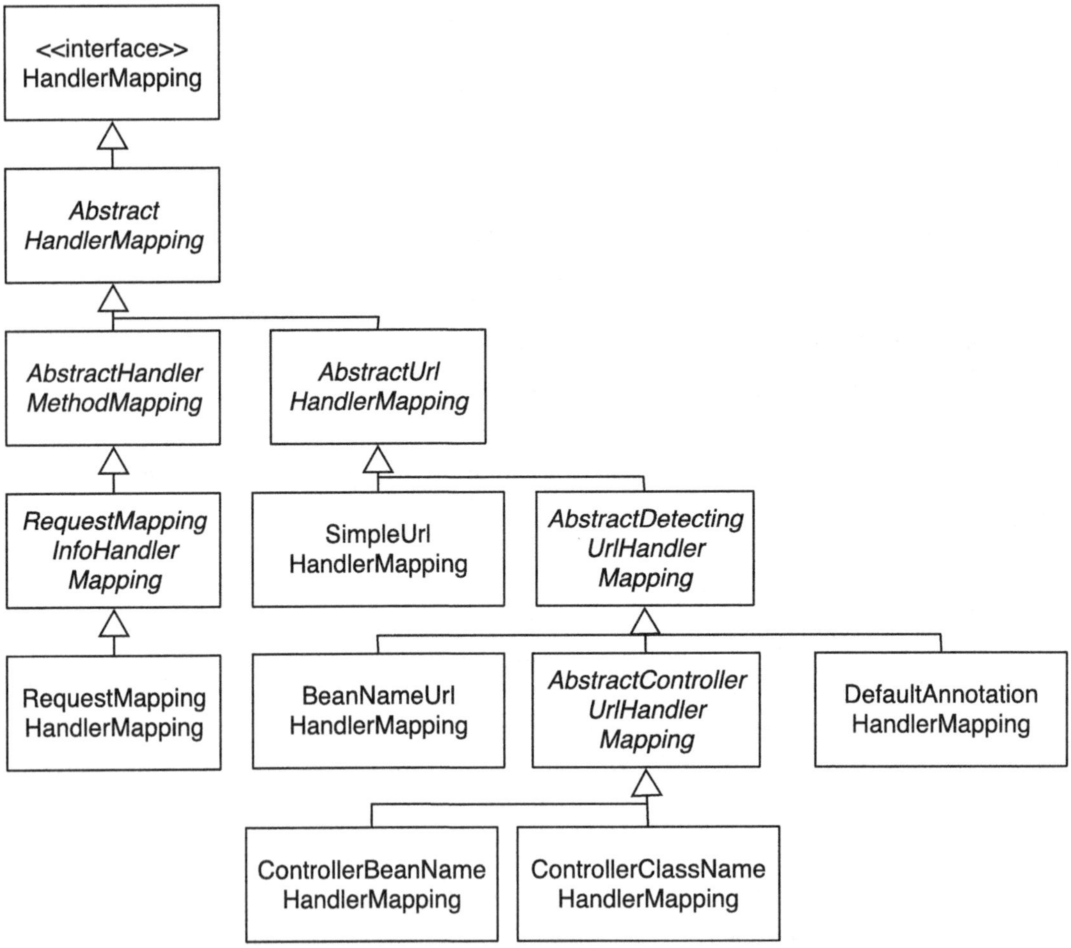

Figure 4-10. *HandlerMapping implementations*

Out of the box, Spring MVC provides four different implementations. Most of them are based on URL mappings. One of the implementations offers a more sophisticated mapping strategy, which you'll learn about momentarily. However, before looking at the different implementations, take a closer look at a URL to see which parts are important.

A request URL consists of several parts. Let's dissect the URL http://www.example. org/bookstore/app/home. A URL consists of four parts (see Figure 4-11).

1. The hostname of the server, consisting of protocol + :// + hostname or domain name + : + port

2. The name of the application (none, if it is the root application)

3. The name of the servlet mapping (in the sample app, it is mapped to /)

4. The path inside the servlet

Figure 4-11. *URL mapping*

By default, all the provided handler-mapping implementations use the path relative to the servlet context inside the servlet (the servlet context relative path) to resolve handlers. Setting the alwaysUseFullPath property to true can change this behavior. The servlet mapping is then included, which (for the example at hand) leads to */app/home* resolving a request handler; otherwise, */home* is used.

A final feature shared among all implementations is that a default handler can be configured. This is done by setting the defaultHandler property. When no handler can be found for an incoming request, it is always mapped to the default handler. This is optional, and it should be used with caution, especially when chaining multiple handler mappings. Only the last handler mapping should specify a default handler, or else the chain breaks.

BeanNameUrlHandlerMapping

The org.springframework.web.servlet.handler.BeanNameUrlHandlerMapping implementation is one of the default strategies used by the dispatcher servlet. This implementation treats any bean with a name that starts with a / as a potential request handler. A bean can have multiple names, and names can also contain a wildcard, expressed as an *.

This implementation uses ant-style regular expressions to match the URL of the incoming request to the name of a bean. It follows this algorithm.

1. Attempt exact match; if found, exit.

2. Search all registered paths for a match; the most specific one wins.

3. If no matches are found, return the handler mapped to /* or to the default handler (if configured).

ℹ️   The name of the bean is different from the ID. Historically, it is defined by the XML specification, and it cannot contain special characters such as /. This means you need to use the name of the bean. You can provide the name for a bean by setting the name attribute on the `org.springframework.context.annotation.Bean` annotation. A bean can have multiple names, and names can be written like an ant-style regular expression.

Listing 4-10 shows how to use a bean name and map it to the /index.htm URL. In the sample application, you could now use http://localhost:8080/chapter4-bookstore/index.htm to call this controller.

Listing 4-10. The BeanNameUrlHandlerMapping sample Configuration

```
package com.apress.prospringmvc.bookstore.web.config;

import java.util.Properties;
import org.springframework.context.annotation.Bean;
import org.springframework.context.annotation.Configuration;
import com.apress.prospringmvc.bookstore.web.IndexController;

@Configuration
public class WebMvcContextConfiguration {

  @Bean(name = { "/index.htm" })
  public IndexController indexController() {
    return new IndexController();
  }
}
```

SimpleUrlHandlerMapping

This implementation requires explicit configuration, as opposed to `org.springframework.web.servlet.handler.BeanNameUrlHandlerMapping`, and it doesn't autodetect mappings. Listing 4-11 shows a sample configuration. Again, you map the controller to the /index.htm.

Listing 4-11. The SimpleUrlHandlerMapping Sample Configuration

```
package com.apress.prospringmvc.bookstore.web.config;

// Other imports omitted see Listing 4-10

import org.springframework.web.servlet.HandlerMapping;
import org.springframework.web.servlet.handler.SimpleUrlHandlerMapping;

@Configuration
public class WebMvcContextConfiguration {

  @Bean
  public IndexController indexController() {
    return new IndexController();
  }

  @Bean
  public HandlerMapping simpleUrlHandlerMapping() {
    var mappings = new Properties();
    mappings.put("/index.htm", "indexController");
    var urlMapping = new SimpleUrlHandlerMapping();
    urlMapping.setMappings(mappings);
    return urlMapping;
  }
}
```

You need to explicitly configure the `SimpleUrlHandlerMapping` and pass it the mappings (see the code in bold). You map the /index.htm URL to the controller named indexController. If you have a lot of controllers, this configuration grows considerably. The advantage of this approach is that you have all your mapping in a single location.

RequestMappingHandlerMapping

The RequestMappingHandlerMapping implementation is more sophisticated. It uses annotations to configure mappings. The annotation can be on either the class and/or the method level. To map the com.apress.prospringmvc.bookstore.web.IndexController to /index.htm, you need to add the @RequestMapping annotation. Listing 4-12 is the controller, and Listing 4-13 shows the sample configuration.

Listing 4-12. The IndexController with RequestMapping

```java
package com.apress.prospringmvc.bookstore.web;

import org.springframework.stereotype.Controller;
import org.springframework.web.bind.annotation.RequestMapping;
import org.springframework.web.servlet.ModelAndView;

@Controller
public class IndexController {

  @RequestMapping(value = "/index.htm")
  public ModelAndView indexPage() {
    return new ModelAndView("/WEB-INF/views/index.jsp");
  }
}
```

Listing 4-13. An annotation-based sample Configuration

```java
package com.apress.prospringmvc.bookstore.web.config;

// Other imports omitted see Listing 4-10

@Configuration
public class WebMvcContextConfiguration {

  @Bean
  public IndexController indexController() {
    return new IndexController();
  }
}
```

RouterFunctionMapping

The org.springframework.web.servlet.function.support.HandlerFunctionAdapter implementation is a functional way to define handlers. Listing 4-14 shows the functional style of writing a handler to render the index page.

Listing 4-14. A Functional-Style Sample Configuration

```
package com.apress.prospringmvc.bookstore.web.config;

// Other imports omitted see Listing 4-10
import org.springframework.web.servlet.function.RouterFunction;
import org.springframework.web.servlet.function.ServerRequest;
import org.springframework.web.servlet.function.ServerResponse;

@Configuration
public class WebMvcContextConfiguration {

  @Bean
  public RouterFunction<ServerResponse> routes() {
    return route()
      .GET("/", response -> ok().render("index"))
      .build();
  }
}
```

HandlerAdapter

org.springframework.web.servlet.HandlerAdapter is the glue between the dispatcher servlet and the selected handler. It removes the actual execution logic from the dispatcher servlet, which makes the dispatcher servlet infinitely extensible. Consider this component the glue between the servlet and the actual handler implementation. Listing 4-15 shows the HandlerAdapter API.

Listing 4-15. The HandlerAdapter API

```
package org.springframework.web.servlet;

import javax.servlet.http.HttpServletRequest;
import javax.servlet.http.HttpServletResponse;

public interface HandlerAdapter {

  boolean supports(Object handler);
  ModelAndView handle(HttpServletRequest request, HttpServletResponse
response, Object handler) throws Exception;
  long getLastModified(HttpServletRequest request, Object handler);
}
```

As Listing 4-15 shows, the API consists of three methods. The supports method is called on each handler in the context by the dispatcher servlet; this is done to determine which HandlerAdapter can execute the selected handler. If the handler adapter can execute the handler, the handle method is called to execute the selected handler. The execution of the handler can lead to org.springframework.web.servlet.ModelAndView being returned. However, some implementations always return null, indicating the response was already sent to the client.

If the incoming request is a GET or HEAD request, the getLastModified method is called to determine when the underlying resource was last modified (–1 means the content is always regenerated). The result is sent back to the client as a Last-Modified request header and compared with the If-Modified-Since request header. If there was a modification, the content is regenerated and resent to the client; otherwise, an HTTP Response Code 304 (Not Modified) is sent back to the client. This is particularly useful when the dispatcher servlet serves static resources, which save bandwidth.

Out of the box, Spring MVC provides five implementations of the HandlerAdapter (see Figure 4-12).

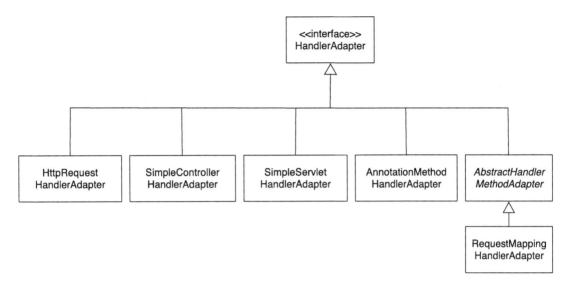

Figure 4-12. *HandlerAdapter implementations*

HttpRequestHandlerAdapter

`org.springframework.web.servlet.mvc.HttpRequestHandlerAdapter` knows how to execute `org.springframework.web.HttpRequestHandler` instances. This handler adapter is mostly used by Spring Remoting to support some of the HTTP remoting options. However, there are two implementations of the `org.springframework.web.HttpRequestHandler` interface that you also use. One serves static resources, and the other forwards incoming requests to the servlet container's default servlet (see Chapter 5 for more information).

SimpleControllerHandlerAdapter

`org.springframework.web.servlet.mvc.SimpleControllerHandlerAdapter` knows how to execute `org.springframework.web.servlet.mvc.Controller` implementations. It returns `org.springframework.web.servlet.ModelAndView` from the `handleRequest` method of the controller instance.

SimpleServletHandlerAdapter

It can be convenient to configure `javax.servlet.Servlet` instances in the application context and put them behind the dispatcher servlet. To execute those servlets, you need `org.springframework.web.servlet.handler.SimpleServletHandlerAdapter`. It knows how to execute `javax.servlet.Servlet`, and it always returns `null` because it expects the servlet to handle the response itself.

HandlerFunctionAdapter

`org.springframework.web.servlet.function.support.HandlerFunctionAdapter` knows how to execute `org.springframework.web.servlet.function.HandlerFunction` instances. It returns `org.springframework.web.servlet.ModelAndView` based on `org.springframework.web.servlet.function.ServerResponse` from the handler function.

RequestMappingHandlerAdapter

`org.springframework.web.servlet.mvc.method.annotation.RequestMappingHandlerAdapter` executes methods annotated with `org.springframework.web.bind.annotation.RequestMapping`. It converts method arguments and gives easy access to the request parameters. The return value of the method is converted or added to the `org.springframework.web.servlet.ModelAndView` implementation internally created by this handler adapter. The whole binding and converting process is configurable and flexible; the possibilities are explained in Chapters 5 and 6.

MultipartResolver

The `org.springframework.web.multipart.MultipartResolver` strategy interface determines whether an incoming request is a multipart file request (for file uploads), and if so, it wraps the incoming request in `org.springframework.web.multipart.MultipartHttpServletRequest`. The wrapped request can then get easy access to the underlying multipart files from the form. File uploading is explained in Chapter 7. Listing 4-16 shows the `MultipartResolver` API.

Listing 4-16. The MultipartResolver API

```
package org.springframework.web.multipart;

import javax.servlet.http.HttpServletRequest;

public interface MultipartResolver {

  boolean isMultipart(HttpServletRequest request);

  MultipartHttpServletRequest resolveMultipart(HttpServletRequest request)
```

```
throws MultipartException;

void cleanupMultipart(MultipartHttpServletRequest request);
}
```

The org.springframework.web.multipart.MultipartResolver component's three methods are called during the preparation and cleanup of the request. The isMultipart method is invoked to determine whether an incoming request is a multipart request. If it is, then the resolveMultipart method is called, which wraps the original request in MultipartHttpServletRequest. Finally, when the request has been handled, the cleanupMultipart method is invoked to clean up any used resources. Figure 4-13 shows the two out-of-the-box implementations of MultipartResolver.

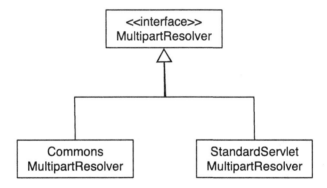

Figure 4-13. *The MultipartResolver implementations*

CommonsMultipartResolver

org.springframework.web.multipart.commons.CommonsMultipartResolver uses the Commons FileUpload library[1] to handle multipart files. It enables easy configuration of several aspects of the Commons FileUpload library.

StandardServletMultipartResolver

The Servlet 3.0 specification introduced a standard way of handling multipart forms. org.springframework.web.multipart.support.StandardServletMultipartResolv er merely serves as a wrapper around this standard approach, so that it is transparently exposed.

---

[1]https://commons.apache.org/fileupload/

LocaleResolver

The org.springframework.web.servlet.LocaleResolver strategy interface determines which java.util.Locale to render the page. In most cases, it resolves validation messages or labels in the application. The different implementations are shown in Figure 4-14 and described in the following subsections.

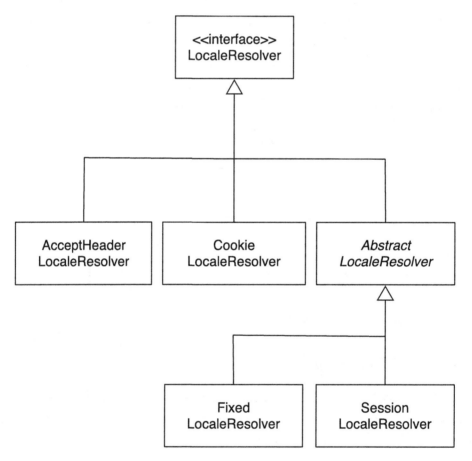

Figure 4-14. *LocaleResolver implementations*

Listing 4-17 shows the API for org.springframework.web.servlet.LocaleResolver.

Listing 4-17. The `LocaleResolver` API

```
package org.springframework.web.servlet;

import java.util.Locale;
import javax.servlet.http.HttpServletRequest;
import javax.servlet.http.HttpServletResponse;

public interface LocaleResolver {

  Locale resolveLocale(HttpServletRequest request);
  void setLocale(HttpServletRequest request,HttpServletResponse response,
              Locale locale);
}
```

The API consists of two methods that each play a role in storing and retrieving the current `java.util.Locale`. The `setLocale` method is called when you want to change the current locale. If the implementation doesn't support this, `java.lang.UnsupportedOperationException` is thrown. The `Spring Framework uses the resolveLocale method`—usually internally—to resolve the current locale.

AcceptHeaderLocaleResolver

The `org.springframework.web.servlet.i18n.AcceptHeaderLocaleResolver` implementation simply delegates to the `getLocale` method of the current `javax.servlet.HttpServletRequest`. It uses the `Accept-Language` HTTP header to determine the language. The client sets this header value; this resolver doesn't support changing the locale.

CookieLocaleResolver

The `org.springframework.web.servlet.i18n.CookieLocaleResolver` implementation uses `javax.servlet.http.Cookie` to store the locale to use. This is particularly useful in cases where you want an application to be as stateless as possible. The actual value is stored on the client side, and it is sent to you with each request. This resolver allows the locale to be changed (you can find more information on this in Chapter 6). This resolver also allows you to configure the name of the cookie and a default locale to use. If no value can be determined for the current request (i.e., there is neither a cookie nor a default locale), this resolver falls back to the request's locale (see `AcceptHeaderLocaleResolver`).

FixedLocaleResolver

org.springframework.web.servlet.i18n.FixedLocaleResolver is the most basic
implementation of org.springframework.web.servlet.LocaleResolver. It allows you
to configure a locale to use throughout the whole application. This configuration is fixed;
as such, it cannot be changed.

SessionLocaleResolver

The org.springframework.web.servlet.i18n.SessionLocaleResolver
implementation uses the javax.servlet.http.HttpSession to store the value of
the locale. The name of the attribute, as well as a default locale, can be configured.
If no value can be determined for the current request (i.e., there is neither a value
stored in the session nor a default locale), then it falls back to the request's locale (see
AcceptHeaderLocaleResolver). This resolver also lets you change the locale (see
Chapter 6 for more information).

ThemeResolver

The org.springframework.web.servlet.ThemeResolver strategy interface determines
which theme to render the page. There are several implementations; these are shown
in Figure 4-15 and explained in the following subsections. How to apply theming is
explained in Chapter 8. If no theme name can be resolved, then this resolver uses the
hardcoded default theme.

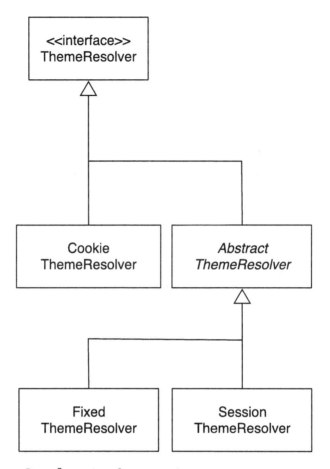

Figure 4-15. *ThemeResolver implementations*

Listing 4-18 shows the API for org.springframework.web.servlet.ThemeResolver, which is similar to the org.springframework.web.servlet.LocaleResolver API.

Listing 4-18. The ThemeResolver API

```
package org.springframework.web.servlet;

import javax.servlet.http.HttpServletRequest;
import javax.servlet.http.HttpServletResponse;
```

```
public interface ThemeResolver {

  String resolveThemeName(HttpServletRequest request);
  void setThemeName(HttpServletRequest request, HttpServletResponse
  response, String themeName);
}
```

You call the setThemeName method when you want to change the current theme. If changing the theme is not supported, it throws java. lang.UnsupportedOperationException. The Spring Framework invokes the resolveThemeName method when it needs to resolve the current theme. This is mainly done by using the theme JSP tag.

CookieThemeResolver

org.springframework.web.servlet.theme.CookieThemeResolver uses javax. servlet.http.Cookie to store the theme to use. This is particularly useful where you want your application to be as stateless as possible. The actual value is stored on the client side and sent to you with each request. This resolver allows the theme to be changed; you can find more information on this in Chapters 6 and 8. This resolver also allows you to configure the name of the cookie and a theme locale to use.

FixedThemeResolver

org.springframework.web.servlet.theme.FixedThemeResolver is the most basic implementation of org.springframework.web.servlet.ThemeResolver. It allows you to configure a theme to use throughout the whole application. This configuration is fixed; as such, it cannot be changed.

SessionThemeResolver

org.springframework.web.servlet.theme.SessionThemeResolver uses javax. servlet.http.HttpSession to store the value of the theme. The name of the attribute, as well as a default theme, can be configured.

HandlerExceptionResolver

In most cases, you want to control how you handle an exception that occurs during the handling of a request. You can use a `HandlerExceptionResolver` for this. The API (see Listing 4-19) consists of a single method that is called on the `org.springframework.web.servlet.HandlerExceptionResolvers` detected by the dispatcher servlet. The resolver can choose to handle the exception itself or to return an `org.springframework.web.servlet.ModelAndView` implementation that contains a view to render and a model (generally containing the exception thrown).

Listing 4-19. The HandlerExceptionResolver API

```
package org.springframework.web.servlet;

import javax.servlet.http.HttpServletRequest;
import javax.servlet.http.HttpServletResponse;

public interface HandlerExceptionResolver {

  ModelAndView resolveException(HttpServletRequest request,
                                HttpServletResponse response, Object
                                handler, Exception ex);
}
```

Figure 4-16 shows the different implementations provided by the Spring Framework. Each works in a slightly different way, just as each is configured differently (see Chapter 6 for more information).

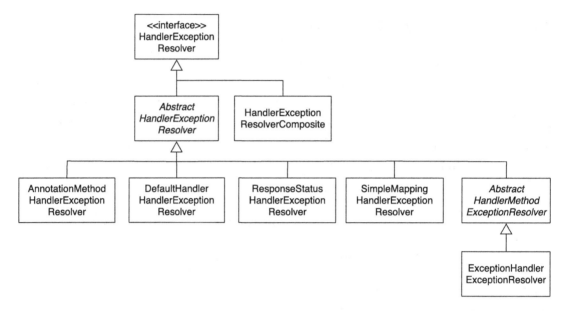

Figure 4-16. *The HandlerExceptionResolver implementations*

The `org.springframework.web.servlet.handler.`
`HandlerExceptionResolverComposite` implementation is used internally by Spring
MVC. It chains several `org.springframework.web.servlet.HandlerExceptionResolver`
implementations together. This resolver does not provide an actual implementation
or added functionality; instead, it merely acts as a wrapper around multiple
implementations (when multiple implementations are configured).

RequestToViewNameTranslator

When a handler returns no view implementation or view name and did not send a
response itself to the client, then `org.springframework.web.servlet.RequestToV`
`iewNameTranslator` tries to determine a view name from the incoming request. The
default implementation (see Figure 4-17), `org.springframework.web.servlet.`
`view.DefaultRequestToViewNameTranslator`, simply takes the URL, strips the
suffix and context path, and then uses the remainder as the view name (i.e., `http://`
`localhost:8080/bookstore/admin/index.html` becomes `admin/index`). You can find
more information about views in Chapter 8.

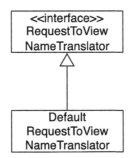

Figure 4-17. *The RequstToViewNameTranslator hierarchy*

The `RequestToViewNameTranslator` API is shown in Listing 4-20.

Listing 4-20. The RequestToViewNameTranslator API

```
package org.springframework.web.servlet;

import javax.servlet.http.HttpServletRequest;

public interface RequestToViewNameTranslator {

  String getViewName(HttpServletRequest request) throws Exception;

}
```

ViewResolver

Spring MVC provides a very flexible view resolving mechanism. It simply takes the view name returned from the handler and tries to resolve it to an actual view implementation (if no concrete `org.springframework.web.servlet.View` is returned). The actual implementation could be a JSP, but it could just as easily be an Excel spreadsheet or PDF file. For more information on view resolving, refer to Chapter 8.

This API (see Listing 4-21) is pretty simple and consists of a single method. This method takes the view name and currently selected locale (see also the `LocaleResolver`). This can resolve an actual View implementation. When there are multiple `org.springframework.web.servlet.ViewResolvers` configured, the dispatcher servlet calls them in turn until one of them returns a View to render.

Listing 4-21. The ViewResolver API

package org.springframework.web.servlet;

import java.util.Locale;

public interface ViewResolver {

　View resolveViewName(String viewName, Locale locale) **throws** Exception;

}

　　The ViewResolver implementations are shown in Figure 4-18. Out of the box, Spring provides several implementations (see Chapter 8 for more information).

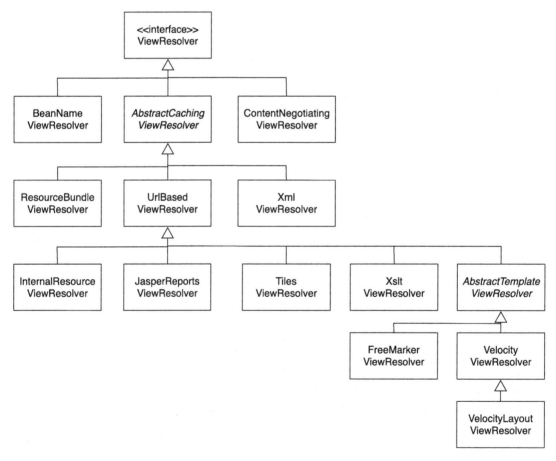

Figure 4-18. *The ViewResolver implementations*

FlashMapManager

`org.springframework.web.servlet.FlashMapManager` enables a flash "scope" in Spring MVC applications. You can use this mechanism to put attributes in a flash map that are then retrieved after a redirect (the flash map survives a request/response cycle). The flash map is cleared after the view is rendered. Spring provides a single implementation, `org.springframework.web.servlet.support.SessionFlashMapManager` (see Figure 4-19).

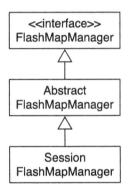

Figure 4-19. *The FlashMapManager hierarchy*

Listing 4-22 shows the `FlashMapManager` API.

Listing 4-22. The FlashMapManager API

```
package org.springframework.web.servlet;

import javax.servlet.http.HttpServletRequest;
import javax.servlet.http.HttpServletResponse;

public interface FlashMapManager {

  FlashMap retrieveAndUpdate(HttpServletRequest request,
                          HttpServletResponse response);

  void saveOutputFlashMap(FlashMap flashMap, HttpServletRequest request,
                          HttpServletResponse response);

}
```

Summary

This chapter started by looking at the request processing workflow, identifying which components play a role. The `DispatcherServlet` can be considered the main component in Spring MVC. It plays the most crucial role—that of the front controller. The MVC pattern in Spring MVC is explicit; you have a model, a view, and a controller (handler). The controller processes the request, fills the model, and selects the view to render.

While processing a request, `DispatcherServlet` uses a lot of different components to play its role. The most important components are `HandlerMapping` and `HandlerAdapter`; these components are the core components used to map and handle requests, respectively. To apply crosscutting concerns, you can use `HandlerInterceptor`. After handling a request, a view needs to be rendered. A handler can return a `View` or the name of a view to render. In the latter situation, this name is passed to a `ViewResolver` to resolve to an actual view implementation.

There is also basic support for flash-scoped variables. To make this possible, there is `FlashMapManager`. Sometimes, the request processing doesn't progress the way you'd like it to. For example, you might encounter exceptions. To handle those, you can use the `HandlerExceptionResolver`. The final components that play a role here are the `LocaleResolver` and `ThemeResolver`. Together, these enable internationalization and theming in your application.

Upcoming chapters explain how to build controllers to handle requests and take a closer look at how to configure Spring MVC through Spring Boot.

CHAPTER 5

Implementing Controllers

Controllers play a crucial role in a web application: they execute the actual request, prepare the model, and select a view to render. In conjunction with the dispatcher servlet, controllers also play a crucial role in the request processing workflow. The controller is the glue between the core application and the web interface to the application. This chapter looks at the two different controller approaches and covers the out-of-the-box implementations provided with the Spring Framework and as configured by Spring Boot.

This chapter also looks at the supporting components for request processing. For example, we cover form submission and how to apply internationalization (I18N).

In this chapter, we work with Thymeleaf HTML templates. JSP views are supported with Spring MVC using Apache Tiles, but we do not recommend that you use JSP views when using Spring Boot and an embedded container.[1]

Introducing Controllers

The controller is the component that is responsible for responding to the action the user takes. This action could be a form submission, clicking a link, or simply accessing a page. The controller selects or updates the data needed for the view. It also selects the name of the view to render or can render the view itself. With Spring MVC, we have two options when writing controllers. We can either implement an interface or put an annotation on the class. The interface is `org.springframework.web.servlet.mvc.Controller`, and the annotation is `org.springframework.stereotype.Controller`. The main focus of this

---

[1]`https://docs.spring.io/spring-boot/docs/current/reference/htmlsingle/#boot-features-jsp-limitations`

© Marten Deinum and Iuliana Cosmina 2021
M. Deinum and I. Cosmina, *Pro Spring MVC with WebFlux*, https://doi.org/10.1007/978-1-4842-5666-4_5

book is the annotation-based approach for writing controllers. However, we feel that we still need to mention the interface-based approach.

Although both approaches work for implementing a controller, there are two major differences between them. The first difference is about flexibility, and the second is about mapping URLs to controllers. Annotation-based controllers allow very flexible method signatures, whereas the interface-based approach has a predefined method on the interface that we must implement. Getting access to other interesting collaborators is harder (but not impossible!).

For the interface-based approach, we must do explicit external mapping of URLs to these controllers; in general, this approach is combined with `org.springframework.web.servlet.handler.SimpleUrlHandlerMapping`, so that all the URLs are in a single location. Having all the URLs in a single location is one advantage the interface-based approach has over the annotation-based approach. The annotation-based approach has its mappings scattered throughout the codebase, which makes it harder to see which URL is mapped to which request-handling method. The advantage of annotation-based controllers is that you can see which URLs it is mapped to when you open a controller.

This section shows how to write both types of controllers and how to configure basic view controllers.

Interface-based Controllers

To write an interface-based controller, we need to create a class that implements the `org.springframework.web.servlet.mvc.Controller` interface. Listing 5-1 shows the API for that interface. When implementing this interface, we must implement the handleRequest method. This method needs to return an `org.springframework.web.servlet.ModelAndView` object or `null` when the controller handles the response itself.

Listing 5-1. The `Controller` Interface

```
package org.springframework.web.servlet.mvc;

import javax.servlet.http.HttpServletRequest;
import javax.servlet.http.HttpServletResponse;
import org.springframework.web.servlet.ModelAndView;
```

```
@FunctionalInterface
public interface Controller {

  ModelAndView handleRequest(HttpServletRequest request,
  HttpServletResponse response) throws Exception;

}
```

Let's look at a small sample. If we take com.apress.prospringmvc.bookstore.
web.IndexController and create an interface-based controller out of it, it would look
something like what you see in Listing 5-2. We implement the handleRequest method
and return an instance of ModelAndView with a view name.

Listing 5-2. An Interface-based IndexController

```
package com.apress.prospringmvc.bookstore.web;

// javax.servlet imports omitted

import org.springframework.web.servlet.ModelAndView;
import org.springframework.web.servlet.mvc.Controller;

public class IndexController implements Controller {

  @Override
  public ModelAndView handleRequest(HttpServletRequest request,
                                     HttpServletResponse response)
  throws Exception {
    return new ModelAndView("index");
  }
}
```

In addition to writing this controller, we would need to configure an instance of
org.springframework.web.servlet.HandlerMapping to map /index.htm to this
controller (see Chapter 3 for more information). We would also need to make sure
that org.springframework.web.servlet.mvc.SimpleControllerHandlerAdapter is
registered to execute the interface-based controllers (this is registered by default).

The sample given here is straightforward. Now imagine a controller that has some page flow. In that case, we would need to check whether the request is a GET or POST request; based on that, we would need to execute different controller logic. With large controllers, this can become cumbersome.

Table 5-1 shows the `Controller` implementations that ship with the framework.

Table 5-1. *A List of Existing Controller Implementations*

Controller implementation	Description
UrlFilenameViewController	A controller implementation that takes the path of a URL and transforms that into a view name. It can be configured to append a prefix and/or suffix to the view name.
ParameterizableViewController	A controller that returns a configured view name.
ServletForwardingController	A controller implementation that forwards the request to a named servlet, which can be a servlet without any mapping. It is useful if you want to use the Spring MVC infrastructure to dispatch requests and apply interceptors.
ServletWrappingController	A controller implementation that wraps and manages a servlet implementation. It is useful if you want to use the Spring MVC infrastructure to dispatch requests and apply interceptors.

> **ⓘ**   All controllers listed in Table 5-1 reside in the `org.springframework.web.servlet.mvc` package.

Annotation-based Controllers

To write an annotation-based controller, we need to write a class and put the `org.springframework.stereotype.Controller` annotation on that class. Also, we need to add an `org.springframework.web.bind.annotation.RequestMapping` annotation to the class, a method, or both. Listing 5-3 shows an annotation-based approach to our `IndexController`.

Listing 5-3. An Annotation-based IndexController

```java
package com.apress.prospringmvc.bookstore.web;

import org.springframework.stereotype.Controller;
import org.springframework.web.bind.annotation.RequestMapping;
import org.springframework.web.servlet.ModelAndView;

@Controller
public class IndexController {

  @RequestMapping(value = "/index.htm")
  public ModelAndView indexPage() {
    return new ModelAndView("index");
  }
}
```

The controller contains a method with the @RequestMapping annotation, and it specifies that it should be mapped to the /index.htm URL, which is the request-handling method. The method has no required parameters, and we can return anything we want; for now, we want to return a ModelAndView.

The mapping is in the controller definition, and we need an instance of org.springframework.web.servlet.mvc.method.annotation. RequestMappingHandlerMapping to interpret these mappings (registered by default).

Configuring View Controllers

The two controller samples we have written so far are called *view controllers*. They don't select data; rather, they only select the view name to render. If we had a large application with more of these views, it would become cumbersome to maintain and write these. Spring MVC can help us here. Enabling us simply to add org.springframework.web. servlet.mvc.ParameterizableViewController to our configuration and to configure it accordingly. We would need to configure an instance to return index as a view name and map it to the /index.htm URL. Listing 5-4 shows what needs to be added to make this work.

Listing 5-4. A ParameterizableViewController Configuration

```
package com.apress.prospringmvc.bookstore.web.config;

import org.springframework.web.servlet.mvc.ParameterizableViewController;

// Other imports omitted

@Configuration
public class WebMvcContextConfiguration implements WebMvcConfigurer {

// Other methods omitted

  @Bean(name = "/index.htm")
  public Controller index() {

    ParameterizableViewController index = new
    ParameterizableViewController();
    index.setViewName("index");
    return index;
  }
}
```

So how does it work? We create the controller, set the view name to return, and then explicitly give it the name of /index.htm (see the highlighted parts). The explicit naming makes it possible for org.springframework.web.servlet. handler.BeanNameUrlHandlerMapping to pick up our controller and map it to the URL. However, if this were to grow significantly larger, then we would need to create a few of these methods. Again, Spring MVC is here to help us. We can override the addViewControllers method (one of the methods of org.springframework.web. servlet.config.annotation.WebMvcConfigurer) and simply register our view names to certain URLs. Listing 5-5 shows how to do this.

Listing 5-5. A ViewController Configuration

```
package com.apress.prospringmvc.bookstore.web.config;

import org.springframework.web.servlet.config.annotation.
ViewControllerRegistry;
import org.springframework.web.servlet.config.annotation.WebMvcConfigurer;
```

```
// Other imports omitted

@Configuration
public class WebMvcContextConfiguration implements WebMvcConfigurer {

// Other methods omitted

  @Override
  public void addViewControllers(final ViewControllerRegistry registry) {
    registry.addViewController("/index.htm").setViewName("index");
  }
}
```

The result is the same. `ParameterizableViewController` is created and mapped to the `/index.htm` URL (see Figure 5-1). However, the second approach is easier and less cumbersome to use than the first one.

Figure 5-1. *The index page*

Request-Handling Methods

Writing request-handling methods can be a challenge. For example, how should a method be mapped to an incoming request? Several things could be a factor here, including the URL, the method used (e.g., GET or POST),[2] the availability of parameters

---

[2]`http://www.w3.org/Protocols/rfc2616/rfc2616-sec9.html`

or HTTP headers,[3] or even the request content type or the content type (e.g., XML, JSON, or HTML) to be produced. These and more can influence which method is selected to handle the request.

The first step in writing a request-handling method is to put an `org.springframework.web.bind.annotation.RequestMapping` annotation on the method. This mapping is detected by the `org.springframework.web.servlet.mvc.method.annotation.RequestMappingHandlerMapping` to create the mapping of incoming URLs to the correct method (see the "Spring MVC Components" section in Chapter 4 for more information on handler mapping). Next, we need to specify which web request we want to execute the specified handler.

The annotation can be put on both the type (the controller) and the method level. We can use the one on the type level to do some coarse-grained mapping (e.g., the URL), and then use the annotation on the method level to further specify when to execute the method (e.g., a GET or POST request).

Table 5-2 shows the attributes that can be set on the RequestMapping annotation and how they influence mapping.

Table 5-2. *The RequestMapping Attributes*

Attribute	Description
name	The name to use for this mapping. The name can be used with the `MvcUriComponentsBuilder` to generate dynamic links.
value or path	Specifies to which URL or URLs this controller reacts, such as `/order.htm`. We can also use ant-style expressions to specify the URLs.
method	Binds the method on specific HTTP methods. Supported methods include GET, POST, PUT, DELETE, HEAD, OPTIONS, and TRACE. By default, OPTIONS and TRACE are handled by `org.springframework.web.servlet.DispatcherServlet`. To have those methods passed onto controllers, we need to set `dispatchOptionsRequest` and/or `dispatchTraceRequest` to `true` respectively on the servlet.

(continued)

---

[3]`http://www.w3.org/Protocols/rfc2616/rfc2616-sec14.html`

Table 5-2. (*continued*)

Attribute	Description	
params	Narrows on the existence or absence of request parameters. Supported expressions include the following:	
	`param-name=param-value`	The specified param must have a certain value
	`param-name!=param-value`	The specified param must not have a certain value.
	`!param-name`	The specified param must be absent from the request.
headers	Narrows on the existence or absence of HTTP request headers.[4] Supported expressions include the following:	
	`header-name=header-value`	The specified header must have a certain value.
	`header-name!=header-value`	The specified header must not have a certain value.
	`!header-name`	The specified header must be absent from the request header.
	The value in the expression can also contain a wildcard (*) in Content-Type or Accept headers (i.e., content-type="text/*" will match all text-based content types).	

(*continued*)

---

[4]`http://www.w3.org/Protocols/rfc2616/rfc2616-sec14.html`

Table 5-2. (*continued*)

Attribute	Description
consumes	Specifies the consumable media types of the mapped request. We use this to narrow the primary mapping. For instance, `text/xml` maps all requests for the content-type of XML, but we could also specify `text/*` to match all textual content types. We can also negate it: `!text/xml` matches all content types except this one. This parameter is preferred over using the headers parameter to specify a `Content-Type` header because it is more explicit.
produces	Specifies the producible media types this request-handling method accepts. It narrows the primary mapping. The same rules that apply to the consumes parameter also apply to this parameter. This parameter is preferred over using the headers parameter to specify an Accept header because it is more explicit.

In Table 5-3, there are a couple of sample mappings that also show the effect of class- and method-level matching. As mentioned, the RequestMapping annotation on the class applies to *all* methods in the controller. This mechanism can do coarse-grained mapping on the class level and finer-grained mapping on the method level.

Table 5-3. *Sample Mappings*

Class	Method	Description
	`@RequestMapping(value="/order.htm")`	Maps to all requests on the order.htm URL
`@RequestMapping("/order.htm")`	`@RequestMapping(method=RequestMethod.GET)`	Maps to all GET requests to the order.html URL
`@RequestMapping("/order.*")`	`@RequestMapping(method={RequestMethod.PUT, RequestMethod.POST})`	Maps to all PUT and POST requests to the order.* URL. * means any suffix or extension such as .htm, .doc, .xls, and so on
`@RequestMapping(value="/customer.htm", consumes="application/json")`	`@RequestMapping(produces="application/xml")`	Maps to all requests that post JSON and accept XML as a response
`@RequestMapping(value="/order.htm")`	`@RequestMapping(params="add-line", method=RequestMethod.POST)`	Maps to all POST requests to the order.htm URL that include an add-line parameter
`@RequestMapping(value="/order.htm")`	`@RequestMapping(headers="!VIA")`	Maps to all requests to the order.htm URL that don't include a VIA HTTP header

Supported Method Argument Types

A request-handling method can have various method arguments and return values. Most arguments mentioned in Table 5-4 can be used in arbitrary order. However, there is a single exception to that rule: the `org.springframework.validation.BindingResult` argument. That argument must follow a model object that we use to bind request parameters.

Table 5-4. *The Supported Method Argument Types*

Argument Type	Description
`javax.servlet.ServletRequest`	The request object that triggered this method.
`javax.servlet.http.HttpServletRequest`	The HTTP request object that triggered this method.
`org.springframework.web.multipart.MultipartRequest`	The request object that triggered this method only works for multipart requests. This wrapper allows easy access to the uploaded files(s). Only exposes methods for multipart file access.
`org.springframework.web.multipart.MultipartHttpServletRequest`	The `MultipartHttpServletRequest` exposes both the `HttpServletRequest` and `MultipartRequest` methods.
`javax.servlet.ServletResponse`	The response associated with the request. It is useful if we need to write the response ourselves.
`javax.servlet.http.HttpServletResponse`	The response associated with the request. It is useful if we need to write the response ourselves.
`javax.servlet.http.HttpSession`	The underlying http session. If no session exists, one is initiated. This argument is therefore never `null`.
`org.springframework.web.context.request.WebRequest`	Allows more generic access to request and session attributes without ties to an underlying native API(e.g., Servlet or JSF).
`org.springframework.web.context.request.NativeWebRequest`	WebRequest extension that has accessor methods for the underlying request and response.
`java.util.Locale`	The currently selected locale as determined by the configured `org.springframework.web.servlet.LocaleResolver`.
`java.io.InputStream`	The stream as exposed by the `getInputStream` method on the `ServletRequest`
`java.io.Reader`	The reader exposed by the `getReader` method on the `ServletRequest`.

(continued)

Table 5-4. (*continued*)

Argument Type	Description
java.io.OutputStream	The responses stream as exposed by the getOutputStream method on the ServletResponse. It can write a response directly to the user.
java.io.Writer	The responses writer exposed by the getWriter method on the ServletResponse. It can write a response directly to the user.
javax.security.Principal	The currently authenticated user (can be null).
java.util.Map	The implicit model belonging to this controller/request.
org.springframework. ui.Model	The implicit model belonging to this controller/request. Model implementations have methods to add objects to the model for added convenience. When adding objects allows method chaining as each method returns the model.
org.springframework. ui.ModelMap	The implicit model belonging to this controller/request. The ModelMap is a map implementation that includes some methods to add objects to the model for added convenience.
org.springframework.web. multipart.MultipartFile	Binds the uploaded file(s) to a method parameter (multiple files are only supported by the multipart support of Spring). It works only when the request is a multipart form submission. The name of the request attribute to use is either taken from an optional org.springframework.web.bind.annotation. RequestPart annotation or derived from the name of the argument (the latter works only if that information is available in the class).
javax.servlet.http.Part	Binds the uploaded file(s) to a method parameter (multiple files are only supported by the multipart support of Spring). It works only when the request is a multipart form submission. The name of the request attribute to use is either taken from an optional org. springframework.web.bind.annotation.RequestPart annotation or derived from the name of the argument (the latter works only if that information is available in the class).

(continued)

Table 5-4. (*continued*)

Argument Type	Description

`org.springframework.web.`
`servlet.mvc.support.`
`RedirectAttributes`
	Enables specification of the exact list of attributes in case you want to issue a redirect. It can also add flash attributes. This argument is used instead of the implicit model in a redirect.

`org.springframework.` `validation.Errors`	The binding and validation results for a *preceding* model object.
`org.springframework.` `validation.BindingResult`	The binding and validation results for a *preceding* model object. Has accessor methods for the model and underlying infrastructure for type conversion. (For most use cases this isn't needed, use Errors instead).
`org.springframework.web.` `bind.support.SessionStatus`	A handler used to mark handling as complete, which triggers the cleanup of session attributes indicated by `org.springframework.web.bind.annotation.` `SessionAttributes`. See the "Using SessionAttributes" section later in this chapter for more information.
`org.springframework.web.` `util.UriComponentsBuilder`	A URI builder for preparing a URL relative to the current request URL.
`org.springframework.http.` `HttpEntity<?>`	Represents an HTTP request or response entity. It consists of headers and a body of the request or response.
Form objects	Binds request parameters to bean properties using type conversion. These objects are exposed as model attributes. Can optionally be annotated with `org.springframework.` `web.bind.annotation.ModelAttribute`.
Request body object	Binds the request body to bean properties using message conversion. These objects need to be annotated with `org.springframework.web.bind.annotation.` `RequestBody`.

RedirectAttributes

The `org.springframework.web.servlet.mvc.support.RedirectAttributes` deserve a little more explanation than what is shown in Table 5-4. With `RedirectAttributes`, it is possible to declare exactly which attributes are needed for the redirect. By default, all model attributes are exposed when doing a redirect. Because a redirect always leads to a GET request, all primitive model attributes (or collections/arrays of primitives) are encoded as request parameters. However, with annotated controllers, there are objects in the model (like path variables and other implicit values) that don't need to be exposed and are outside of our control.

The `RedirectAttributes` can help us out here. When this is a method argument, and a redirect is issued, only the attributes added to the RedirectAttributes instance are added to the URL.

In addition to specifying attributes encoded in the URL, it is also possible to specify *flash attributes*, which are stored before the redirect and retrieved and made available as model attributes after the redirect. This is done by using the configured `org.springframework.web.servlet.FlashMapManager`. Flash attributes are useful for objects that cannot be encoded (non-primitive objects) or to keep URLs clean.

UriComponentsBuilder

The `UriComponentsBuilder` provides a mechanism for building and encoding URIs. It can take a URL pattern and replace or extend variables. This can be done for relative or absolute URLs. This mechanism is particularly useful when creating URLs instead of cases where we need to think about encoding parameters or doing string concatenation ourselves. This component consistently handles these things for us. The code in Listing 5-6 creates the /book/detail/42 URL.

Listing 5-6. The `UriComponentsBuilder` Sample Code

```
UriComponentsBuilder
  .fromPath("/book/detail/{bookId}")
  .buildAndExpand("42")
  .encode();
```

The sample given is simple; however, it is possible to specify more variables (e.g., bookId) and replace them (e.g., specify the port or host). There is also the `ServletUri ComponentsBuilder` subclass, which we can use to operate on the current request. For example, we might use it to replace, not only path variables, but also request parameters.

Supported Method Argument Annotations

In addition to explicitly supported types (as mentioned in the previous section), there are also a couple of annotations that we can use to annotate our method arguments (see Table 5-5). Some of these can also be used with the method argument types mentioned in Table 5-4. In that case, they specify the name of the attribute in the request, cookie, header, or response, as well as whether the parameter is required.

Table 5-5. *The Supported Method Argument Annotations*

Argument Type	Description
RequestParam	Binds the argument to a single request parameter or all request parameters.
RequestHeader	Binds the argument to a single request header or all request headers.[5]
RequestBody	Gets the request body for arguments with this annotation. The value is converted using org.springframework.http.converter.HttpMessageConverter.
RequestPart	Binds the argument to the part of a multipart form submission.
ModelAttribute	Binds and validates arguments with this annotation. The parameters from the incoming request are bound to the given object.
PathVariable	Binds the method parameter to a path variable specified in the URL mapping (the value attribute of the RequestMapping annotation).
CookieValue	Binds the method parameter to a javax.servlet.http.Cookie.
SessionAttribute	Binds the method parameter to a session attribute.
RequestAttribute	Binds the method parameter to a request attribute (not to be confused with a request parameter).
MatrixVariable	Binds the method parameter to a name-value pair within a path-segment.

---

[5]http://en.wikipedia.org/wiki/List_of_HTTP_header_fields

All the parameter values are converted to the argument type by using type conversion. The type-conversion system uses `org.springframework.core.convert. converter.Converter` or `java.beans.PropertyEditor` to convert from a `String` type to the actual type.

ℹ️   All annotations live in the `org.springframework.web.bind. annotation` package.

All these different method argument types and annotations allow us to write very flexible request-handling methods. However, we could extend this mechanism by extending the framework. Resolving those method argument types is done by various `org.springframework.web.method.support.HandlerMethodArgumentResolver` implementations. Listing 5-7 shows that interface. We can create our own implementation of this interface and register it with the framework if we want. You can find more information on this in Chapter 7.

Listing 5-7. The `HandlerMethodArgumentResolver` Interface

```
package org.springframework.web.method.support;

import org.springframework.core.MethodParameter;
import org.springframework.web.bind.WebDataBinder;
import org.springframework.web.bind.support.WebDataBinderFactory;
import org.springframework.web.context.request.NativeWebRequest;

public interface HandlerMethodArgumentResolver {

  boolean supportsParameter(MethodParameter parameter);

  Object resolveArgument(MethodParameter parameter,
                         ModelAndViewContainer mavContainer,
                         NativeWebRequest webRequest,
                         WebDataBinderFactory binderFactory)
  throws Exception;
}
```

Let's take a closer look at all the different annotation types we can use. All these annotations have a few attributes that we can set and that have default values or may be required.

All the annotations in Table 5-5 have a value attribute. This value attribute refers to the name of the object to use (what it applies to depends on the annotation). If this value isn't filled, then the fallback uses the name of the method argument. This fallback is only usable if the classes are compiled with parameter information.[6] An exception to this rule occurs when using the ModelAttribute annotation. Instead of the name of the method argument, it infers the name from the type of argument, using the simple classname as the argument name. If the type is an array or collection, it makes this plural by adding List. If we were to use our com.apress.prospringmvc.bookstore.domain.Book as an argument, the name would be book; if it were an array or collection, it would become bookList.

RequestParam

The @RequestParam annotation can be placed on any argument in a request-handling method. When present, it retrieves a parameter from the request. When put on a map, there is some special handling, depending on whether the name attribute is set. If the name is set, the value is retrieved and converted into a map. For conversion (see the "Data Binding" section and Table 5-6 for more information), if no name is given, all request parameters are added to the map as key/value pairs.

---

[6]http://docs.oracle.com/javase/6/docs/technotes/tools/windows/javac.html

Table 5-6. *The RequestParam Attributes*

Attribute	Default Value	Description
required	true	Indicates whether the parameter is required. If it is required and the parameter is missing, then org.springframework.web. bind.MissingServletRequestParameterException is thrown.
defaultValue	null	Indicates the default value to use when the parameter is missing from the request. Setting a default value is implicitly setting required to false. The value can either be a hardcoded value or a SpEL expression.
value or name	Empty string	Indicates the name of the parameter to look up from the request. If no name is specified, then the name is derived from the method argument name. If no name can be found, java.lang. IllegalArgumentException is thrown.

RequestHeader

The @RequestHeader annotation can be placed on any method argument. It binds a method argument to a request header. When placed on a map, all available request headers are put on the map as key/value pairs. If it is placed on another type of argument, then the value is converted into the type using org.springframework.core. convert.converter.Converter or PropertyEditor (see the "Data Binding" section and Table 5-7 for more information).

Table 5-7. *The RequestHeader Attributes*

Attribute	Default Value	Description
required	True	Indicates whether the parameter is required. If it is required and the parameter is missing, `org.springframework.web.bind.ServletRequestBindingException` is thrown. When set to `false`, `null` is used as the value; alternatively, the `defaultValue` is used when specified.
defaultValue	Null	Indicates the default value to use when the parameter is missing from the request. Setting a default value is implicitly setting required to false. The value can either be a hardcoded value or a SpEL expression.
value or name	Empty string	Indicates the name of the request header to bind to. If no name is specified, then the name is derived from the method argument name. If no name can be found, `java.lang.IllegalArgumentException` is thrown.

RequestBody

The @RequestBody annotation marks a method parameter we want to bind to the body of the web request. The body is converted into the method parameter type by locating and calling `org.springframework.http.converter.HttpMessageConverter`. This converter is selected based on the requests content-type. If no converter is found, `org.springframework.web.HttpMediaTypeNotSupportedException` is thrown. By default, this leads to a response with code 415 (`SC_UNSUPPORTED_MEDIA_TYPE`) sent to the client.

Optionally, method parameters can also be annotated with javax.validation.Valid or org.springframework.validation.annotation.Validated to enforce validation for the created object. You can find more information on validation in the "Validation of Model Attributes" section later in this chapter.

RequestPart

When the @RequestPart annotation is put on a method argument of type `javax.servlet.http.Part`, `org.springframework.web.multipart.MultipartFile` (or on a collection or array of the latter), we get the content of that file (or group of files) injected. If it is put on any other argument type, the content is passed through `org.springframework.http.converter.HttpMessageConverter` for the content type detected on the file. If no suitable converter is found, then `org.springframework.web.HttpMediaTypeNotSupportedException` is thrown. (see the "Data Binding" section and Table 5-8 for more information).

Table 5-8. *The RequestPart Attributes*

Attribute	Default Value	Description
required	true	Indicates whether the parameter is required. If it is required and the parameter is missing, `org.springframework.web.bind.ServletRequestBindingException` is thrown. When set to `false`, `null` is used as a value; alternatively, `defaultValue` is used when specified.
value or name	Empty string	The name of the request header to bind to. If no name is specified, the name is derived from the method argument name. If no name is found, `java.lang.IllegalArgumentException` is thrown.

ModelAttribute

The @ModelAttribute annotation can be placed on method arguments, as well as on methods. When placed on a method argument, it binds this argument to a model object. When placed on a method, that method constructs a model object, and this method is called before any request-handling methods are called. These methods can create an object to be edited in a form or to supply data needed by a form to render itself. (see the "Data Binding" section and Table 5-9 for more information).

Table 5-9. *The ModelAttribute Attributes*

Attribute	Default Value	Description
value or name	Empty string	The name of the model attribute to bind to. If no name is specified, the name is derived from the method argument type.

PathVariable

The @PathVariable annotation can be used in conjunction with path variables. Path variables can be used in a URL pattern to bind the URL to a variable. Path variables are denoted as {name} in our URL mapping. If we were to use a URL mapping of /book/ {isbn}/image, ISBN would be available as a path variable. (see the "Data Binding" section and Table 5-10 for more information).

Table 5-10. *The PathVariable Attribute*

Attribute	Default Value	Description
value or name	Empty string	The name of the path variable to bind to. If no name is specified, then the name is derived from the method argument name. If no name is found, java.lang.IllegalArgumentException is thrown.

CookieValue

This @CookieValue annotation can be placed on any argument in the request-handling method. When present, it retrieves a cookie. When placed on an argument of type javax.servlet.http.Cookie, we get the complete cookie; otherwise, the value of the cookie is converted into the argument type. (see the "Data Binding" section and Table 5-11 for more information).

Table 5-11. *The CookieValue Attributes*

Attribute	Default Value	Description
required	true	Indicates whether the parameter is required. If it is required and the parameter is missing, org.springframework.web.bind. ServletRequestBindingException is thrown. When set to false, null is used as a value; alternatively, defaultValue is used when specified.
defaultValue	null	Indicates the default value to use when the parameter is missing from the request. Setting a default value is implicitly setting required to false. The value can either be a hardcoded value or a SpEL expression.
value or name	Empty string	Indicates the name of the cookie to bind to. If no name is specified, the name is derived from the method argument name. If no name is found, java.lang.IllegalArgumentException is thrown.

SessionAttribute

This @SessionAttribute annotation can be placed on any argument in the request-handling method. When present, it retrieves an attribute from the HttpSession. (see the "Data Binding" section and Table 5-12 for more information).

Table 5-12. *The SessionAttribute Attributes*

Attribute	Default Value	Description
required	true	Indicates whether the parameter is required. If it is required and the parameter is missing, org.springframework.web.bind. ServletRequestBindingException is thrown. When set to false, null is used as a value.
value or name	Empty string	Indicates the name of the cookie to bind to. If no name is specified, the name is derived from the method argument name. If no name is found, java.lang.IllegalArgumentException is thrown.

RequestAttribtue

This @RequestAttribtue annotation can be placed on any argument in the request-handling method. When present, it retrieves an attribute from the HttpServletRequest. Attributes are obtained using the getAttribute method of the request and shouldn't be confused with parameters. For the latter, use the @RequestParam annotation. (see the "Data Binding" section and Table 5-13 for more information).

Table 5-13. *The RequestAttribtue Attributes*

Attribute	Default Value	Description
required	true	Indicates whether the parameter is required. If it is required and the parameter is missing, org.springframework.web.bind. ServletRequestBindingException is thrown. When set to false, null is used as a value.
value or name	Empty string	Indicates the name of the cookie to bind to. If no name is specified, the name is derived from the method argument name. If no name is found, java.lang.IllegalArgumentException is thrown.

145

Supported Method Return Values

In addition to all the different method argument types, a request handling method can also have several different return values. Table 5-14 lists the default supported and handling of method return values for request handling methods.

Table 5-14. *The Supported Method Return Values*

Argument Type	Description
org.springframework.web.servlet.ModelAndView	When a ModelAndView is returned, this is used as-is. It should contain the full model to use and the name of a view (or the View) to render (the latter is optional).
org.springframework.ui.Model	Indicates that this method returned a model. Objects in this model are added to the controller's implicit model and made available for view rendering. The name of the view is determined by org.springframework.web.servlet.RequestToViewNameTranslator.
java.util.Map org.springframework.ui.ModelMap	The map elements are added to the controller's implicit model and made available for view rendering. The name of the view is determined by org.springframework.web.servlet.RequestToViewNameTranslator.
org.springframework.web.servlet.View	The view to render.
java.lang.CharSequence (generally java.lang.String)	The name of the view to render. If annotated with @ModelAttribute, it is added to the model.
java.lang.Void	The model is already prepared by the controller, and the name of the view is determined by org.springframework.web.servlet.RequestToViewNameTranslator.

(continued)

Table 5-14. (*continued*)

Argument Type	Description
`org.springframework.http.HttpEntity<?>` `org.springframework.http.ResponseEntity<?>`	Specifies the headers and entity body to return to the user. The entity body is converted and sent to the response stream through `org.springframework.http.converter.HttpMessageConverter`. Optionally, the `HttpEntity` can also set a status code to send to the user.
`org.springframework.http.HttpHeaders`	Specifies the headers to return to the user.
`org.springframework.web.servlet.mvc.method.annotation.StreamingResponseBody`	Asynchronously write a result to the client. Requires async processing to be enabled (on by default).
`org.springframework.web.context.request.async.DeferredResult` `org.springframework.util.concurrent.ListenableFuture` `java.util.concurrent.CompletionStage` `java.util.concurrent.Callable`	Async result types for use in a async processing environment. Requires async processing to be enabled (on by default).
Any other return type	All other return types are used as model attributes. The name is either derived from the return type or the name specified in `org.springframework.web.bind.annotation.ModelAttribute`. Unless the method return value is annotated with @ResponseBody, it is written to client using a `HttpMessageConverter` instead of being used as a model attribute. For more insights, see Chapter 7 on REST controllers.

When an arbitrary object is returned, and there is no `ModelAttribute` annotation present, the framework tries to determine a name for the object in the model. It takes the simple name of the class (the classname without the package) and lowercases the first letter—for example, the name of our com.apress.prospringmvc.bookstore.domain.Book becomes book. When the return type is a collection or array, it becomes the simple name of the class, suffixed with List. Thus a collection of `Book` objects becomes `bookList`.

This same logic is applied when we use a `Model` or `ModelMap` to add objects without an explicit name. This also has the advantage of using the specific objects, instead of a plain `Map` to gain access to the underlying implicit model.

Although the list of supported return values is already extensive, we can use the framework's flexibility and extensibility to create our own handler. The method's return values are handled by an implementation of the `org.springframework.web.method.support.HandlerMethodReturnValueHandler` interface (see Listing 5-8).

Listing 5-8. The HandlerMethodReturnValueHandler Interface

```
package org.springframework.web.method.support;

import org.springframework.core.MethodParameter;
import org.springframework.web.context.request.NativeWebRequest;

public interface HandlerMethodReturnValueHandler {

  boolean supportsReturnType(MethodParameter returnType);

  void handleReturnValue(Object returnValue,
                         MethodParameter returnType,
                         ModelAndViewContainer mavContainer,
                         NativeWebRequest webRequest)
                throws Exception;

}
```

Writing Annotation-based Controllers

Let's take some of the theory we've developed thus far and apply it to our controllers. For example, all the menu options we have on our page lead to a 404 error, which indicates that the page cannot be found.

In this section, we add some controllers and views to our application. We start by creating a simple login controller operating with the request and request parameters. Next, we add a book search page that uses an object. And finally, we conclude by building a controller that retrieves and shows the details of a book.

A Simple Login Controller

Before we can start writing our controller, we need to have a login page. In the WEB-INF/ views directory, we create a file named login.html. The resulting structure should look like the one shown in Figure 5-2.

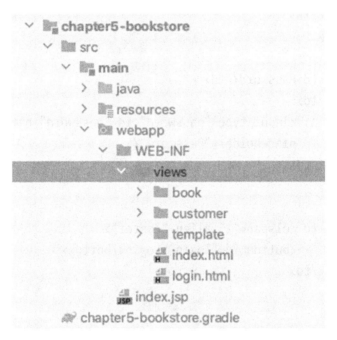

Figure 5-2. *The directory structure after adding* login.html

The login page needs some content. The content common to all pages of the site is declared in the template/layout.html template. The login.html is declared to inherit some of that content and replace some of it using special Thymeleaf constructs like th:fragment and th:replace. The most important part of the login.html page is the login form shown in Listing 5-9.

Listing 5-9. The Login Page, `login.html`

```
<form action="#" th:action="@{/login}" method="POST" id="loginForm">
    <fieldset>
        <legend>Login</legend>
        <table>
            <tr>
                <td>Username</td>
                <td>
                    <input type="text" id="username" name="username"
                        placeholder="Username"/>
                </td>
            </tr>
            <tr>
                <td>Password</td>
                <td>
                    <input type="password" id="password" name="password"
                        placeholder="Password"/>
                </td>
            </tr>
            <tr>
                <td colspan="2" align="center">
                    <button id="login">Login</button>
                </td>
            </tr>
        </table>
    </fieldset>
</form>
```

In addition to the page, we need to have a controller and map it to /login. Let's create the `com.apress.prospringmvc.bookstore.web.controller.LoginController` and start by having it render our page (see Listing 5-10).

Listing 5-10. The Initial LoginController

```
package com.apress.prospringmvc.bookstore.web.controller;

import org.springframework.stereotype.Controller;
import org.springframework.web.bind.annotation.GetMapping;
import org.springframework.web.bind.annotation.RequestMapping;
import org.springframework.web.bind.annotation.RequestMethod;

@Controller
@RequestMapping("/login")
public class LoginController {

  @GetMapping
  public String login() {
    return "login";
  }
}
```

After the application has been restarted, and we click the Login button, we should see a page like the one shown in Figure 5-3.

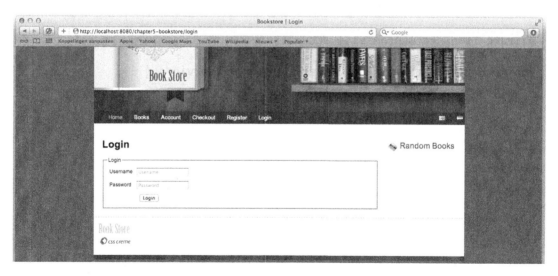

Figure 5-3. *The login page*

If we now enter the username and password (jd/secret) and press the Login button, we are greeted with an error page (error code 405) that indicates that the method (POST) is not supported. This is correct because our controller doesn't yet have a method that handles a POST request. So, let's add a method to our controller that handles our login. Listing 5-11 shows the modified controller.

Listing 5-11. The Modified LoginController

```
package com.apress.prospringmvc.bookstore.web.controller;

import com.apress.prospringmvc.bookstore.domain.Account;

import org.springframework.stereotype.Controller;
import org.springframework.web.bind.annotation.*;
import org.springframework.web.servlet.mvc.support.RedirectAttributes;

import javax.servlet.http.HttpSession;

@Controller
@RequestMapping("/login")
public class LoginController {

  private static final String ACCOUNT_ATTRIBUTE = "account";

  private final AccountService accountService;

  public LoginController(AccountService accountService) {
    this.accountService = accountService;
  }

  @GetMapping
  public String login() {
    return "login";
  }

  @PostMapping
  public String handleLogin(HttpServletRequest request, HttpSession
  session) {
    try {
      var username = request.getParameter("username");
      var password = request.getParameter("password");
```

```java
        var account = this.accountService.login(username, password);
        session.setAttribute(ACCOUNT_ATTRIBUTE, account);
        return "redirect:/index.htm";
      } catch (AuthenticationException ae) {
        request.setAttribute("exception", ae);
        return "login";
      }
    }
  }
}
```

Before we move on, let's drill down on how the handleLogin method works. The username and password parameters are retrieved from the request; they call the login method on the AccountService. If the correct credentials are supplied, we get an Account instance for the user (which we store in the session), and then we redirect to the index page. If the credentials are not correct, the service throws an authentication exception, which is handled by the controller for now. The exception is stored as a request attribute, and we return the user to the login page.

Although the current controller does its work, we are still operating directly on the HttpServletRequest. This is a cumbersome (but sometimes necessary) approach; however, we would generally want to avoid this and use the flexible method signatures to make our controllers simpler. With that in mind, let's modify the controller and limit our use of directly accessing the request (see Listing 5-12).

Listing 5-12. The LoginController with RequestParam

```java
package com.apress.prospringmvc.bookstore.web.controller;

import org.springframework.web.bind.annotation.RequestParam;

// Other imports omitted, see Listing 5-11

@Controller
@RequestMapping(value = "/login")
public class LoginController {

// Other methods omitted

  @PostMapping
```

```java
public String handleLogin(@RequestParam String username, @RequestParam
String password, HttpServletRequest request, HttpSession session)
                            throws AuthenticationException {
  try {
    var account = this.accountService.login(username, password);
    session.setAttribute(_ACCOUNT_ATTRIBUTE_, account);
    return "redirect:/index.htm";
  } catch (AuthenticationException ae) {
    request.setAttribute("exception", ae);
    return "login";
  }
 }
}
```

Using the @RequestParam annotation simplified our controller. However, our exception handling dictates that we still need access to the request. This changes in the next chapter when we implement exception handling.

There is one drawback with this approach: the lack of support for the Back button in a browser. If we go back a page, we get a nice popup asking if we want to resubmit the form. It is a common approach to redirect after a POST[7] request; that way, we can work around the double submission problem. In Spring, we can address this by using RedirectAttributes. Listing 5-13 highlights the final modifications to our controller in bold.

Listing 5-13. The LoginController with RedirectAttributes

```java
package com.apress.prospringmvc.bookstore.web.controller;

// Other imports omitted, see Listing 5-11

import org.springframework.web.servlet.mvc.support.RedirectAttributes;

@Controller
@RequestMapping(value = "/login")
public class LoginController {
```

---

[7]www.theserverside.com/news/1365146/Redirect-After-Post

```java
// Other methods omitted

  @PostMapping
  public String handleLogin(@RequestParam String username,
                            @RequestParam String password,
                            RedirectAttributes redirect,
                            HttpSession session)
                              throws AuthenticationException {

    try {
      var account = this.accountService.login(username, password);
      session.setAttribute(ACCOUNT_ATTRIBUTE, account);
      return "redirect:/index.htm";
    } catch (AuthenticationException ae) {
      redirect.addFlashAttribute("exception", ae);
      return "redirect:/login";
    }
  }
}
```

When the application is redeployed, and we log in, typing in the wrong username/
password combination raises an error message; however, when we press the Back
button, the popup request for a form submission is gone.

Until now, everything we have done is low level. Our solutions include working
with the request and/or response directly or through a bit of abstraction with `org.`
`springframework.web.bind.annotation.RequestParam`. However, we work in an
object-oriented programming language, and where possible, we want to work with
objects. We explore this in the next section.

Book Search Page

We have a bookstore, and we want to sell books. At the moment, however, there is
nothing in our web application that allows the user to search for or even see a list
of books. Let's address this by creating a book search page so that the users of our
application can search for books.

First, we create a directory book in the /WEB-INF/views directory. In that directory, we create a file called search.html. This file is our search form, and it also displays the results of the search. The code for the search form and the result table can be seen in Listing 5-14.

Listing 5-14. The Search Page Form

```html
<form action="#" th:action="@{/book/search}"
        method="GET" id="bookSearchForm">
    <fieldset>
        <legend>Search Criteria</legend>
        <table>
            <tr>
                <td><label>Title</label></td>
                <td><input type="text"/></td>
            </tr>
        </table>
    </fieldset>
    <button id="search"">Search</button>
</form>
<!-- other HTML and JavaScript code omitted -->

<table id="bookSearchResults">
    <thead>
        <tr>
            <th>Title</th>
            <th>Description</th>
            <th>Price</th>
        </tr>
    </thead>
    <tbody>
    <th:block th:each="book : ${bookList}">
        <tr>
            <td th:text="${book.title}"></td>
            <td th:text="${book.description}"></td>
            <td th:text="${book.price}"></td>
        </tr>
```

```
      </th:block>
    </tbody>
</table>
```

The page consists of a form with a field to fill in a (partial) title that searches for books. When there are results, we show a table to the user containing the results. Now that we have a page, we also need a controller that can handle the requests. Listing 5-15 shows the initial com.apress.prospringmvc.bookstore.web.controller.BookSearchController.

Listing 5-15. The BookSearchController with Search

```java
package com.apress.prospringmvc.bookstore.web.controller;

import org.springframework.beans.factory.annotation.Autowired;
import org.springframework.stereotype.Controller;
import org.springframework.ui.Model;
import org.springframework.web.bind.annotation.RequestMapping;
import org.springframework.web.bind.annotation.RequestMethod;
import com.apress.prospringmvc.bookstore.domain.BookSearchCriteria;
import com.apress.prospringmvc.bookstore.service.BookstoreService;
import javax.servlet.http.HttpServletRequest;

@Controller
public class BookSearchController {

  private final BookstoreService bookstoreService;

  public BookSearchController(BookstoreService bookstoreService) {
    this.bookstoreService=bookstoreService;
  }

  @GetMapping("/book/search")
  public String list(Model model, HttpServletRequest request) {
    var criteria = new BookSearchCriteria();
    criteria.setTitle(request.getParameter("title"));
    model.addAttribute(this.bookstoreService.findBooks(criteria));
    return "book/search";
  }
}
```

The controller reacts to the URL, retrieves the title parameter from the request (this is the name of the field in our page, as shown in Listing 5-13), and finally, proceeds with a search. The results of the search are put in the model. Initially, it displays all the books; however, as soon as a title is entered, it limits the results based on that title (see Figure 5-4).

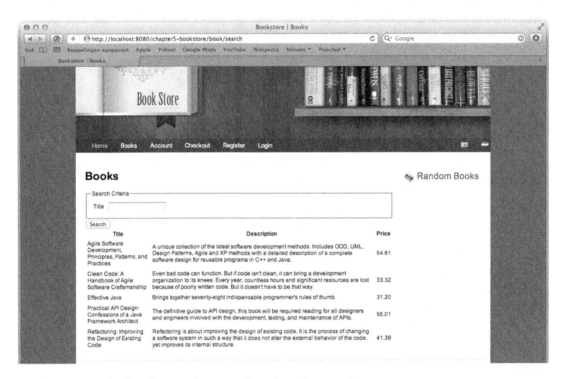

Figure 5-4. *The book search page showing the results*

As mentioned earlier, working with the `HttpServletRequest` directly isn't necessary in most cases. Let's make our search method a little simpler by putting the `com.apress.prospringmvc.bookstore.domain.BookSearchCriteria` in the list of method arguments (see Listing 5-16).

Listing 5-16. The `BookSearchController` with `BookSearchCriteria` as a Method Argument

```
package com.apress.prospringmvc.bookstore.web.controller;

import org.springframework.web.bind.annotation.RequestParam;

// Other imports omitted, see listing 5-15
```

```
@Controller
public class BookSearchController {

  @GetMapping("/book/search")
  public String list(Model model, BookSearchCriteria criteria) {
    model.addAttribute(this.bookstoreService.findBooks(criteria));
    return "book/search";
  }
}
```

In Spring MVC, this is called *data binding*. To enable data binding, we needed to modify com.apress.prospring.bookstore.web.controller.BookSearchController, so it uses a method argument, instead of working with the request directly (see Listing 5-14). Alternatively, it could use RequestParam to retrieve the parameters and set them on the object. This forces Spring to use data binding on the criteria method argument. Doing so maps all request parameters with the same name as one of our object's properties to that object (i.e., the request parameter title is mapped to the property title). Using data binding simplifies our controller (you can find more in-depth information on this in the "Data Binding" section of this chapter).

We can do even better! Instead of returning a String, we could return something else. For example, let's modify our controller to return a collection of books. This collection is added to the model with the name bookList, as explained earlier in this chapter. Listing 5-16 shows this controller, but where do we select the view to render? It isn't explicitly specified. In Chapter 4, we mentioned that org.springframework.web. servlet.RequestToViewNameTranslator kicks in if there is no explicitly mentioned view to render. We see that mechanism working here. It takes the URL (http:// [server]:[port]/chapter5-bookstore/book/search); strips the server, port, and application name; removes the suffix (if any); and then uses the remaining book/search as the name of the view to render (exactly what we have been returning).

Listing 5-17. The BookSearchController Alternate Version

```
package com.apress.prospringmvc.bookstore.web.controller;

// Other imports omitted, see listing 5-15

@Controller
public class BookSearchController {

  @GetMapping(value = "/book/search")
  public Collection<Book> list(BookSearchCriteria criteria ) {
    return this.bookstoreService.findBooks(criteria);
  }
}
```

Book Detail Page

Now let's put some more functionality into our search page. For example, let's make the title of a book a link that navigates to a book's details page that shows an image and some information about the book. We start by modifying our search.html and adding links (see Listing 5-18).

Listing 5-18. The Modified Search Page

```
<form action="#" th:action="@{/book/search}"
         method="GET" id="bookSearchForm">
    <fieldset>
        <legend >Search Criteria</legend>
        <table>
            <tr>
                <td><label for="title">Title</label></td>
                <td><input type="text" th:field="*{title}"/></td>
            </tr>
        </table>
    </fieldset>
    <button id="search">Search</button>
</form>
```

```
<!-- other HTML and JavaScript code omitted -->

<table id="bookSearchResults">
    <thead>
        <tr>
            <th>Title</th>
            <th>Description</th>
            <th>Price</th>
        </tr>
    </thead>
    <tbody>
    <th:block th:each="book : ${bookList}">
        <tr>
            <td><a th:href="@{/book/detail/} + ${book.id}"
                th:text="${book.title}"></a></td>
            <td th:text="${book.description}"></td>
            <td th:text="${book.price}"></td>
        </tr>
    </th:block>
    </tbody>
</table>
```

The highlighted line is the only change we need to make to this page. At this point, we have generated a URL based on the ID of the book, so we should get a URL like /book/detail/4 that shows us the details of the book with ID 4. Let's create a controller to react to this URL and extract the ID from the URL (see Listing 5-19).

Listing 5-19. The BookDetailController

```
package com.apress.prospringmvc.bookstore.web.controller;

import org.springframework.beans.factory.annotation.Autowired;
import org.springframework.stereotype.Controller;
import org.springframework.ui.Model;
import org.springframework.web.bind.annotation.GetMapping;
import org.springframework.web.bind.annotation.PathVariable;

import com.apress.prospringmvc.bookstore.domain.Book;
import com.apress.prospringmvc.bookstore.service.BookstoreService;
```

```
@Controller
public class BookDetailController {

  @GetMapping(value = "/book/detail/{bookId}")
  public String details(@PathVariable("bookId") long bookId, Model model) {
    var book = this.bookstoreService.findBook(bookId);
    model.addAttribute(book);
    return "book/detail";
  }
}
```

The highlighted code is what makes the extraction of the ID possible. This is `org.springframework.web.bind.annotation.PathVariable` in action. The URL mapping contains the {bookId} part, which tells Spring MVC to bind that part of the URL to a path variable called bookId. We can then use the annotation to retrieve the path variable again. In addition to the controller, we also need an HTML page to show the details. The code in Listing 5-20 creates a detail.html in the book directory.

Listing 5-20. The Book's detail.html Page

```
<img th:src="@{'/resources/images/books/' + ${book.isbn} + '/book_front_
cover.png'}"
    align="left" alt="${book.title}" width="250"/>
<table>
    <tr>
        <td>Title</td>
        <td th:text="${book.title}"></td>
    </tr>
    <tr>
        <td >Description</td>
        <td th:text="${book.description}"></td>
    </tr>
    <tr>
        <td>Author</td>
        <td th:text="${book.author}"></td>
    </tr>
```

```
<tr>
    <td>Year</td>
    <td th:text="${book.year}"></td>
</tr>
<tr>
    <td>ISBN</td>
    <td th:text="${book.isbn}"></td>
</tr>
<tr>
    <td >Price</td>
    <td th:text="${book.price}"></td>
</tr>
</table>
```

If we click one of the links from the search page after redeployment, we should be greeted with a details page that shows an image of and some information about the book (see Figure 5-5).

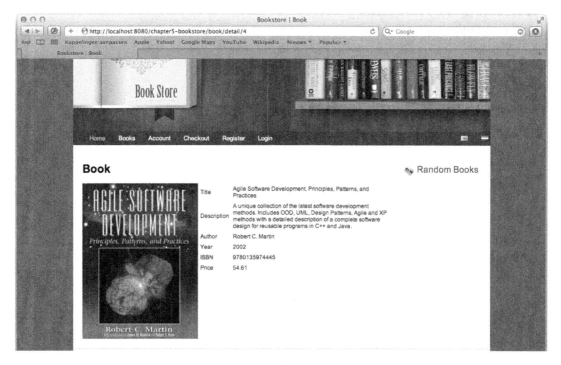

Figure 5-5. *The book's details page*

Data Binding

This section explores the benefits of using data binding, including how to configure and extend it. However, we begin by explaining the basics of data binding. Listing 5-21 shows our `com.apress.prospringmvc.bookstore.domain.BookSearchCriteria` class. It is a simple object with two properties: `title` and `category`.

Listing 5-21. The BookSearchCriteria JavaBean

```
package com.apress.prospringmvc.bookstore.domain;

public class BookSearchCriteria {

private String title;
private Category category;

  public String getTitle() {
    return this.title;
  }

  public void setTitle(String title) {
    this.title = title;
  }

  public void setCategory(Category category) {
    this.category = category;
  }

  public Category getCategory() {
    return this.category;
  }
}
```

Assume we receive the following request: `http://localhost:8080/chapter5-bookstore/book/search?title=Agile`. In this case, the title property receives the value of Agile. Behind the scenes, Spring calls the `setTitle` method on our JavaBean, which we specified as a method argument in the list method on our controller. If there were a parameter named category in the request, Spring would call the setCategory method; however, it would first try to convert the parameter (which is always a `String`) to `com.apress.prospring.bookstore.domain.Category` JavaBean.

However, data binding isn't limited to simple setter methods. We can also bind to nested properties and even indexed collections like maps, arrays, and lists. Nested binding happens when the parameter name contains a *dot* (.); for instance, `address.street=Somewhere` leads to `getAddress().setStreet("Somewhere")`.

To bind to indexed collections, we must use a notation with square brackets to enclose the index. When using a map, this index doesn't have to be numeric. For instance, `list[2].name` would bind a name property on the third element in the list. Similarly, `map['foo'].name` would bind the name property to the value under the key foo in the map.

Customizing Data Binding

We have two options for customizing the behavior of data binding: globally or per controller. We can mix both strategies by performing a global setup and then fine-tuning it per controller.

Global Customization

To customize data binding globally, we need to create a class that implements the `org.springframework.web.bind.support.WebBindingInitializer` interface. Spring MVC provides a configurable implementation of this interface, `org.springframework.web.bind.support.ConfigurableWebBindingInitializer`. An instance of the interface must be registered with the handler mapping implementation to be used. After an instance of `org.springframework.web.bind.WebDataBinder` is created, the `initBinder` method of `org.springframework.web.bind.support.WebBindingInitializer` is called.

The provided implementation allows us to set a couple of properties. When a property is not set, it uses the defaults as specified by `org.springframework.web.bind.WebDataBinder`. If we were to want to specify more properties, it would be easy to extend the default implementation and add the desired behavior. It is possible to set the same properties here as in the controller (see Table 5-15).

Table 5-15. *The ConfigurableWebBindingInitializer Properties*

Attribute	Description
autoGrowNestedPaths	If set to true, a path containing a null value is populated with a default object value instead of resulting in an exception. Moreover, this default value is used for further traversal of the expression. This property also controls auto growing of collections when an out-of-bounds index is accessed. The default value is true.
bindingErrorProcessor	Sets the org.springframework.validation.BindingErrorProcessor implementation.
conversionService	Sets the instance of org.springframework.core.convert.ConversionService.
directFieldAccess	When set to true, we don't need to write getters/setters to access the fields. The default is false.
messageCodesResolver	Sets org.springframework.validation.MessageCodesResolver.
propertyEditorRegistrar propertyEditorRegistrars	Registers one or more org.springframework.beans.PropertyEditorRegistrars. It is useful when we have old-style PropertyEditors that we want to use for type conversion.
Validator	Sets the org.springframework.validation.Validator implementation.

Spring Boot makes configuring and reusing the ConfigurableWebBindingInitializer easier. It detects a bean of the specific type and uses that for further configuring the handler adapters.

Listing 5-22. Configure the ConfigurableWebBindingInitializer

```
@Bean
public ConfigurableWebBindingInitializer configurableWebBindingInitializer(
        Validator mvcValidator,
        FormattingConversionService conversionService) {
  var initializer = new ConfigurableWebBindingInitializer();
  initializer.setDirectFieldAccess(true);
```

```
   initializer.setValidator(mvcValidator);
   initializer.setConversionService(conversionService);
   return initializer;
}
```

💡 Notice the Validator and FormattingConversionService dependencies in the method signature. These are needed to enable validation and type conversion from the incoming String parameter to the actual type needed.

Per Controller Customization

For the per controller option, we must implement a method in the controller and put the `org.springframework.web.bind.annotation.InitBinder` annotation on that method. The method must have no return value (`void`) and at least `org.springframework.web.bind.WebDataBinder` as a method argument. The method *can* have the same arguments as a request-handling method. However, it *cannot* have a method argument with the `org.springframework.web.bind.annotation.ModelAttribute` annotation. This is because the model is available after binding, and in this method, we configure the way we bind.

The `org.springframework.web.bind.annotation.InitBinder` annotation has a single attribute named value that can take the model attribute names or request parameter names that this init-binder method applies to. The default is to apply to all model attributes and request parameters.

To customize binding, we need to configure our `org.springframework.web.bind.WebDataBinder`. This object has several configuration options (setter methods) that we can use, as shown in Table 5-16.

Table 5-16. *WebDataBinder properties.*

Attribute	Description
allowedFields	Specifies the fields that are allowed for binding. It is a white list; only fields included in this list are used for binding. Field names can also contain an asterisk (*) for matching field names with a certain pattern. By default, all fields are allowed. See the disallowedFields attribute for information on excluding fields from binding.
autoGrowCollectionLimit	Sets the maximum size to auto grow a collection when binding. This setting can prevent out of memory errors when binding on large collections. By default, it is set to 256.
autoGrowNestedPaths	If set to true, populates a path containing a null value with a default object value instead of raising an exception. This default object value is used for further traversal of the expression. This property also controls auto growing of collections when an out-of-bounds index is being accessed. By default, it is set to true.
bindEmptyMultipartFiles	By default, replaces the already bound multipart files with an empty multipart file holder if the user resubmits a multipart form without choosing a different file. If this isn't desired and you want null instead, then turn this property off.
bindingErrorProcessor	Sets the org.springframework.validation. BindingErrorProcessor implementation. Spring provides org.springframework.validation. DefaultBindingErrorProcessor as a default implementation.
conversionService	Sets org.springframework.core.convert.ConversionService.
disallowedFields	Specifies the fields that aren't allowed for binding. It is a blacklist of request parameter names to ignore during binding. In general, it is wise to put fields like the ID and version fields in there. Like allowedFields, this property can contain an * for matching field names with a certain pattern.

(continued)

Table 5-16. (*continued*)

Attribute	Description
extractOldValueForEditor	Specifies whether to extract the old values for editors and converters. By default, the old values are kept in the binding result. If this isn't desired, set this property to `false`. It is also useful to set this to `false` if you have getters with side effects (e.g., they set other properties or default values).
fieldDefaultPrefix	Specifies the prefix to identify parameters that contain default values for empty fields. The default value is !.
fieldMarkerPrefix	Specifies the prefix to identify parameters that mark fields that aren't submitted. Generally, this is useful with checkboxes. A checkbox that isn't checked isn't submitted as part of the request. Note that this mechanism still lets us receive a value. The default marker is _ (underscore).
ignoreInvalidFields	If set to `true`, ignores invalid fields. Should we ignore bind parameters with corresponding fields in our model object, but which aren't accessible? Generally this happens with a nested path, when part of that path resolves to `null`. The default is false (i.e., it does *not* ignore these fields).
ignoreUnknownFields	Indicates whether to ignore parameters that aren't represented as parameters on our model objects. When set to `false`, all the parameters that are submitted must be represented on our model objects. The default is `true`.
messageCodesResolver	Sets `org.springframework.validation.MessageCodesResolver`. Spring provides `org.springframework.validation.DefaultMessageCodesResolver` as the default implementation.
requiredFields	Sets the fields that are required. When a required field is not set, this leads to a bind error.
validator	Sets the `org.springframework.validation.Validator` implementation.

In addition to setting these properties, we can also tell `org.springframework.web.`
`bind.WebDataBinder` to use bean property access (the default) or direct field access.
This can be done by calling the `initBeanPropertyAccess` or `initDirectFieldAccess`
method to set property access or direct field access, respectively. The advantage of direct
field access is that we don't have to write getter/setters for each field we want to use for
binding. Listing 5-23 shows an example init-binder method.

Listing 5-23. An Example init-binder Method

```
package com.apress.prospringmvc.bookstore.web.controller;

//Imports omitted

@Controller
@RequestMapping("/customer")
public class RegistrationController {

// Other methods omitted

  @InitBinder
  public void initBinder(WebDataBinder binder) {
    binder.initDirectFieldAccess();
    binder.setDisallowedFields("id");
    binder.setRequiredFields("username", "password", "emailAddress");
  }
}
```

ModelAttributes

To fully utilize data binding, we have to use model attributes. Furthermore, we should
use one of these model attributes as the object our form fields are bound to. In our `com.`
`apress.prospringmvc.bookstore.web.controller.BookSearchController`, we added
an object as a method argument, and Spring used that as the object to bind the request
parameters to. However, it is possible to have more control over our objects and how we
create objects. For this, we can use the `org.springframework.web.bind.annotation.`
`ModelAttribute` annotation. This annotation can be put both on a method and method
arguments.

Using ModelAttribute on Methods

We can use the @ModelAttribute annotation on methods to create an object to be used in our form (e.g., when editing or updating) or to get reference data (i.e., data that is needed to render the form like a list of categories). Let's modify our controller to add a list of categories to the model and an instance of a com.apress.prospring.bookstore. domain.BookSearchCriteria object (see Listing 5-24).

When an @ModelAttribute annotation is put on a method, this method is called before the request-handling method is called!

Listing 5-24. The BookSearchController with ModelAttribute Methods

```
package com.apress.prospringmvc.bookstore.web.controller;

// Other imports omitted.

import org.springframework.web.bind.annotation.ModelAttribute;

@Controller
public class BookSearchController {

  private final BookstoreService bookstoreService;

  @ModelAttribute
  public BookSearchCriteria criteria() {
    return new BookSearchCriteria();
  }

  @ModelAttribute("categories")
  public List<Category> getCategories() {
    return this.bookstoreService.findAllCategories();
  }

  @GetMapping("/book/search")
  public Collection<Book> list(BookSearchCriteria criteria) {
    return this.bookstoreService.findBooks(criteria);
  }
}
```

Methods annotated with @ModelAttribute have the same flexibility in method argument types as request-handling methods. Of course, they shouldn't operate on the response and cannot have @ModelAttribute annotation method arguments. We could also have the method return void; however, we would need to include org.springframework.ui.Model, org.springframework.ui.ModelMap, or java.util.Map as a method argument and explicitly add its value to the model.

The annotation can also be placed on request-handling methods, indicating that the method's return value is a model attribute. The name of the view is then derived from the request that uses the configured org.springframework.web.servlet.RequestToViewNameTranslator.

Using ModelAttribute on Method Arguments

When using the annotation on a method argument, the argument is looked up from the model. If it isn't found, an instance of the argument type is created using the default constructor.

Listing 5-25 shows com.apress.prospring.bookstore.web.controller.BookSearchController with the annotation.

Listing 5-25. The BookSearchController with ModelAttribute Annotation on a Method Argument

```
package com.apress.prospringmvc.bookstore.web.controller;

// Imports omitted see listing 5-22

@Controller
public class BookSearchController {

// Methods omitted see listing 5-22

  @GetMapping("/book/search")
  public Collection<Book> list(@ModelAttribute("bookSearchCriteria")
    BookSearchCriteria criteria) {
    return this.bookstoreService.findBooks(criteria);
  }
}
```

Using SessionAttributes

It can be beneficial to store a model attribute in the session between requests. For example, imagine we need to edit a customer record. The first request gets the customer from the database. It is then edited in the application, and the changes are submitted back and applied to the customer. If we don't store the customer in the session, then the customer record must be retrieved from the database. This can be inconvenient.

In Spring MVC, you can tell the framework to store certain model attributes in the session. For this, you can use the `org.springframework.web.bind.annotation.SessionAttributes` annotation (see Table 5-17). You should use this annotation to store model attributes in the session to survive multiple HTTP requests. However, you should not use this annotation to store something in the session and then use the `javax.servlet.http.HttpSession` to retrieve it. The session attributes are also only usable from within the same controller, so you should not use them as a transport to move objects between controllers. If you need that, we suggest using plain access to the `HttpSession`.

Table 5-17. *The SessionAttributes Attributes*

Argument Name	Description
value	The names of the model attributes that should be stored in the session.
types	The fully qualified classnames (types) of model attributes should be stored in the session. All attributes in a model of this type are stored in the session, regardless of their names.

When using the `org.springframework.web.bind.annotation.SessionAttributes` annotation to store model attributes in the session, we also need to tell the framework when to remove those attributes. For this, we need to use the `org.springframework.web.bind.support.SessionStatus` interface (see Listing 5-26). When we finish using the attributes, we need to call the `setComplete` method on the interface. To access that interface, we can simply include it as a method argument (see Table 5-4).

Listing 5-26. The SessionStatus Interface

```
package org.springframework.web.bind.support;

public interface SessionStatus {

  void setComplete();
  boolean isComplete();

}
```

Thymeleaf expressions

To use all the data binding features provided by the framework, we rely on the view technology, in this case, Thymeleaf. Thymeleaf parses the search.html template and evaluates the various template expressions to render the form. Spring Framework can be used with JSP views, and in this case, the Spring Tag Library can write forms and bind form elements to Spring objects.

When using Thymeleaf views, regardless of template types (HTML, text, etc.), you can use five types of standard expressions (or constructs). They are listed in Table 5-18.

Table 5-18. *The Thymeleaf standard expression types.*

Construct	Expression Type	Comment
${...}	Variable expressions.	OGNL expressions or Spring EL executed on the *model attributes*.
*{...}	Selection expressions.	OGNL expressions or Spring EL executed on an object previously selected with a variable expression.
#{...}	Message (i18n) expressions.	Also called *internationalization expressions* to allow retrieval of locale-specific messages.
@{...}	Link (URL) expressions.	Builds URLs and adds useful context and session info.
~{...}	Fragment expressions.	An easy way to represent fragments of markup and move them around templates. Can specify inheritance or overriding of template elements.

A number of these expressions have been used in the examples in this chapter. Table 5-19 lists a few of these with a short explanation for each.

Table 5-19. *Thymeleaf expressions used in the Bookstore project.*

Expression	Description
`<head th:replace="~{template/ layout :: head('Search books')}"></head>`	Parametrizable fragment expression: the `<head../>` element in the current template is replaced with the one from `template/layout.html`, and the argument value is injected wherever required in this `<head../>` element declaration.
`<div id="header" th:replace="~{template/layout :: header}" ></div>`	Fragment expression: this div element is replaced with the one with the same ID from template `template/layout.html`.
`<h1 id="pagetitle" th:text="#{book.search. title}">SEARCH TITLE</h1>`	Message expression: the value of the `<h1>` element is replaced with the message value matching the `book.search.title` message key. The resulting HTML element, for and EN locale is `<h1 id="pagetitle">Search Books</h1>`.
`th:action="@{/book/search}"`	Link expression: this generates a full URL by adding the protocol, domain name, and application context in front of the value provided as argument (e.g., `http:// localhost:8080/chapter5-bookstore/book/ search`). It provides a POST endpoint for a form.
`th:object="${bookSearch Criteria}"`	Variable expression: this declares the model object to use for collecting the form data.
`<th:block th:each="book : ${bookList}"> </th:block>`	Variable expression – iteration: the content within the block is repeated for each element in the `bookList`
`<td><input type="text" th:field="{title}"/> <span th:if="${#fields. hasErrors('title')}" class="error" th:errors= "{title}"></span></td>`	Variable expression – validation: within a `bean-backed form`, secondary elements can display validation errors. In general, if the user enters a title that violates the @ `Valid` constraints, it bounces back to this page with the error message displayed.

Given all the information introduced about the Thymeleaf expressions, if we load the search page and issue a search, we see that our title field keeps the previously entered value (see Figure 5-6). This is due to our use of data binding in combination with the Thymeleaf expressions.

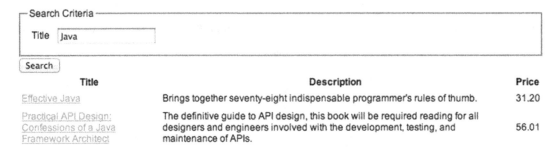

Figure 5-6. *The Title field remains filled*

Now it's time to make things a bit more interesting by adding a drop-down box (an HTML select) to select a category to search for in addition to the title. First, we already have the categories in our model (see Listing 5-27).

Listing 5-27. Adding Categories to the `search.html` Model

```
package com.apress.prospringmvc.bookstore.web.controller;
// other import statements omitted

@Controller
public class BookSearchController {

    @ModelAttribute("categories")
    public Iterable<Category> getCategories() {
        return this.bookstoreService.findAllCategories();
    }
    // other code omitted
}
```

We simply want to add a drop-down and bind it to the `category`'s ID field (see Listing 5-28). We add a select tag and tell it which model attribute contains the items to render.

We also specify the value and label to show for each of the items. The value is bound to the model attribute used for the form.

Listing 5-28. The Search Page with a Category Drop-down Element

```
<form action="#" th:action="@{/book/search}"
      th:object="${bookSearchCriteria}"
      method="GET" id="bookSearchForm">
   <fieldset>
      <legend>Search Criteria</legend>
      <table>
         <tr>
            <td>
               <label for="title">Title</label>
            </td>
            <td><input type="text" th:field="*{title}"/></td>
         </tr>
         <tr>
            <td>
               <label for="category">Category</label>
            </td>
            <td>
               <select th:field="*{category}">
                  <option th:each="c : ${categories}"
                          th:value="${c.id}" th:text="${c.name}"
                          th:selected="${c.id==1}">
                  </option>
               </select>
            </td>
         </tr>
      </table>
   </fieldset>
   <button id="search">Search</button>
</form>

// Result table omitted
```

Type Conversion

An important part of data binding is type conversion. When we receive a request, the only thing we have is String instances. However, in the real world, we use many different object types, not only text representations. Therefore, we want to convert those String instances into something we can use, which is where type conversion comes in. With Spring, there are three ways to do type conversion.

- Property editors

- Converters

- Formatters

Property editors are old-style type conversion, whereas converters and formatters are the new way. Converters and formatters are more flexible; as such, they are also more powerful than property editors. Also, relying on property editors pulls in the whole java.beans package, including all its support classes, which you don't need in a web environment.

Property Editors

Support for property editors has been part of the Spring Framework since its inception. To use this kind of type conversion, we create a PropertyEditor implementation (typically by subclassing PropertyEditorSupport). Property editors take a String and convert it into a strongly typed object—and vice versa. Spring provides several implementations for accomplishing this out of the box (see Table 5-20).

Table 5-20. *Spring's Default Property Editors in use by Spring MVC*

Class	Explanation
`ByteArrayPropertyEditor`	An editor for byte arrays that converts Strings to their corresponding byte representations.
`CharterEditor`	An editor for `Character` or `char` fields. It converts a (Unicode) String into a character. Throws `java.lang.IllegalArgumentException` if more than one character is being parsed. Registered by default.
`CharsetEditor`	An editor for `java.nio.charset.Charset` that expects the same name syntax as the name method of `java.nio.charset.Charset`.
`ClassEditorClass ArrayEditor`	An editor that parses Strings representing classes into actual classes and vice versa. When a class is not found, `java.lang.IllegalArgumentException` is thrown.
`CurrencyEditor`	An editor for Currency that translates currency codes into Currency objects. It also exposes the currency code as the text representation of a `Currency` object.
`CustomBooleanEditor`	A customizable property editor for `Boolean` properties.
`CustomCollectionEditor`	A property editor for collections that converts any source `Collection` into a given target Collection type.
`CustomMapEditor`	Property editor for Map that converts any source Map into a given target Map type.
`CustomDateEditor`	A customizable property editor for `java.util.Date` that supports a custom `DateFormat`. It is *not* registered by default, and it must be user registered as needed with the appropriate format.
`CustomNumberEditor`	A customizable property editor for any `Number` subclass like `Integer`, `Long`, `Float`, and so on. It is registered by default, but can be overridden by registering a custom instance of it as a custom editor.

(*continued*)

Table 5-20. (*continued*)

Class	Explanation
FileEditor	An editor capable of resolving Strings to java.io.File objects. It is registered by default.
InputStreamEditor	A one-way property editor capable of taking a text string and producing java.io.InputStream, so that InputStream properties may be directly set as Strings. Note that the default usage does not close the InputStream for you! It is registered by default.
LocaleEditor	An editor capable of resolving to Locale objects and vice versa (the String format is *[country][*variant], which is the same behavior the toString() method of Locale provides). It is registered by default.
PatternEditor	An editor capable of resolving Strings to JDK 1.5 Pattern objects and vice versa.
PropertiesEditor	An editor capable of converting Strings (formatted using the format as defined in the Javadoc for the Properties class) to Properties objects. It is registered by default.
StringTrimmerEditor	A property editor that trims Strings. Optionally, it allows transforming an empty String into a null value. It is *not* registered by default; it must be registered by the user as needed.
TimeZoneEditor	An editor for Timezone that translates timezone IDs into TimeZone objects. Note that it does not expose a text representation for TimeZone objects.
URIEditor	An editor for java.net.URI that directly populates a URI property instead of using a String property as a bridge. By default, this editor encodes String into URIs.
URLEditor	An editor capable of resolving a String representation of a URL into an actual java.net.URL object. It is registered by default.
UUIDEditor	Converts a String into java.util.UUID and vice versa, registered by default.
ZoneId	Converts a String into java.time.ZoneId and vice versa, registered by default.

> ⓘ   All property editors are in the org.springframework.beans.propertyeditors package.

Converters

The converter API in Spring is a general-purpose type-conversion system. Within a Spring container, this system is used as an alternative to property editors to convert bean property value strings into the required property type. We can also use this API to our advantage in our application whenever we need to do type conversion. The converter system is a strongly typed conversion system and uses generics to enforce this.

Four different interfaces can implement a converter, all of which are in the org. springframework.core.convert.converter package.

- Converter

- ConverterFactory

- GenericConverter

- ConditionalGenericConverter

Let's explore the four different APIs.

Listing 5-29 shows the Converter API, which is very straightforward. It has a single convert method that takes a source argument and transforms it into a target. The source and target types are expressed by the S and T generic type arguments.

Listing 5-29. The Converter API

```
package org.springframework.core.convert.converter;

public interface Converter<S, T> {

  T convert(S source);

}
```

Listing 5-30 shows the ConverterFactory API, which is useful when you need to have conversion logic for an entire class hierarchy. For this, we can parameterize S to be the type we are converting from (the source), and we parameterize R as the base type we want to convert to. We can then create the appropriate converter inside the implementation of this factory.

Listing 5-30. The ConverterFactory API

```
package org.springframework.core.convert.converter;

public interface ConverterFactory<S, R> {

  <T extends R> Converter<S, T> getConverter(Class<T> targetType);

}
```

When we require more sophisticated conversion logic, we can use org. springframework.core .convert.converter.GenericConverter (see Listing 5-31). It is more flexible, but less strongly typed than the previous converter types. It supports converting between multiple sources and target types. During a conversion, we have access to the source and target type descriptions, which is useful for complex conversion logic. This also allows type conversion to be driven by annotation (i.e., we can parse the annotation at runtime to determine what needs to be done).

Listing 5-31. The GenericConverter API

```
package org.springframework.core.convert.converter;

import org.springframework.core.convert.TypeDescriptor;
import org.springframework.util.Assert;
import java.util.Set;

public interface GenericConverter {

  Set<ConvertiblePair> getConvertibleTypes();
  Object convert(Object source, TypeDescriptor sourceType, TypeDescriptor
  targetType);

}
```

An example of this type of conversion logic would be a converter that converts from an array to a collection. A converter first inspects the type of element being converted to apply additional conversion logic to different elements.

Listing 5-32 shows a specialized version of `GenericConverter` that allows us to specify a condition for when it should execute. For example, we could create a converter that uses one of the BigDecimals `valueOf` methods to convert a value, but this would only be useful if we could invoke that method with the given `source type`.

Listing 5-32. The ConditionalGenericConverter API

```
package org.springframework.core.convert.converter;

import org.springframework.core.convert.TypeDescriptor;

  boolean matches(TypeDescriptor sourceType, TypeDescriptor targetType);

}
```

The converters are executed behind the `org.springframework.core.convert.ConversionService` interface (see Listing 5-33); typical implementations of this interface also implement the `org.springframework.core.convert.converter.ConverterRegistry` interface, which enables the easy registration of additional converters. When using Spring MVC, there is a preconfigured instance of `org.springframework.format.support.DefaultFormattingConversionService` (which also allows executing and registering formatters).

Listing 5-33. The ConversionService API

```
package org.springframework.core.convert;

public interface ConversionService {
  boolean canConvert(Class<?> sourceType, Class<?> targetType);
  boolean canConvert(TypeDescriptor sourceType, TypeDescriptor targetType);
  <T> T convert(Object source, Class<T> targetType);
  Object convert(Object source, TypeDescriptor sourceType, TypeDescriptor
  targetType);

}
```

Formatters

The Converter API is a general-purpose type-conversion system. It is strongly typed and can convert from any object type to another object type (if there is a converter available). However, this is not something we need in our web environment because we only deal with String objects there. On the other hand, we probably want to represent our objects as String to the client, and we might even want to do so in a localized way. This is where the Formatter API comes in (see Listing 5-34). It provides a simple and robust mechanism to convert from a String to a strongly typed object. It is an alternative to property editors, but it is also lighter (e.g., it doesn't depend on the `java.beans` package) and more flexible (e.g., it has access to the Locale for localized content).

Listing 5-34. The Formatter API

```
package org.springframework.format;

public interface Formatter<T> extends Printer<T>, Parser<T> {

}

import java.util.Locale

public interface Printer<T> {

  String print(T object, Locale locale);

}

import java.util.Locale

import java.text.ParseException;

public interface Parser<T> {

  T parse(String text, Locale locale) throws ParseException;

}
```

To create a formatter, we need to implement the `org.springframework.format.Formatter` interface and specify the type T as the type we want to convert. For example, imagine we had a formatter that could convert `java.util.Date` instances to text, and vice versa. We would specify T as Date and use the Locale to determine the specific date format for performing the conversion (see Listing 5-35).

Listing 5-35. The Sample DateFormatter

```java
package com.apress.prospringmvc.bookstore.formatter;

// java.text and java.util imports omitted

import org.springframework.format.Formatter;

import org.springframework.util.StringUtils;

public class DateFormatter implements Formatter<Date> {

  private String format;

  @Override
  public String print(Date object, Locale locale) {
    return getDateFormat(locale).format(object);
  }

  @Override
  public Date parse(String text, Locale locale) throws ParseException {
    return getDateFormat(locale).parse(text);
  }

  private DateFormat getDateFormat(Locale locale) {
    if (StringUtils.hasText(this.format)) {
      return new SimpleDateFormat(this.format, locale);
    } else {
      return SimpleDateFormat.getDateInstance(SimpleDateFormat.MEDIUM,
      locale);
    }
  }

  public void setFormat(String format) {
    this.format = format;
  }
}
```

Formatters can also be driven by annotations instead of by field type. If we want to bind a formatter to an annotation, we have to implement `org.springframework.format.AnnotationFormatterFactory` (see Listing 5-36).

Listing 5-36. The AnnotationFormatterFactory Interface

```
package org.springframework.format;

public interface AnnotationFormatterFactory<A extends Annotation> {

  Set<Class<?>> getFieldTypes();
  Printer<?> getPrinter(A annotation, Class<?> fieldType);
  Parser<?> getParser(A annotation, Class<?> fieldType);

}
```

We need to parameterize A with the annotation type we want to associate with it. The getPrinter and getParser methods should return `org.springframework.format.Printer` and `org.springframework.format.Parser`, respectively. We can then use these to convert from or to the annotation type. Let's imagine we have a `com.apress.prospringmvc.bookstore.formatter.DateFormat` annotation that we can use to set the format for a date field. We could then implement the factory shown in Listing 5-37.

Listing 5-37. The DateFormatAnnotationFormatterFactory Class

```
package com.apress.prospringmvc.bookstore.formatter;

import java.util.Date;
import java.util.Set;
import org.springframework.format.AnnotationFormatterFactory;
import org.springframework.format.Parser;
import org.springframework.format.Printer;

public class DateFormatAnnotationFormatterFactory
    implements AnnotationFormatterFactory<DateFormat> {

  @Override
  public Set<Class<?>> getFieldTypes() {
    return Set.of(Date.class);
  }
```

```java
@Override
public Printer<?> getPrinter(DateFormat annotation, Class<?> fieldType) {
  return createFormatter(annotation);
}

@Override
public Parser<?> getParser(DateFormat annotation, Class<?> fieldType) {
  return createFormatter(annotation);
}

private DateFormatter createFormatter(DateFormat annotation) {
  var formatter = new DateFormatter();
  formatter.setFormat(annotation.format());
  return formatter;
}
}
```

Configuring Type Conversion

If we want to use org.springframework.core.convert.converter.Converter or
org.springframework.format.Formatter in Spring MVC, then we need to add some
configuration.

org.springframework.web.servlet.config.annotation.
WebMvcConfigurerAdapter has a method for this. The addFormatters method can be
overridden to register additional converters and/or formatters. This method has org.
springframework.format.FormatterRegistry (see Listing 5-38) as an argument, and
it can register the additional converters and/or formatters. (The FormatterRegistry
extends org.springframework.core.convert.converter.ConverterRegistry, which
offers the same functionality for Converter implementations).

Listing 5-38. The FormatterRegistry Interface

```java
package org.springframework.format;

import java.lang.annotation.Annotation;

import org.springframework.core.convert.converter.ConverterRegistry;
```

```java
public interface FormatterRegistry extends ConverterRegistry {

void addFormatter(Formatter<?> formatter);

void addFormatterForFieldType(Class<?> fieldType, Formatter<?> formatter);

void addFormatterForFieldType(Class<?> fieldType, Printer<?> printer,
Parser<?> parser);

void addFormatterForFieldAnnotation(AnnotationFormatterFactory
    <? extends Annotation> annotationFormatterFactory);

}
```

To convert from a String to a com.apress.prospringmvc.bookstore.domain. Category, we implement org.springframework.core.convert.converter. GenericConverter (see Listing 5-39) and register it in our configuration (see Listing 5-40). The com.apress.prospringmvc.bookstore.converter.StringToEntityConverter takes a String as its source and transforms it into a configurable entity type. It then uses a javax.persistence.EntityManager to load the record from the database.

Listing 5-39. The StringToEntityConverter

```java
package com.apress.prospringmvc.bookstore.converter;

import org.springframework.core.convert.TypeDescriptor;
import org.springframework.core.convert.converter.GenericConverter;
import org.springframework.util.ReflectionUtils;
import org.springframework.util.StringUtils;

import javax.persistence.EntityManager;
import javax.persistence.PersistenceContext;
import java.util.Set;

public class StringToEntityConverter implements GenericConverter {

    private static final String ID_FIELD = "id";

    private final Class<?> clazz;

    @PersistenceContext
    private EntityManager em;
```

```java
    public StringToEntityConverter(Class<?> clazz) {
        super();
        this.clazz = clazz;
    }

    @Override
    public Set<ConvertiblePair> getConvertibleTypes() {
        return Set.of(
                new ConvertiblePair(String.class, this.clazz),
                    new ConvertiblePair(this.clazz, String.class));
    }

    @Override
    public Object convert(Object source, TypeDescriptor sourceType,
    TypeDescriptor targetType) {
        if (String.class.equals(sourceType.getType())) {
            if (!StringUtils.hasText((String) source)) {
                return null;
            }
            var id = Long.parseLong((String) source);
            return this.em.find(this.clazz, id);
        } else if (this.clazz.equals(sourceType.getType())) {
                if (source == null) {
                        return "";
                } else {
                        var field = ReflectionUtils.findField(source.
                        getClass(), ID_FIELD);
                        if (field != null) {
                            ReflectionUtils.makeAccessible(field);
                            return ReflectionUtils.getField(field, source);
                        }
                }
        }
        throw new IllegalArgumentException("Cannot convert " + source + "
        into a suitable type!");
    }
}
```

Listing 5-40. The CategoryConverter Configuration

```
package com.apress.prospringmvc.bookstore.web.config;
// other imports omitted

@Configuration
public class WebMvcContextConfiguration implements WebMvcConfigurer {

// other code omitted

  @Bean
  public StringToEntityConverter categoryConverter() {
    return new StringToEntityConverter(Category.class);
  }

  @Override
  public void addFormatters(final FormatterRegistry registry) {
    registry.addConverter(categoryConverter());
    registry.addFormatter(new DateFormatter("dd-MM-yyyy"));
  }
}
```

In addition to the category conversion, we also need to do date conversions. Therefore, Listing 5-38 also includes `org.springframework.format.datetime.DateFormatter` with a pattern for converting dates.

Using Type Conversion

Now that we have covered type conversion, let's see it in action. We create the user registration page that allows us to enter the details for the `com.apress.prospringmvc.bookstore.domain.Account` object. First, we need a web page under `WEB-INF/views`. Next, we need to create a customer directory and place a `register.html` file in it. The content included in Listing 5-41 has been simplified, because there is a lot of repetition on this page for all the different fields.

Listing 5-41. The Registration Page

```html
<html xmlns:th="http://www.thymeleaf.org">
<head th:replace="~{template/layout :: head('Register')}"></head>
<!-- other HTML elements omitted -->

<form action="#" th:action="@{/customer/register}"
  th:object="${account}" method="POST" id="registerForm">
<fieldset>
<legend >Personal</legend>
<table>
    <tr>
        <td><label for="firstName">Firstname</label></td>
        <td><input type="text" th:field="*{firstName}"/>
            <span th:if="${#fields.hasErrors('firstName')}"
                class="error" th:errors="*{firstName}"></span>
        </td>
    </tr>
    <tr>
        <td><label for="lastName" >Lastname</label></td>
        <td><input type="text" th:field="*{lastName}"/>
            <span th:if="${#fields.hasErrors('lastName')}"
                class="error" th:errors="*{lastName}"></span>
        </td>
    </tr>
<tr>
        <td><label for="title" >date of Birth</label></td>
        <td><input type="date" th:field="*{dateOfBirth}"/>
            <span th:if="${#fields.hasErrors('dateOfBirth')}"
                class="error" th:errors="*{dateOfBirth}"></span>
        </td>
    </tr>
</table>
 <button id="search" >Save</button>
<!-- other form elements omitted -->

</fieldset>
</form>
```

We also need a controller for this, so we create the `com.apress.prospringmvc.` `bookstore.web.controller.RegistrationController`. In this controller, we use a couple of data binding features. First, we disallow the submission of an ID field (to prevent someone from editing another user). Then, we preselect the user's country based on the current Locale. Listing 5-42 shows our controller.

Listing 5-42. The RegistrationController

```java
package com.apress.prospringmvc.bookstore.web.controller;

import java.util.Locale;
import java.util.Map;
import java.util.TreeMap;
import org.springframework.beans.factory.annotation.Autowired;
import org.springframework.stereotype.Controller;
import org.springframework.validation.BindingResult;
import org.springframework.web.bind.WebDataBinder;
import org.springframework.web.bind.annotation.InitBinder;
import org.springframework.web.bind.annotation.ModelAttribute;
import org.springframework.web.bind.annotation.RequestMapping;
import org.springframework.web.bind.annotation.RequestMethod;
import com.apress.prospringmvc.bookstore.domain.Account;

@Controller
@RequestMapping("/customer/register")
public class RegistrationController {

    private final AccountService accountService;

    public RegistrationController(AccountService accountService) {
        this.accountService = accountService;
    }

    @ModelAttribute("countries")
    public Map<String, String> countries(Locale currentLocale) {
      var countries = new TreeMap<String,String>();
```

```java
  for (var locale : Locale.getAvailableLocales()) {
    countries.put(locale.getCountry(), locale.getDisplayCountry(
    currentLocale));
  }
  return countries;
}

@InitBinder
public void initBinder(WebDataBinder binder) {
  binder.setDisallowedFields("id");
  binder.setRequiredFields("username","password","emailAddress");
}

@GetMapping
@ModelAttribute
public Account register(Locale currentLocale) {
  var account = new Account();
  account.getAddress().setCountry(currentLocale.getCountry());
  return account;
}

@RequestMapping(method = { RequestMethod.POST, RequestMethod.PUT })
public String handleRegistration(@ModelAttribute Account account,
BindingResult result) {
  if (result.hasErrors()) {
    return "customer/register";
  }
  this.accountService.save(account);
  return "redirect:/customer/account/" + account.getId();
}

}
```

The controller has a lot going on. For example, the initBinder method configures our binding. It disallows the setting of the ID property and sets some required fields. We also have a method that prepares our model by adding all the available countries in the JDK to the model. Finally, we have two request-handling methods, one for a GET request (the initial request when we enter our page) and one for POST/PUT requests when we submit our form. Notice the org.springframework.validation.BindingResult attribute next to the model attribute. This is what we can use to detect errors, and based on that, we can redisplay the original page. Also, remember that the error expressions in the Thymeleaf template display error messages for fields or objects (this is covered in the upcoming sections). When the application is redeployed, and you click the Register link, you should see the page shown in Figure 5-7.

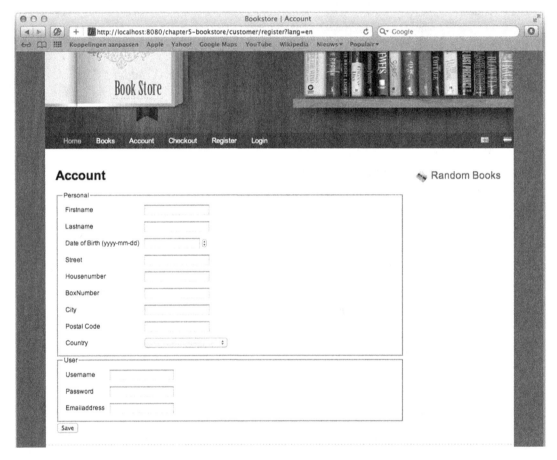

Figure 5-7. *The account registration page*

If we now enter an invalid date, leave the username, password, and e-mail address fields blank, and then submit the form, the same page redisplays with some error messages (see Figure 5-8).

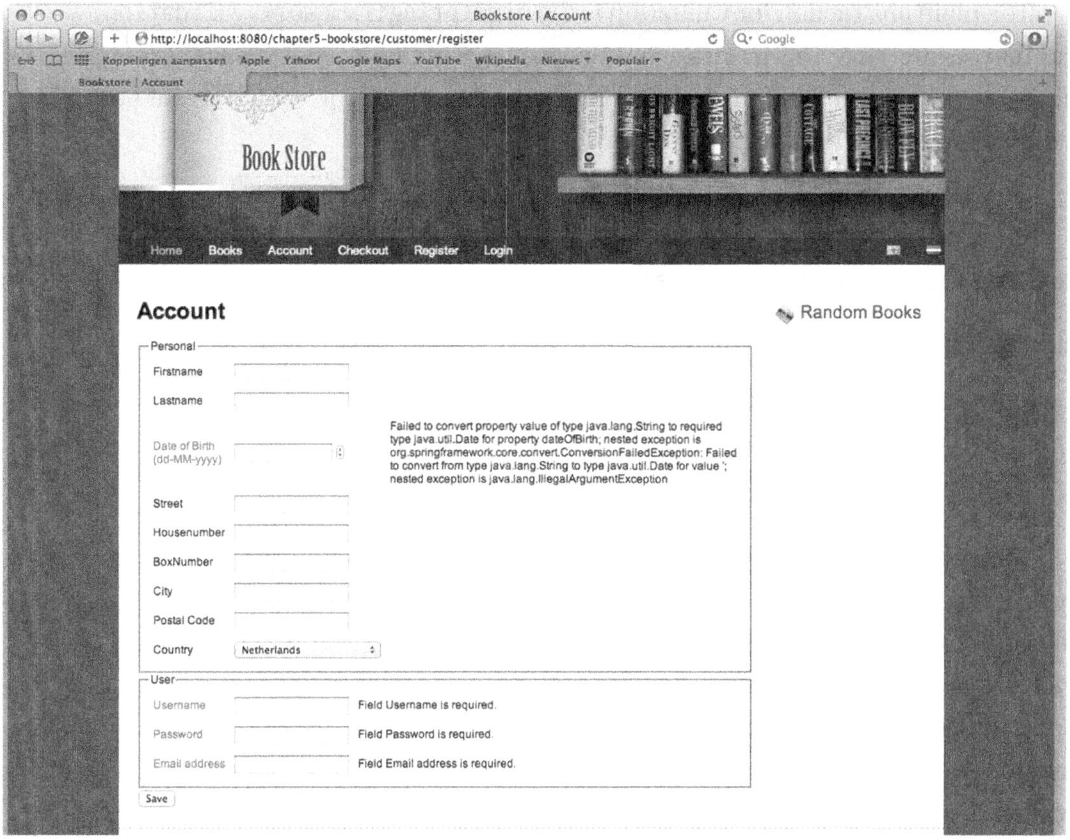

Figure 5-8. *The account registration page showing some errors*

The error messages are created by the data binding facilities in Spring MVC. Later in this chapter, you see how we can influence the messages displayed. For now, let's leave them intact. If we fill in proper information and click Save, we are redirected to an account page (for which we already have provided the basic controller and implementation).

Validating Model Attributes

We've already mentioned validation a couple of times. We've also referred to the `org.springframework.validation` package a couple of times. Validating our model attributes is easy to accomplish with the validation abstraction from the Spring Framework. Validation isn't bound to the web; it is about validating objects. Therefore, validation can also be used outside the web layer; in fact, it can be used anywhere.

The main abstraction for validation is the `org.springframework.validation.` `Validator` interface. This interface has two callback methods. The `supports` method determines if the validator instance can validate the object. The `validate` method validates the object (see Listing 5-43).

Listing 5-43. The `Validator` Interface

```
package org.springframework.validation;

public interface Validator {

  boolean supports(Class<?> clazz);
  void validate(Object target, Errors errors);
}
```

The supports method is called to see if a validator can validate the current object type. If that returns true, the framework calls the validate method with the object to validate and an instance of an implementation of the `org.springframework.` `validation.Errors` interface. When binding, this is an implementation of `org.` `springframework.validation.BindingResult`. When doing validation, it is good to include an `Errors` or `BindingResult` (the latter extends Errors) method attribute. This way, we can handle situations where there is a bind or validation error. If this is not the case, `org.springframework.validation.BindException` is thrown.

When using Spring MVC, we have two options for triggering validation. The first is to inject the validator into our controller and call the validate method on the validator. The second is to add the `javax.validation.Valid` (JSR-303) or `org.springframework.` `validation.annotation.Validated` annotation to our method attribute. The annotation from the Spring Framework is more powerful than the one from the javax.validation package. The Spring annotation enables us to specify *hints*; when combined with a JSR-303 validator (e.g., hibernate-validation), we can specify validation groups.

Validation and bind errors lead to message codes that are registered with the `Errors` instance. In general, simply showing an error code to the user isn't very informative, so the code must be resolved to a message. This is where `org.springframework.context.` `MessageSource` comes into play. The error codes are passed as message codes to the configured message source and retrieve the message. If we don't configure a message source, we are greeted with a nice stack trace, indicating that a message for error code cannot be found. So, before we proceed, let's configure the `MessageSource` shown in Listing 5-44.

Listing 5-44. The MessageSource Configuration Bean

```
package com.apress.prospringmvc.bookstore.web.config;

import org.springframework.context.support.ResourceBundleMessageSource;

// Other imports omitted

@Configuration
public class WebMvcContextConfiguration extends WebMvcConfigurer {

  @Bean
  public MessageSource messageSource() {
    var messageSource = new ResourceBundleMessageSource();
    messageSource.setBasename("messages");
    messageSource.setUseCodeAsDefaultMessage(true);
    return messageSource;
  }

// Other methods omitted

}
```

We configure a message source and then configure it to load a resource bundle with basename messages (you learn more about this in the "Internationalization" section later in this chapter). When a message is not found, we return the code as the message. This is especially useful during development because we can quickly see which message codes are missing from our resource bundles.

Let's implement validation for our com.apress.prospringmvc.bookstore.domain. Account class. We want to validate whether an account is valid, and for that, we need a username, password, and a valid e-mail address. To handle shipping, we also need an address, city, and country. Without this information, the account isn't valid. Now let's see how to use the validation framework to our advantage.

Implementing Our Validator

We begin by implementing our own validator. In this case, we create a com.apress. prospringmvc.bookstore.validation.AccountValidator (see Listing 5-45) and use an init-binder method to configure it.

Listing 5-45. The AccountValidator Implementation

```
package com.apress.prospringmvc.bookstore.validation;

import java.util.regex.Pattern;
import org.springframework.validation.Errors;
import org.springframework.validation.ValidationUtils;
import org.springframework.validation.Validator;
import com.apress.prospringmvc.bookstore.domain.Account;

public class AccountValidator implements Validator {

private static final String EMAIL_PATTERN = "^[_A-Za-z0-9-]+(\\.
[_A-Za-z0-9-]+)*@"
  +"[A-Za-z0-9]+(\\.[A-Za-z0-9]+)*(\\.[A-Za-z]\\{2,})$";

  @Override
  public boolean supports(Class<?> clazz) {
    return Account.class.isAssignableFrom(clazz);
  }

  @Override
  public void validate(Object target, Errors errors) {
    ValidationUtils.rejectIfEmpty(errors, "username","required", new
    Object[] {"Username"});
    ValidationUtils.rejectIfEmpty(errors, "password","required", new
    Object[] {"Password"});
    ValidationUtils.rejectIfEmpty(errors, "emailAddress","required", new
    Object[] {"Emailaddress"});
    ValidationUtils.rejectIfEmpty(errors, "address.street","required", new
    Object[] {"Street"});
    ValidationUtils.rejectIfEmpty(errors, "address.city","required", new
    Object[] {"City"});
    ValidationUtils.rejectIfEmpty(errors, "address.country","required", new
    Object[] {"Country"});
```

```
  if (!errors.hasFieldErrors("emailAddress")) {
    var account = (Account) target;
    var email = account.getEmailAddress();
    if (!emai.matches(EMAIL_PATTERN)) {
      errors.rejectValue("emailAddress", "invalid");
    }
  }
 }
}
```

> Specifying `requiredFields` on `org.springframework.web.bind.`
> `WebDataBinder` would result in the same validation logic as with the
> `ValidationUtils.rejectIfEmptyOrWhiteSpace`. In our case, however, we
> have all the validation logic in one place, rather than having it spread over two
> places.

This validator implementation checks if the fields are not null and non-empty. If the field is empty, it registers an error for the given field. The error is a collection of message codes determined by an `org.springframework.validation.MessageCodesResolver` implementation. The default implementation, `org.springframework.validation.DefaultMessageCodesResolver`, resolves to four different codes (see Table 5-21). The order in the table is also how the error codes are resolved to a proper message.

Table 5-21. *The Error Codes for Field Errors*

Pattern	Example
code + object name + field	`required.newOrder.name`
code + field	`required.name`
code + field type	`required.java.lang.String`
Code	`required`

The final part of this validation is that we need to configure our validator and tell the controller to validate our model attribute on submission. In Listing 5-46, we show the modified order controller. We only want to trigger validation on the final submission of our form.

Listing 5-46. The RegistrationController with Validation

```
package com.apress.prospringmvc.bookstore.web.controller;

import com.apress.prospringmvc.bookstore.domain.AccountValidator;

import javax.validation.Valid;
// Other imports omitted

@Controller
@RequestMapping("/customer/register")
public class RegistrationController {

  @InitBinder
  public void initBinder(WebDataBinder binder) {
    binder.setDisallowedFields("id");
    binder.setValidator(new AccountValidator());
  }

  @RequestMapping(method = { RequestMethod._POST_, RequestMethod._PUT_ })
  public String handleRegistration(@Valid @ModelAttribute Account account,
BindingResult result) {
     if (result.hasErrors()) {
       return "customer/register";
     }
     this.accountService.save(account);
     return "redirect:/customer/account/" + account.getId();
  }

// Other methods omitted

}
```

If we submit illegal values after redeployment, we are greeted with some error codes, as shown in Figure 5-9.

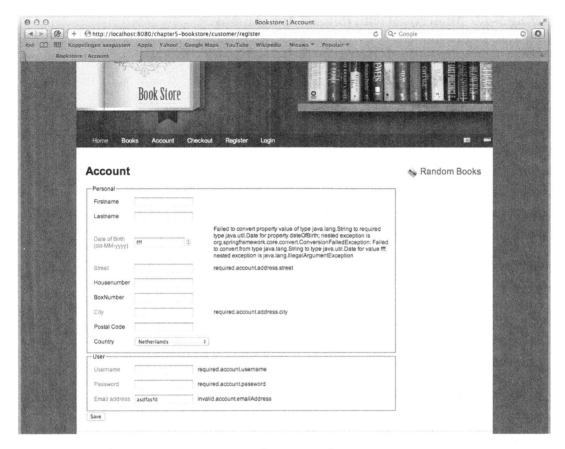

Figure 5-9. *The registration page with error codes*

Using JSR-303 Validation

Instead of implementing our own validator, we could also use the JSR-303 annotations to add validation. For this, we would only need to annotate our `com.apress.prospringmvc.bookstore.domain.Account` object with JSR-303 annotations (see Listing 5-47) and then leave the `javax.validation.Valid` annotation in place. When using these annotations, the error code used is slightly different than the one used in our custom validator (see Table 5-22). However, the registration page doesn't need to change, so it remains the same as before. Our init-binder method does not need to set the validator because a JSR-303 capable validator is automatically detected (the sample project uses the one from Hibernate).

Listing 5-47. An Account with JSR-303 Annotations

```java
package com.apress.prospringmvc.bookstore.domain;

import java.io.Serializable;
import java.util.ArrayList;
import java.util.Date;
import java.util.List;
import javax.persistence.*;
import javax.validation.Valid;
import javax.validation.constraints.Email;
import javax.validation.constraints.NotEmpty;

@Entity
public class Account {

  @Id
  @GeneratedValue(strategy = GenerationType.AUTO)
  private Long id;

  private String firstName;
  private String lastName;
  private Date dateOfBirth;

  @Embedded
  @Valid
  private Address address = new Address();

  @NotEmpty
  @Email
  private String emailAddress;

  @NotEmpty
  private String username;

  @NotEmpty
  private String password;

// getters and setters omitted

}
```

Table 5-22. *The Error Codes for Field Errors with JSR-303 Annotations*

Pattern	Example
annotation name + object name + field	`NotEmpty.newOrder.name`
annotation name + field	`NotEmpty.name`
annotation name + field type	`NotEmpty.java.lang.String`
annotation name	`NotEmpty`

When using JSR-303 annotations, if we submit the form with invalid values, we get a result like the one shown in Figure 5-10. As you can see, there are messages displayed instead of codes. How is that possible? There are some default messages shipped with the validator implementation we use. We can override these if we want by specifying one of the codes from Table 5-22 in our resource bundle (see the next section).

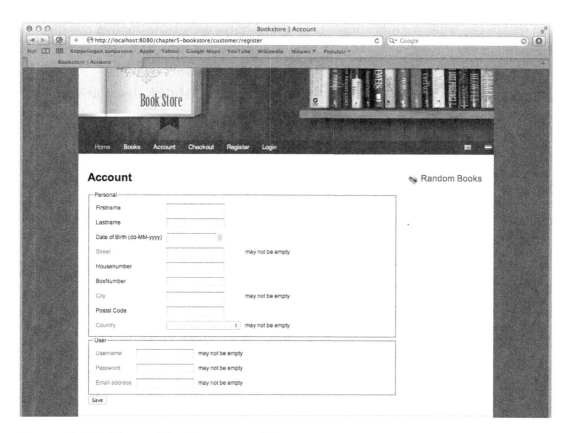

Figure 5-10. *The registration page with error messages*

Internationalization

For internationalization to work, we need to configure different components to resolve messages based on the language (locale) of the user. For example, there is `org.springframework.context.MessageSource`, which lets us resolve messages based on message codes and locale. To resolve the locale, we also need `org.springframework.web.servlet.LocaleResolver`. Finally, to change the locale, we also need to configure `org.springframework.web.servlet.i18n.LocaleChangeInterceptor` (the next chapter covers interceptors in more depth).

Message Source

The message source is the component that resolves our message based on a code and the locale. Spring provides a couple of implementations of the `org.springframework.context.MessageSource` interface. Two of those implementations are implementations that we can use, while the other implementations simply delegate to another message source.

The two implementations provided by the Spring Framework are in the `org.springframework.context.support` package. Table 5-23 briefly describes both of them.

Table 5-23. *A MessageSource Overview*

Class	Description
ResourceBundleMessageSource	Uses the ResourceBundle facility available on the JVM. It can only load resources from the classpath.
ReloadableResourceBundleMessageSource	Works similarly to the ResourceBundleMessageSource but adds reloading and caching capabilities. It allows the resources to be anywhere on the file system; it uses the resource loading mechanism in Spring.

We configure both beans more or less the same way. One thing we need is a bean named messageSource. Which implementation we choose doesn't matter. For example, we could even create our own implementation that uses a database to load the messages.

The configuration in Listing 5-48 configures org.springframework.context. support.ReloadableResourceBundleMessageSource, which loads a file named *messages.properties* from the classpath. It also tries to load the messages_[locale]. properties for the locale we are currently using to resolve the messages.

Listing 5-48. The MessageSource Configuration in WebMvcContext

```java
package com.apress.prospringmvc.bookstore.web.config;

import org.springframework.context.support.
ReloadableResourceBundleMessageSource;

// Other imports omitted

@Configuration
public class WebMvcContextConfiguration extends WebMvcConfigurer {

  @Bean
  public MessageSource messageSource() {
    var messageSource = new ReloadableResourceBundleMessageSource();
    messageSource.setBasename("classpath:/messages");
    messageSource.setUseCodeAsDefaultMessage(true);
    return messageSource;
  }

}
```

The following snippets show two properties files (resource bundles) that are loaded. The messages in the *messages.properties* (see Listing 5-49) file are treated as the defaults, and they can be overridden in the language-specific *messages_nl.properties* file (see Listing 5-50).

Listing 5-49. The messages.properties Snippet

```
home.title=Welcome
invalid.account.emailaddress=Invalid email address.
required=Field {0} is required.
```

Listing 5-50. messages_nl.properties

```
home.title=Welkom
invalid.account.emailaddress=Ongeldig emailadres.
required=Veld {0} is verplicht.
```

LocaleResolver

For the message source to do its work correctly, we also need to configure `org.springframework.web.servlet.LocaleResolver` (this can be found this in the `org.springframework.web.servlet.i18n` package). Several implementations ship with Spring that can make our lives easier. The locale resolver is a strategy that detects which `Locale`. The different implementations each use a different way of resolving the locale (see Table 5-24).

Table 5-24. *The LocaleResolver Overview*

Class	Description
FixedLocaleResolver	Always resolves to a fixed locale. All the users of our website use the same locale, so changing the locale isn't supported.
SessionLocaleResolver	Resolves (and stores) the locale in the user's HttpSession. The attribute stores the locale can be configured and the default locale to use if no locale is present. The drawback to this is that the locale isn't stored between visits, so it must be set at least once on the user's session.
AcceptHeaderLocaleResolver	Uses the HTTP accept header to resolve the locale. In general, this is the locale of the user's operating system, so changing the locale isn't supported. It is also the default LocalResolver used by the DispatcherServlet.
CookieLocaleResolver	Uses a cookie to store the user's locale. The advantage of this resolver is that the locale is kept on the client's machine, so it is available on subsequent visits to the website. The cookie name and timeout can be configured, as well as the default locale.

LocaleChangeInterceptor

If we want our users to change the locale, we need to configure org.springframework.web.servlet.i18n.LocaleChangeInterceptor (see Listing 5-51). This interceptor inspects the current incoming requests and checks whether a parameter named locale is on the request. If this is present, the interceptor uses the earlier configured locale resolver to change the current user's Locale. The parameter name can be configured.

Listing 5-51. The Full Internationalization Configuration

```
package com.apress.prospringmvc.bookstore.web.config;

import org.springframework.context.MessageSource;
import org.springframework.context.support.
ReloadableResourceBundleMessageSource;
import org.springframework.web.servlet.HandlerInterceptor;
```

```
import org.springframework.web.servlet.LocaleResolver;
import org.springframework.web.servlet.config.annotation.
InterceptorRegistry;
import org.springframework.web.servlet.config.annotation.
ResourceHandlerRegistry;
import org.springframework.web.servlet.i18n.CookieLocaleResolver;
import org.springframework.web.servlet.i18n.LocaleChangeInterceptor;

// Other imports omitted

@Configuration
public class WebMvcContextConfiguration implements WebMvcConfigurer {

  @Override
  public void addInterceptors(InterceptorRegistry registry) {
    registry.addInterceptor(localeChangeInterceptor());
  }

  @Bean
  public HandlerInterceptor localeChangeInterceptor() {

    var localeChangeInterceptor = new LocaleChangeInterceptor();
    localeChangeInterceptor.setParamName("lang");
    return localeChangeInterceptor;
  }

  @Bean

  public LocaleResolver localeResolver() {
    return new CookieLocaleResolver();
  }
}
```

💡 In general, it is a good idea to have LocaleChangeInterceptor as one of the first interceptors. If something goes wrong, we want to inform the user in the correct language.

If we redeploy our application, we should get localized error messages if we switch the language (of course, this works only if we add the appropriate error codes to the resource bundles). However, using the MessageSource for error messages isn't its only use; we can also use MessageSource to retrieve our labels, titles, error messages, and so on from our resource bundles. We can use Thymeleaf's message expressions for that. Listing 5-52 shows a modified book search page, which uses message expressions to fill the labels, titles, and headers. If we switch the language, we should get localized messages (see Figures 5-11 and 5-12).

Listing 5-52. The Book Search Page with the Message Tag

```
<form action="#" th:action="@{/book/search}"
    th:object="${bookSearchCriteria}"
    method="GET" id="bookSearchForm">
    <fieldset>
        <legend th:text="#{book.searchcriteria}">SEARCH CRITERIA</legend>
        <table>
            <tr>
                <td><label for="title" th:text="#{book.title}">TITLE</
                label></td>
                <td><input type="text" th:field="*{title}"/></td>
            </tr>
            <tr>
                <td><label for="category" th:text="#{book.
                category}">CATEGORY</label></td>
                <td>
                    <select th:field="*{category}">
                        <option th:each="c : ${categories}"
                        th:value="${c.id}"
                                th:text="${c.name}" th:selected="${c.
                                id==1}">
                        </option>
                    </select>
                </td>
            </tr>
        </table>
    </fieldset>
```

```html
        <button id="search" th:text="#{button.search}">SEARCH</button>
</form>

  <table id="bookSearchResults">
    <thead>
    <tr>
        <th th:text="#{book.title}">TITLE</th>
        <th th:text="#{book.description}">DESCRIPTION</th>
        <th th:text="#{book.price}">PRICE</th>
        <th></th>
    </tr>
    </thead>
    <tbody>
    <th:block th:each="book : ${bookList}">
        <tr>
            <td><a th:href="@{/book/detail/} + ${book.id}"
                th:text="${book.title}">TITLE</a></td>
            <td th:text="${book.description}">DESC</td>
            <td th:text="${book.price}">PRICE</td>
            <td><a th:href="@{/cart/add/} + ${book.id}"
                th:text="#{book.addtocart}">CART</a></td>
        </tr>
    </th:block>
    </tbody>
</table>
```

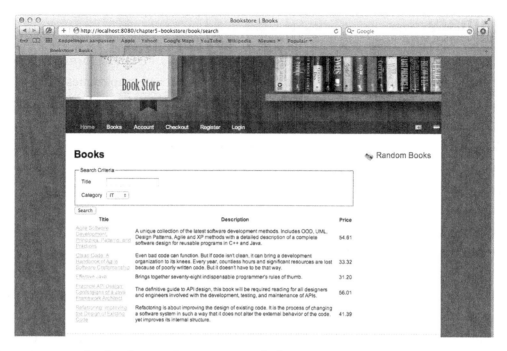

Figure 5-11. *The book search page in English*

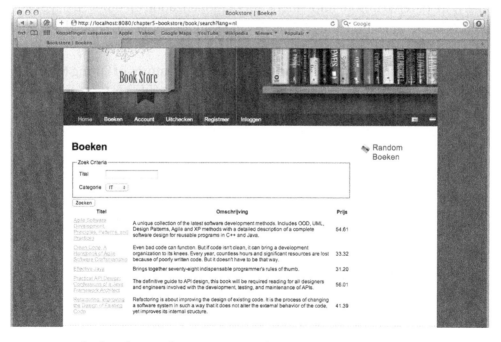

Figure 5-12. *The book search page in Dutch*

Summary

This chapter covered all things we need to write controllers and handle forms. We began by exploring the @RequestMapping annotation and how that can map requests to a method to handle a request. We also explored flexible method signatures and covered which method argument types and return values are supported out of the box.

Next, we dove into the deep end and started writing controllers and modifying our existing code. We also introduced form objects and covered how to bind the properties to fields. And we explained data binding and explored Spring's type-conversion system and how that converts from and to certain objects. We also wrote our own implementation of a Converter to convert from text to a Category object.

In addition to type conversion, we also explored validation. There are two ways to validate: we can create our own implementation of a Validator interface or use the JSR-303 annotations on the objects we want to validate. Enabling validation is done with either the @Valid or the @Validated annotation.

To make it easier to bind certain fields to a form object's attributes, there is the Spring Form Tag library, which helps us to write HTML forms. This library also helps us to display bind and validation errors to the user.

Finally, we covered how to implement internationalization on our web pages and how to convert the validation and error codes to proper messages to show to the end user.

In the next chapter, we explore some more advanced features of Spring MVC. Along the way, you see how to further extend and customize the existing infrastructure.

CHAPTER 6

Implementing Controllers: Advanced

This chapter looks at some of the more advanced parts of Spring MVC and then shows how to tap into the framework to extend it to suit our needs.

We begin by examining scoped beans and how we can use them to our advantage. Next, we explore how we can add generic functionality (cross-cutting concerns) to our application. For this, we look at interceptors, including how to create them and how to wire them into our application.

No matter how robust or well-thought-out our application is, there will be a time when our application doesn't behave as expected (e.g., maybe someone trips over the wire to our database server), which results in exceptions in our application. In general, we want to prevent the user from seeing cryptic stack traces; and for this, we explore the exception-handling facilities in Spring MVC.

After we cover all these topics, we dive into the internals of Spring @MVC and explore a couple of APIs we can extend; we then use these extended APIs to augment the framework's functionality.

Using Scoped Beans

In Chapter 2, we mentioned the different scopes for beans that are supported by the Spring Framework. Table 6-1 lists them again. This section uses scopes to our advantage. Specifically, we walk through a practical example that leverages a scoped bean to create an online shopping cart.

© Marten Deinum and Iuliana Cosmina 2021
M. Deinum and I. Cosmina, *Pro Spring MVC with WebFlux*, https://doi.org/10.1007/978-1-4842-5666-4_6

Table 6-1. *An Overview of Scopes*

Prefix	Description
singleton	The default scope. A single instance of a bean is created and shared throughout the application. The life cycle of the bean is tied to the application context it is constructed in.
prototype	Each time a certain bean is needed, a fresh instance of the bean is returned.
thread	The bean is created when needed and bound to the currently executing thread. If the thread dies, the bean is destroyed.
request	The bean is created when needed and bound to the lifetime of the incoming `javax.servlet.ServletRequest`. If the request is over, the bean instance is destroyed.
session	The bean is created when needed and stored in `javax.servlet.http.HttpSession`. When the session is destroyed, so is the bean instance.
application	This scope is very similar to the singleton scope. The major difference is that beans with this scope are also registered in `javax.servlet.ServletContext`.

We've already worked with the singleton scope—as that is the default for bean creation in the Spring Framework. The `org.springframework.context.annotation.Scope` annotation specifies the scope of a bean; its properties are listed in Table 6-2.

This annotation can be used as a type-level or method-level annotation. When you use Scope as a type-level annotation, all beans of this type have the scope specified by the annotation. When you use it as a method-level annotation, beans created by this annotated method have the scope specified by the annotation. You must put it on a method annotated with the `org.springframework.context.annotation.Bean` annotation.

Table 6-2. *The Scope Annotation Properties*

Property	Description
value + scopeName	The name of the scope to use (see Table 6-1). Defaults to singleton.
proxyMode	Indicates whether scoped proxies should be created and by which proxy mechanism. This property defaults to NO unless another default proxy mode has been set through the component-scan tag or annotation.

Adding Something to the Cart

This section takes the first step in enabling site visitors to buy books from our bookstore. Specifically, we implement logic that lets us add books to our shopping cart. For this, we first need to define a session-scoped cart bean.

Listing 6-1 shows how to define a bean (our shopping cart) with session scope. This bean can be injected into other beans, just like any other bean in the framework. Spring handles the complexity of managing the life cycle of the bean. The life cycle of the bean depends on the scope of the bean (see Table 6-1). For example, a singleton-scoped bean (the default) is tied to the life cycle of the application context, whereas a session-scoped bean is tied to the life cycle of the `javax.servlet.http.HttpSession` object.

Listing 6-1. Cart Session Scoped Bean

```
package com.apress.prospringmvc.bookstore.web.config;

//Other imports omitted

import org.springframework.context.annotation.Scope;
import org.springframework.context.annotation.ScopedProxyMode;
import com.apress.prospringmvc.bookstore.domain.Cart;

@Configuration
public class WebMvcContextConfiguration implements WebMvcConfigurer {

//Other methods omitted

  @Bean
  @Scope(value = "session", proxyMode = ScopedProxyMode.TARGET_CLASS)
  public Cart cart() {
    return new Cart();
  }

}
```

In this case, we have a bean declaration with the annotation, and we are using session scope. We want to use class-based proxies (`com.apress.prospringmvc.bookstore.domain.Cart` doesn't implement an interface, so we need class-based proxies). We can now simply have this bean injected into other beans and use it like any other bean. Let's create a controller that uses this bean: com.apress.prospringmvc. bookstore.web.controller.CartController (see Listing 6-2).

Listing 6-2. The CartController Bean

```java
package com.apress.prospringmvc.bookstore.web.controller;

import com.apress.prospringmvc.bookstore.domain.Book;
import com.apress.prospringmvc.bookstore.domain.Cart;
import com.apress.prospringmvc.bookstore.service.BookstoreService;
import org.springframework.stereotype.Controller;
import org.springframework.web.bind.annotation.PathVariable;
import org.springframework.web.bind.annotation.PostMapping;
import org.springframework.web.bind.annotation.RequestHeader;

@Controller
public class CartController {

    private final Cart cart;
    private final BookstoreService bookstoreService;

    public CartController(Cart cart, BookstoreService bookstoreService) {
        this.cart = cart;
        this.bookstoreService = bookstoreService;
    }

    @PostMapping("/cart/add/{bookId}")
    public String addToCart(@PathVariable("bookId") long bookId,
                            @RequestHeader("referer") String referer) {
        Book book = this.bookstoreService.findBook(bookId);
        this.cart.addBook(book);
        return "redirect:" + referer;
    }
}
```

In this case, we simply autowire the session-scoped bean cart, as we would for any other bean. The addToCart method contains the logic for adding a book to the cart. After the book has been added, we redirect to the page from which we came (the referer request header).

This controller is mapped to the URL, /cart/add/{bookId}; however, currently, nothing invokes our controller because we have nothing pointing to that URL. Let's modify our book search page and add a link to add a book to our shopping cart (see Listing 6-3). The parts highlighted in bold show the changes.

Listing 6-3. The Book Search Page with an Add to Cart Link

```jsp
<%@ taglib prefix="c" uri="http://java.sun.com/jsp/jstl/core"%>
<%@ taglib prefix="spring" uri="http://www.springframework.org/tags" %>
<%@ taglib prefix="form" uri="http://www.springframework.org/tags/form" %>

// Search Form Omitted

<c:if test="${not empty bookList}">
<table>
<tr>
    <th><spring:message code="book.title"/></th>
    <th><spring:message code="book.description"/></th>
    <th><spring:message code="book.price" /></th>
    <th></th>
</tr>

<c:forEach items="${bookList}" var="book">
    <tr>
        <td>
            <a href="<c:url value="/book/detail/${book.id}"/>">$
            {book.title}</a>
        </td>
        <td>${book.description}</td>
        <td>${book.price}</td>
        <td>
            <a href="<c:url value="/cart/add/${book.id}"/>">
                <spring:message code="book.addtocart" />
            </a>
        </td>
    </tr>
</c:forEach>
</table>
</c:if>
```

217

After restarting our application, we should have an Add to Cart link on the Books page (see Figure 6-1). If we click that link, we should stay on the Books page. We did add something to our shopping cart, however.

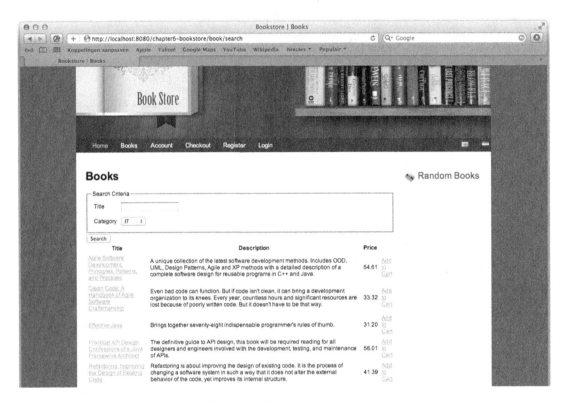

Figure 6-1.   *A book search with an Add to Cart link*

Implementing the Checkout

To finalize the ordering process, we allow our customers to check out their carts. This creates an actual `com.apress.prospringmvc.bookstore.domain.Order` object and entry in the database. The checkout is a combination of a lot of things we covered in the previous chapter and the previous section. The controller is `com.apress.prospringmvc.bookstore.web.controller.CheckoutController` (see Listing 6-4), and it contains a lot of logic. The `checkout.jsp` file is the JSP that contains our screen; it can be found in `/WEB-INF/views/cart`.

Listing 6-4. The CheckoutController

```java
package com.apress.prospringmvc.bookstore.web.controller;

//Other imports omitted

import com.apress.prospringmvc.bookstore.validation.OrderValidator;

@Controller
@SessionAttributes(types = { Order.class })
@RequestMapping("/cart/checkout")
public class CheckoutController {

    private final Cart cart;
    private final BookstoreService bookstoreService;

    public CheckoutController(Cart cart, BookstoreService bookstoreService)
{
        this.cart = cart;
        this.bookstoreService = bookstoreService;
    }

    @ModelAttribute("countries")
    public Map<String, String> countries(Locale currentLocale) {
        var countries = new TreeMap<String, String>();
        for (Locale locale : Locale.getAvailableLocales()) {
            countries.put(locale.getCountry(),locale.getDisplayCountry
            (currentLocale));
        }
        return countries;
    }

    @GetMapping
    public void show(HttpSession session, Model model) {
        var account = (Account) session.getAttribute(LoginController.
        ACCOUNT_ATTRIBUTE);
        var order = this.bookstoreService.createOrder(this.cart, account);
        model.addAttribute(order);
    }
```

```java
@PostMapping(params = "order")
public String checkout(SessionStatus status,
                       @Validated @ModelAttribute Order order,
                       BindingResult errors) {

    if (errors.hasErrors()) {
        return "cart/checkout";
    } else {
        this.bookstoreService.store(order);
        status.setComplete(); //remove order from session
        this.cart.clear(); // clear the cart
        return "redirect:/index.htm";
    }
}

@PostMapping(params = "update")
public String update(@ModelAttribute Order order) {
    order.updateOrderDetails();
    return "cart/checkout";
}

@InitBinder
public void initBinder(WebDataBinder binder) {
    binder.setValidator(new OrderValidator());
}
}
```

The first method called on the controller when we click checkout is the show method. It takes our cart and uses the account stored in the session to create an order and add that to the model. The order is stored in the session in between requests; this due to the use of SessionAttributes. When this is done, the checkout page is rendered (see Figure 6-2).

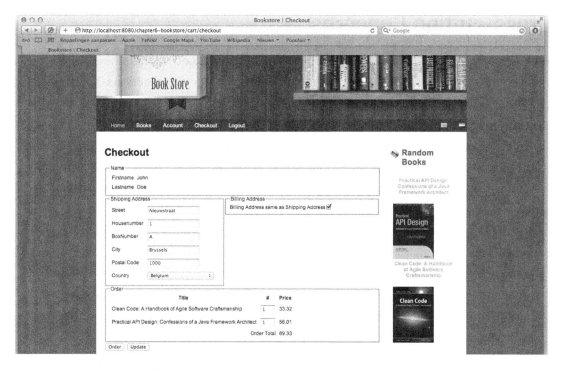

Figure 6-2. *The Checkout page*

When the form is filled in, the customer can do two things: he can press the Order button or the Update button. When the Update button is pressed, the update method is called. This submits the form and then updates the order (and recalculates the total price). When the Order button is pressed, the order is submitted and then validated by `com.apress.prospringmvc.bookstore.validation.OrderValidator`. When an error occurs, the page is redisplayed, and error messages are shown to the customer. The interesting part occurs when there are no errors. First, the order is stored in the database. When we are finished with the order, we need to remove it from the session, which we accomplish by calling the `setComplete` method on the `org.springframework.web.bind.support.SessionStatus` object (see Chapter 5's "Supported Method Argument Types" section). Finally, before redirecting to the index page again, we need to clear the shopping cart. We do this so that the customer can add new books to the cart. Because we cannot simply replace the session-scoped object, we need to call a method to clear it. If we were to replace the cart with a fresh instance, we would destroy the scoped proxy object.

Cross-cutting Concerns

When developing an enterprise application, we are often faced or challenged with cross-cutting concerns. These are concerns that affect many objects and actions. Examples of cross-cutting concerns include transaction management and security and actions such as exposing generic data for each incoming web request.

In general, these concerns are hard to implement in our codebase by using traditional object-oriented approaches. If we were to implement them in traditional ways, it would lead to code duplication and hard-to-maintain code. For our general objects, we can use aspect-oriented programming (AOP) to address these cross-cutting concerns; however, we need a slightly different approach when it comes to applying it to requests.

Spring MVC gives us two ways of implementing cross-cutting concerns. The first approach uses *interceptors* to implement generic logic, while the second relies on exception handling. This section looks at both techniques for applying cross-cutting concerns in our web application.

Interceptors

Interceptors are to request handlers what filters are to servlets. According to the servlet specification,[1] a filter is a reusable piece of code that can transform the content of HTTP requests, responses, and header information. Filters modify or adapt the requests for a resource and modify or adapt responses from a resource. Examples of filtering include authentication, auditing, and encryption.

Filters and interceptors both implement common functionality (cross-cutting concerns) to apply to all (or a selection) of incoming HTTP requests. Filters are more powerful than interceptors because they can replace (or wrap) the incoming request/response, whereas an interceptor cannot do this. On the other hand, the interceptor has more life cycle methods than the filter (see Table 6-3).

---

[1]See Servlet Specification, Chapter 6.

Table 6-3. *Interceptor Callbacks*

Method	Description
preHandle	Called before the handler is invoked.
postHandle	Called when the handler method has been successfully invoked and just before the view is rendered. It can place shared objects in the model.
afterCompletion	Called when the request processing is done, after view rendering. This method is always called on interceptors in which the preHandle method was called successfully, even when there was an error during request processing. It can clean up resources.

Spring MVC has two interceptor strategies.

- org.springframework.web.servlet.HandlerInterceptor (see Listing 6-5)

- org.springframework.web.context.request. WebRequestInterceptor (see Listing 6-6)

Listing 6-5. The HandlerInterceptor Interface (in module spring-webmvc)

```
package org.springframework.web.servlet;

import javax.servlet.http.HttpServletRequest;
import javax.servlet.http.HttpServletResponse;

public interface HandlerInterceptor {

    boolean preHandle(HttpServletRequest request,
                    HttpServletResponse response, Object handler) throws
                    Exception;

    void postHandle(HttpServletRequest request, HttpServletResponse response,
                    Object handler, ModelAndView modelAndView) throws
                    Exception;
```

```
    void afterCompletion(HttpServletRequest request, HttpServletResponse
    response, Object handler, Exception ex) throws Exception;

}
```

Listing 6-6. The WebRequestInterceptor Interface (in module spring-web)

```
package org.springframework.web.context.request;

import org.springframework.ui.ModelMap;

public interface WebRequestInterceptor {

    void preHandle(WebRequest request) throws Exception;

    void postHandle(WebRequest request, ModelMap model) throws Exception;

    void afterCompletion(WebRequest request, Exception ex) throws
Exception;

}
```

As is often the case within the Spring Framework, both strategies are expressed as interfaces to provide an implementation. The main difference between the strategies is that WebRequestInterceptor is independent of the underlying technology. It can be used in a JSF or Servlet environment without changing the implementation. A handler interceptor is only usable in a Servlet environment. An advantage of HandlerInterceptor is that we can use it to prevent the handler from being called. We do this by returning false from the preHandle method.

Configuring Interceptors

To use an interceptor, you need to configure it in the configuration. Configuring an interceptor consists of two steps.

1. Configure the interceptor.

2. Connect it to the handlers.

Connecting an interceptor to our handlers can be done in two ways. It is possible to use both approaches together, but we don't recommend this. First, we can explicitly add the interceptors to our handler mappings in using BeanPostProcessor. Second, we can use org.springframework.web.servlet.config.annotation.InterceptorRegistry to add interceptors.

In general, it is preferable to use InterceptorRegistry to add the interceptors, simply because that is a very convenient way to add them. It is also very easy to limit which URLs the interceptors are matched to (explained in the section about the InterceptorRegistry.)

Explicitly Configuring a Handler Mapping with Interceptors Using BeanPostProcessor

To register the interceptors with the handler mapping, we first need to get the handler mappings involved. To do this, we need to either explicitly add them or extend the Spring base classes to get a reference to them (see Listing 6-7). Next, we simply add all interceptors to the instances. Using multiple handler mappings can be cumbersome, especially if we want to apply the interceptor only to certain URLs.

Listing 6-7. A Sample of Explicit HandlerMapping BeanPostProcessor for Interceptors

```
package com.apress.prospringmvc.bookstore.web.config;

import org.springframework.beans.BeansException;
import org.springframework.beans.factory.config.BeanPostProcessor;
import org.springframework.web.servlet.HandlerInterceptor;
import org.springframework.web.servlet.mvc.method.annotation.
RequestMappingHandlerMapping;

import java.util.List;

public class InterceptorAddingPostProcessor implements BeanPostProcessor {

    private final List<HandlerInterceptor> interceptors;

    public InterceptorAddingPostProcessor(List<HandlerInterceptor>
    interceptors) {
        this.interceptors = interceptors;
    }
```

```
@Override
public Object postProcessBeforeInitialization(Object bean, String
beanName) throws BeansException {
    if (bean instanceof RequestMappingHandlerMapping) {
        RequestMappingHandlerMapping handlerMapping =
        (RequestMappingHandlerMapping) bean;
        handlerMapping.setInterceptors(this.interceptors);
    }
    return bean;
}
}
```

Using the InterceptorRegistry

A more powerful and flexible way to register interceptors is to use `org.springframework.web.servlet.config.annotation.InterceptorRegistry`. The interceptors added to this registry are added to all configured handler mappings. Additionally, mapping to certain URLs is very easy to accomplish with this approach. To get access to the registry, we need to implement the `org.springframework.web.servlet.config.annotation.WebMvcConfigurer` interface on the configuration class that configures our web resources. This interface has several callback methods that are called during the configuration of Spring MVC.

The `InterceptorRegistry` has two methods (one for each interceptor type) that we can use to add interceptors (see Listing 6-8). Both methods return an instance of `org.springframework.web.servlet.config.annotation.InterceptorRegistration` that we can use to fine-tune the mapping of the interceptor. We can use ant-style path patterns [2] to configure a fine-grained mapping for the registered interceptor. If we don't supply a pattern, the interceptor is applied to all incoming requests.

---

[2]See Chapter 3 for information about ant-style expressions.

Listing 6-8. The InterceptorRegistry Interface

```
package org.springframework.web.servlet.config.annotation;

import java.util.ArrayList;
import java.util.List;
import org.springframework.web.context.request.WebRequestInterceptor;
import org.springframework.web.servlet.HandlerInterceptor;
import org.springframework.web.servlet.handler.
WebRequestHandlerInterceptorAdapter;

public class InterceptorRegistry {

    public InterceptorRegistration addInterceptor(HandlerInterceptor
    interceptor) { .. }

    public InterceptorRegistration addWebRequestInterceptor(WebRequestInter
    ceptor interceptor) { ..
}

}
```

Listing 6-9 shows our current configuration. At this point, we have configured an interceptor to change the locale, and this interceptor is being applied to all incoming requests (we didn't specify a URL pattern to match against). Next, we configure the interceptor and use the `addInterceptor` method to add it to the registry. The framework takes care of the additional details for registering the interceptors with the configured handler mappings.

Listing 6-9. Using the InterceptorRegistry to Add Interceptors

```
package com.apress.prospringmvc.bookstore.web.config;

//Other imports omitted

import org.springframework.web.servlet.HandlerInterceptor;
import org.springframework.web.servlet.config.annotation.
InterceptorRegistry;

@Configuration
public class WebMvcContextConfiguration implements WebMvcConfigurer {
```

```java
  @Override
  public void addInterceptors(InterceptorRegistry registry) {
    registry.addInterceptor(localeChangeInterceptor());
  }

  @Bean
  public HandlerInterceptor localeChangeInterceptor() {
    var localeChangeInterceptor = new LocaleChangeInterceptor();
    localeChangeInterceptor.setParamName("lang");
    return localeChangeInterceptor;
  }

//... Other methods omitted
}
```

Listing 6-10 shows a snippet of code in which we change the mapping from all URLs to only URLs starting with /customers.

Listing 6-10. Limiting an Interceptor to Certain URLs

```java
package com.apress.prospringmvc.bookstore.web.config;

//Imports omitted

@Configuration
public class WebMvcContextConfiguration implements WebMvcConfigurer {

  @Override
  public void addInterceptors(InterceptorRegistry registry) {
      var registration = registry.addInterceptor(localeChangeInterceptor());
      registation.addPathPatterns("/customers/**");
  }

//Other methods omitted


}
```

Implementing an Interceptor

Thus far, we have covered different types of interceptors and how to register them to be used. Now let's implement interceptors for our store. We implement two different interceptors. The first adds some commonly used data to our model to show it to the user. The second addresses a security need: we want the account and checkout page to be accessible only by registered users.

Implement WebRequestInterceptor

In this section, we implement `org.springframework.web.context.request.WebRequestInterceptor`. If you look at our web page in Figure 6-3, you see a Random Books section. This section on our web page has remained empty thus far. Now we create an interceptor that adds some random books to the model. For this, we implement the postHandle method (see Listing 6-11).

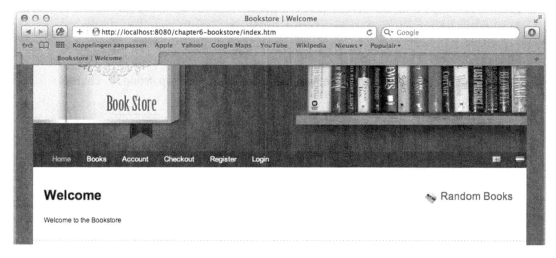

Figure 6-3. *The welcome page without random books listed*

In a real webshop, you would probably call this section "New Books" or "Suggested Books."

Listing 6-11. The CommonDataInterceptor

```java
package com.apress.prospringmvc.bookstore.web.interceptor;

import com.apress.prospringmvc.bookstore.service.BookstoreService;
import org.springframework.ui.ModelMap;
import org.springframework.web.context.request.WebRequest;
import org.springframework.web.context.request.WebRequestInterceptor;

public class CommonDataInterceptor implements WebRequestInterceptor {
    private final BookstoreService bookstoreService;

    public CommonDataInterceptor(BookstoreService bookstoreService) {
        this.bookstoreService = bookstoreService;
    }

    @Override
    public void preHandle(WebRequest request) throws Exception {
    }

    @Override
    public void postHandle(WebRequest request, ModelMap model) throws
    Exception {
        if (model != null) {
            model.addAttribute("randomBooks", this.bookstoreService.
            findRandomBooks());
        }
    }

    @Override
    public void afterCompletion(WebRequest request, Exception ex) throws
    Exception {
    }
}
```

The postHandle method adds some random books to the model, but only when this model is available. This is why our code includes a null check. The model can be null when we use AJAX or write the response ourselves.

To have our interceptor applied to the incoming request, we need to register it. The interceptor needs to be called for every incoming request, so it doesn't require much additional configuration (see the highlighted line in Listing 6-12).

Listing 6-12. The CommondDataInterceptor Configuration

```
package com.apress.prospringmvc.bookstore.web.config;

import org.springframework.web.context.request.WebRequestInterceptor;
import org.springframework.web.servlet.config.annotation.
InterceptorRegistry;

com.apress.prospringmvc.bookstore.web.interceptor.CommonDataInterceptor;

// Other imports omitted
@Configuration
public class WebMvcContextConfiguration implements WebMvcConfigurer {

  private final BookstoreService bookstoreService;

  public WebMvcContextConfiguration(BookstoreService bookstoreService) {
    this.bookstoreService = bookstoreService;
  }

  @Override
  public void addInterceptors(InterceptorRegistry registry) {
    registry.addInterceptor(localeChangeInterceptor());
    registry.addWebRequestInterceptor(commonDataInterceptor());
  }

  @Bean
  public WebRequestInterceptor commonDataInterceptor() {
    return new CommonDataInterceptor(this.bookstoreService);
  }

// Other methods omitted
}
```

Now when we redeploy our application and access a page, we should see random books displayed in the Random Books section on our page (see Figure 6-4). (The logic used in our template for selecting the random books is shown in Listing 6-13.)

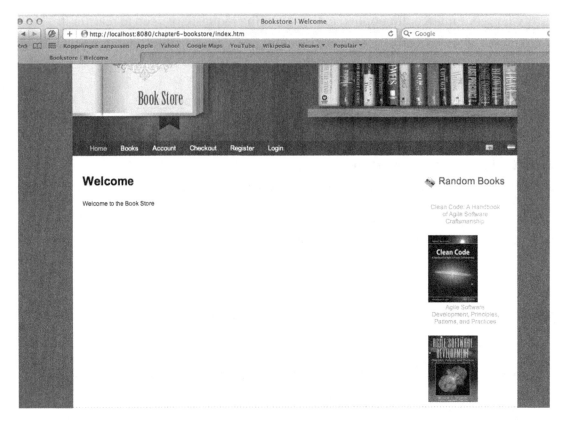

Figure 6-4. *The Welcome page with titles in the Random Books section*

Listing 6-13. The Random Books Section from the Template

```
<div class="right_box">
    <div class="title">
        <span class="title_icon">
            <img src="<c:url value="/resources/images/bullet4.gif"/>"
            alt="" title="" />
        </span>
        <spring:message code="main.title.randombooks"/>
    </div>

    <c:forEach items="${randomBooks}" var="book">
        <div class="new_prod_box">
            <c:url value="/book/detail/${book.id}" var="bookUrl" />
            <a href="${bookUrl}">${book.title}</a>
```

```
<div class="new_prod_img">
    <c:url value="/resources/images/books/${book.isbn}/book_
    front_cover.png" var="bookImage"/>
        <a href="${bookUrl}">
            <img src="${bookImage}" alt="${book.title}"
            title="${book.title}" class="thumb" border="0"
            width="100px"/>
        </a>
    </div>
</div>
</c:forEach>
</div>
```

Implementing a Handler Interceptor

Currently, our account pages aren't secure. For example, someone could simply change the ID in the URL to see the content of another account. Let's use the interceptor approach to apply security to our pages. We will create an interceptor that checks whether we are already logged in (our account is available in the HTTP session). If not, it throws com.apress.prospringmvc.bookstore.service.AuthenticationException (see Listing 6-14). We also store the original URL in a session attribute; that way, we can redirect the user to the URL he wants to visit after he logs in.

When implementing or adding Security to your application it is generally better to use a framework like Spring Security[3] (see Chapter 12) or Apache Shiro[4] instead of rolling your own security solution!

Listing 6-14. SecurityHandlerInterceptor

```
package com.apress.prospringmvc.bookstore.web.interceptor;

// javax.servlet imports omitted

import org.springframework.web.servlet.HandlerInterceptor;
import org.springframework.web.servlet.handler.HandlerInterceptorAdapter;
import org.springframework.web.util.WebUtils;
```

---

[3]https://spring.io/projects/spring-security
[4]https://shiro.apache.org

```java
import com.apress.prospringmvc.bookstore.domain.Account;
import com.apress.prospringmvc.bookstore.service.AuthenticationException;
import com.apress.prospringmvc.bookstore.web.controller.LoginController;

public class SecurityHandlerInterceptor implements HandlerInterceptor {

  @Override
  public boolean preHandle(HttpServletRequest request, HttpServletResponse
  response, Object handler) throws Exception {
    var account= (Account) WebUtils.getSessionAttribute(request,
    LoginController.ACCOUNT_ATTRIBUTE);
    if (account == null) {
      //Retrieve and store the original URL.
      var url = request.getRequestURL().toString();
      WebUtils.setSessionAttribute(request, LoginController.
      REQUESTED_URL, url);
      throw new AuthenticationException("Authentication required.",
      "authentication.required");
    }
    return true;
  }
}
```

Our configuration is a bit more complex for this interceptor because we want to map
it to certain URLs (see the highlighted part in Listing 6-15).

Listing 6-15. SecurityHandlerInterceptor Configuration

```java
package com.apress.prospringmvc.bookstore.web.config;

import com.apress.prospringmvc.bookstore.web.interceptor.
SecurityHandlerInterceptor;

//Other imports omitted

@Configuration
public class WebMvcContextConfiguration extends WebMvcConfigurerAdapter {
```

```
@Override
public void addInterceptors(InterceptorRegistry registry) {
  registry.addInterceptor(localeChangeInterceptor());
  registry.addWebRequestInterceptor(commonDataInterceptor());
  registry.addInterceptor(new SecurityHandlerInterceptor()).
      addPathPatterns("/customer/account*", "/cart/checkout");

}

// Other methods omitted

}
```

Finally, we also need to make a modification to our com.apress.prospringmvc. bookstore.web.controller.AccountController. Currently, we expect an ID as part of the URL. However, instead of retrieving the account from the database, we restore it from the session. Listing 6-16 shows the necessary modifications.

Listing 6-16. The AccountController

```
package com.apress.prospringmvc.bookstore.web.controller;

// Imports omitted

@Controller
@RequestMapping("/customer/account")
@SessionAttributes(types = Account.class)
public class AccountController {

//Fields and other methods omitted

    @GetMapping
    public String index(Model model, HttpSession session) {
        var account = (Account) session.getAttribute(LoginController.
        ACCOUNT_ATTRIBUTE);
        model.addAttribute(account);
        model.addAttribute("orders", this.orderRepository.
        findByAccount(account));
        return "customer/account";
    }
```

```
@PostMapping
@PutMapping
public String update(@ModelAttribute Account account) {
    this.accountRepository.save(account);
    return "redirect:/customer/account";
}
}
```

When we redeploy our application and click Account in the menu bar, we are greeted
with an error page (see Figure 6-5). We use the default exception-handling mechanism
to send an error code back to the client so that the browser can act upon it. In the next
section, we cover exception handling in more detail.

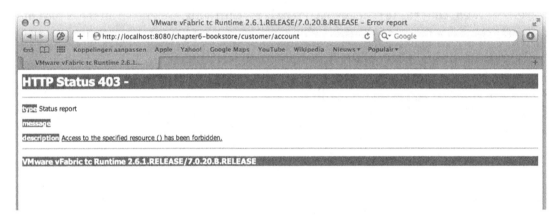

Figure 6-5. *A 403 error page after clicking a secured link*

While we have protected our resources, it would be nicer to show the login page to
the user with a message that she needs to log in to see the requested page. This is what
we do in the next section.

Exception Handling

As mentioned in Chapter 4, when an exception occurs during the request processing,
Spring tries to handle the exception. To give us a generic way of handling exceptions,
Spring uses yet another strategy that can be utilized by implementing the org.
springframework.web.servlet.HandlerExceptionResolver interface.

`org.springframework.web.servlet.HandlerExceptionResolver` provides a callback method for the dispatcher servlet (see Listing 6-17). This method is called when an exception occurs during the request processing workflow. The method can return `org.springframework.web.servlet.ModelAndView`, or it can choose to handle the Exception itself.

Listing 6-17. The HandlerExceptionResolver Interface

```
package org.springframeowork.web.servlet;

import javax.servlet.http.HttpServletRequest;
import javax.servlet.http.HttpServletResponse;

public interface HandlerExceptionResolver {
    ModelAndView resolveException(HttpServletRequest request,
    HttpServletResponse response, Object handler, Exception ex);

}
```

By default, the dispatcher servlet looks for all beans in the application context of the type `org.springframework.web.servlet.HandlerExceptionResolver` (see the "Configuring the DispatcherServlet" section in Chapter 4). When multiple resolvers are detected, the dispatcher servlet consults them until a viewname is returned or the response is written. If the exception cannot be handled, then the exception is rethrown so that the servlet container can handle it. The servlet container uses the error-pages configuration from its configuration or simply propagate the exception to the user. (In most cases, you get an error 500 with a stack trace on the screen.)

Spring MVC comes with several implementations of the `org.springframework.web.servlet.HandlerExceptionResolver` interface, as you can see in Figure 6-6. Note that each of these implementations works differently. Table 6-4 gives a short overview of how the different implementations work.

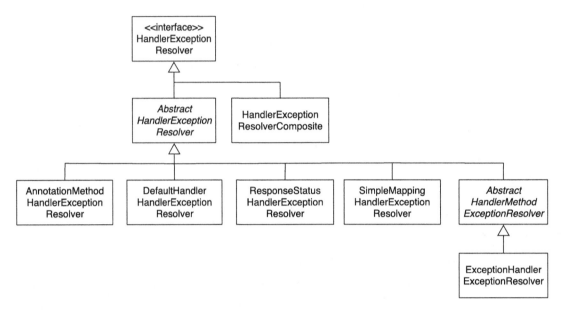

Figure 6-6. *The HandlerExceptionResolver hierarchy*

Table 6-4. *The HandlerExceptionResolver Implementations*

HandlerExceptionResolver	Description
ExceptionHandler ExceptionResolver	Searches the current controller for methods annotated with @ ExceptionHandler and selects the best exception-handling method to handle the exception. It then invokes the selected method.
DefaultHandler ExceptionResolver	Translates well-known exceptions to a proper response for the client. Returns an empty ModelAndView and sends the appropriate HTTP Response Code to the client.
ResponseStatus ExceptionResolver	Looks for the org.springframework.web.bind. annotation.ResponseStatus annotation on the exception and uses that to send a response to the client.
SimpleMapping ExceptionResolver	Maps exceptions to view names by the exception class name or part (substring) of that class name. This implementation can be configured either globally or for certain controllers.
HandlerException ResolverComposite	Used internally by the MVC configuration to chain exception resolvers. Only the framework can use it.

As the class diagram in Figure 6-6 illustrates, most usable implementations for resolving exceptions extend `org.springframework.web.servlet.handler.` `AbstractHandlerExceptionResolver`. This is a convenient superclass that provides common features and configuration options to all implementations. Table 6-5 lists and briefly describes its common properties.

All attributes are defined on the `AbstractHandlerExceptionResolver`.

Table 6-5. *Common AbstractHandlerExceptionResolver Properties*

Property	Description
mappedHandlerClasses	A set of handler classes for which HandlerExceptionResolver should handle exceptions. Exceptions propagated from handlers of a type, not in the set, are not handled by this HandlerExceptionResolver.
mappedHandlers	Similar to mappedHandlerClasses, but instead of classes, it contains actual handlers (controllers, in this case).
preventResponseCaching	Enables us to prevent caching for the views resolved by this HandlerExceptionResolver. The default value is false, which allows browsers to cache the error pages.
warnLogCategory	Sets the category used for logging the exceptions (the log level is WARN). The default is no category, which translates to no logging.

DefaultHandlerExceptionResolver

The `DefaultHandlerExceptionResolver` implementation always returns an empty `ModelAndView` and sends an HTTP response code to the client. In Table 6-6, you can see the exception to the HTTP response code and description mapping.

Table 6-6. *Exception HTTP Response Code Mapping*

Exception	HTTP Code	Description
NoSuchRequestHandlingMethodException	404	Not Found
HttpRequestMethodNotSupportedException	405	Method not Allowed
HttpMediaTypeNotSupportedException	415	Unsupported Media Type
HttpMediaTypeNotAcceptableException	406	Not Acceptable
ConversionNotSupportedException HttpMessageNotWritableException	500	Internal Server Error
MissingServletRequestParameterException ServletRequestBindingException TypeMismatchException HttpMessageNotReadableException MethodArgumentNotValidException MissingServletRequestPartException	400	Bad Request

ResponseStatusExceptionResolver

ResponseStatusExceptionResolver checks if the thrown exception is annotated with an org.
springframework.web.bind.annotation.ResponseStatus annotation (see Listing 6-18).
If that is the case, it handles the exception, sends the HTTP response code from the
annotation to the client, and then returns an empty ModelAndView indicating the exception
was handled. If that annotation isn't present, it simply returns null to indicate that the
exception wasn't handled.

Listing 6-18. Handling an AuthenticationException

```
package com.apress.prospringmvc.bookstore.service;

import org.springframework.http.HttpStatus;
import org.springframework.web.bind.annotation.ResponseStatus;

@ResponseStatus(value = HttpStatus.FORBIDDEN)
public class AuthenticationException extends Exception {

    private final String code;
```

```java
    public AuthenticationException(String message, String code) {
        super(message);
        this.code = code;
    }

    public String getCode() {
        return this.code;
    }
}
```

When we throw this exception, `org.springframework.web.servlet.mvc.`
`annotation.ResponseStatusExceptionResolver` detects that it has been annotated
with `org.springframework.web.servlet.bind.annotation.ResponseStatus`. This
is the mechanism we use to have the framework handle `com.apress.prospringmvc.`
`bookstore.service.AuthenticationException`. This annotation has two properties we
can use to specify information (see Table 6-7).

Table 6-7. `ResponseStatus` *Properties*

Property	Description
Value	Sends the HTTP response code to send to the client. It is required.
Reason	Sends the reason to the client. This is optional. It also provides additional information.

SimpleMappingExceptionResolver

`SimpleMappingExceptionResolver` can be configured to translate certain exceptions to a
view. For example, we can map (partial) exception class names to a view. We say *partial*
here because matching is done based on the name of the class and not on its concrete
type. The matching is done with a simple substring mechanism; wildcards (ant-style
regular expressions) aren't supported.

Listing 6-19 shows the configuration for `SimpleMappingExceptionResolver`. It is
configured to map an `AuthenticationException` to the view with the name login. We
also set an HTTP response code to send with the login view.

Listing 6-19. A SimpleMappingExceptionResolver Configuration

```
package com.apress.prospringmvc.bookstore.web.config;

import org.springframework.web.servlet.HandlerExceptionResolver;
import org.springframework.web.servlet.handler.
SimpleMappingExceptionResolver;

// Imports omitted

@Configuration

public class WebMvcContextConfiguration implements WebMvcConfigurer {

    @Override
    public void configureHandlerExceptionResolvers(List<HandlerException
    Resolver> exceptionResolvers {
        exceptionResolvers.add(simpleMappingExceptionResolver());
    }

    @Bean
    public SimpleMappingExceptionResolver simpleMappingExceptionResolver()
{

        var mappings = new Properties();
        mappings.setProperty("AuthenticationException", "login");

        var statusCodes = new Properties();
        mappings.setProperty("login", String.valueOf(HttpServletResponse.
        SC_UNAUTHORIZED));

        var exceptionResolver = new SimpleMappingExceptionResolver();
        exceptionResolver.setExceptionMappings(mappings);
        exceptionResolver.setStatusCodes(statusCodes);
        return exceptionResolver;
    }
// Other methods omitted
}
```

The matching is done based on the class name rather than the concrete type. If the class name of the exception thrown matches the specified pattern, then the corresponding view name is used. The pattern doesn't support wildcards; it is merely a substring that matches the class name. We need to choose the pattern carefully. For instance, `Exception` matches almost all exceptions thrown (because most exceptions have *Exception* as part of their class name). Similarly, `DataAccessException` more or less matches all of Spring's exceptions for data access.

We need to make one final adjustment; namely, we need to modify our `com.apress.prospringmvc.bookstore.web.controller.LoginController`. At the moment, there is exception handling inside the controller; however, this can be removed because the `AuthenticationException` is handled by our recently configured `HandlerExceptionResolver` (see Listing 6-20 for the improved controller).

Listing 6-20. The Improved Login Controller

```
package com.apress.prospringmvc.bookstore.web.controller;

// Imports omitted

@Controller
@RequestMapping(value = "/login")
public class LoginController {

public static final String ACCOUNT_ATTRIBUTE = "account";
public static final String REQUESTED_URL = "REQUESTED_URL";

private final AccountService accountService;

    @GetMapping
    public void login() {}

    @PostMapping
    public String handleLogin(@RequestParam String username, @RequestParam
    String password, HttpSession session) throws AuthenticationException {

        var account = this.accountService.login(username, password);
        session.setAttribute(ACCOUNT_ATTRIBUTE, account);
        var url = (String) session.getAttribute(REQUESTED_URL);
        session.removeAttribute(REQUESTED_URL);
```

```
    if (StringUtils.hasText(url) && !url.contains("login")) {
        return "redirect:" + url;
    } else {
        return "redirect:/index.htm";
    }
  }
}
```

If we click Account on the menu bar after redeployment, we are greeted with a login page (see Figure 6-7).

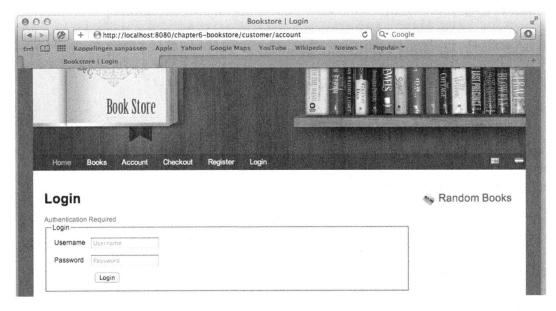

Figure 6-7. *The Login page*

ExceptionHandlerExceptionResolver

The ExceptionHandlerExceptionResolver looks in the current controller or on an @ControllerAdvice annotated class for methods annotated with org.springframework. web.bind.annotations.ExceptionHandler.

Exception-handling methods are very much like controller methods (as explained in Chapter 5); they can use the same method parameters and the same return values. An exception-handling method uses the same underlying infrastructure to detect the return types and method-argument types. However, there is one addition to these methods that we can also pass in the thrown exception; namely, we can specify an argument of type Exception (or a subclass).

The method in Listing 6-21 handles all exceptions thrown in the controller it is defined in. It causes an error code 500 to be sent back to the client, along with the given reason. This is the most basic exception-handling method we can write. As mentioned, we can use multiple parameters in the method signature, which also goes for the method arguments because of the method return types. (See Tables 5-3 and 5-4 in the preceding chapter for an overview.)

Listing 6-21. A Basic Exception-handling Method Sample

```
@ExceptionHandler
@ResponseStatus(value=HttpStatus.INTERNAL_SERVER_ERROR, reason="Exception
while handling request.")
public void handleException() {}
```

Listing 6-22 shows a more elaborate example. When `org.springframework.dao. DataAccessException` occurs, it fills the model with as much information as possible. After that, the view named `db-error` is rendered.

Listing 6-22. An Advanced Exception-handling Method Sample

```
@ExceptionHandler
public ModelAndView handle(DataAccessException ex, Principal principal,
WebRequest request) {
    var mav = new ModelAndView("db-error");
    mav.addObject("exception", ex);
    mav.addObject("username", principal.getName());
    mav.addAllObjects(request.getParameterMap());
    for(Iterator<String> names = request.getHeaderNames();
    names.hasNext(); ) {
        var name = names.next();
        var value = request.getHeaderValues(name);
        mav.addObject(name, value);
    }
    return mav;
}
```

Extending Spring @MVC

In previous chapters, we explained how Spring MVC works and how we can write controllers. However, there might come a time when the support from the framework out-of-the-box isn't sufficient, and we want to change or add to the framework's behavior. In general, the Spring Framework is flexible due to the way it is built. It uses many strategies and delegation, which we can use to extend or modify the framework's behavior. In this section, we dive into the internals of request mapping, request handling, and form rendering. Finally, we cover how to extend these features.

Extending `RequestMappingHandlerMapping`

To map incoming requests to controller methods, Spring uses a handler mapping. For our use case, we have been using `org.springframework.web.servlet.mvc.method. annotation.RequestMappingHandlerMapping`, and we already have mentioned a couple of times that it is flexible. To match the requests based on methods with the `org. springframework.web.bind.annotation.RequestMapping` annotation, the handler mapping consults several `org.springframework.web.servlet.mvc.condition. RequestCondition` implementations (see Figure 6-8).

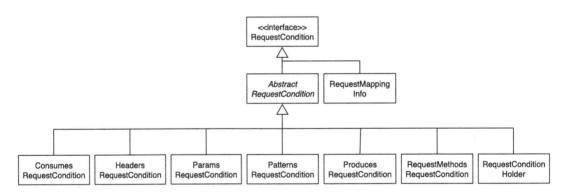

Figure 6-8. *The RequestCondition class diagram*

As the diagram illustrates, there is an implementation for each of the attributes (i.e., consumes, headers, methods, params, produces, and value; for more details, see Table 5-2) of the `org.springframework.web.bind.annotation.RequestMapping` annotation. The `RequestConditionHolder` and `RequestMappingInfo` are two implementations used internally by the framework.

To create an implementation, we need two things. First, we need an implementation of the interface (see Listing 6-23 for the API). Second, we need to extend `org.springframework.web.servlet.mvc.method.annotation.RequestMappingHandlerMapping`. This class contains two callback methods that act as factory methods for our custom request method (see Listing 6-24). The `getCustomTypeCondition` method is called to create an instance to match the type-level condition, while the `getCustomMethodCondition` method is used for method-level conditions.

Listing 6-23. The RequestCondition API

```
package org.springframework.web.servlet.mvc.condition;

import javax.servlet.http.HttpServletRequest;

import org.springframework.web.bind.annotation.RequestMapping;

public interface RequestCondition<T> {

T combine(T other);

T getMatchingCondition(HttpServletRequest request);

int compareTo(T other, HttpServletRequest request);

}
```

Listing 6-24. The RequestMappingHandlerMapping

```
package org.springframework.web.servlet.mvc.method.annotation;

import java.lang.reflect.Method;
import org.springframework.context.EmbeddedValueResolverAware;
//other imports omitted

public class RequestMappingHandlerMapping extends
RequestMappingInfoHandlerMapping implements MatchableHandlerMapping,
EmbeddedValueResolverAware {

// Other methods omitted.
```

```
    protected RequestCondition<?> getCustomMethodCondition(Method method) {
        return null;
    }

    protected RequestCondition<?> getCustomTypeCondition(Class<?>
    handlerType) {
        return null;
    }
}
```

Extending the RequestMappingHandlerAdapter

Like the RequestMappingHandlerMapping, the RequestMappingHandlerAdapter uses a couple of different strategies to do its work. To determine what to inject into a method argument, the adapter consults several org.springframework.web. method.support.HandlerMethodArgumentResolver implementations. For the return types, it consults the registered org.springframework.web.method.support. HandlerMethodReturnValueHandler implementations.

HandlerMethodArgumentResolver

HandlerMethodArgumentResolver is used by the RequestMappingHandlerAdapter to determine what to use for a method argument. There is one implementation for each of the supported method-argument types or annotations (see Chapter 5's "Supported Method Argument Types" section). The API is simple, as you can see in Listing 6-25.

Listing 6-25.   The HandlerMethodArgumentResolver API

```
package org.springframework.web.method.support;

import org.springframework.core.MethodParameter;
import org.springframework.web.bind.WebDataBinder;
import org.springframework.web.bind.support.WebDataBinderFactory;
import org.springframework.web.context.request.NativeWebRequest;
```

```java
public interface HandlerMethodArgumentResolver {

    boolean supportsParameter(MethodParameter parameter);

    Object resolveArgument(MethodParameter parameter, ModelAndViewContainer
    mavContainer, NativeWebRequest webRequest, WebDataBinderFactory
    binderFactory)throws Exception;

}
```

The supportsParameter method is called on each registered
HandlerMethodArgumentResolver. The one that returns true detects or creates the
actual value to use for that method argument. We do this by calling the resolveArgument
method.

HandlerMethodReturnValueHandler

HandlerMethodReturnValueHandler is similar to HandlerMethodArgumentResolver, but
with one important difference. As its name implies, HandlerMethodReturnValueHandler
works for method return values. There is an implementation for each of the supported
return values or annotations (see Chapter 5's "Supported Return Values" section). This
API is also simple, as you can see in Listing 6-26.

Listing 6-26. HandlerMethodReturnValueHandler

```java
package org.springframework.web.method.support;

import org.springframework.core.MethodParameter;

import org.springframework.web.context.request.NativeWebRequest;

public interface HandlerMethodReturnValueHandler {

    boolean supportsReturnType(MethodParameter returnType);

    void handleReturnValue(Object returnValue, MethodParameter returnType,
                        ModelAndViewContainer mavContainer,
                        NativeWebRequest webRequest)
                        throws Exception;

}
```

The supportsReturnType method for each registered HandlerMethodReturnValueHandler is called with the return type of the method. The one that returns true handles the return value, which is accomplished by calling the handleReturnValue method.

Implementing Your Own

We can use the strategies used by RequestMappingHandlerAdapter to our advantage. For example, we want an easy way to store and retrieve objects in javax.servlet.http. HttpSession. For this, we first need an annotation to mark a method argument or return type as something we want to retrieve or put in the HttpSession. Listing 6-27 describes the annotation we use.

Listing 6-27. The SessionAttribute Annotation

```
package com.apress.prospringmvc.bookstore.web.method.support;

import java.lang.annotation.Documented;
import java.lang.annotation.ElementType;
import java.lang.annotation.Retention;
import java.lang.annotation.RetentionPolicy;
import java.lang.annotation.Target;

@Target({ ElementType.PARAMETER, ElementType.METHOD })
@Retention(RetentionPolicy.RUNTIME)
@Documented
public @interface SessionAttribute {

    String value() default "";

    boolean required() default true;

    boolean exposeAsModelAttribute() default false;

}
```

However, all by itself, adding an annotation isn't much help because we still need a class that uses that annotation. Because we want to retrieve from and store in the HttpSession, we create a class that implements both the HandlerMethodReturnValueHandler and HandlerMethodArgumentResolver interfaces (see Listing 6-28).

Listing 6-28. The SessionAttributeProcessor

```
package com.apress.prospringmvc.bookstore.web.method.support;

import org.springframework.core.MethodParameter;
import org.springframework.web.bind.
MissingServletRequestParameterException;
import org.springframework.web.bind.support.WebDataBinderFactory;
import org.springframework.web.context.request.NativeWebRequest;
import org.springframework.web.context.request.WebRequest;
import org.springframework.web.method.support.
HandlerMethodArgumentResolver;
import org.springframework.web.method.support.
HandlerMethodReturnValueHandler;
import org.springframework.web.method.support.ModelAndViewContainer;

public class SessionAttributeProcessor implements
HandlerMethodReturnValueHandler, HandlerMethodArgumentResolver {

    @Override
    public boolean supportsReturnType(MethodParameter returnType) {
        return returnType.getMethodAnnotation(SessionAttribute.class) !=
        null;
    }

    @Override
    public void handleReturnValue(Object returnValue, MethodParameter
    returnType,
                                    ModelAndViewContainer mavContainer,
                                    NativeWebRequest webRequest) throw
                                    Exception {

        var annotation = returnType.getMethodAnnotation(SessionAttribute.
        class);
        webRequest.setAttribute(annotation.value(), returnValue,
        WebRequest.SCOPE_SESSION);
        exposeModelAttribute(annotation, returnValue, mavContainer);
    }
```

```
    @Override
    public boolean supportsParameter(MethodParameter parameter) {
        return parameter.hasParameterAnnotation(SessionAttribute.class);
    }

    private void exposeModelAttribute(SessionAttribute annotation, Object
    value, ModelAndViewContainer mavContainer) {
        if (annotation.exposeAsModelAttribute()) {
            mavContainer.addAttribute(annotation.value(), value);
        }
    }
    @Override
    public Object resolveArgument(MethodParameter parameter,
    ModelAndViewContainer mavContainer,
                                    NativeWebRequest webRequest,
                                    WebDataBinderFactory binderFactory)
                                    throws Exception {

        var annotation = parameter.getParameterAnnotation(SessionAttribute.
        class);
        var value = webRequest.getAttribute(annotation.value(), WebRequest.
        SCOPE_SESSION);
        if (value == null && annotation.required()) {
            throw new MissingServletRequestParameterException(annotation.
            value(), parameter.getParameterType().getName());
        }
        exposeModelAttribute(annotation, value, mavContainer);
        return value;
    }

}
```

Before we can use the processor, we need to configure it. For this, we need to modify our configuration class. Specifically, we need to add the processor as a bean and make the environment aware of the bean's existence (see Listing 6-29).

Listing 6-29. The Modified WebMvcContextConfiguration

```
package com.apress.prospringmvc.bookstore.web.config;

com.apress.prospringmvc.bookstore.web.method.support.
SessionAttributeProcessor;

// Other imports omitted

@Configuration
public class WebMvcContextConfiguration implements WebMvcConfigurer {

    @Bean
    public SessionAttributeProcessor sessionAttributeProcessor() {
        return new SessionAttributeProcessor();
    }

    @Override
    public void addArgumentResolvers(List<HandlerMethodArgumentResolver>
    argumentResolvers) {
        argumentResolvers.add(sessionAttributeProcessor());
    }

    @Override
    public void addReturnValueHandlers(List<HandlerMethodReturnValueHandler>
    returnValueHandlers) {
        returnValueHandlers.add(sessionAttributeProcessor());
    }

// Other methods omitted
}
```

Now that we have configured our processor, we are finally ready to use it. Let's begin by modifying the controllers for accounts, as shown in Listing 6-30. We removed the need for directly accessing the session and adding the account to the model; this is now all handled by the processor. Bold font reflects the changes; it is simply an annotation on a method argument. At this point, we no longer need direct access to the HTTP session.

Listing 6-30. The Modified AccountController

```java
package com.apress.prospringmvc.bookstore.web.controller;

// Imports omitted

@Controller
@RequestMapping("/customer/account")
@SessionAttributes(types = Account.class)
public class AccountController {

    @RequestMapping(method = RequestMethod.GET)
    public String index(Model model,@SessionAttribute(value =
    LoginController.ACCOUNT_ATTRIBUTE, exposeAsModelAttribute = true)
    Account account) {
        model.addAttribute("orders", this.orderRepository.
        findByAccount(account));
        return "customer/account";

    }

// Other methods omitted

}
```

If we now relaunch the application and click Account (after logging in), we are greeted by our Account page (see Figure 6-9).

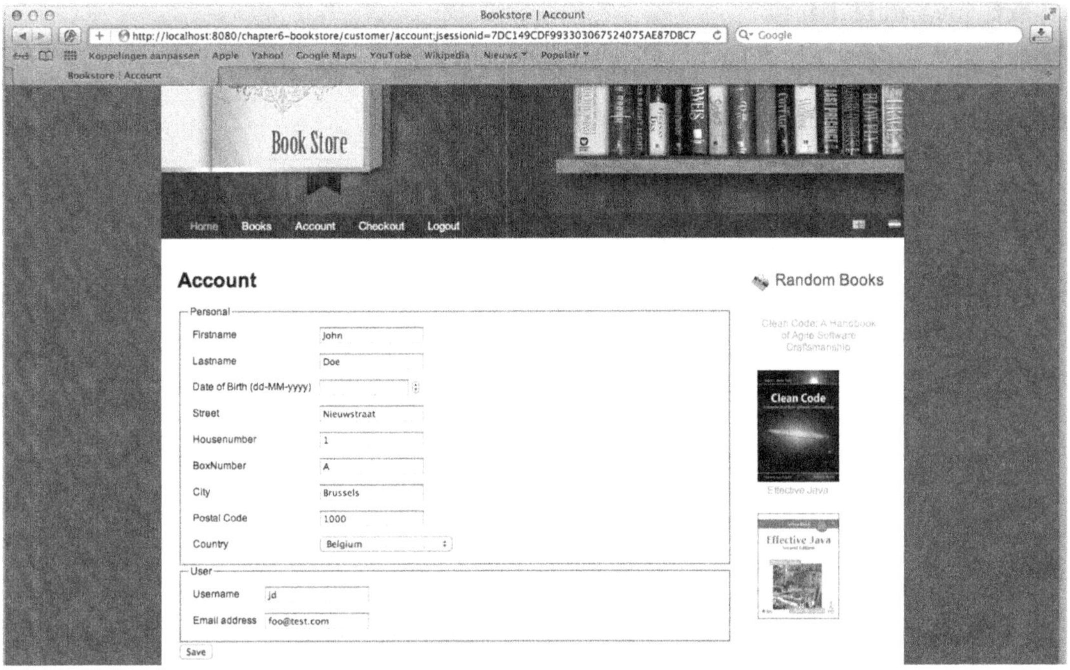

Figure 6-9. *The Account page*

Using the RequestDataValueProcessor

The org.springframework.web.servlet.support.RequestDataValueProcessor component is optional in that we can use to inspect or modify request parameter values before they are rendered or before a redirect is issued.

We can use this component as part of a solution[5] to provide data integrity, confidentiality, and protection against cross-site request forgery (CSRF).[6] We can also use it to automatically add hidden fields to all forms and URLs.

The RequestDataValueProcessor API consists of four methods (see Listing 6-31).

---

[5]http://www.hdiv.org
[6]http://www.owasp.org

Listing 6-31. The RequestDataValueProcessor API

```
package org.springframework.web.servlet.support;

import java.util.Map;
import javax.servlet.http.HttpServletRequest;

public interface RequestDataValueProcessor {

    String processAction(HttpServletRequest request, String action, String
    httpMethod);

    String processFormFieldValue(HttpServletRequest request, String name,
    String value, String type);

    Map<String, String> getExtraHiddenFields(HttpServletRequest request);

    String processUrl(HttpServletRequest request, String url);

}
```

We can use this interface to do some interesting things. For example, we might create a checksum over the not editable fields (like ID) in the controller (or an interceptor) and then review this checksum to see whether any fields have been tampered with.

The `<c:/url ../>` tag uses the `processUrl` method. On a redirect, we could use it to encode or add extra parameters to the URL to secure our URLs (for instance, we could add a checksum to check the validity of our parameters).

There is no default instance provided by the framework. Therefore, an implementation needs to be tailored for our application (the HDIV[7] website has a plugin to protect a site from a whole range of vulnerabilities). To configure `RequestDataValueProcessor`, we need to add it to the application context and then register it with the name `requestDataValueProcessor`, which is the name the framework uses to detect the registered instance.

---

[7]http://www.hdiv.org

Summary

This chapter covered some more advanced techniques to build web applications. For example, we started by looking at scoped beans and using them to our advantage. To that end, we implemented a shopping cart in our sample application.

At times we find ourselves in need of reusing code or executing code across many classes or URLs. These cross-cutting concerns can be addressed using aspect-oriented programming; however, this isn't always a good fit in a web application. In Spring MVC, we can use interceptors and an advanced exception-handling strategy to address those cross-cutting concerns. For example, we can use interceptors to execute a piece of code for many controllers. When configuring these interceptors, we can specify whether to map to all controllers or only to certain controllers based on the URL.

Although we all try to build our applications to be as robust as possible, there is always a chance that things go wrong. When things do go wrong, we want to handle the problems gracefully. For example, we might want to show the user an error page or login page when we need the user's credentials. For this, we took an in-depth look at the exception-handling strategies inside Spring MVC.

We followed this by diving deeper into the infrastructure classes of Spring MVC and examined how to extend the framework if the need arises. We also explained how to expand the request matching by specifying an additional request condition. Next, we explained (and showed) how to write a processor to handle method-argument types and return values for request-handling methods.

Finally, we ended the chapter with a brief introduction to the request data value processor, covering how to use this to protect against CSFR and provide data integrity.

CHAPTER 7

REST and AJAX

Until now, we have been building a classic web application: we send a request to the server, the server processes the request, and we render the result and show it to the client. Over the last decade, however, the way we build web applications has changed considerably. Now we have JavaScript and JSON/XML, which allow AJAX-based web applications and push more and more behavior push to the client, including validation, rendering parts of the screen, and so on.

This chapter starts with REST[1] (REpresentational State Transfer), an architectural style that has influenced how developers think of web resources and handle them. Later, we discuss AJAX and consider it in combination with REST.

The second part of this chapter covers file uploads. You learn how to do file uploading with the Spring Framework and handle the task in our controllers. However, before we get into this, let's look at REST.

REpresentational State Transfer (REST)

This section briefly explains the topic of REST, which essentially has two parts: first, the resources and how to identify them, and how we operate or work with these resources. REST was described in 2000 by Roy Thomas Fielding in a paper titled "Architectural Styles and the Design of Network-based Software Architectures."[2] It describes how to work with resources using the HTTP protocol and the features offered by this protocol.

---

[1]https://www.ics.uci.edu/~fielding/pubs/dissertation/rest_arch_style.htm
[2]https://www.ics.uci.edu/~fielding/pubs/dissertation/top.htm

© Marten Deinum and Iuliana Cosmina 2021
M. Deinum and I. Cosmina, *Pro Spring MVC with WebFlux*, https://doi.org/10.1007/978-1-4842-5666-4_7

Identifying Resources

Chapter 4 briefly discussed the parts of a URL (Uniform Resource Locator)[3] consists of. For REST, this doesn't change; however, the URL is important as it points to a unique resource. That is why, when talking about REST APIs, URL is replaced with URI (Uniform Resource Identifier).[4] Table 7-1 gives a couple of samples of resource locations.

Table 7-1. *Resource Locators*

URI	Description
`http://www.example.com/books`	A list of books
`http://www.example.com/books/9781430241553`	The details of the book with ISBN 978-1-4302-4155-3

> ℹ️   It is a best practice that URIs use the plural of the objects they describe in operations.

In REST, it is all about a *representation* of a resource, and hence the URI is important. It gives us the location of an actual resource (web page, the image on the web page, mp3 file, or whatever). What we see in our web browser isn't the actual resource but a representation of that resource. The next section explains how we can use this resource location to work with (modify, delete, etc.) that resource.

Working with Resources

The HTTP protocol specifies several methods (HTTP methods)[5] to work with information from our application. Table 7-2 gives an overview of the methods.

---

[3]https://en.wikipedia.org/wiki/URL
[4]https://en.wikipedia.org/wiki/Uniform_Resource_Identifier
[5]https://www.w3.org/Protocols/rfc2616/rfc2616-sec9.html

Table 7-2. *Available HTTP Methods*

Method	Description
GET	Retrieves a representation of a resource (for example, a book) from the given location.
HEAD	Similar to GET; however, the actual representation is not returned, but only the headers belonging to that resource. Useful to identify if something has changed and if a GET request needs to be sent.
PUT	Stores a representation of a resource (book) on the server. Usually, resources have a unique identifier. When the body of a PUT request contains an object with an identifier, the body's content updates an existing resource with the specified ID. If the PUT request body does not have an identifier, a new resource is created. If a user issues the same PUT request multiple times, the result should always be the same.
POST	Similar to PUT but the server is in control of creating resources or initiating actions. A POST is useful for creating new resources (such as a user) or for triggering an action (in our example, adding a book to the cart). Issuing the same request multiple times does not produce the same result (that is, the book would be added twice). That is why the result of a successful POST request is usually a redirect to a page containing the created resource.[6]
DELETE	Deletes the addressed resource (in this case, delete the book).
OPTIONS	Determines the options associated with this resource or the capabilities of the server. (For example, the supported HTTP methods, whether security is enabled, any versions, and so on).
TRACE	Performs a message loop-back test along the path to the target resource, providing a useful debugging mechanism.
PATCH	Intended for making partial changes to an existing resource. A PATCH is useful for updating resources when bandwidth is limited. This method is neither safe nor idempotent.

The TRACE and OPTIONS methods aren't used in REST but are mentioned here for completeness.

The PATCH method isn't used in REST since it is a good practice for an API to apply patches atomically using the PUT method.

---

[6]https://en.wikipedia.org/wiki/Post/Redirect/Get

In the "Identifying Resources" section, we mentioned how a URI points to a resource. If we combine REST with the resources from Table 7-1, we could work with them, as outlined in Table 7-3.

Table 7-3. *REST API*

URL	Method	Description
`http://www.example.com/books`	GET	Get a list of books.
`http://www.example.com/books`	PUT	Update a list of books.
`http://www.example.com/books`	POST	Create a new list of books.
`http://www.example.com/books`	DELETE	Delete all the books.
`http://www.example.com/books/9781430241553`	GET	Get a representation of the book with ISBN 978-1-4302-4155-3.
`http://www.example.com/books/9781430241553`	PUT	Update the book with ISBN 978-1-4302-4155-3.
`http://www.example.com/books/9781430241553`	POST	Create the book with ISBN 978-1-4302-4155-3.
`http://www.example.com/books/9781430241553`	DELETE	Delete the book with ISBN 978-1-4302-4155-3.

The list of HTTP methods is larger than most web browsers support. In general, they only support the GET and POST methods, and not the other methods identified. To use the different methods in a classic web application, we need to use a workaround; for this, Spring MVC has `HiddenHttpMethodFilter`.

HiddenHttpMethodFilter

The `org.springframework.web.filter.HiddenHttpMethodFilter` component masks a POST request as another specified type of request. It uses a request parameter to determine which method to use for the incoming request. This works well with forms created using The Spring tag library and Thymeleaf. By default, it uses a request parameter with the name _method; however, this name can be configured by extending the `HiddenHttpMethodFilter` class and overriding `setMethodParam(String)` to set a different name for the parameter.

A POST request can be "transformed" to a PUT or DELETE by ensuring the request parameter is there; the request is then wrapped in `HttpMethodRequestWrapper` (which is an inner class of `HiddenHttpMethodFilter`). A GET request is processed as is; it is not transformed into another type of request. This is because a GET request, unlike the other types, has all parameters encoded in the URL. By contrast, the POST and PUT requests have them encoded in the request body.

Enabling `HiddenHttpMethodFilter` for our web application requires adding a property to `application.properties` (see Listing 7-1).

Listing 7-1. Enable `HiddenHttpMethodFilter`

```
spring.mvc.hiddenmethod.filter.enabled=true
```

Having enabled the filter, we need to modify our account page. Open the `account.jsp` file and make sure there is a hidden field with the name `_method,` and the value `PUT`. Listing 7-2 shows the start of the page; as you can see, the opening of the form has this hidden field defined.

Listing 7-2. Account.jsp Heading

```
<%@ taglib prefix="c" uri="http://java.sun.com/jsp/jstl/core"%>
<%@ taglib prefix="spring" uri="http://www.springframework.org/tags" %>
<%@ taglib prefix="form" uri="http://www.springframework.org/tags/form" %>

<form:form method="POST" modelAttribute="account" id="accountForm">
    <!-- filter to transform POST method in PUT -->
    <input type="hidden" name="_method" value="PUT" />

    <fieldset>
    <legend><spring:message code="account.personal"/></legend>

// Remainder of page omitted
```

When submitting the page, `HiddenHttpMethodFilter` does its work and transform our POST request into a PUT request. For simple applications, the controller can handle both request methods using the same handler method (see Listing 7-3). For more complex applications, they can be handled separately.

Listing 7-3. AccountController Update Method

```
package com.apress.prospringmvc.bookstore.web.controller;

//Imports omitted

@Controller
@RequestMapping("/customer/account")
@SessionAttributes(types = Account.class)
public class AccountController {

@PostMapping
@PutMapping
public String update(@ModelAttribute Account account) {
    this.accountRepository.save(account);
    return "redirect:/customer/account";
}

// Other methods omitted

}
```

The filter is still a workaround to make REST possible with browsers and normal forms, which can be useful if we choose to use progressive enhancement or graceful degradation for our website. Progressive enhancement means adding rich behavior to a basic page and first making sure our basic page works as we want it to. Graceful degradation is the other way around—we develop a rich website and try to make sure the whole site still works even if certain features aren't available.

Asynchronous JavaScript and XML (AJAX)

Jesse James Garrett coined the term **AJAX** in 2005. By itself, AJAX isn't a technology. It is a collection of technologies working together to create a rich user experience for our web application. AJAX incorporates the following technologies.

- Standards-based presentation by using HTML and CSS

- Dynamic display and interaction by using the Document Object Model (DOM)

- Data interchange and manipulation (using XML or JSON)

- Asynchronous data retrieval using the XMLHttpRequest

- JavaScript to bring all this together

Although the acronym stands for **Asynchronous JavaScript and XML**, it is often used with JavaScript Object Notation (JSON) to pass data between the client and server.

As AJAX has already been in use for a couple of years, there are a lot of JavaScript frameworks and libraries out there that make it easier to create a rich user experience. For Spring MVC, it doesn't matter which JavaScript framework or library you choose, and it is beyond the scope of the book to discuss the abundance of JavaScript frameworks and libraries out there. For our example, we use jQuery[7] because it is one of the most widely used libraries. To use jQuery, we need to load the JavaScript file containing this library. For this, we modify the template.jsp file to include jQuery (see Listing 7-4).

Listing 7-4. Modified `template.jsp` Header

```
<!DOCTYPE HTML>

<%@ taglib prefix="c" uri="http://java.sun.com/jsp/jstl/core"%>
<%@ taglib prefix="spring" uri="http://www.springframework.org/tags" %>
<%@ taglib prefix="tiles" uri="http://tiles.apache.org/tags-tiles" %>

<html>
<head>
    <meta charset="utf-8">
    <c:set var="titleKey">
        <tiles:getAsString name="title" />
    </c:set>

    <title> Bookstore |
      <spring:message code="${titleKey}" text="Your Home in Books"/>
    </title>

    <link rel="stylesheet" type="text/css"
      href="<c:url value="/resources/css/style.css"/>" >
```

---

[7]https://jquery.org

```
<script
    src="<c:url value="/resources/jquery/jquery-3.5.1.min.js"/>">
</script>
</head>

//Body Omitted
</html>
```

If you have a good and constant Internet connection, you do not have to download jQuery; you can directly link the publicly available minified version.

```
<script src="https://code.jquery.com/jquery-3.5.1.min.js"/>
```

This adds the jQuery JavaScript library to all the pages (if added to the commons layout); however, by itself, it doesn't do much. We still need to add logic to our page, meaning calling the now available functions when users interact with HTML elements. In the next sections, we add AJAX behavior to our sample application. We start with a simple form submit and, along the way, explore the features that Spring MVC offers to work with AJAX and how it helps us build REST applications.

Adding AJAX to Our Application

Thanks to the flexibility of Spring MVC, it is easy to add AJAX behavior to our application and integrate it nicely with Spring MVC. In this section, you learn how to change the form submit into an AJAX-based form submit (with and without JSON). AJAX is more suitable for submitting a search form since it prevents the full reload on the page. However, a form submit isn't the only possible use for AJAX; it merely serves our sample application; it is also possible to create autocompletion fields, automatic field/form validation, and so on.

AJAX Form Submit with HTML Result

Let's look at our book search page and transform that into a more dynamic web page. We start by changing the normal form submit into an AJAX form submit. Open the search.jsp file and add the script as shown in Listing 7-5 right after the form or at the bottom of the page to ensure that the HTML code was rendered and JS can manipulate it.

Listing 7-5. Book Search Page with AJAX Form Submit

```
<script>
  $('#bookSearchForm').submit(function(evt){
    evt.preventDefault();
    formData = $('#bookSearchForm').serialize();
    $.ajax({
      url: $('#bookSearchForm').action,
      type: 'GET',
      data: formData
    });
  });
</script>
```

This script replaces the actual form submit. It first prevents the actual submit from happening, and then builds an AJAX request that passes the data to the server. If we now redeploy our application, navigate to our book search page, and press Submit, it looks like nothing happens. At least we don't see anything change on the screen. If we debug our application, we can see the request arrive at the server and the search being issued. So why isn't the result being rendered?

At the beginning of this section, we mentioned that AJAX is a collection of technologies, and one of those is asynchronous data retrieval using the XMLHttpRequest. This is also where our current problem lies. We send a request to the server, but we haven't included anything to handle the response from the server.

Listing 7-6 shows the modified script (see the highlighted part) to render the returned page.

Listing 7-6. Book Search Page with Success Handler

```
<script>
  $('#bookSearchForm').submit(function(evt) {
    evt.preventDefault();
    formData = $('#bookSearchForm').serialize();
    $.ajax({
      url: $('#bookSearchForm').action,
      type: 'GET',
      data: formData,
```

```
  success: function(html) {
    resultTable = $('#bookSearchResults', html);
    $('#bookSearchResults').html(resultTable);
  }
});
});
</script>
```

We added the success handler for this script and what it does is render the result we receive from the server. The result is the whole page as it is normally rendered. We select the table with the results, and we replace the current table on screen with the detected table. If the application is redeployed and a search is issued, the page would work again.

AJAX Form Submit with JSON Result

The previous section showed a basic AJAX form submit from which we got back HTML. We send data to the server, and we get an HTML page fragment page to render. The other way to do it is to get the data we need to render and process that on the client. This complicates the JavaScript code a little, but we also need to extend our server side. We need an additional method to return JSON-encoded data to the client (see Listing 7-7).

Listing 7-7. BookSearch Controller with JSON Producing Method

```
package com.apress.prospringmvc.bookstore.web.controller;

import org.springframework.http.MediaType;
import org.springframework.web.bind.annotation.ResponseBody;

// Other imports omitted

@Controller
public class BookSearchController {

// Other methods omitted

    @GetMapping(value = "/book/search", produces = MediaType.APPLICATION_
    JSON_VALUE )
    public @ResponseBody Collection<Book> listJSON(
        @ModelAttribute("bookSearchCriteria") BookSearchCriteria criteria) {
```

```
      return this.bookstoreService.findBooks(criteria);
    }
}
```

The method does the same as the original list method on the same controller; however, there are two important differences, which are highlighted. The first is that this method is invoked whenever an incoming request has specified that it wants to receive JSON (by setting the Accept headers, as explained in Chapter 4). Next, we use the @ResponseBody annotation to instruct Spring MVC to use the returned value as the body of the response (see the "Supported Method Argument Annotations" section in Chapter 5). The returned value is converted by using org.springframework.http. converter.HttpMessageConverter<T>.

Spring MVC automatically registers org.springframework.http.converter.json. MappingJackson2HttpMessageConverter when the Jackson Java JSON processor[8] is found on the classpath.

In addition to the controller, we need to modify our JavaScript to specify that we want to receive JSON from the server. Because we receive JSON, we need to use JSON to replace the content of our result table. In Listing 7-8, you can see the result for the search.jsp file.

Listing 7-8. Book Search Page with JSON Success Handler

```
<script>
  $('#bookSearchForm').submit(function(evt){
  evt.preventDefault();
  formData = $('#bookSearchForm').serialize();
  $.ajax({
    url: $('#bookSearchForm').action,
    type: 'GET',
    dataType: 'json',
    data: formData,
    success: function(data){
      var content = '';
      var books = data;
```

---

[8]https://github.com/FasterXML

```
var baseDetailUrl = '<c:url value="/book/detail/"/>';
var baseAddCartUrl = '<c:url value="/cart/add/" />';
for (var i = 0; i<books.length; i++) {
  content += '<tr>';
  content += '<td><a href="'
   + baseDetailUrl + books[i].id+'">'
   + books[i].title+'</a></td>';
  content += '<td>'+books[i].description+'</td>';
  content += '<td>'+books[i].price+'</td>';
  content += '<td><a href="'+ baseAddCartUrl +books[i].id
     +'"><spring:message code="book.addtocart"/></a></td></tr>';
  }
  $('#bookSearchResults tbody').html(content);

 }
 });
 });
</script>
```

When the application is redeployed and a search is issued, our new method is invoked, and JSON is returned to the client. The client uses the JSON objects to create a new table body, and when the body is created, it replaces the current table body.

Sending and Receiving JSON

It is possible to send JSON to the server as well as to receive JSON from the server. The advantage of sending JSON is that it is compact and faster to send and process (both client and server side) than XML. A drawback can be that you need some hand-coding to prepare the JSON for sending to the server, especially when reusing existing objects (as you can see in our sample).

To make this possible, we need to modify our client-side JavaScript and make some changes to our request handling method. The controller needs to know that we aren't using a normal model attribute but instead want to use JSON for our BookSearchCriteria. To enable this, we annotate our method argument with @RequestBody; it is analogous to @ResponseBody, but for incoming requests. To make it clear that the handler method requires a certain type of data input, the consumes attribute can be added to the @PostMapping annotation.

Listing 7-9 highlights the changes that need to be made to the controller.

Listing 7-9. BookSearchController with RequestBody Annotation

```
package com.apress.prospringmvc.bookstore.web.controller;

import org.springframework.web.bind.annotation.RequestBody;

// Other imports omitted

@Controller
public class BookSearchController {

// Other methods omitted

    @PostMapping(value = "/book/search", produces = MediaType.APPLICATION_
    JSON_VALUE
        ,consumes = MediaType.APPLICATION_JSON_VALUE)
    public @ResponseBody Collection<Book> listJSON(
        @RequestBody BookSearchCriteria criteria) {
        return this.bookstoreService.findBooks(criteria);
    }
}
```

Notice the change from a GET request to a POST request; this is needed because we use the @RequestBody annotation. The annotation operates on the body of a request, but a GET request generally encodes the data in the URL instead of the body.

ⓘ   When using the @RequestBody and @ResponseBody annotations, everything used to represent/build the resource should be part of the request. Spring MVC deserializes the request body to a Java object processed in the handler method and serializes the returned result to the type specified by the produces attribute.

Having modified our controller, we also need to modify our JavaScript again. We need to convert the data from the form into a JSON string that we can send to the server. Listing 7-10 shows what needs to be changed.

Listing 7-10. Book Search Page with JSON Form Submit

```
<script>
  $('#bookSearchForm').submit(function(evt){
    evt.preventDefault();
    var title = $('#title').val();
    var category = $('#category').val();
    var json = { "title" : title, "category" : { "id" : category}};
    $.ajax({
      url: $('#bookSearchForm').action,
      type: 'POST',
      dataType: 'json',
      contentType: 'application/json',
      data: JSON.stringify(json),
      success: function(books) {
        var content = '';
        var baseDetailUrl = '<c:url value="/book/detail/"/>';
        var baseAddCartUrl = '<c:url value="/cart/add/" />';
        for (var i = 0; i<books.length; i++) {
         content += '<tr>';
         content += '<td><a href="'+ baseDetailUrl + books[i].id+'">'
          +books[i].title+'</a></td>';
         content += '<td>'+books[i].description+'</td>';
         content += '<td>'+books[i].price+'</td>';
         content += '<td><a href="'+ baseAddCartUrl +books[i].id
         +'"><spring:message code="book.addtocart"/></a></td></tr>';
        }
        $('#bookSearchResults tbody').html(content);
      }
    });
  });
</script>
```

As you can see, the contentType property was added to convert the form data into a JSON object, and the type of request was changed to POST. This is needed because the content is the body of the request, and a GET request doesn't have a body but encodes everything into the URL.

The data property value is for converting the JSON object into a JSON string, which can be sent to the server. Everything else remains the same.

If the application is redeployed, and we issue a search, the search results are shown to the user again.

ℹ️   jQuery has a plugin architecture, and there are a couple of plugins out there that make form-to-JSON (Dream.js,[9] JsonView[10]) conversion easier. We choose not to use a plugin to avoid focus on the plugin itself.

Combining AJAX and REST

We briefly covered REST, and we also touched on AJAX, but we covered each topic separately. However, it is also very easy to combine the two. In the REST section, we changed the account update form into a form issued with a PUT request, but this was a simulation using POST. With the JavaScript library we use, it is possible to create a real PUT request instead of a POST request used as a PUT request.

To issue and handle PUT requests, two things must be done: AJAX must submit the form as a PUT request, and we need to prepare the server to handle PUT requests. There are some differences between the POST and PUT requests. A major difference is that a POST request must have the form data available (the specification requires this), but that is not the case for the PUT request. Spring provides `org.springframework.web.filter.FormContentFilter`, which can help us here.

The filter kicks in when a PUT request with a content-type of `application/x-www-form-urlencoded` is detected. It parses the body of the incoming request (delegated to `org.springframework.http.converter.support.AllEncompassingFormHttpMessageConverter`), and the result is a map of parameters that can be used just like normal form parameters. To enable the filter in a Spring Boot application, the `spring.mvc.formcontent.filter.enabled` property must be set to `true` in the application configuration (see Listing 7-11).

---

[9]https://github.com/adleroliveira/dreamjs
[10]https://github.com/yesmeck/jquery-jsonview

Listing 7-11. Enable the `FormContentFilter`

```
spring.mvc.formcontent.filter.enabled=true
```

Next, we need to add some JavaScript to our `account.jsp file`. It is similar to the script we first added to our book search page, with one major difference: we now use a PUT instead of a GET. See Listing 7-12 for the JavaScript that is added right after the form or at the end of the page. The controller method (see Listing 7-3) remains the same, as it still is a PUT request for the controller.

Listing 7-12. Account Page PUT AJAX Form Submit

```
<script>
  $('#accountForm').submit(function(evt){
   evt.preventDefault();
   formData = $('#accountForm').serialize();
    $.ajax({
      url: $('#accountForm').action,
      type: 'PUT',
      data: formData
    });
  });
</script>
```

Progressive Enhancement

The way we have been applying the AJAX features is a technique called **progressive enhancement**. It means that one builds a simple web page that functions as it is and then add dynamic and rich behavior to the page with JavaScript.

The opposite approach is also possible; this technique is called **graceful degradation**, which means that we start with a page with all the behavior we want. Depending on the features offered by the browser, we scale down on the rich behavior used.

The trend nowadays is to use progressive enhancement because it is easier to build and maintain. It also has the advantage that we can enhance based on the device's capabilities that connect to our application (an iPhone has different features than a Windows 7 PC with Internet Explorer 9).

Handling File Uploads

HTTP file uploading or form-based file upload in HTML is defined in RFC 1867.[11] After adding an HTML input field with a type file to the form and setting the encoding to `multipart/form-data`, the browser can send text and/or binary files to the server as part of a POST request.

To handle file uploads, we first need to register `org.springframework.web. multipart.MultipartResolver`. Out of the box, Spring provides two ways of handling file uploads. The first is the multipart support described in the Servlet API specification, and the second is by using the features offered by the Commons FileUpload[12] project from Apache.

The Spring Framework provides two implementations.

- `org.springframework.web.multipart.support. StandardServletMultipartResolver`

- `org.springframework.web.multipart.commons. CommonsMultipartResolver`

The first implementation can be used in a Servlet API environment with multipart enabled on the servlet, and the second uses the Commons FileUpload library.

For the actual handling of file uploads, we need to modify the controller. These modifications are mostly independent of the file uploading technology used. Spring provides several abstractions to handle file uploads.

- We can write a request-handling method that takes an argument of type `org.springframework.web.multipart.MultipartFile` (or `Collection<MultipartFile>`), or we could use `org. springframework.web.multipart.MultipartHttpServletRequest` and retrieve the files ourselves.

- When we are in a Servlet API environment and use the multipart parsing support. We can also use the `javax.servlet.http.Part` interface to get the file.

---

[11]`https://www.ietf.org/rfc/rfc1867.txt`

[12]`http://commons.apache.org/proper/commons-fileupload/`

The final way to indicate something with a file upload is to annotate the method argument with `org.springframework.web.bind.annotation.RequestPart` (see Chapter 4). When put on anything else described earlier, Spring uses the type conversion system to transform the file's content.

We first discuss the configuration for the two different strategies. After that, we look at how to handle file uploads inside a controller.

Configuration

The first step in enabling file uploads is to configure our environment. As Spring provides two different technologies out of the box, each requires a different set of configuration items. We look at the Servlet API multipart support and Commons FileUpload.

Configuring Servlet API File Uploading

Spring Boot supports the Servlet API way of doing file uploads by default, simply because that is always available in a servlet container. It can be enabled or disabled by setting `spring.servlet.multipart.enabled` to `true`/`false` in the application configuration (see Listing 7-13).

Listing 7-13. Explicitly Enable Multipart File Upload

```
spring.servlet.multipart.enabled=true
```

When using Spring vanilla configuration, the first step in multipart parsing on `org.springframework.web.servlet.DispatcherServlet` is to add a multipart-config section to XML configuration or include `javax.servlet.MultipartConfigElement` in our `org.springframework.web.WebApplicationInitializer` implementation.

In a Spring Boot web application, other properties can configure things like max file size, request size, and so forth (see Table 7-4).

Table 7-4. *Spring Boot Properties for File Upload*

Property	Description	Default
`spring.servlet.multipart.enabled`	Enable or disable file uploads	`true`
`spring.servlet.multipart.location`	Temporary location for the uploaded files, when not specified, a temporary directory is used.	
`spring.servlet.multipart.max-file-size`	Maximum size of the file to be uploaded	1 megabyte
`spring.servlet.multipart.max-request-size`	Maximum size of the request for uploading, when the request contains more than one file	10 megabytes
`spring.servlet.multipart.file-size-threshold`	How much of the file is kept in memory before writing to disk	0 bytes
`spring.servlet.multipart.resolve-lazily`	Should files be resolved/parsed immediately or delayed until being accessed as a parameter	`false`

Configuring Apache Commons File Uploading

To use the Commons FileUpload support in Spring Boot, it requires the registration of CommonsMultipartResolver to enable file uploads (see Listing 7-14). The parameters, as used in a configuration like `spring.servlet.multipart.location`, do not automatically apply to the Commons FileUpload configuration—although we could reuse the configuration properties for manual configuration!

Listing 7-14. Configuration with CommonsMultipartResolver

```
package com.apress.prospringmvc.bookstore.web.config;

import org.springframework.web.multipart.MultipartResolver;
import org.springframework.web.multipart.commons.CommonsMultipartResolver;
```

```
// Other imports omitted

@Configuration
public class WebMvcContextConfiguration implements WebMvcConfigurer {

    @Bean
    public MultipartResolver multipartResolver(MultipartProperties
    multipartProperties) {
        CommonsMultipartResolver multipartResolver = new
        CommonsMultipartResolver();
        multipartResolver.setMaxUploadSize(multipartProperties.
        getMaxFileSize().toBytes());
        return multipartResolver;
    }
}
```

Request Handling Method for File Upload

In addition to configuring the upload, we also need a page with a form to submit a file. For this, we need to create a form that has its encoding set to multipart/form-data (see Listing 7-15).

This form doesn't change if we change the different techniques available; only the way the uploads are handled changes. When adding an input element with the type file, it is important to give it a name, especially if we do a single file upload. This name is also needed to retrieve the file from the request.

Listing 7-15. Upload Order Form for Account Page

```
<form id="orderForm"
      action="<c:url value="/order/upload"/>"
      method="POST"
      enctype="multipart/form-data">
    <fieldset>
        <legend>Upload order</legend>
        <input type="file" placeholder="Select File"
               id="order" name="order"/>
```

```
<button id="upload"><spring:message code="button.upload"/></button>
  </fieldset>
</form>
```

We add this form to the `account.jsp` file right after the already existing form. When we now render the account page, it looks like Figure 7-1.

Figure 7-1. *Account page with file upload*

In the following sections, we explore the different ways of handling file uploads in a controller. Most of the methods are portable between the two different file upload technologies; however, the last one is only available when using the Servlet API multipart support. Each of the different request handling methods has the same output when a file is uploaded; it prints the name of the uploaded file and the size of the file, as shown in Figure 7-2.

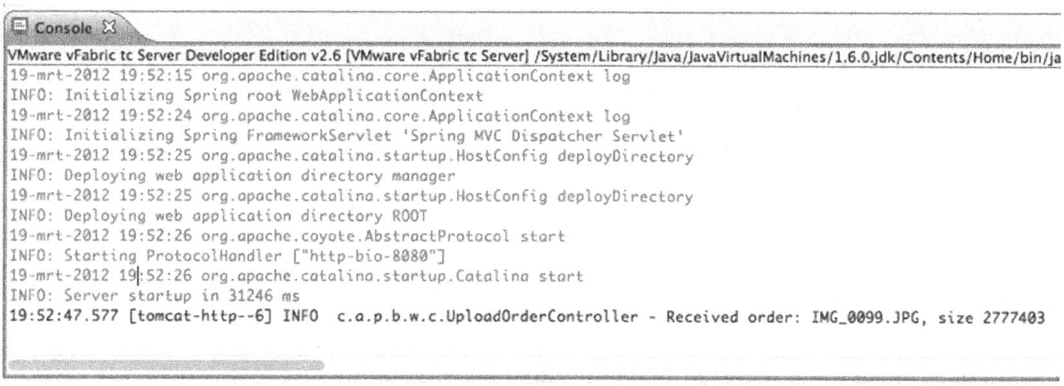

Figure 7-2. *Sample file upload output*

Writing a Request Handling Method with Multipart File

When writing a request handling method, if we want to do file upload and use the multipart file abstraction from Spring, we need to create a method, annotate it, and make sure it has `MultipartFile` as a method argument. When there are multiple files uploaded with the same name, we can also receive a `Collection<MultipartFile>` of files instead of a single element. Listing 7-16 shows a controller with a method that can handle file uploads using this technique.

Listing 7-16. UploadOrderController with `MultipartFile`

```java
package com.apress.prospringmvc.bookstore.web.controller;

// Other imports omitted
import org.springframework.web.multipart.MultipartFile;

@Controller
public class UploadOrderController {

    private Logger logger =
        LoggerFactory.getLogger(UploadOrderController.class);

    @PostMapping(path = "/order/upload", consumes = MediaType.MULTIPART_
    FORM_DATA_VALUE)
    public String handleUpload(final MultipartFile order) {
        logFile(order.getOriginalFilename(), order.getSize());
        return "redirect:/customer/account";
    }

    private void logFile(String name, long size) {
        this.logger.info("Received order: {}, size {}", name, size);
    }
}
```

Using MultipartHttpServletRequest to Handle File Uploads

Instead of accessing the file(s) directly, it is also possible to use `MultipartHttpServletRequest` to access the multipart files (see Listing 7-17). The methods exposed to access the multipart files are defined in the `org.springframework.web.multipart.MultipartRequest` super interface.

Listing 7-17. UploadOrderController with `MultipartHttpServletRequest`

```
package com.apress.prospringmvc.bookstore.web.controller;

// Other imports omitted

import org.springframework.web.multipart.MultipartFile;
import org.springframework.web.multipart.MultipartHttpServletRequest;

@Controller
public class UploadOrderController {

    private Logger logger =
      LoggerFactory.getLogger(UploadOrderController.class);

    @PostMapping("/order/upload")
    public String handleUpload(final MultipartHttpServletRequest request) {
        Map<String, MultipartFile> files = request.getFileMap();
        for (MultipartFile file : files.values()) {
            logFile(file.getOriginalFilename(), file.getSize());
        }

        return "redirect:/customer/account";
    }

    private void logFile(String name, long size) {
        this.logger.info("Received order: {}, size {}", name, size);
    }
}
```

Using a Form Object to Handle Uploads

Instead of handling the upload directly, we could also make it part of a form object
(model attribute). This can be convenient if the upload is part of a form that includes
more fields (like our customer account page, including a picture). To do this, we
need to create a class that can be used as the form object, with an attribute of type
`MultipartFile` (see Listing 7-18).

Listing 7-18. UploadOrderForm Class

```java
package com.apress.prospringmvc.bookstore.web;

import org.springframework.web.multipart.MultipartFile;

public class UploadOrderForm {

private MultipartFile order;

    public MultipartFile getOrder() {
        return this.order;
    }

    public void setOrder(MultipartFile order) {
        this.order = order;
    }
}
```

We need to modify the controller to take the form as a method argument (see Listing 7-19).

Listing 7-19. UploadOrderController with UploadOrderForm Object

```java
package com.apress.prospringmvc.bookstore.web.controller;

// Other imports omitted
import com.apress.prospringmvc.bookstore.web.UploadOrderForm;

@Controller
public class UploadOrderController {

    private Logger logger =
        LoggerFactory.getLogger(UploadOrderController.class);

    @PostMapping(path = "/order/upload", consumes = MediaType.MULTIPART_
    FORM_DATA_VALUE)
    public String handleUpload(UploadOrderForm form) {
        logFile(form.getOrder().getOriginalFilename(), form.getOrder().
        getSize());
        return "redirect:/customer/account";
    }
```

```
    private void logFile(String name, long size) {
        this.logger.info("Received order: {}, size {}", name, size);
    }
}
```

Writing a Request Handling Method Using the Servlet API

In a strict Servlet API environment, we can use the standard `javax.servlet.http.Part` interface to get access to the uploaded file. We simply create a method that takes the Part as an argument (see Listing 7-20). We need to create a method, annotate it, and give it a method argument. This technique only works in a Servlet API environment (so if you are writing a reactive application using a Netty server, this approach is not available) and is in that regardless portable than using the `MultipartFile` argument.

Listing 7-20. UploadOrderController with Part

```
package com.apress.prospringmvc.bookstore.web.controller;

// Other imports omitted
import javax.servlet.http.Part;

@Controller
public class UploadOrderController {

    private Logger logger =
        LoggerFactory.getLogger(UploadOrderController.class);

    @PostMapping(path = "/order/upload", consumes = MediaType.MULTIPART_
    FORM_DATA_VALUE)
    public String handleUpload(final Part order) {
        logFile(order.getName(), order.getSize());
        return "redirect:/customer/account";
    }

    private void logFile(String name, long size) {
        this.logger.info("Received order: {}, size {}", name, size);
    }
}
```

Exception Handling

Uploading a file can also fail. The file could be too large to handle (larger than the configured maximum file size), or our disks could be full. There are many reasons it might fail. If possible, we want to handle the errors and show a nice error page to the users. We can use the exception handling (as explained in Chapter 6) to handle the exception and show a nice error page. When an exception occurs, the multipart support throws org.springframework.web.multipart.MultipartException, and we can use this exception to show an error page.

Summary

This chapter covered Representational State Transfer (REST), as explained by Roy Thomas Fielding. You learned how to configure Spring MVC to facilitate the different methods used by REST. We discussed the configuration of HiddenHttpMethodFilter and the use-case for this filter.

Next, we briefly explained Asynchronous JavaScript and XML (AJAX) and how we can use that on the client and have controllers react to those requests. Although AJAX was originally about XML, it is now about JSON. We explored the JSON features offered by Spring MVC by using the @RequestBody and @ResponseBody annotations.

The final part of this chapter looked at uploading files to our application. For this purpose, we looked at the configuration needed for Servlet API multipart support and Commons FileUpload support. We then explored the different ways of writing a controller that can handle file uploads.

CHAPTER 8

Resolving and Implementing Views

So far, we have mainly used JavaServer Pages (JSP) and HTML templates as our view technology; however, Spring MVC provides a very powerful and flexible mechanism to resolve and implement views. You had a brief look at the view resolving mechanism in Chapter 4. This chapter looks at the different `ViewResolver` implementations and shows how to create and use our own implementation. You see which view technologies Spring MVC supports out of the box. And we create some custom implementations. Before we dive into the internals, however, let's recap the view rendering process and API.

View Resolvers and Views

Chapter 4 discussed the request processing workflow of the dispatcher servlet. Resolving and rendering a view is part of that process. Figure 8-1 shows the view rendering process (see the "Render View" section in Chapter 4).

© Marten Deinum and Iuliana Cosmina 2021
M. Deinum and I. Cosmina, *Pro Spring MVC with WebFlux*, https://doi.org/10.1007/978-1-4842-5666-4_8

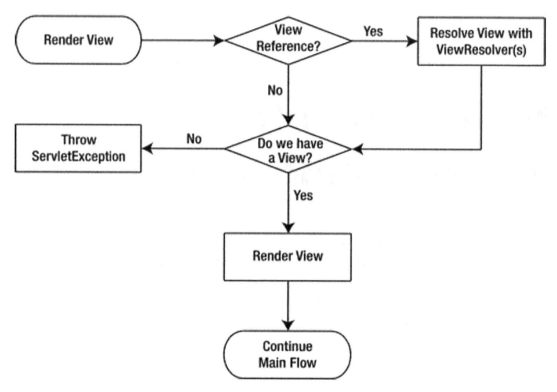

Figure 8-1. *View rendering process*

The controller can return an org.springframework.web.servlet.View
implementation or a reference to a view (view name). In the latter case, the configured
ViewResolvers are consulted to translate the reference into a concrete implementation.
When an implementation is available, it is instructed to render; otherwise, javax.
servlet.ServletException is thrown.

ViewResolver (see Listing 8-1) has only a single method to resolve to a view.

Listing 8-1. ViewResolver API

```
package org.springframework.web.servlet;

import java.util.Locale;

public interface ViewResolver {
    View resolveViewName(String viewName, Locale locale) throws Exception;
}
```

When a view has been selected, the dispatcher servlet calls the render method (see Listing 8-2) on the view instance. The getContentType() method is invoked on the View instance to determine the type of content. This value sets the content type on the response; it is also used by org.springframework.web.servlet.view. ContentNegotiatingViewResolver to determine the best matching view (see the upcoming section for more information).

Listing 8-2. View API

```
package org.springframework.web.servlet;

import java.util.Map;

import javax.servlet.http.HttpServletRequest;
import javax.servlet.http.HttpServletResponse;

public interface View {

    String getContentType();

    void render(Map<String, ?> model,
        HttpServletRequest request,
        HttpServletResponse response) throws Exception;
}
```

View Resolvers

Chapter 4 showed the hierarchy for the different ViewResolver implementations. Let's take a closer look at the generic usable implementations, how they work, and how they can be configured. Figure 8-2 shows the different implementations again. The implementations specific to particular view technologies are explained in the "View Technologies" section later in this chapter.

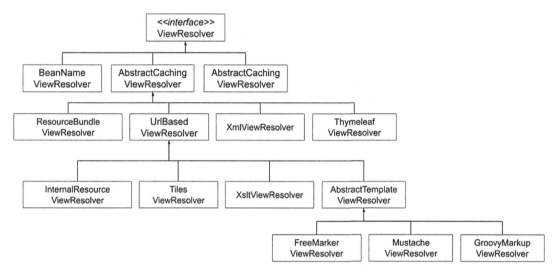

Figure 8-2. *ViewResolver hierarchy*

BeanNameViewResolver

The org.springframework.web.servlet.view.BeanNameViewResolver implementation is the most basic available and configured by default. It takes the name of the view and looks in org.springframework.context.ApplicationContext to see if there is a View with that name. If there is, the resolver returns it; otherwise, it returns null. This view resolver is useful in small(er) applications; however, it has one big drawback: each view needs to be configured using a bean in the application context. It has a single property that can be configured, and that is the order in which it is being called (see Table 8-1).

Table 8-1. BeanNameViewResolver *Properties*

Property	Purpose
Order	The order in which this view resolver is called in the chain. The higher the number, the lower the order in the chain.

Listing 8-3 shows the configuration for how our index page is served and resolved by this view resolver. We also need to add a View instance, and as we are using a JSP with JSTL support, we are returning org.springframework.web.servlet.view.JstlView.

Listing 8-3. BeanNameViewResolver Configuration

```
package com.apress.prospringmvc.bookstore.web.config;

import org.springframework.web.servlet.view.BeanNameViewResolver;
import org.springframework.web.servlet.view.JstlView;
// Other imports omitted

@Configuration
public class ViewConfiguration {

    @Bean
    public ViewResolver viewResolver() {
        BeanNameViewResolver viewResolver = new BeanNameViewResolver();
        viewResolver.setOrder(1);
        return viewResolver;
    }

    @Bean
    public View index() {
        JstlView view = new JstlView();
        view.setUrl("/WEB-INF/views/index.jsp");
        return view;
    }
}
```

UrlBasedViewResolver

org.springframework.web.servlet.view.UrlBasedViewResolver expects the view name to map directly to a URL. It can optionally modify the URL by adding a prefix and/or suffix to the view name. In general, this class serves as a base class to the different view technologies like JSP and template-based view technologies (see the "View Technologies" section later in this chapter). Table 8-2 describes the properties for this type of view resolver.

Table 8-2. `UrlBasedViewResolver` *Properties*

Property	Purpose
staticAttributes	Attributes to be included in each view resolved by this view resolver. The attributes and their values provide as a `Properties` or `Map<String,?>` instance via methods `setAttributes(Properties)` and `setAttributeMap(Map<String,?>)`.
cacheUnresolved	Should unresolved views be cached? That is, if a view has resolved to null, should it be put into the cache? The default is true. (Inherited from `AbstractCachingViewResolver`.)
contentType	Sets the content type[1] (text/HTML, application/JSON, etc.) for all views resolved by this view resolver, except for view implementations that determine or return the content-type themselves and ignore this property (like JSPs).
exposePathVariables	Should the path variables (see Chapter 5) be added to the model or not? In general, the views decide for themselves; setting this property can override that behavior.
Order	The order in which this view resolver is called in the chain. The higher the number, the lower the order in the chain.
Prefix	The prefix to add to the view name to generate a URL.
redirectContextRelative	Should a redirect URL starting with a / be interpreted as relative to the servlet context or not? The default is true. When this property is set to false, the URL is resolved relative to the current URL.
redirectHttp10Compatible	Should the redirect be HTTP 1.0 compatible? When true, an HTTP status code 302 issues a redirect; otherwise, an HTTP status code 303 to redirect. The default value is `true`.

(continued)

---

[1]https://www.iana.org/assignments/media-types/media-types.xhtml

Table 8-2. (*continued*)

Property	Purpose
requestContextAttribute	Sets the name of the org.springframework.web. servlet.support.RequestContext attribute for all views. The default is null, which means you are not exposing the RequestContext. Exposing a RequestContext can be useful when using standard JSP tags like useBean or technologies that don't have access to the request, like Velocity. The RequestContext is a context holder for the request-specific state.
Suffix	The suffix to add to the view name to generate a URL.
viewClass	The type of view to create; this needs to be a subclass of org.springframework.web.servlet.view. AbstractUrlBasedView. This property is required.
viewNames	The names of the views that can be handled by this view resolver. Names can include the * wildcard for matching names. The default is null, indicating to resolve all views.

Listing 8-4 is a sample configuration for this view resolver. We need to specify the view class (required). In general, it is also necessary to add a prefix and/or suffix to generate a URL pointing to the actual view implementation. The advantage of using UrlBasedViewResolver is that we don't need a bean for each View instance in our configuration. We rely on UrlBasedViewResolver to create a View using the configured properties and a symbolic view name.

Listing 8-4. UrlBasedViewResolver Configuration

```
package com.apress.prospringmvc.bookstore.web.config;

// Other imports omitted

import org.springframework.web.servlet.view.JstlView;
import org.springframework.web.servlet.view.UrlBasedViewResolver;
```

```
@Configuration
public class ViewConfiguration {

    @Bean
    public ViewResolver viewResolver() {
        UrlBasedViewResolver viewResolver = new UrlBasedViewResolver();
        viewResolver.setOrder(1);
        viewResolver.setPrefix("/WEB-INF/views/");
        viewResolver.setSuffix(".jsp");
        viewResolver.setViewClass(JstlView.class);
        return viewResolver;
    }
}
```

InternalResourceViewResolver

This extension of the `UrlBasedViewResolver` is a convenience subclass that preconfigures the view class to `org.springframework.web.servlet.view.InternalResourceView` and its subclasses. Listing 8-5 shows a sample configuration for `org.springframework.web.servlet.view.InternalResourceViewResolver`. The result is essentially the same as in Listing 8-4.

Listing 8-5. InternalResourceViewResolver configuration

```
package com.apress.prospringmvc.bookstore.web.config;

// Other imports omitted*
import org.springframework.web.servlet.view.InternalResourceViewResolver;

@Configuration
public class ViewConfiguration {

    @Bean
    public ViewResolver viewResolver() {
        InternalResourceViewResolver viewResolver;
        viewResolver = new InternalResourceViewResolver();
        viewResolver.setOrder(1);
```

```
        viewResolver.setPrefix("/WEB-INF/views/");
        viewResolver.setSuffix(".jsp");
        return viewResolver;
    }
}
```

XsltViewResolver

`org.springframework.web.servlet.web.view.xslt.XsltViewResolver` can resolve the view name to an XSLT stylesheet to transform the model into something to show to the user. To work with this view resolver and views, we need an XSLT template for transforming our model to a view. The returned view, an instance of `org.springframework.web.servlet.view.xslt.XsltView` detects which model object to render. It supports the following types.

- `javax.xml.transform.Source`

- `org.w3c.dom.Document`

- `org.w3c.dom.Node`

- `java.io.Reader`

- `java.io.InputStream`

- `org.springframework.core.io.Resource`

`XsltView` takes the supported type and uses the XSLT stylesheet to transform it. Although this mechanism can be powerful, we believe that this isn't something to create a view layer for a web application. In general, it is easier to return XML (or JSON) from the controller and directly process that on the client with JavaScript.

ContentNegotiatingViewResolver

`org.springframework.web.servlet.view.ContentNegotiatingViewResolver` is a very special view resolver; it can resolve views by name and content-type. It works by first determining which content-type is requested. There are three ways to do it.

- Check the file extension.

- Check the Accept header.

- Check a request parameter named *format* by default (the parameter name is configurable; see Table 8-3).

After the content-type is determined, the resolver consults all configured view resolvers to collect the candidate views by name. Finally, it selects the best matching view by checking if the requested content-type is supported. Table 8-3 shows the configurable properties of the view resolver.

Table 8-3. *ContentNegotiatingViewResolver Properties*

Property	Purpose
contentNegotiationManager	ContentNegotiationManager bean determines requested media types.
cnmFactoryBean	ContentNegotiationManagerFactoryBean bean creates a ContentNegotiationManager instance.
defaultViews	Sets the default views to consult. It is used when no specific view can be found. Very useful when using a marshaling view or returning JSON.
useNotAcceptableStatusCode	When no suitable view can be found, should we send an HTTP response code of 406 to the client? The default is false.
viewResolvers	List of view resolvers to consult. By default, it detects all view resolvers in the application context.
Order	The order in which this view resolver is called in the chain. The higher the number, the lower the order in the chain.

ⓘ   When multiple view resolvers are used, the ContentNegotiating ViewResolver must have the highest order to function correctly. It is already set by default, but if you change the order, keep this in mind.

Implementing Your Own ViewResolver

This section explains how to implement our own view resolver. We create a simple implementation that resolves the view name from a map of configured views.

Implementing your own view is easy to do; you create a class and let it implement the ViewResolver interface (see Listing 8-1) and provide the necessary implementation. Listing 8-6 shows our com.apress.prospringmvc.bookstore.web.view. SimpleConfigurableViewResolver.

Listing 8-6. SimpleConfigurableViewResolver

```
package com.apress.prospringmvc.bookstore.web.view;

// Other imports omitted*
import org.springframework.web.servlet.View;
import org.springframework.web.servlet.ViewResolver;

public class SimpleConfigurableViewResolver implements ViewResolver {
    private Map<String, ? extends View> views = new HashMap<>();

    @Override
    public View resolveViewName(String viewName, Locale locale) {
        return this.views.get(viewName);
    }
    public void setViews(Map<String, ? extends View> views) {
        this.views = views;
    }
}
```

We use this implementation in the next section to add views for PDF and Excel.

View Technologies

Spring MVC supports many different technologies, and if there isn't support, you can probably add it yourself by implementing org.springframework.web.servlet.View or by extending one of the provided View classes. This section discusses several view technologies and shows how Spring MVC supports them. For some, there is extensive support; for others, very little. Figure 8-3 shows the View class hierarchy, where you can see some of the supported view technologies. For some technologies, we need to specify a specific `ViewResolver` to work; others work together with the configured view resolvers.

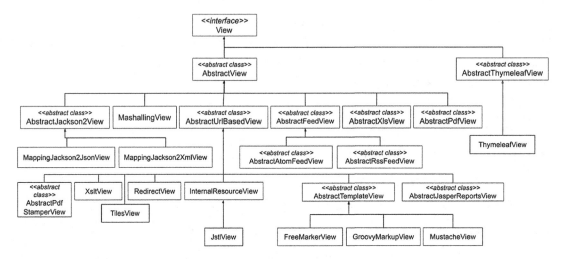

Figure 8-3. *View hierarchy*

The next part of this section briefly covers some of the supported view technologies. It shows the support classes and how to set up Spring to work with the specified technology. It does not provide in-depth coverage of all the different supported view technologies; other books are available for most of the technologies mentioned here.

ℹ   The `TilesViewResolver` has order 2 in most listings in this section to ensure it is executed at the right moment, especially when using the `ContentNegotiatingViewResolver`, which should execute before (which is the default) the `TilesViewResolver`.

JavaServer Pages

Until now, we have been using JavaServer Pages for our application. Spring has excellent support for it, including its own tag library (see Chapters 5 and 6). Spring has support and integration classes, and in general, it is the tool used with `org.springframework.web.servlet.view.InternalResourceViewResolver` to enable JSTL support and integrate with the default formatting and functions library from Sun.

Tiles

Apache Tiles[2] is a powerful page composition framework that allows you to compose your page of different page components (the *tiles*). The project has now been retired, and the Spring Framework team is very fond of Thymeleaf[3] and Mustache,[4] but Tiles was a Spring favorite for a long time and still deserves attention. These page components can be reused and configured in different page layouts. Originally it was designed as a JSP composition framework; however, it can also compose FreeMarker-based views.

Configuring Tiles

To get started with Tiles, we must configure and bootstrap the engine for it. Next, we need to configure the view resolver to return Tiles-based views, and finally, we need to specify our page composition and add the different templates (tiles).

We need to add `org.springframework.web.servlet.view.tiles3.TilesConfigurer` to our configuration. Next to that we need the special org.springframework.web.servlet.view.tiles3.TilesViewResolver. Finally, we need to specify our page compositions and add the templates. Listing 8-7 shows the most basic configuration for tiles.

Listing 8-7. ViewConfiguration for Tiles

```
package com.apress.prospringmvc.bookstore.web.config;

*// Other imports omitted*

import org.springframework.web.servlet.view.tiles3.TilesConfigurer;
import org.springframework.web.servlet.view.tiles3.TilesViewResolver;

@Configuration
public class ViewConfiguration {

    @Bean
    public TilesConfigurer tilesConfigurer() {
        return new TilesConfigurer();
    }
```

---

[2]https://attic.apache.org/projects/tiles.html
[3]https://www.thymeleaf.org/
[4]https://mustache.github.io/

```
@Bean
public TilesViewResolver tilesViewResolver() {
    TilesViewResolver tilesViewResolver = new TilesViewResolver();
    tilesViewResolver.setOrder(2);
    return tilesViewResolver;
}
}
```

The TilesConfigurer loads a file called tiles.xml from the WEB-INF directory by default; this file contains the page definitions. Before we look at the definition file, let's look at the properties of the configurer in Table 8-4.

Table 8-4. *TilesConfigurer Properties*

Property	Purpose
checkRefresh	Should we check the Tiles definitions for changes? The default is false; setting it to true impacts performance but can be useful during development.
completeAutoload	When set to true (the default is false), the initialization of Tiles is completely left to Tiles itself. It renders the other properties of this configurer class useless.
definitions	The list of files containing the definitions. The default refers to /WEB-INF/tiles.xml.
definitionsFactoryClass	Sets an org.apache.tiles.definition. DefinitionsFactory implementation to use to create the Tiles definitions. By default uses the org.apache.tiles. definition.UrlDefinitionsFactory class.
preparerFactoryClass	Sets an org.apache.tiles.preparer. PreparerFactory implementation to use. By default uses the org.apache.tiles.preparer. BasicPreparerFactory class.

(continued)

Table 8-4. (*continued*)

Property	Purpose
tilesInitializer	Sets the custom initializer to initialize Tiles. When setting a custom implementation, the initializer should initialize Tiles completely, as setting this property renders the other properties on this class useless.
useMutableTilesContainer	Should we use a mutable tiles container? The default is false.
validateDefinitions	Specifies whether we should validate the definitions XML file. The default is true.

The TilesViewResolver has no additional properties to set; it has the same set of properties as the UrlBasedViewResolver. It is a convenience subclass that automatically configures the correct view type to return. For Tiles, we need to create instances of org.springframework.web.servlet.view.tiles3.TilesView.

Configuring and Creating Templates

Tiles require one or more files to define our pages; these are called the **definitions files**. The default file loaded by the TilesConfigurer is the /WEB-INF/tiles.xml (see Listing 8-8).

Listing 8-8. Tiles Definitions

```
<?xml version="1.0" encoding="UTF-8" ?>
<!DOCTYPE tiles-definitions PUBLIC
    "-//Apache Software Foundation//DTD Tiles Configuration 3.0//EN"
    "http://tiles.apache.org/dtds/tiles-config_3_0.dtd">

<tiles-definitions>
    <!-- definition 1 -->
    <definition name="template" template="/WEB-INF/templates/template.jsp">
        <put-attribute name="header" value="/WEB-INF/templates/header.jsp"/>
        <put-attribute name="footer" value="/WEB-INF/templates/footer.jsp"/>
    </definition>
```

```
<!-- definition 2 -->
<definition name="*" extends="template">
    <put-attribute name="title" value="{1}.title" />
    <put-attribute name="body" value="/WEB-INF/views/{1}.jsp" />
</definition>

<!-- definition 3 -->
<definition name="*/*" extends="template">
    <put-attribute name="title" value="{1}.{2}/title" />
    <put-attribute name="body" value="/WEB-INF/views/{1}/{2}.jsp" />
</definition>

</tiles-definitions>
```

We have created three definitions.

1. The definition with the name template is the general layout
   configuration.

2. The other definitions extend this general layout (and could
   override the predefined attributes). Multiple definitions are
   declared by using a wildcard(*) in the definition name. The {1}
   placeholder refers to the star's value.

3. More definitions extend this general layout but are located
   in a deeper hierarchy of directories. The location hierarchy is
   represented by the /. The {1} placeholder refers to the first star's
   value, and the {2} refers to the second star's value.[5]

For Spring to select the correct definition, our definition name must match the view
(or a * wildcard as we did in our sample). Our template page (template.jsp) consists
of three tiles (header, footer, and body), and we need a property title that contains a
message key so that we can use our message source (see the Chapter 5 discussion of
internationalization) to resolve the actual title. Listing 8-9 shows template.jsp, which is
for the general layout.

---

[5]https://tiles.apache.org/framework/tutorial/advanced/wildcard.html

Listing 8-9. `template.jsp` content

```
<!DOCTYPE HTML>
<%@ taglib prefix="c" uri="http://java.sun.com/jsp/jstl/core"%>
<%@ tagib prefix="spring" uri="http://www.springframework.org/tags" %>
<%@ taglib prefix="tiles" uri="http://tiles.apache.org/tags-tiles" %>

<html>
  <head>
      <meta charset="utf-8">
      <c:set var="titleKey">
        <tiles:getAsString name="title" />
      </c:set>
      <title>
        Bookstore | <spring:message code="${titleKey}"
          text="Your Home in Books"/>
      </title>
      <link rel="stylesheet" type="text/css"
          href="<c:url value="/resources/css/style.css"/>" >
  </head>

  <body>
      <div id="wrap">
        <tiles:insertAttribute name="header"/>
        <div class="center_content">
          <div class="left_content">
              <h1>
                <spring:message code="${titleKey}"
                    text="${titleKey}"/>
              </h1>
              <tiles:insertAttribute name="body" />
          </div><!--end of left content-->
        <div class="right_content">
        <div class="right_box">
          <div class="title">
              <span class="title_icon">
```

```
        <img
            src="<c:url value="/resources/images/bullet4.gif"/>"
            alt="" title="" />
        </span>
        <spring:message code="main.title.randombooks"/>
    </div>
    <c:forEach items="${randomBooks}" var="book">
        <div class="new_prod_box">
            <c:url value="/book/${book.id}" var="bookUrl" />
            <a href="${bookUrl}">${book.title}</a>
            <div class="new_prod_img">
              <c:url
                value="/book/${book.isbn}/image" var="bookImage"/>
              <a href="${bookUrl}">
                  <img src="${bookImage}" alt="${book.title}"
                    title="${book.title}" class="thumb"
                    border="0" width="100px"/>
              </a>
            </div>
        </div>
    </c:forEach>
  </div><!--end of right box-->
  </div><!--end of right content-->
  <div class="clear"></div>
  </div><!--end of center content-->

    <tiles:insertAttribute name="footer" />
    </div>
  </body>
</html>
```

The highlighted code sets a variable based on the content of the title attribute from our tiles.xml. That way, we can specify a key on the tiles configuration and use the Spring message tag to retrieve the internationalized value. Listing 8-10 shows our index.jsp, which is used as the body for the welcome page.

Listing 8-10. `index.jsp` Used as Content

```
<p>Welcome to the Book Store</p>
```

Figure 8-4 shows the resulting page.

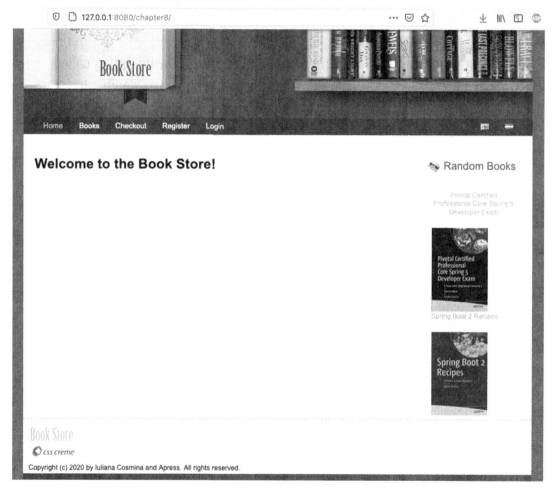

Figure 8-4. *Resulting Welcome page*

FreeMarker and Thymeleaf

Both FreeMarker[6] and Thymeleaf are templating frameworks written in Java. You can use them, among others, to create templates for HTML pages. They are text-based templating engines, and both are widely used in applications for all kinds of templating solutions.

> ❗   There was another HTML templating framework used with Spring called Velocity, but it is no longer supported. The Velocity package was deprecated in Spring 4.3 and removed completely in 5.0.1[7] in favor of FreeMarker. Velocity is quite old; the most recent version was released in 2010.

FreeMarker and Thymeleaf templates aren't compiled into Java code as JSPs are. They are interpreted at runtime by their templating engines, which is much like the XSLT processing we discussed earlier. You might think that this interpretation, instead of compilation, could lead to performance degradation of our application, but this is often not true. Both engines have extensive caching of interpreted templates, which make them fast.

Another advantage of using a templating approach over JSP is that in the latter case, you might be tempted to put Java code in your JSPs. Putting Java code in your pages, although possible, is not an approach that you should take. It generally leads to pages that are hard to maintain, debug, and modify.

When using FreeMarker and Thymeleaf templates, extra configuration is needed to set up the correct templating engine and View resolver. First, we need to configure the templating engine of our choice. Then, we need to configure view resolving for that templating engine.

Configuring the Template Engine

The Spring Framework extensively supports both FreeMarker and Thymeleaf, and there are some helper classes to make configuring the engines easier. For FreeMarker there is `org.springframework.web.servlet.view.freemarker.FreeMarkerConfigurer` (see Table 8-5).

---

[6]https://freemarker.apache.org/
[7]https://github.com/spring-projects/spring-framework/issues/18368

Table 8-5. *FreeMarkerConfigurer Properties*

Property	Purpose
configLocation	The location of the configuration file containing the FreeMarker engine settings.
defaultEncoding	Sets the encoding for the FreeMarker configuration file. The default is to use the platform encoding.
freemarkerSettings	Directly sets the properties for the templating engine. It can override properties from the configuration file or to fully configure the template engine.
freemarkerVariables	Sets the map of well-known FreeMarker objects. These objects are passed as variables to the FreeMarker configuration.
postTemplateLoaders	Specifies freemarker.cache.TemplateLoader to load templates. They are registered after the default template loaders.
preferFileSystemAccess	Should we prefer file system access for loading the FreeMarker templates? The default is true; set this to false if your templates aren't on the file system but, for instance, on the classpath in a jar file.
preTemplateLoaders	Specifies freemarker.cache.TemplateLoader to load templates. They are registered before the default template loaders.
templateLoaderPathtemplate LoaderPaths	Sets the path to the FreeMarker templates. The value for templateLoaderPaths can be a comma-separated list of paths. It can mix different resource paths (see "Resource Loading" in Chapter 2).

The most important property in this table is the one that sets the location from which to load the templates: the templateLoaderPath. It is a best practice to make them inaccessible for web clients, which can be done by putting them inside the WEB-INF directory.

ℹ️   There is also `org.springframework.beans.factory.FactoryBean` to configure the FreeMarker templating engine for bootstrapping the engine to use for non-web templates, like email.

Thymeleaf engine integrates easily with the Spring Framework via two types: `org.thymeleaf.spring5.templateresolver.SpringResourceTemplateResolver` and `org.thymeleaf.spring5.SpringTemplateEngine` (see Table 8-6). A `SpringResourceTemplateResolver` bean is needed to support Thymeleaf template resources.

Table 8-6. *Properties for the Thymeleaf* `SpringResourceTemplateResolver`

Property	Purpose
`applicationContext`	This property needs to be set to the Spring `ApplicationContext` instance so that template resources become accessible to it.
`prefix`	The prefix added to all template names to convert *template names* into *resource names*.
`suffix`	The suffix added to all template names to convert *template names* into *resource names*.
`forceSuffix`	Should the suffix be enforced on a template? If set to `true`, regardless of the template name's extension, the configured suffix is applied. The default is `false`.
`templateMode`	The template mode to be applied to the templates resolved by the Thymeleaf resolver. The default is HTML.
`forceTemplateMode`	Should the template mode be enforced on a template resource? If set to `true`, the resolution is not on the template resource name but the configured `suffix`. The default is `false`.
`characterEncoding`	The character encoding for reading the resource.
`cacheable`	Should the templates resolved by the Thymeleaf resolver be cached? The default is `true`, but during development, we recommend that you set this property to `false`.
`order`	The order in which this view resolver is called in the chain. The higher the number, the lower the order in the chain. The default is 1.

The most important properties in the previous table are the ones that define the location where the template resources are (`suffix` and `prefix`), and the `applicationContext` that must have access to them. It is a best practice to make them inaccessible for web clients, which can be done by putting them inside the `WEB-INF` directory.

ⓘ   There is another implementation that is specific to Spring provided by the `org.thymeleaf.templateresolver.ServletContextTemplateResolver` class that implements `ServletContextAware`, and is dependent of the servlet context. This implementation resolves templates using the Servlet Resource Resolution mechanism, while the `SpringResourceTemplateResolver` resolves templates using Spring's Resource Resolution mechanism. The classes are mostly interchangeable, but `SpringResourceTemplateResolver` is recommended because it automatically integrates with Spring's resource resolution infrastructure.

In addition to setting up the different engines, we also need to configure a view resolver to resolve correct view implementations. Spring ships with `org.springframework.web.servlet.view.freemarker.FreemarkerViewResolver`. The Thymeleaf framework provides `org.thymeleaf.spring5.view.ThymeleafViewResolver` for the same purpose. It isn't required to use these specialized view resolvers; an extensively configured `InternalResourceViewResolver` would also do. However, using these specialized view resolvers makes our life easier. Listing 8-11 shows a FreeMarker configurations sample.

Listing 8-11. FreeMarker Configuration

```
package com.apress.prospringmvc.bookstore.web.config;

// Other imports omitted
import org.springframework.web.servlet.view.freemarker.
FreeMarkerConfigurer;
import org.springframework.web.servlet.view.freemarker.
FreeMarkerViewResolver;
```

```java
@Configuration
public class ViewConfiguration {

    @Bean
    public FreeMarkerConfigurer freeMarkerConfigurer() {
        FreeMarkerConfigurer freeMarkerConfigurer;
        freeMarkerConfigurer = new FreeMarkerConfigurer();
        freeMarkerConfigurer.setTemplateLoaderPath("WEB-INF/freemarker");
        return freeMarkerConfigurer;
    }

    @Bean
    public ViewResolver freeMarkerViewResolver() {
        FreeMarkerViewResolver viewResolver = new FreeMarkerViewResolver();
        viewResolver.setSuffix(".ftl");
        return viewResolver;
    }
}
```

When a controller now returns index as the view name, for a FreeMarker template, it becomes WEB-INF/freemarker/index.ftl. The templateLoaderPath is prefixed to the view name. The view resolver also allows setting an additional prefix (inherited from the AbstractTemplateViewResolver). Table 8-7 describes the different properties for the view resolver.

Table 8-7. *Additional Properties for the FreeMarker View Resolver*

Property	Purpose
allowRequestOverride	Should request attributes override model attributes when we merge the model? When set to true, request attributes can override model attributes when stored under the same name. The default is false, which leads to an exception when an attribute with the same name is encountered.
allowSessionOverride	Should session attributes override model attributes when we merge the model? When set to true, session attributes can override model attributes when stored under the same name. The default is false, which leads to an exception when an attribute with the same name is encountered.
exposeRequestAttributes	Should all request attributes be put in the model? The default is false.
exposeSessionAttributes	Should all session attributes be put in the model? The default is false.
exposeSpringMacroHelpers	Should the macros (see Table 8-8) be exposed so that they are available for rendering? The default is true.

Listing 8-12 shows a Thymeleaf configuration sample.

Listing 8-12. Thymeleaf Configuration

```
package com.apress.prospringmvc.bookstore.web.config;

// Other imports omitted
import org.thymeleaf.spring5.SpringTemplateEngine;
import org.thymeleaf.spring5.templateresolver.
SpringResourceTemplateResolver;
import org.thymeleaf.spring5.view.ThymeleafViewResolver;

@Configuration
public class ViewConfiguration implements ApplicationContextAware {

    private ApplicationContext applicationContext;
```

```java
@Override
public void setApplicationContext(ApplicationContext
applicationContext) {
    this.applicationContext = applicationContext;
}

@Bean
public SpringResourceTemplateResolver templateResolver() {
    var resolver = new SpringResourceTemplateResolver();
    resolver.setApplicationContext(applicationContext);
    resolver.setPrefix("/WEB-INF/thymeleaf/");
    resolver.setSuffix(".html");
    //HTML is the default value, added here for clarity
    resolver.setTemplateMode(TemplateMode.HTML);
    resolver.setCharacterEncoding("UTF-8");
    return resolver;

}

@Bean
@Description("Thymeleaf Template Engine")
public SpringTemplateEngine templateEngine() {
    var templateEngine = new SpringTemplateEngine();
    templateEngine.setTemplateResolver(templateResolver());
    return templateEngine;
}

@Bean
@Description("Thymeleaf View Resolver")
public ThymeleafViewResolver viewResolver() {
    var viewResolver = new ThymeleafViewResolver();
    viewResolver.setTemplateEngine(templateEngine());
    return viewResolver;
}
}
```

When a controller now returns index as the view name, for a Thymeleaf template, it becomes WEB-INF/AbstractTemplateViewResolver/index.html. The prefix value is added before the view name, and the suffix value right after.

The Templating Language

Now that we have configured our environment, we also need to write a template that shows the page. FreeMarker and Thymeleaf are somewhat similar. Listings 8-13 and 8-14 show the book search page written for FreeMarker and Thymeleaf, respectively.

Listing 8-13. books/search.ftl FreeMarker Template.

```
<#ftl>
<#import "/spring.ftl" as spring />
<!DOCTYPE HTML>
<html>
 <head>
    <title>Booksearch</title>
 </head>
 <body>
    <h1><@spring.message code="book.title" /></h1>
    <p>
     <form method="POST">
     <fieldset>
        <legend><@spring.message code="book.searchcriteria" /></legend>
        <table>
         <tr>
            <td><@spring.message code="book.title" /></td>
            <td><@spring.formInput"searchCriteria.title" /></td>
         </tr>
         <tr>
         <td><@spring.message code="book.category" /></td>
         <td><@spring.formSingleSelect
             "searchCriteria.category", categories, "" /></td>
         </tr>
        </table>
     </fieldset>
```

```
    <button id="search"><@spring.message code="book.search" /></button>
    </form>
<!-- Javascript functions ommitted -->
    <#if bookList?has_content>
    <table>
        <tr>
         <th><@spring.message code="book.title"/></th>
         <th><@spring.message
                    code="book.description"/></th>
         <th><@spring.message code="book.price" /></th>
        </tr>
        <#list bookList as book>
        <tr>
         <td>${book.title}</td>
         <td>${book.description}</td>
         <td>${book.price}</td>
         <td><a
           href="<@spring.url "/cart/add/${book.id}"/>">
               <@spring.message code="book.addtocart"/></a></td>
        </tr>
        </#list>
    </table>
    </#if>
    </p>
 </body>
</html>
```

Listing 8-14. books/search.html Thymeleaf Template

```
<html xmlns:th="http://www.thymeleaf.org">

  <head th:replace="~{template/layout :: head('Search books')}"></head>
  <body>
    <div id="header" th:replace="~{template/layout :: header}" ></div>
    <h1 id="pagetitle" th:text="#{book.searchcriteria}">SEARCH TITLE</h1>
    <form action="#" th:action="@{/book/search}" th:object="${bookSearch
    Criteria}" method="GET" id="bookSearchForm">
```

```html
<fieldset>
  <legend th:text="#{book.searchcriteria}">SEARCH CRITERIA</legend>
    <table>
      <tr>
        <td><label for="title" th:text="#{book.title}">TITLE
        </label></td>
        <td><input type="text" th:field="*{title}"/></td>
      </tr>
      <tr>
        <td><label for="category" th:text="#{book.
        category}">CATEGORY</label></td>
        <td>
          <select th:field="*{category}">
            <option th:each="c : ${categories}"
            th:value="${c.id}" th:text="${c.name}"
            th:selected="${i==1}">
            </option>
          </select>
        </td>
      </tr>
    </table>
</fieldset>
<button id="search" th:text="#{button.search}">SEARCH</button>
</form>
<!-- Javascript functions ommitted -->
<table id="bookSearchResults" th:if="${bookList ne null and not #lists.
isEmpty(bookList)}">
  <thead>
  <tr>
    <th th:text="#{book.title}">TITLE</th>
    <th th:text="#{book.description}">DESCRIPTION</th>
    <th th:text="#{book.price}">PRICE</th>
    <th></th>
  </tr>
  </thead>
```

313

```
<tbody>
<th:block th:each="book : ${bookList}">
    <tr>
        <td><a th:href="@{/book/detail/} + ${book.id}"
        th:text="${book.title}">TITLE</a></td>
        <td th:text="${book.description}">DESC</td>
        <td th:text="${book.price}">PRICE</td>
        <td><a th:href="@{/cart/add/} + ${book.id}"
        th:text="${book.addtocart}">CART</a></td>
    </tr>
</th:block>
</tbody>
</table>
</body>
</html>
```

The FreeMarker templates are similar to Apache Tiles templates. The FreeMarker (see Listing 8-13) template also has tag libraries available (in the listings bound to Spring). Both libraries offer the same support as the Spring Form Tag library for JSP.

Thymeleaf is different from FreeMarker. Thymeleaf is a modern server-side Java Template engine for both web and standalone environments. When Spring started to move away from Apache Tiles, it moved toward Thymeleaf because its creator designed this templating framework for Spring.

Thymeleaf supports multiple kinds of templates: HTML, XML, JavaScript, CSS, and even plain text, but the easiest to design and use are the HTML templates. Thymeleaf templates are elegant and natural to the development flow and since they are written in HTML can be tested during the design phase using a browser. The strongest point of Thymeleaf is that it easily integrates with Spring controllers, localization, and validation.

The previous template contains a few Thymeleaf tags that naturally fit into the HTML content. They are prefixed with th: and those are interpreted by the Thymeleaf Template engine to generate the corresponding HTML page.

Table 8-8 provides an overview of the different FreeMarker tags. The Thymeleaf equivalents constructs are just enriched HTML tags, so a comparison is not necessary.

Table 8-8. *Tage Available for FreeMarker and Thymeleaf Equivalent HTML Constructs*

Macro	FreeMarker
message (output a string from a resource bundle based on the code parameter)	<@spring.message code/>
messageText (output a string from a resource bundle based on the code parameter, falling back to the value of the default parameter)	<@spring.messageText code, text/>
url (prefix a relative URL with the application's context root)	<@spring.url relativeUrl/>
formInput (standard input field for gathering user input)	<@spring.formInput path, attributes, fieldType/>
formHiddenInput * (hidden input field for submitting non-user input, e.g. CSRF tokens)	<@spring.formHiddenInput path, attributes/>
formPasswordInput * (standard input field for gathering passwords)	<@spring.formPasswordInput path, attributes/>
formTextarea (large text field for gathering long, freeform text input)	<@spring.formTextarea path, attributes/>
formSingleSelect (drop-down box of options allowing a single required value to be selected)	<@spring.formSingleSelect path, options, attributes/>
formMultiSelect (a list box of options allowing the user to select 0 or more values)	<@spring.formMultiSelect path, options, attributes/>
formRadioButtons (a set of radio buttons allowing a single selection to be made from the available choices)	<@spring.formRadioButtons path, options separator, attributes/>
formCheckboxes (a set of checkboxes allowing 0 or more values to be selected)	<@spring.formCheckboxes path, options, separator, attributes/>
formCheckbox (a single checkbox)	<@spring.formCheckbox path, attributes/>
showErrors	<@spring.showErrors separator, classOrStyle/>

The parameters to any of the macros listed have consistent meanings.

- **path**: The name of the field to bind to (that is, `searchCriteria.title`).

- **options**: A map containing all the available values that can be selected from in the input field. The map's keys represent the values that are POSTed back from the form and bound to the command object. The values belonging to the key are used as the labels to show to the user. Usually, such a map is supplied as reference data by the controller. Any Map implementation can be used, depending on the required behavior.

- **separator**: Where multiple options are available as discrete elements (radio buttons or checkboxes), the sequence of characters separate each one in the list (for example, `<br/>`).

- **attributes**: An additional string of arbitrary tags or text to be included within the HTML tag itself. This string is echoed literally by the macro. For example, in a textarea field you may supply attributes as `rows="5" cols="60"` or you could pass style information such as `style="border:1px solid silver"`.

- **classOrStyle**: For the showErrors macro, the name of the CSS class that the span tag wrapping each error uses. If no information is supplied (or the value is empty), the errors are wrapped in `<b></b>` tags.

The two macros marked (*) in the table exist for FreeMarker; however, they are not required because you can use the normal `formInput` macro specifying hidden or password as the value for the `fieldType` parameter.

Using FreeMarker, you can specify which library to use. In FreeMarker, we need to specify the library using the import directive (see Listing 8-13).

Thymeleaf does not use any special tag library that needs to be referred to in a template. The Thymeleaf template engine looks for `th:` constructs and dynamically resolves them. The most important Thymeleaf constructs are used for the following purposes.

- **th:fragment** declares an HTML element that is part of a layout and can be inherited or overridden by a child page. A fragment can receive a parameter. For example, `<head th:fragment="head(title)"/>`.

- **th:replace** declares an HTML element that replaces an element inherited from a layout. If the fragment is parametrized, an argument is required. For example, `<head th:replace="~{template/layout :: head('Search')}"/>`.

- **th:text** (for HTML elements with text values) tells the Thymeleaf engine to replace the value of this construct with a dynamically obtained value. When writing HTML templates, the default value for the HTML element is usually written in uppercase letters. This helps when opening the template in the browser because a proper view is depicted. It also helps with spotting engine configuration issues when the default text is depicted instead of the dynamically resolved one. The value in the `th:text` construct is either a value of a model attribute `<title th:text="${title}"> TITLE </title>` or an internationalized text `<title th:text="#{book.title}"> TITLE </title>`.

- **th:href** sets the `href` attribute with a contextual URL for `<a/>` and `<link />` HTML elements. The element `<link rel="stylesheet" type="text/css" th:href="@{/resources/css/style.css}" >` has the `href` attribute populated with a URL that points to the `style.css` file within the context of the application.

- **th:if** decides if an HTML element or text should be displayed on the page. For example, we can use a construction like this `<li th:if="${session.account ne null}"><a th:href="@{/logout}" th:text="#{nav.logout}">LOGOUT</a></li>` to condition the presence of the Logout option on the presence of an account instance in the user session.

Thymeleaf uses Spring Expression Language for expression evaluation, and there is an extension of this library for Spring Security support. Such a strong integration with the Spring Framework makes it clear why this templating framework is perfect for Spring web applications.

PDF

Spring can be integrated with either iText[8] or OpenPDF[9] to support rendering PDF Views. The Spring team recommends OpenPDF since it is actively maintained and fixes an important vulnerability for untrusted PDF content.

To enable rendering PDF views this, we need to write our own view implementation, and for that, we need to extend `org.springframework.web.servlet.view.document.AbstractPdfView`. When we extend this class, we must implement the `buildPdfDocument` method.

We create a PDF that gives an overview of one of our orders on our account page. Listing 8-15 shows the view implementation.

Listing 8-15. View Implementation to Create a PDF

```
package com.apress.prospringmvc.bookstore.web.view;

// Other imports omitted
import org.springframework.web.servlet.view.document.AbstractPdfView;
import com.lowagie.text.Document;
import com.lowagie.text.Paragraph;
import com.lowagie.text.Table;
import com.lowagie.text.pdf.PdfWriter;

public class OrderPdfView extends AbstractPdfView {

    @Override
    protected void buildPdfDocument(Map<String, Object> model,
        Document document,
        PdfWriter writer,
        HttpServletRequest request,
        HttpServletResponse response)
    throws Exception {
        Order order = (Order) model.get("order");
        document.addTitle("Order :" + order.getId());
        document.add(new Paragraph("Order date: " + order.getOrderDate()));
```

---

[8]https://itextpdf.com/
[9]https://github.com/LibrePDF/OpenPDF

```
document.add(new Paragraph("Delivery date: " + order.
getDeliveryDate()));
Table orderDetails = new Table(4);
orderDetails.addCell("Title");
orderDetails.addCell("Price");
orderDetails.addCell("#");
orderDetails.addCell("Total");

for (OrderDetail detail : order.getOrderDetails()) {
    orderDetails.addCell(detail.getBook().getTitle());
    orderDetails.addCell(detail.getBook().getPrice().toString());
    orderDetails.addCell(String.valueOf(detail.getQuantity()));
    orderDetails.addCell(detail.getPrice().toString());
}
document.add(orderDetails);
    }
}
```

Next, let's add `org.springframework.web.servlet.view.`
`ContentNegotiatingViewResolver` to our view configuration. We do this to have our
order page rendered in HTML or PDF, and we don't want to change `com.apress.`
`prospringmvc.bookstore.web.controller.OrderController` because it is already
doing what we want—adding the selected order to the model. Listing 8-16 shows the
changed `com.apress.prospringmvc.bookstore.web.config.ViewConfiguration`. This
is also where we start using our custom view resolver.

Listing 8-16. ViewConfiguration with ContentNegotiatingViewResolver

```
package com.apress.prospringmvc.bookstore.web.config;

// Other imports omitted

import org.springframework.web.servlet.view.ContentNegotiatingViewResolver;
import org.springframework.web.servlet.view.document.AbstractPdfView;
import com.apress.prospringmvc.bookstore.web.view.OrderPdfView;
import com.apress.prospringmvc.bookstore.web.view.
SimpleConfigurableViewResolver;
```

```java
@Configuration
public class ViewConfiguration {

    @Bean
    public ContentNegotiatingViewResolver contentNegotiatingViewResolver()
    {
        ContentNegotiatingViewResolver viewResolver;
        viewResolver = new ContentNegotiatingViewResolver();
        List<ViewResolver> viewResolvers = new ArrayList<ViewResolver>();
        viewResolvers.add(pdfViewResolver());
        viewResolver.setViewResolvers(viewResolvers);
        return viewResolver;
    }

    @Bean
    public ViewResolver pdfViewResolver() {
        SimpleConfigurableViewResolver viewResolver;
        viewResolver = new SimpleConfigurableViewResolver();
        Map<String, AbstractPdfView> views;
        views = new HashMap<String, AbstractPdfView>();
        views.put("order", new OrderPdfView());
        viewResolver.setViews(views);
        return viewResolver;
    }

// Other methods omitted
}
```

The changed configuration contains our view resolver, and we use it to resolve `com.apress.prospringmvc.bookstore.web.view.OrderPdfView`. This configuration also allows us to resolve an order view for an Excel document (see the "Excel" section).

After these changes, we need to redeploy our application. If we log in and navigate to our account page, we can now click the PDF link and get a PDF instead of the HTML version. Figure 8-5 shows the result of clicking the PDF link.

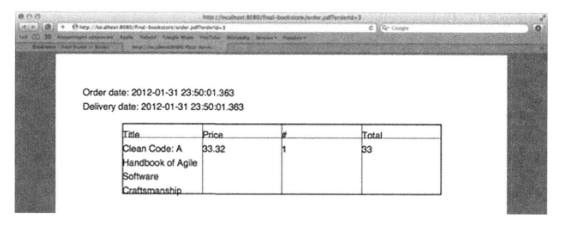

Figure 8-5. *Generated PDF*

Although this approach is very flexible, the drawback is that we need to code the construction of PDFs for each PDF we want. If we have some complex PDF or need to apply a certain style, this is cumbersome and hard to maintain. It might be worthwhile to look at solutions like JasperReports (see the "JasperReports" section) in such cases.

Excel

Spring has two ways of rendering an Excel document. The first is by using the JExcel library,[10] and the other is using the Apache POI library.[11] Both approaches need us to implement a view (as with a PDF); to do that, we extend either `org.springframework.web.servlet.view.document.AbstractXlsView` or `org.springframework.web.servlet.view.document.AbstractXlsxView`. They are for XLS and XLSX formats, respectively. Both implementations hide the setup and allow an XLS template to be loaded and processed; we need to add the view-specific rendering. We need to implement the buildExcelDocument method for that. Listing 8-17 shows a `View` implementation example of an order as an Excel document that uses Apache POI.

---

[10]`http://jexcelapi.sourceforge.net`
[11]`https://poi.apache.org/`

Listing 8-17. OrderExcelView

```java
package com.apress.prospringmvc.bookstore.web.view;

// Other imports omitted

import org.apache.poi.ss.usermodel.Row;
import org.apache.poi.ss.usermodel.Sheet;
import org.springframework.web.servlet.view.document.AbstractXlsView;

public class OrderExcelView extends AbstractXlsView {

    @Override
    protected void buildExcelDocument(Map<String, Object> model,
        WritableWorkbook workbook,
        HttpServletRequest request,
        HttpServletResponse response)
    throws Exception {
        response.setHeader("Content-Disposition",
            "attachment; filename=\"order.xls\"");
        Order order = (Order) model.get("order");
        Sheet sheet = workbook.createSheet();
        sheet.createRow(1).createCell(0)
            .setCellValue("Order: " + order.getId());
        sheet.createRow(2).createCell(0)
            .setCellValue("Order Date: " + order.getOrderDate());
        sheet.createRow(3).createCell(0)
            .setCellValue("Delivery Date: " + order.getDeliveryDate());
        sheet.createRow(4).createCell(0)
            .setCellValue("Order: " + order.getId());

        Row header = sheet.createRow(5);
        header.createCell(0).setCellValue("Quantity");
        header.createCell(1).setCellValue("Title");
        header.createCell(2).setCellValue("Price");
```

```
    int row = 5;
    for (OrderDetail detail : order.getOrderDetails()) {
        row++;
        Row detailRow = sheet.createRow(row);
        detailRow.createCell(0).setCellValue(detail.getQuantity());
        detailRow.createCell(1)
                .setCellValue(detail.getBook().getTitle());
        detailRow.createCell(2).setCellValue(
                detail.getPrice().doubleValue() * detail.getQuantity());
    }

    row++;
    Row footer = sheet.createRow(row);
    footer.createCell(0).setCellValue("Total");
    footer.createCell(1).setCellValue(
            order.getTotalOrderPrice().doubleValue());
    }
}
```

Next to the view, we need to add a view resolver. In our sample application, we add this (just like the PDF view) to our ViewConfiguration class. We add another instance of our custom implementation (see Listing 8-18) and let the ContentNegotiatingViewResolver decide what to do.

Listing 8-18. ViewConfiguration with OrderExcelView

```
package com.apress.prospringmvc.bookstore.web.config;

//Other imports omitted
import org.springframework.web.servlet.view.document.AbstractJExcelView;
import org.springframework.web.servlet.view.document.AbstractPdfView;
import com.apress.prospringmvc.bookstore.web.view.OrderExcelView;

@Configuration

public class ViewConfiguration {
```

```java
@Bean
public ContentNegotiatingViewResolver contentNegotiatingViewResolver() {
    ContentNegotiatingViewResolver viewResolver;
    viewResolver = new ContentNegotiatingViewResolver();
    List<ViewResolver> viewResolvers = new ArrayList<ViewResolver>();
    viewResolvers.add(pdfViewResolver());
    viewResolvers.add(xlsViewResolver());
    viewResolver.setViewResolvers(viewResolvers);
    return viewResolver;
}

@Bean
public ViewResolver xlsViewResolver() {
    SimpleConfigurableViewResolver viewResolver;
    viewResolver = new SimpleConfigurableViewResolver();
    Map<String, AbstractJExcelView> views;
    views = new HashMap<String, AbstractJExcelView>();
    views.put("order", new OrderExcelView());
    viewResolver.setViews(views);
    return viewResolver;
}
// Other methods omitted
}
```

But, wait, isn't our application going to break because we have multiple view implementations resolving to the order view name? The special view resolver ContentNegotiatingViewResolver can help us here. It determines which of the resolved views best matches the content-type requested using the Accept header. Without changing our controller and simply adding some configuration (and view implementations), we can differentiate which view is being served.

To test, click the XLS link, and an Excel document is downloaded for you to view.

XML and JSON

Spring MVC has another way of serving XML or JSON to our clients. We can use the ContentNegotiatingViewResolver to our advantage. Spring has two special view implementations to convert objects to XML or JSON, respectively, org.springframework.web.servlet.view.xml.MarshallingView and org. springframework.web.servlet.view.json.MappingJackson2JsonView. The XML-based view uses the Spring XML support to marshal our model to XML. The JSON view uses the Jackson library.[12] We can easily configure our view resolver to expose XML and/ or JSON to our clients. We simply can add a default view for XML and JSON (we can also add additional view resolvers, as we did for the PDF and Excel documents). Listing 8-19 is the modified configuration (see the highlighted parts).

Listing 8-19. ViewConfiguration for XML and JSON

```
package com.apress.prospringmvc.bookstore.web.config;

// Other imports omitted
import org.springframework.oxm.Marshaller;
import org.springframework.oxm.xstream.XStreamMarshaller;
import org.springframework.web.servlet.view.json.MappingJackson2JsonView;
import org.springframework.web.servlet.view.xml.MarshallingView;
import com.apress.prospringmvc.bookstore.web.view.OrderExcelView;
import com.apress.prospringmvc.bookstore.web.view.OrderPdfView;

@Configuration
public class ViewConfiguration {

    @Bean
    public ContentNegotiatingViewResolver contentNegotiatingViewResolver() {
    ContentNegotiatingViewResolver viewResolver;
    viewResolver = new ContentNegotiatingViewResolver();
    List<ViewResolver> viewResolvers = new ArrayList<ViewResolver>();
        viewResolvers.add(pdfViewResolver());
        viewResolvers.add(xlsViewResolver());
```

---

[12]https://github.com/FasterXML/jackson

```java
        viewResolver.setViewResolvers(viewResolvers);
        List<View> defaultViews = new ArrayList<View>();
        defaultViews.add(jsonOrderView());
        defaultViews.add(xmlOrderView());
        viewResolver.setDefaultViews(defaultViews);
        return viewResolver;
    }

    @Bean
    public MappingJackson2JsonView jsonOrderView() {
        MappingJackson2JsonView jsonView = new MappingJackson2JsonView();
        jsonView.setModelKey("order");
        return jsonView;
    }

    @Bean

    public MarshallingView xmlOrderView() {
        MarshallingView xmlView = new MarshallingView(marshaller());
        xmlView.setModelKey("order");
        return xmlView;
    }

    @Bean
    public Marshaller marshaller() {
        return new XStreamMarshaller();
    }

// Other methods omitted, see previous listings
}
```

For XML to work, we also need to configure an `org.springframework.oxm.`
`Marshaller` implementation. We choose here to use the XStream[13] library because
is quick and easy to use. To use another solution, simply configure the appropriate
marshaller. More information on marshaling and XML can be found in the *Spring
Reference Guide*. The `modelKey` property is set to the object to be marshaled. If not
specified, the model map is searched for a supported value type.

---

[13]https://x-stream.github.io/

When using this type of view with an ORM implementation (like in our sample), you can experience lazy loading or loading half the database due to collections being initialized.

If we now change the URL in the browser to end in either .json or .xml, we get a JSON or XML representation of our order (see Figure 8-6 is the JSON sample). We now have five different ways of viewing our order (HTML, PDF, Excel, JSON, and XML) without touching our controller and by simply changing our configuration.

Figure 8-6. *JSON representation of our order*

Summary

This chapter covered the view part of Spring MVC. We looked at view resolving by covering several general-purpose ViewResolver implementations. We also covered several view technologies supported by Spring MVC and explained how to configure Spring to use them. We started with JSPs, and we briefly touched on JSF and how you can integrate Spring into a JSF application. Next, you saw several templating solutions; specifically, Tiles, Velocity, and FreeMarker.

After the web-based views, we looked at different view technologies like how to create PDF and Excel without changing our controllers but by simply adding ContentNegotiatingViewResolver and an appropriate View implementation.

The previous chapter covered JSON, and this chapter covered another way to expose (part) of our model as JSON or XML. Finally, we looked at rendering PDF and Excel views.

One important thing to take away from this chapter is the separation of controller logic and view logic (demonstrated by the different representations of our order). This shows the power of applying separation of concerns and the flexibility it gives one.

You will probably never use all the technologies in a single application. You will likely use only two or three different technologies (for our pages and probably creating a PDF or Excel file). But it is nice to have the flexibility to change or simply add a new view layer to our application.

CHAPTER 9

Introduction to Spring WebFlux

In previous chapters, typical Java web applications were built and run on an instance of Apache Tomcat server that was external or embedded in the application. Whatever the case, the Spring `DispatcherServlet` was responsible for directing incoming HTTP requests to all the handlers declared in the application. But, can an application like the ones we developed so far be used in a real production environment? How many HTTP requests can `DispatcherServlet` handle at the same time? Can that number be increased? Will they be handled within an acceptable time frame? These questions and many others need to be answered before sharing a web application with the world.

Production web applications are expected to handle a large number of users and to handle huge amounts of data in a manner that is resilient in the face of more information coming in, errors within the systems, or mere slowdowns in the system. Think about Twitter, Facebook, or YouTube and how much content is being uploaded or downloaded at any time of the day. When opening your Facebook page, you expect it to be responsive even if there are millions of other users logged in and doing the same things as you do: reading messages, or posting messages, videos, or pictures, or playing games. This amounts to an insane number of simultaneous requests being processed. These requests might require data from a database or file, or data from other services, which introduce the possibility of blocking I/O operations.

If any of these applications are developed using Spring, `DispatcherServlet` is the entry point for all requests. `DispatcherServlet` does not really have a say in the number of requests it can handle. The servlet container defines that; in our case, is the Apache Tomcat server.

© Marten Deinum and Iuliana Cosmina 2021
M. Deinum and I. Cosmina, *Pro Spring MVC with WebFlux*, https://doi.org/10.1007/978-1-4842-5666-4_9

These next few chapters focus on using Spring WebFlux to build reactive web applications run on non-blocking servers like Netty, Undertow, and Servlet 3.1+ containers. To understand why reactive applications are most suitable for handling large amounts of users and data, it is necessary to explain how HTTP requests have been handled since the beginning of the Internet.

HTTP Request Handling

HTTP is the acronym for Hypertext Transfer Protocol and loads web pages using hypertext links. A typical flow over HTTP involves a client machine making a **request** to a server, which then sends a **response** message. In the initial version of HTTP (1.0) a connection is needed for each request/response pair. You can see why this is inefficient, since establishing a new connection includes the TCP handshake process to introduce the communication parties to each other.[1]

In HTTP 1.1 persistent HTTP connections were introduced.[2] This means a connection is kept alive and reused for multiple HTTP requests, thus reducing the communication lag between two parties.

What does this mean for a servlet container such as Apache Tomcat? Apache Tomcat is a popular choice for building and maintaining dynamic websites and applications based on the Java software platform. The Java Servlet API is what enables a web server to handle dynamic Java-based web content using the HTTP protocol. Older versions of Tomcat had an HTTP connector that was blocking and followed a **thread-per-connection** model. This means it assigns a Java thread for each HTTP connection being handled. Thus, the number of users that can be connected to the application at the same time is limited by the number of threads supported by the application server. The threads are not created when an HTTP connection is established and destroyed after the HTTP connection is closed, because that is inefficient. Instead, the server manages a thread pool that provides threads for HTTP connections. When an HTTP connection is established, a thread from the pool is assigned to it. The thread does its job of receiving requests and providing responses and when the HTTP connection is closed, the thread is recycled back into the pool and is ready to be assigned to another request.

---

[1]https://en.wikipedia.org/wiki/TCP_congestion_control#Slow_start
[2]https://www.w3.org/Protocols/rfc2616/rfc2616-sec8.html#sec8.1

The problem with this approach is that a thread sits idle when is not being used, as long as an HTTP connection is open. If one or more users take their time between requests, or forget to close the connection, eventually, the server runs out of threads and stops accepting new connections. One solution is to increase the number of threads in the pool; but, the size of the thread pool is limited by the characteristics (memory, CPU, etc.) of the VM/computer the server is installed on. The obvious solution is to get a more powerful server. In software development this is called **vertical scaling** and it works up to a point, being limited by the existent hardware and its cost. The smart solution is to have the application installed on more than one server. This is easily done nowadays by deploying your application to a cloud platform like AWS[3] or GCP[4] and set up a cloud configuration that includes an automated load balancer that spans up VMs as necessary. This method is called **horizontal scaling** and it works, but it can get very expensive too, especially when your application gets popular.

The newer versions of Tomcat (after Java 4), and other popular web servers, all use the **thread-per-request** model which means a persistent HTTP connection doesn't require that a thread be constantly assigned to it. The reason why this was not possible before Java 4 is because there was no non-blocking IO API in the JDK. Threads can be assigned to HTTP connections only when requests are being processed. If the connection is idle, the thread can be recycled, and the connection is placed in a centralized NIO[5] select set to detect new requests without consuming a separate thread. This means that a lower number of threads is required to handle the same number of users, and since threads use considerably less resources, scaling your application requires less financial investment.

There are a few things to consider. For a big number of users connecting at the same time, resource consumption is still high. For short-duration requests it has the same behavior and performance as the thread-per-connection model. When there are long pauses during processing of each request, the threads still stay idle. The only advantage is that the thread-per-request mode scales slightly better than thread-per-connection.

Applications handling HTTP Requests concurrently have also to be designed to share resources, and for resources that cannot be shared synchronized access has to be implemented, which might lead to blocking. How do we avoid blocking in Java applications? By using asynchronous processing. Servlet API 3.0 introduced Async servlet-

---

[3]https://aws.amazon.com
[4]https://cloud.google.com
[5]http://tutorials.jenkov.com/java-nio/nio-vs-io.html

handling support, so slow tasks (e.g., waiting for some resource to become available) can be handled in a separate thread without blocking the server-managed thread pool, and when finished, the container is notified to assign a new container-managed thread to send the result back to the client.

These are typical solutions to typical web problems, but they still require a response to be fully constructed before being sent to the client. Take a search engine web application, for example. How would you implement the solution to respond to a search query? Considering the amount of content available on the Internet, putting your client on hold until you scan all your indexed content would take forever, and the size of the response so big it would take forever to transfer. Sending a complete response to your client is not an option. For a situation such as this a streaming approach is more suitable. You scan a few indexed resources, then you send a partial response to the client, then scan some more, send another piece, and so on until nothing else is found. Another issue that might come up is that if you send your partial results, but you are sending them to fast and the client cannot process them, you risk blocking the client. So, your solution needs to provide a data flow that allows the client to regulate the flow.

If the software example is too puzzling for you, imagine the following scenario. You have a friend named Jim. You also have a bucket of differently colored balls. Jim tells you to give him all the red balls. You have two ways of doing this.

- You pick all the red balls, put them in another bucket, and hand the bucket to Jim. This is the typical **request-complete response model**. It is an asynchronous model, if selecting the red balls takes too long, Jim does other things while you do the sorting, and when you are done, you notify him that his bucket of red balls is ready. It is asynchronous because Jim is not blocked by you sorting the balls; he does other things until they are ready.

- You get the red balls one by one from your bucket and throw them at Jim. This is your data flow, or a ball flow in this case. If you are faster at finding them and throwing them than Jim is at catching them, you have a blockage. Jim tells you to slow down; he is regulating the flow of balls.

This translates to software as a **reactive application**.

Building Reactive Applications

Reactive applications are the solution when it comes to handling large amounts of data. Reactive applications are applications designed with resilience, responsiveness, and scalability as a priority. The Reactive Manifesto[6] describes the characteristics of reactive applications. The Reactive Streams API specification[7] provides a minimum set of interfaces that application components should implement, so that applications can be considered reactive. Thus, the Reactive Streams API is an interoperability specification that ensures that reactive components integrate flawlessly and keep the operations non-blocking and asynchronous.

There are four key terms that describe reactive applications.

- **Responsive**: Characterized by fast and consistent response times.

- **Resilient**: Remains responsive during failures and able to recover.

- **Elastic**: Remains responsive during high loads.

- **Message-driven**: Communication is asynchronous, and backpressure is applied to prevent producers of messages from overwhelming the consumers.

Reactive applications are supposed to be more flexible, loosely coupled, and scalable, but at the same time easier to develop, more malleable to change and more tolerant of failure. Building reactive applications requires following the principles of the reactive programming paradigm.

Introduction to Reactive Programming

Reactive programming is programming with asynchronous data streams. Reactive Streams is an initiative to provide a standard for asynchronous stream processing with non-blocking back pressure. They are extremely useful for solving problems that require complex coordination across thread boundaries. The operators allow you to gather your data on to the desired threads and ensures thread-safe operations without requiring, in most cases, excessive uses of `synchronized` and volatile `constructs`.

---

[6]https://www.reactivemanifesto.org/
[7]https://www.reactive-streams.org/

Java took a step toward reactive programming after introducing the Streams API in version 8, but Reactive Streams was not available until version 9. Reactive programming became popular in a world that needed to efficiently handle huge quantities of data. While Oracle was working on making Reactive Streams and modules happen within the JDK, projects like RxJava,[8] Akka,[9] and Project Reactor[10] appeared to provide alternatives for the missing implementation of the Reactive Stream API in the Java world.

Unable to wait for JDK 9, which was released with a six months delay, the Pivotal open source team,[11] the same one that created Spring, build the Spring WebFlux[12] using Project Reactor, their own reactive library. Spring WebFlux is a framework designed for building reactive, non-blocking, server-based web applications that require a small number of threads to solve a big number of requests.

Before fully diving into Spring WebFlux, you need however to scratch the surface on programming with Reactive Streams looks like in Java.

Programming with Streams

The first step to switch from imperative to reactive programming is to switch your thinking from variables to streams.

Imagine that you need to calculate the sum of two numbers. In imperative programming, you declare the two variables and then the statement to be executed to add them. The program executes the statement one after the other. And if the two variables are modified after the sum was calculated, the variable that holds the sum doesn't get modified.

When using streams, you have the two values to be added provided to you as a stream. You declare the operation to be performed on the values emitted by the - in this case the adding operation. Any extra value emitted by the stream affects the result.

A stream is a succession of events ordered in time. Those events can be one of the following:

---

[8]https://github.com/ReactiveX/RxJava

[9]https://doc.akka.io/docs/akka/current/stream/reactive-streams-interop.html

[10]https://projectreactor.io/

[11]https://tanzu.vmware.com/open-source

[12]https://docs.spring.io/spring/docs/current/spring-framework-reference/web-reactive.html

- **Emitted values** are values of some type that are to be consumed.

- **An error** is an unexpected invalid value that is to be processed differently than a value.

- **A completed signal** is a notification that no more values will be emitted.

Most times, the last two can be omitted and developers write functions only to process emitted values. The functions that are supposed to process values emitted by a stream, or perform some action when values are emitted must **subscribe** to the stream. Then they **listen** to the stream. They are **observing**[13] the stream and waiting to **consume** the emitted values.

It might look weird that the term **function** was used instead of **method**, but when it comes to reactive programming, you rarely can have one without the other. Functional programming is based on pure functions. **Pure functions** are functions that do not mutate the input, always return a value and the returned value is based solely on the input (they have no side effects). Because their action is atomic, functions can be easily composed. And Lambda expressions are suitable for this kind of writing code too. Thus, **functional reactive programming** is a programming paradigm that involves providing solutions by applying pure functions to Reactive Streams.[14]

Anyway, back to streams. A stream has a source, an entity providing the values to be emitted. You can also view a stream as **data on the move** from its source to a destination. That source can be anything: a variable, user input, properties, data structures (like collections), and even another stream. The stream emits values until the source is depleted, or an error happens.

Functions that are subscribing to streams use the values and return results as part of a new stream. These types of functions are sometimes called **transformers**, **processors**, or **operators**. They do not modify the initial stream, because streams are immutable. The functions that end a chain are called **terminal operators** or **final transformers**. The functions that process multiple streams emitted values and compute a single value are called **reductors** and those that accumulate stream emitted values in a collection are called **collectors**.

A chain of pure functions is sometimes referred to as a **pipeline**.

---

[13]https://en.wikipedia.org/wiki/Observer_pattern
[14]https://blog.danlew.net/2017/07/27/
  an-introduction-to-functional-reactive-programming/

In Figure 9-1, you see a bad drawing depicting stream processing with a bucket of colored balls and an occasional apple that represents the error signal.

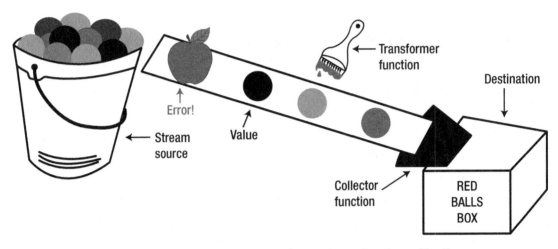

Figure 9-1. *Stream processing representation using a bucket of balls*

The representation is not that fully accurate since painting the ball red should create a new red ball, but it is close enough to the idea of how a stream works and is supposed to be used.

If it helps, imagine writing your code using streams as being analogous to designing a Rube Goldberg machine.[15]

Before streams being introduced all developers had to work with to manage sets of data were collections. Let's take a simple task: given a collection of balls of different colors and different sizes select all blue balls with diameter bigger than three, paint them red and calculate the sum of their diameters. Before Java 8 the code would look similar to the snippet in Listing 9-1.

Listing 9-1. Filtering Balls and Adding Their Diameters Before Java 8

```
List<Ball> bucket = List.of(
    new Ball("BLUE",9),
    new Ball("RED", 4),
    // other instances omitted
    );
```

---

[15]https://en.wikipedia.org/wiki/Rube_Goldberg_machine

```
Integer sum = 0;

for(Ball ball : bucket) {
    if (ball.getColor().equals("BLUE") && ball.getDiameter() >= 3) {
        ball.setColor("RED");
        sum += ball.getDiameter();
    }
}

System.out.println("Diameter sum is " + sum);
```

This is a depiction of imperative code. It uses a sequence of statements to be executed to change the state of the list of balls. It describes **how** the program should accomplish the state change.

Starting with Java 8, using streams the same code can be written as depicted in Listing 9-2.

Listing 9-2. Filtering Balls and Adding Their Diameters Starting with Java 8

```
import java.util.function.Function;
import java.util.function.Predicate;

// other imports and code omitted

Predicate<Ball> predicate = ball -> ball.getColor().equals("BLUE")
    && ball.getDiameter() >= 3;
Function<Ball, Ball> redBall =
    ball -> new Ball("RED", ball.getDiameter());
Function<Ball, Integer> quantifier = Ball::getDiameter;

int sum  = bucket.stream()
        .filter(predicate)
        .map(redBall)
        .map(quantifier)
        .reduce(0, Integer::sum);

System.out.println("Diameter sum is " + sum);
```

The pipeline in Listing 9-2 is made of the following method calls.

- **The stream() method** returns an instance of java.util.stream. Stream<Ball> which uses the initial collection as a source.

- The **filter(Predicate<T>) method** uses the predicate provided as argument to filter the stream and returns a stream containing the elements matching the predicate. The predicate consists of the composed boolean condition that balls are tested against.

- The **map(Function<T, R>) method** is a transformer function that takes the elements of the stream, applies the function provided as an argument, and returns the results as a stream.

- The **reduce(T, BinaryOperator<T>) method** is an accumulator function. It takes two parameters: an initial value and a java.util. function.BinaryOperator<T> instance declaring the operation to perform between two operands of the same type, producing a result of the same type. In the previous listing the function being used is the typical summing function for integers declared as a method reference. (Look up Java method references; if you haven't used them before, they are pretty cool.)

The code in Listing 9-2 starts with three statements that require explanation.

- The **predicate instance** is an inline implementation of the Predicate<T> functional interface. This interface exposes a single abstract method named test(..) that must be implemented with the predicate to be evaluated against the provided argument.

- The **redBall instance** is an inline implementation of the Function<T, R> functional interface. This interface exposes a single abstract method named apply(..) that must be implemented with the code to apply to the provided argument. In this case we are creating a new Ball instance.

- The **quantifier instance** is a reference to the method named getDiameter() from the Ball instance. And in Java they are called **method references** because it apparently sounds cooler.

These three instances are introduced to externalize **how** the stream should be modified. They are necessary for a declarative programming approach.[16] By declaring them outside the pipeline, the result is a code snippet that declares **what** needs to be achieved. The **how** has become a parameter, and changing what those references point to don't affect the **what**. You can think of the code pipeline as an assembly line where the operators are workstations. Changing something internal to a workstation (a predicate or a function) should not affect the pipeline setup.

The stream API introduced in Java 8 provides a lot of utility methods for stream processing, and the reactive stream APIs extends that set even more. Depending on the problem you are trying to solve, a combination of lambda expressions and streams might lead to a more readable and elegant solution.

And now that you know how to write code using streams, you are ready for the icing on the cake: Reactive Streams.

Reactive Streams

Reactive Streams provide a common API for reactive programming in Java. It is composed of four simple interfaces that provide a standard for asynchronous stream processing with non-blocking back pressure. If you want to write a component that can integrate with other reactive components, you need to implement one of these.

On an abstract level, the components and the relationships between them, as described in the Reactive Streams specification, looks like Figure 9-2.

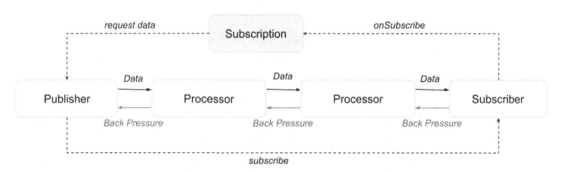

Figure 9-2. *Reactive Streams specification abstract representation*

And now, the long explanation.

---

[16]https://ui.dev/imperative-vs-declarative-programming/

- A **publisher** is a potentially infinite producer of data. In Java a producer of data must implement `org.reactivestreams.Publisher<T>`.

- A **subscriber** registers with the publisher to consume data. In Java a data consumer must implement `org.reactivestreams.Subscriber<T>`.

- Upon subscribing, a **subscription** object is created to represent the one-to-one relationship between the publisher and the subscriber. This object is used to request data from the publisher but also to cancel the demand for data. In Java a subscription class must implement `org.reactivestreams.Subscription`.

- The publisher emits values, on demand from the subscriber.

- A **processor** is a special component that has the same properties as a publisher and subscriber. In Java a processor of data must implement `org.reactivestreams.Processor<T,R>`. Processors can be chained to form stream processing pipeline.

- A processor consumes data from the publisher/processor in front of it in the chain and emits data for the processor/subscriber after it in the chain to consume.

- The subscriber/processor applies back pressure to slow down the producer/processor when emitting data if it cannot consume it fast enough.

That is the basic idea of how Reactive Streams works. In the basic case there is a publisher, a subscriber, and a stream of events they react to. In more complex cases, there are processors involved.

You can check out the code in your IDE or on GitHub.[17]

ℹ️   Most reactive implementations for the JVM were developed in parallel. Different teams of developers chose different names for their implementations of Reactive Streams interfaces. That is why when first introducing streams, more than one name to each component was mentioned.

---

[17]https://github.com/reactive-streams/reactive-streams-jvm/tree/master/api/src/main/java/org/reactivestreams

When the Reactive Streams specification was adopted in the JDK, the decision was made to copy all the interfaces from the `org.reactivestreams` package into the `java.util.concurrent.Flow` class. Most of the libraries now support adapters to integrate with the JDK too. Table 9-1 shows the names of the Reactive Streams implementations in most used Java Reactive libraries.

Table 9-1. *Reactive Streams Implementation Names*

Reactive Streams API	RxJava	Project Reactor	Akka	JDK*
Publisher	Observable, Single	Flux, Mono	Source	Flow.Publisher*
Subscriber	Observer	CoreSubscriber	Sink	Flow.Subscriber*
Processor	Subject	FluxProcessor, MonoProcessor	Flow	Flow.Processor*
Subscription	-	-	-	-

* The JDK Reactive Streams specification components are marked with a * in Table 9-1 because they do not extend the Reactive Streams API but copy all components in the Flow class.

Code written with Reactive Streams looks pretty similar to the one with for non- reactive streams, but what happens under the covers is different. Reactive streams are asynchronous, but you do not have to write the logic of dealing with that. You need to declare what must happen when some value is emitted on a stream. The code you are writing is invoked when the stream emits an item **asynchronously**, independent of the main program flow. If there is more than one processor involved, each is executed on its own thread.

Since your code runs asynchronously, you must be careful with the functions you are providing as arguments to your transformer methods. Make sure they are pure functions, they should only interact with the program through their arguments and return values, and they should never modify an object that requires synchronization.

Let's see now how Project Reactor implements the Reactive Streams specification and how its classes write reactive code.

Using Project Reactor

Project Reactor is one of the first libraries for reactive programming. It provides a non-blocking stable foundation with efficient demand management for reactive applications. It provides classes that make designing your code using Reactive Streams very practical. It works with Java 8, but provides adapter classes for all JDK9+ versions. Project Reactor is suitable for writing microservices applications and provides a lot more classes designed to make development of reactive applications more practical than the JDK does.

Project Reactor provides two main publisher implementations.

- `reactor.core.publisher.Mono<T>` is a reactive stream publisher representing zero or one element.

- `reactor.core.publisher.Flux<T>` is a reactive stream publisher representing an asynchronous sequence of zero to infinity elements.

`Mono<T>` and `Flux<T>` are similar to `java.util.concurrent.Future<V>`. They represent the result of an asynchronous computation. The difference between them is that `Future<V>`, blocks the current thread until the computation completes when you try to get the result with the `get()` method. `Mono<T>` and `Flux<T>` both provide a family of `block*()` methods used to retrieve the value of an asynchronous computation that do not block the current thread.

Before getting there, let's learn more about `Flux<T>` and `Mono<T>`.

Figure 9-3 depicts the class hierarchy for `Flux<T>` and `Mono<T>` including the root parents from the Reactive Streams specification package.

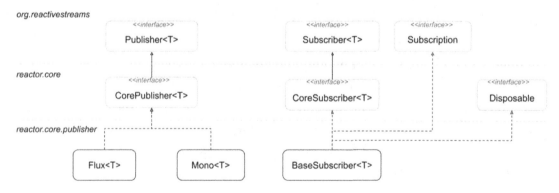

Figure 9-3. *Class hierarchy for Project Reactor core components*

The `CorePublisher<T>` interface declares a single method to be implemented, its own version of the `subscribe(..)` a method that requires an argument of type `CoreSubscriber<T>`.

The `CoreSubscriber<T>` interface declares a default method named `currentContext()` that is used to access the reactive context that contains information shared with downstream or terminal operators. It also declares an abstract method the `onSubscribe(Subscription)` that implementors need to provide an implementation for to initialized the stream state before values are emitted.

Both `Flux<T>` and `Mono<T>` inherit the `Publisher<T>` which means they can be chained with any type of subscriber if it implements `Subscriber<T>`. When writing code using project reactor, it is practical to extend the `BaseSubscriber<T>` abstract class. This class has minimal implementations for all the methods inherited from `Subscriber<T>` but also declares hook methods (interceptor methods) for them, which you can implement to customize the subscriber behavior when one of the three signals mentioned in a previous section are emitted: value, error, or completion. It also contains a hook for the method signaling the subscription to a publisher and a final hook to add behavior to be executed after any termination events: error, complete or cancel. Since all the methods have a minimal implementation (an empty body) this allows you to override only methods you are interested in, and the most often during development there is one method that matters the most: `hookOnNext(T)`.

`Mono<T>` is a special type of reactive stream, it can only return 0 or 1 single value. Knowing the number of values a stream emits leads to more simple code being written to consume them. Also, not all asynchronous processes return a value so to signal the completion of such process a `Mono<Void>` can be used. Since `Mono<T>` has such a low limit on its values, it offers only a small set of operators compared to `Flux<T>`.

Before going further, look at the code in Listing 9-3. It contains the Reactive Streams version of the code in Listing 9-2.

Listing 9-3. Filtering Balls and Adding Their Diameters Using Reactive Streams

```java
import reactor.core.publisher.BaseSubscriber;
import reactor.core.publisher.Flux;

// other imports and code omitted

Subscriber<Integer> subscriber = new BaseSubscriber<Integer>() {
    @Override
```

```
    protected void hookOnNext(Integer sum) {
        System.out.println("Diameter sum is " + sum);
    }
};

  Flux.fromIterable(bucket)  // Flux<Ball>
        .filter(predicate)
        .map(redBall)
        .map(quantifier)  // Flux<Integer>
        .reduce(0, Integer::sum) // Mono<Integer>
        .subscribe(subscriber);
```

A few comments have been added to make it clear when the type of object on the returned stream changes. All the methods in the implementation return either Flux<T> or Mono<T> and that is why they can be chained so nicely. The last component in the chain is the subscriber, the one that consumes the element in the stream returned by the reduce(..) accumulator function. Since this accumulator returns a Mono<T>, more functions could be chained if needed.

For this example, the subscriber object is created by extending the BaseSubscriber<T> type and instantiating it in place. An implementation for the hookOnNext(..) method prints the emitted value in the console. The whole pipeline execution is asynchronous, and the value is printed when it is emitted, without blocking the main thread.

Flux<T> or Mono<T> classes provide an enriched version of the subscribe(..) method that allows the developer to define java.util.function.Consumer<T> functions for error and complete signals too. Assuming something might go wrong in the operator preceding the subscription, this allows errors to be treated properly and perform extra actions after the process has finished successfully.

Thus, using this method the code in Listing 9-3 becomes the one in Listing 9-4.

Listing 9-4. Declaring Consumers for a Different Kind of Signal

```
Flux.fromIterable(bucket)
    .filter(predicate)
    .map(redBall)
    .map(quantifier)
    .reduce(0, Integer::sum)
    .subscribe(
```

```
        sum -> System.out.println("Diameter sum is " + sum),
        error -> System.err.println("Something went wrong " + error),
        () -> System.out.println("Pipeline executed successfully.")
    );
```

Under the covers, a subscriber instance is created and the consumers provided as arguments are called by the appropriate hook methods.

Maybe this code looks more complicated than the previous implementations, but the code is still readable, and it is asynchronous and non-blocking. For simple use-case scenarios, using reactive components is overkill. Reactive Streams show their true powers in reactive applications in which the cost of having a long chain of functions and code that is unreadable is outweighed by the efficiency and reliability of non-blocking processes. And even if you think long chains of reactive functions looks impractical, trust me, the same code written only with the Java concurrency API would be even more so.

To see why reactive programming is inefficient for applications with moderate load and medium complexity (not like Netflix or Facebook ☺) processing, let's modify the previous implementation so that each function prints the thread ID. A delay in processing values is simulated by adding a call to delayElements(Duration.ofSeconds(1)) in the pipeline.

In Listing 9-5 the modified redBall function is depicted, but the modification is similar for all the other functions in the pipeline. The pipeline code doesn't change, and the result returned by the pure functions is not affected by the print statement.

Listing 9-5. Pure Function Modified To Print the ID of Its Executing Thread

```
// other imports and code omitted
Function<Ball, Ball> redBall = ball -> {
    System.out.println("[RedBall]Executing thread: "
        + Thread.currentThread().getId());
    return new Ball("RED", ball.getDiameter());
};

Flux.fromIterable(bucket)
    .delayElements(Duration.ofSeconds(1))
    .filter(predicate)
    .map(redBall)
    .map(quantifier)
```

```
    .reduce(0, Integer::sum)
    .subscribe(
        sum -> System.out.println("Diameter sum is " + sum),
        error -> System.err.println("Something went wrong " + error),
        () -> System.out.println("Pipeline executed successfully.")
    );
```

When we execute the pipeline now, the output in the console should look pretty close to the one depicted in Listing 9-6.

Listing 9-6. Reactive Pipeline Output

```
[Predicate]Executing thread: 17
[GetDiameter]Executing thread: 17
[Predicate]Executing thread: 18
[Predicate]Executing thread: 19
[Predicate]Executing thread: 20
[GetDiameter]Executing thread: 20
[RedBall]Executing thread: 20
[GetDiameter]Executing thread: 20
[GetDiameter]Executing thread: 20
[Predicate]Executing thread: 21
[Predicate]Executing thread: 22
[Predicate]Executing thread: 23
[GetDiameter]Executing thread: 23
[Predicate]Executing thread: 24
...
[Subscriber]Executing thread: 24
```

The different thread IDs means that each pure function is executed by its own thread. The number of threads that are being used is equal to the number of cores the processor has, and the load is distributed evenly: one thread per core. For a simple task, the effort of creating so many threads, and coordinating them is not worth it.

Flux<T> and Mono<T> are powerful and practical. When writing Spring Reactive applications, you rarely need to use anything else. They both provide a rich list of operators that can create, compose, and control Reactive Streams[18] and allow a practical pipeline design.

---

[18]https://projectreactor.io/docs/core/release/api/index.html

One thing to keep in mind, when writing a reactive application, every component of the application must be reactive, otherwise the application is not truly reactive, and the non-reactive component might become a bottleneck and break down the whole flow.

For example: a three-tier application with the typical tiers: presentation, service, database is only reactive if all three are reactive. A reactive Spring WebFlux application must have reactive views, reactive controllers, reactive services, reactive repositories and a reactive database. And the client making calls to the application must be reactive too. An application can consume data exposed reactively by a different application, becoming a client in this case. For the communication to go well, both applications must be reactive. Except the views and the database, if the rest of them are written in Java, the input and output for each method in the APIs must be `Flux<T>` or `Mono<T>` (or any other implementation of Reactive Streams mentioned earlier) instances, so they can be composed without the need to write extra code to encapsulate them in `Flux<T>` or `Mono<T>` instances.

Without further ado, let's see how we can move from writing applications using Spring MVC to do the same using Spring WebFlux.

Introduction to Spring WebFlux

Spring Web MVC is designed around the `DispatcherServlet` which is the gateway that maps HTTP requests to handlers and is set up with themes configurations, internationalization, files upload and view resolution. Spring MVC was built for Servlet API and Servlet containers. This means it mostly uses blocking I/O and one thread per HTTP request. Supporting asynchronous processing of requests is possible but requires a bigger thread pool which in turn requires more resources. Also, it is difficult to scale.

Spring WebFlux is a reactive stack web framework that was added in Spring 5, and it is Spring's response to the rising issue of blocking I/O architecture. It can run on Servlet 3.1+ containers, but it can adapt to other native server APIs. The preferred server of choice is Netty[19] that is well-established in the async, non-blocking space. Spring WebFlux is built with functional reactive programming in mind and allows code to be written in declarative style.

---

[19]`https://netty.io/`

The two frameworks have a few elements in common and can even be used together. Figure 9-4 is a diagram from the official Spring Reference documentation that shows what Spring MVC and Spring WebFlux have in common and how they support each other.

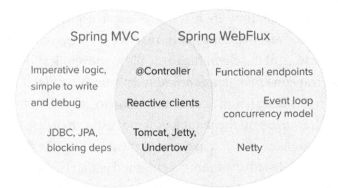

Figure 9-4. *Spring MVC and Spring WebFlux diagram*

Starting with Spring 5, the `spring-web` module was enriched with low level infrastructure and HTTP abstractions to build reactive web applications. All public APIs were modified to support `Publisher<T>` and `Subscriber<T>` as parameters and returned types. This module is dependency of the `spring-webflux` module which is the most important dependency of a Spring Reactive application. So, how do we write a Spring Web Flux application? It's simple, we start with the configuration.

Spring WebFlux Configuration: Reactive Controllers

It was mentioned that reactive applications can be deployed on Servlet 3.1+ containers, such as Tomcat, Jetty, or Undertow. The trick here is not to use `DispatcherServlet`, which is the central dispatcher for HTTP request handlers/controllers. No matter how powerful it is, it is still a blocking component. Tomcat and Jetty are non-blocking at the core, so the key is to use them to handle HTTP requests without the servlet facade.

This is where the new and improved `spring-web` components come to the rescue by introducing `org.springframework.http.server.reactive.HttpHandler`. This interface represents lowest level contract for reactive HTTP request handling and Spring provides server adapters based on it for each supported server. Table 9-2 lists the servers supported by Spring WebFlux and the name of the adapter classes that represent the core of the non-blocking I/O to Reactive Streams bridge for each server.

Table 9-2. *Servers Supported*

Server Name	Spring Adapter	Bridge Used
Netty	ReactorHttpHandlerAdapter	Netty API using the Reactor Netty library
Undertow	UndertowHttpHandlerAdapter	spring-web Undertow to Reactive Streams bridge
Tomcat	TomcatHttpHandlerAdapter	spring-web: Servlet 3.1 non-blocking I/O to Reactive Streams bridge
Jetty	JettyHttpHandlerAdapter	spring-web: Servlet 3.1 non-blocking I/O to Reactive Streams bridge

The HttpHandler interface is very basic. Its content is depicted in Listing 9-7.

Listing 9-7. HttpHandler Interface

```
package org.springframework.http.server.reactive;

import reactor.core.publisher.Mono;
// other comments omitted
public interface HttpHandler {

    /**
    * Handle the given request and write to the response.
    * @param request current request
    * @param response current response
    * @return indicates completion of request handling
    */
    Mono<Void> handle(ServerHttpRequest request, ServerHttpResponse response);

}
```

On top of it, Spring provides the WebHandler interface, which is a slightly higher-level contract describing all general-purpose server APIs with filter chain–style processing and exception handling.

What does this mean for a Spring configuration, compared to a classic Spring Web MVC application? This means instead of org.springframework.web.servlet.DispatcherServlet, you need org.springframework.web.reactive.DispatcherHandler. DispatcherHandler, as the dispatcher servlet, is designed as a front controller. It is the central `WebHandler` implementation and provides an algorithm for request processing performed by configurable components. It delegates to special beans to process requests and render appropriate responses and their implementations are, as expected, non-blocking. Similar to the Spring MVC ecosystem there is a `HandlerMapping` bean to map a request to a handler, a `HandlerAdapter` bean to invoke a handler, an `org.springframework.web.server.WebExceptionHandler` bean to handle exceptions, and a `HandlerResultHandler` bean to get the result from the handler and finalize the response all declared into the `org.springframework.web.reactive` package.

In the Spring typical way, for most cases the configuration of the `DispatcherHandler` does not require code that describes it directly. To configure a Spring WebFlux application that runs in a Servlet 3.1+ container, you need to do the following.

- Declare a Spring WebFlux configuration class and annotate it with @ `Configuration` and `@EnableWebFlux`.

- Extend the `org.springframework.web.server.adapter.` `AbstractReactiveWebInitializer` class, implement the `getConfigClasses()` method, and inject your Spring WebFlux configuration class in it.

Listing 9-8 depicts `AppConfiguration`, a custom configuration class for a Spring WebFlux application.

Listing 9-8. `AppConfiguration` Class

```
package com.apress.prospringmvc.bookstore;

import org.springframework.web.reactive.config.EnableWebFlux;
// other imports omitted

@EnableWebFlux
@Configuration
public class AppConfiguration {
}
```

The `@EnableWebFlux` annotation is part of the `org.springframework.web.reactive.` `config` package, and it enables use of annotated controllers and functional endpoints. When Spring IoC finds this annotation it imports all Spring WebFlux configuration from `org.springframework.web.reactive.config.WebFluxConfigurationSupport`. If you want to customize the imported configuration in any way, all you have to do make the annotated class implement `org.springframework.web.reactive.config.WebFluxConfigurer`. This interface contains methods for configuring static access resource handlers, formatter, validators, message sources, view resolvers, and so forth.

Listing 9-9 depicts `WebAppInitializer,` which extends `AbstractReactiveWebInitializer` to provide integration with a Servlet 3.1+ container.

Listing 9-9. `WebAppInitializer` Class

```
package com.apress.prospringmvc.bookstore;

import org.springframework.web.server.adapter.
AbstractReactiveWebInitializer;

public class WebAppInitializer extends AbstractReactiveWebInitializer {

    @Override
    protected Class<?>[] getConfigClasses() {
        return new Class<?>[]{AppConfiguration.class};
    }
}
```

The `AbstractReactiveWebInitializer` implements `WebApplicationInitializer` and is necessary to install a Spring Web Reactive application on a Servlet container.

To help you make a transition from Spring MVC to Spring WebFlux, look at Table 9-3. This table shows a correspondence of configuration components between a Spring MVC, and a Spring WebFlux application.

Table 9-3. *Spring MVC and WebFlux Comparison*

Spring Web MVC	Spring WebFlux
@EnableWebMvc	@EnableWebFlux
WebMvcConfigurer	WebFluxConfigurer
WebMvcConfigurationSupport	WebFluxConfigurationSupport
WebApplicationInitializer (interface)	AbstractReactiveWebInitializer (class)
DispatcherServlet	DispatcherHandler

Once the two configuration classes were written the next step is to write a reactive controller. And since we are using Spring WebFlux, we know that this can be done by making sure the methods return Flux<T> or Mono<T>. One of the things That I always do when writing a web application is to write an IndexController that prints, "It works!" Listing 9-10 depicts a simple IndexController returning a Mono<T> instance emitting a single value.

Listing 9-10. Reactive IndexController Implementation

```
package com.apress.prospringmvc.bookstore;
import reactor.core.publisher.Mono;
// other imports omitted

@RestController
public class IndexController {

    @ResponseStatus(HttpStatus.OK)
    @GetMapping(path="/", produces = MediaType.TEXT_EVENT_STREAM_VALUE)
    public Mono<String> index(){
        return Mono.just("It works!");
    }

}
```

@RestControllers are used because reactive applications are focused on streaming data but @Controllers can be used too, as you see in the next chapter.

The value of the produces attribute is text/event-stream and it represents the type of the returned content. This content type describes an event stream from the source. If you deploy this application to an Apache Tomcat server and try to open the http:// localhost:8080/ page, some browsers urge you to save the output to a file, because the response is not something that a browser can render. The response is a server-sent event (SSE), which is a server push technology enabling a client to receive a stream of updates from a server via HTTP connection that is part of HTML5.[20] In the classic polling model, the communication between a client and a server requires a succession of request/ response over an HTTP connection because the client had to poll for data repeatedly. Server-sent events allow the server to push data toward the client when it is available, without the client asking for it. And thus, are the best fit for reactive web applications.

---

[20]https://html.spec.whatwg.org/multipage/server-sent-events.html

Except this header, how do we know that our application is reactive? It's easy— instead of returning a Mono<T> we return a Flux<T> and we slow down the rate of the emitted elements.

Slowing down the rate of values being emitted is done by combining two streams using an operation called **zip**. There are three combining operations that can be applied to streams and they are depicted in Figure 9-5.

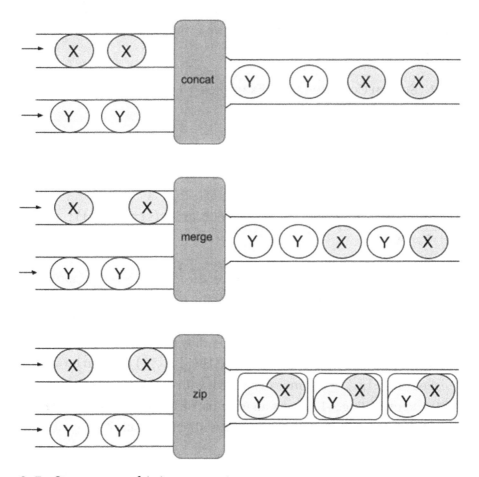

Figure 9-5. *Streams combining operations*

Two or more Flux<T> instances can be combined into a single Flux<T> using one of the operators described in Figure 9-5. The following list describes de operators and the resulting stream.

- **concat** concatenates two streams. The order of the streams is important, since the second flux is only subscribed to after the first flux emits the onComplete signal. For concatenating streams, the Flux.concat(..) utility method can be used. There is also a method named concatWith(Flux<T>) that can be called on a Flux<T> instance to concat it with the stream received as argument. Listing 9-11 shows an example of stream concatenation, using as sources two very convenient streams: that that emits X values and one that emits Y values.

Listing 9-11. Stream Concatenation Examples

```
Flux<String> y =  Flux.just("Y", "Y");
Flux<String> x =  Flux.just("X", "X");

Flux.concat(y,x).subscribe(str -> System.out.print(str + " "));
// or
y.concatWith(x).subscribe(str -> System.out.print(str + " "));
// expect: Y Y X X
```

- **merge** merges two streams. The order of the streams is not important, since both streams are subscribed to at the same time. The resulting stream emits values from either of the source streams randomly. For merging streams, the Flux.merge(..) utility method can be used. There is also a method named mergeWith(Flux<T>) that can be called on a Flux<T> instance to merge it with the stream received as argument. Listing 9-12 shows an example of stream merging, using as sources two very convenient streams: that that emits X values and one that emits Y values.

Listing 9-12. Stream Merging Examples

```
Flux<String> y =  Flux.just("Y", "Y");
Flux<String> x =  Flux.just("X", "X");

Flux.merge(y,x).subscribe(str -> System.out.print(str + " "));
// or
y.mergeWith(x).subscribe(str -> System.out.print(str + " "));
```

// expect multiple X and Y elements being written in any order

- **zip** is a stream emitting values that are created by wrapping together values emitted by each stream. The result of this operation is applied on two to eight streams. When one stream emits the onComplete signal, all values from other streams which cannot be combined are discarded. When zipping streams, the Flux.zip(..) utility method can be used. There is more than one version of this method, and they can zip from two to eight streams. The resulting values are of type reactor.util.function.Tuple*, where the * replaces the number of values being combined. There is also a method named zipWith(Flux<T>) that can be called on a Flux<T> instance to zip it with the stream received as argument.

Listing 9-13 shows an example of stream zipping, using as sources three very convenient streams: that that emits X values, one that emits Y values and one that emits Z values.

Listing 9-13. Zipping Merging Examples

```
Flux<String> y =  Flux.just("Y", "Y");
Flux<String> x =  Flux.just("X", "X");
Flux<String> z =  Flux.just("Z", "Z");

Flux.zip(y,x).subscribe(t -> System.out.print(str + " "));
// or
y.zipWith(x).subscribe(str -> System.out.print(str + " "));
// expect multiple Tuple2 instances: [Y,X]
Flux.zip(y,x,z).subscribe(t -> System.out.print(str + " "));
// expect multiple Tuple3 instances: [Y,X,Z]
```

The zipWith(..) operation slows down the emitting rate of a stream by combining it with a reactive interval stream. A reactive interval stream can be created by calling Flux. interval(Duration). This method takes a Duration instance as argument and creates a Flux<Long> that emits long values starting with 0 and incrementing at specified time intervals on the global timer. The first element is emitted after an initial delay equal to the duration provided as argument.

If we zip a reactive data stream with a reactive interval stream with a `Duration` of one second, this results in a stream with one `Tuple2` instance being emitted per second. We then apply `map` to the stream of tuples to isolate the values we are interested in.

Let's make things interesting and modify `IndexController` and add a handler method for the /debug path that returns a stream containing all bean names and their types at the rate of one per second. Each emitted value is of type `Pair<S,T>` and contains the bean name and its type. The value of the `produces` attribute declares the returned type of the method as being `MediaType.APPLICATION_STREAM_JSON_VALUE` which is a constant with the `application/stream+json` value. This means every value emitted by this stream is converted to JSON.

The proposed implementation is depicted in Listing 9-14.

Listing 9-14. Reactive `IndexController` Implementation Returning a `Flux<T>`

```
package com.apress.prospringmvc.bookstore;
import reactor.core.publisher.Flux;
import reactor.util.function.Tuple2;
import org.springframework.data.util.Pair;
// other imports omitted

@RestController
public class IndexController implements ApplicationContextAware {
    // other code omitted
    @ResponseStatus(HttpStatus.OK)
    @GetMapping(path="/debug", produces =
                          MediaType.APPLICATION_STREAM_JSON_VALUE)
    public Flux<Pair<String,String>> debug() {
        List<Pair<String,String>> info = new ArrayList<>();
        Arrays.stream(ctx.getBeanDefinitionNames())
          .forEach(beanName -> info.add(Pair.of(beanName,
                ctx.getBean(beanName).getClass().getName())));
        return Flux.fromIterable(info)
        .zipWith(Flux.interval(Duration.ofSeconds(1))).map(Tuple2::getT1);
    }
}
```

When accessed in a browser, if the browser can parse it, you see the values being depicted sequentially with a one-second delay between them. If your browser can't do that, after a few seconds (depending how big is the dataset is), you are prompted to save the response as a file. If you have a UNIX-based operating system, you can open that `http://localhost:8080/debug` using the `curl` command.

```
curl -H -v "application/stream+json" http://localhost:8080/debug
```

This command prints the values as they are emitted converted to JSON. But, where is this being configured? It's not done explicitly, although you can declare your own converters if you need to. The conversion of `Flux<T>` and `Mono<T>` to bytes and vice versa is done using `Encoder<T>` and `Decoder<T>` beans. These two interfaces are part of `org.springframework.core.codec` package and basic implementations are part of the `spring-core` and `spring-web` modules.

In a Spring WebFlux application, an `org.springframework.http.codec.HttpMessageWriter<T>` bean is configured by default to use existing encoder implementations to *encode* a stream of objects of type `<T>` and write them to a stream of data buffers to stream the response content. An `org.springframework.http.codec.HttpMessageReader<T>` bean is configured by default to used exiting decoder implementations to *decode* a stream of data buffers containing request data into a stream of objects of type `<T>`.

Configuring a Spring WebFlux application is similar to configuring a Spring MVC application. The only thing that changes is the returned type of the handler methods and the options available as a parameter in methods annotated with `@RequestMapping` and variations.

- Reactive types are supported as arguments, but you should not use reactive types for arguments that do not require non-blocking I/O (For example, for a POST request handler method for saving a book, it does not make sense to declare the argument type as `Mono<Book>`.)

- `org.springframework.web.server.ServerWebExchange` can be used as an argument to provide access to the HTTP request, response, and other server-side properties. In Listing 9-15, the `IndexController.debug(..)` method has been modified to receive `ServerWebExchange` as argument. The request is analyzed to inspect the `user-agent` header of the request, and if the request is made using the `curl` command, a cookie is added to the response. Both the request and response objects are accessed through the `ServerWebExchange` argument.

Listing 9-15. Reactive IndexController Using the ServerWebExchange
Argument

```
package com.apress.prospringmvc.bookstore;

import org.springframework.web.server.ServerWebExchange;
// other imports omitted

@RestController
public class IndexController implements ApplicationContextAware {
    // other code omitted
    @ResponseStatus(HttpStatus.OK)
    @GetMapping(path="/debug", produces = MediaType.APPLICATION_STREAM_
    JSON_VALUE)
    public Flux<Pair<String,String>> debug(ServerWebExchange exchange) {
        if(Objects.requireNonNull(exchange.getRequest()
                .getHeaders().get("user-agent"))
                .stream().anyMatch(v-> v.startsWith("curl"))){
            logger.debug("Development request with id: {}", exchange.
            getRequest().getId());
            ResponseCookie devCookie = ResponseCookie
                .from("Invoking.Environment.Cookie", "dev")
                .maxAge(Duration.ofMinutes(5)).build();
            exchange.getResponse().addCookie(devCookie);
        }
        List<Pair<String,String>> info = new ArrayList<>();
        Arrays.stream(ctx.getBeanDefinitionNames()).forEach(beanName ->
            info.add(Pair.of(beanName,    ctx.getBean(beanName).
                                          getClass().getName()))
        );
        return Flux.fromIterable(info).zipWith(Flux.interval(Duration.
        ofSeconds(1))).map(Tuple2::getT1);
    }
}
```

- A method with a `Mono<Void>` return type is considered to have fully handled the response if it also has a `ServerHttpResponse`, or a `ServerWebExchange` argument, or an `@ResponseStatus` annotation.

- `Flux<ServerSentEvent>`, `Observable<ServerSentEvent>`, or other reactive type are supported as return types. The `ServerSentEvent` wrapper type can be omitted when only simple text needs to be written. In this case the `produces` attribute must be set to the `text/event-stream` value (as it was done for the first version of `IndexController`).

Spring Boot WebFlux Application

When using Spring Boot to build a Spring WebFlux application, things become even more easier. Using `spring-boot-starter-webflux` as a dependency and the Spring Boot dependency injection ensures that the application is already configured by default with all the necessary infrastructure beans.

All that is left to do is to write the reactive controllers and other custom beans required by them, such as repository or service beans. There is one important thing that needs mentioning though. Creation of a deployable war file is not supported.[21]

❗ Because Spring WebFlux does not strictly depend on the Servlet API, and applications are deployed by default on an embedded Reactor Netty server, war deployment is not supported for WebFlux applications.

What does this mean? This means we cannot build a deployable war using Spring Boot, and we cannot deploy it on a Tomcat server, which is not that important, really. Since reactive applications are the best for writing microservices applications, it is more suitable to have an embedded server and package your application as an executable `jar` anyway.

---

[21]`https://docs.spring.io/spring-boot/docs/current/reference/html/howto.html#howto-traditional-deployment`

Spring WebFlux Configuration: Functional Endpoints

Spring WebFlux provides a functional model as an alternative approach to @Controller annotated classes to map requests to handlers. Configurations can be composed nicely, and there is the advantage of immutability.

In this model, requests are handled by a HandlerFunction<T>. This is a simple functional interface declaring a single method. Listing 9-16 shows the code of this interface.

Listing 9-16. HandlerFunction<T> Code

```
// other comments omitted
package org.springframework.web.reactive.function.server;

import org.springframework.web.reactive.function.server.ServerRequest;
import org.springframework.web.reactive.function.server.ServerResponse;
import reactor.core.publisher.Mono;

@FunctionalInterface
public interface HandlerFunction<T extends ServerResponse> {
    Mono<T> handle(ServerRequest request);
}
```

The handle(..) method takes a ServerRequest and returns a Mono<ServerResponse>. It is equivalent to a @Controller method annotated with @RequestMapping.

ServerRequest exposes the request body as a Flux<T> or Mono<T> instance. It also provides access to request parameters, path variables, the HTTP method, and headers. The ServerResponse accepts any Publisher<T> implementation as a body. Both ServerRequest and ServerResponse are immutable. The response is built by calling various static methods (e.g., ok(), badRequest(), etc.) on the ServerResponse class that expose a BodyBuilder. This instance provides multiple methods to customize the response: set the HTTP response status code, add headers, and provide a body.

Handler functions are usually grouped in components specific to the type of object being handled. For example, handler functions that handle requests specific to Book objects should be grouped in a component named BookHandler.

Listing 9-17 depicts the BookHandler class. A bean of this type is declared and is part of the Spring WebFlux application configuration and its methods are used as handler functions for requests managing Book instances.

Listing 9-17. The BookHandler Class

```
package com.apress.prospringmvc.bookstore;
// other imports omitted

@Component
public class BookHandler {

    private final BookService bookService;
    public HandlerFunction<ServerResponse> list;
    public HandlerFunction<ServerResponse> delete;

    public BookHandler(BookService bookService) {
        this.bookService = bookService;

        /* 1 */
        list = serverRequest -> ServerResponse.ok()
                .contentType(MediaType.APPLICATION_JSON)
                .body(bookService.findAll(), Book.class);
        /* 2 */
        delete = serverRequest -> ServerResponse.noContent()
                .build(bookService.delete(serverRequest.
                pathVariable("id")));
    }

    /* 3 */
    public Mono<ServerResponse> findByIsbn(ServerRequest serverRequest) {
        Mono<Book> bookMono = bookService.findByIsbn(serverRequest.
        pathVariable("isbn"));
        return bookMono
                .flatMap(book -> ServerResponse.ok().contentType(MediaType.
                APPLICATION_JSON).bodyValue(book))
                .switchIfEmpty(ServerResponse.notFound().build());
    }
```

```
/* 4 */
public Mono<ServerResponse> save(ServerRequest serverRequest) {
    Mono<Book> bookMono =  serverRequest.bodyToMono(Book.class).
    doOnNext(bookService::save);
    return bookMono
            .flatMap(book -> ServerResponse.created(URI.create("/
            books/" + book.getId())).contentType(MediaType.APPLICATION_
            JSON).bodyValue(book))
            .switchIfEmpty(ServerResponse.status(HttpStatus
                            .INTERNAL_SERVER_ERROR).build());
}
}
```

In Listing 9-17, each handler function is marked with a number. The following list discusses each handler function and the bullet number matches the function number.

1. list is a simple handler function that returns all Book instances returned by the reactive BookService.findAll() method. It is declared as a field of type HandlerFunction and it is a member of the BookHandler class. It cannot be initialized in the same line with the declaration because of its dependency on bookService. To initialize this field, the bookService field must be initialized first. Since it is initialized in the constructor, the initialization of the list field is part of the constructor too. The initial ServerResponse.ok() sets the HTTP response status to 200 (OK) and it returns a reference to the internal BodyBuilder that allows other methods to be chained to describe the request. The chain must end with one of the body*(..) methods that returns a Mono<ServerResponse>.

2. delete is a simple handler function deletes a Book instance with the ID matching the path variable. The path variable is extracted by calling serverRequest.pathVariable("id"). The "id" parameter represents the name of the path variable. The bookService.delete() method returns Mono<Void>, so the Mono<ServerResponse> is emitting a response with an empty body and status code 204 (No Content) set by the ServerResponse. noContent().

3. findByIsbn is a handler function that returns a single Book instance
    identified by the ISBN path variable. The instance is being retrieved
    by calling bookService.findByIsbn(..) that returns a Mono<Book>.
    If this stream emits a value, this means a book was found matching
    the path variable, and a response is created with the Status 200
    code and a body represented by the Book instance as JSON. To
    access the Book instance, emitted by the stream without blocking,
    the flatMap(..) function is used. If the stream does not emit a
    value, this means a book with the expected ISBN was not found so
    an empty response is created with the Status 404 (Not Found) by
    calling switchIfEmpty(ServerResponse.notFound().build()).

4. save is a handler function that stores a new Book instance
    contained in the request body. Since the request body is read
    as a Mono<Book> by calling serverRequest.bodyToMono(Book.
    class) the doOnNext(bookService::save) method is chained to
    invoke bookService.save(book) when the value is emitted. The
    method returns a Mono<Book>. This stream emits a value when a
    successful save was executed and the response is populated with
    a Location header pointing to the URL when the created resource
    can be accessed. To access the Book instance, emitted by the stream
    without blocking, the flatMap(..) function is used. This is done by
    calling ServerResponse.created(), which sets the response status
    to 201 (Created) and declares an URI as a parameter. The value
    provided as an argument becomes the value of the location header.
    If the stream does not emit a value, this means the save operation
    failed. The implementation provided here returns an empty
    response body with a 500 (Internal Server Error) response status.

Now that we have handler functions, how are they being mapped to requests? Well,
this is the job of a *router* bean.

org.springframework.web.reactive.function.server.RouterFunction<T>
is a simple functional interface describing a function that routes incoming requests
to HandlerFunction<T> instances. RouterFunction<T> takes a ServerRequest and
returns Mono<HandlerFunction<T>>. If a handler function is not found it returns an
empty Mono<Void>. RouterFunction<T> has a similar purpose as the @RequestMapping
annotation in @Controller classes.

org.springframework.web.reactive.function.server.RouterFunctions is a utility abstract class that provides static methods for building simple and nested routing functions and can even transform a RouterFunction<T> into a HttpHandler which makes the application run in a Servlet 3.1+ container.

Before discussing router functions any further, let's first look at an example. Listing 9-18 depicts the BookRouterConfiguration configuration class. It declares a single bean of type RouterFunction<ServerResponse>, which is a router function routes incoming requests to the handler functions declared in the BookHandler bean introduced previously.

Listing 9-18. The BookRouterConfiguration Configuration Class

```
package com.apress.prospringmvc.bookstore;
import org.springframework.web.reactive.function.server.RouterFunction;
import org.springframework.web.reactive.function.server.ServerResponse;

import static org.springframework.web.reactive.function.server.
RequestPredicates.*;
import static org.springframework.web.reactive.function.server.
RouterFunctions.route;
// other imports omitted

@Configuration
public class BookRouterConfiguration {
    private final Logger logger = LoggerFactory.getLogger(BookRouter.
    class);

    @Bean
    RouterFunction<ServerResponse> routerFunction(BookHandler bookHandler)
{
        return route(GET("/books"), bookHandler.list) /* 1 */
            .andRoute(GET("/books/{isbn}"), bookHandler::findByIsbn)  /* 2 */
            .andRoute(POST("/books"), bookHandler::save)  /* 3 */
            .andRoute(DELETE("/books/{id}"), bookHandler.delete)  /* 4 */
            .filter((request, next) -> { /* 5 */
                logger.info("Before handler invocation: " + request.path());
                return next.handle(request);
            });
    }
}
```

In Listing 9-18, each handler function is marked with a number. The following list discusses the content of each line and bullet number matches the function number.

1. `route(GET("/books"), bookHandler.list)` creates a `RouterFunction<T>` based on `org.springframework.web.reactive.function.server.RequestPredicate` and `HandlerFunction<T>`. The `RequestPredicate` instance represents a function that evaluates `ServerRequest` against a set of properties, like the request method and URL template. `GET("/books")` is a static method from the `org.springframework.web.reactive.function.server.RequestPredicates` abstract utility class that creates a `request predicate` that matches GET requests to the /books URL.

2. `.andRoute(GET("/books/{isbn}"), bookHandler::findByIsbn)` takes a predicate and handler function as arguments and creates a router function that gets added to the router function the method is being invoked on. It returns the router function that represents a composition of the two.

3. `.andRoute(POST("/books"), bookHandler::save)` is a static method from the `org.springframework.web.reactive.function.server.RequestPredicates` utility class that creates a `request predicate` that matches POST requests to the /books URL.

4. `.andRoute(DELETE("/books/{id}"), bookHandler.delete)` is a static method from the `org.springframework.web.reactive.function.server.RequestPredicates` utility class that creates a `request predicate` that matches DELETE requests to the /books/{id} URL, where ID is the name of the path variable.

5. `.filter((request, next) → {..})` is a method declared in `RouterFunction` that can be implemented to add a `HandlerFilterFunction<T,S>` to the filter handler functions based on some conditions or to add logging code, as in the example in Listing 9-18. `HandlerFilterFunction<T,S>` functions pretty much as a `@ControllerAdvice` or `javax.servlet.Filter`.

In a Spring WebFlux application, if you want to pick up beans containing handler function definitions, component scanning must be enabled on the packages in which the beans are declared.

Router function beans can be declared in any @Configuration annotated class and are picked up by enabling component scanning for the packages where the configuration classes are declared.

Spring WebFlux applications are suitable for streaming data, which is why most applications do not resolve requests to views and instead return streams of data. The preferred way is to write a web application that is detached from the backend using technologies such as React,[22] TypeScript,[23] and more. This introduces a lot of flexibility when upgrading resources and scaling the application. The preferred way of communication between the client and the server is through the WebSocket Protocol,[24] which allows establishing a two-way communication between a web browser and a server.

WebSocket is the perfect protocol for reactive applications, because both parties can start sending data at any time, which means the client can apply backpressure. But, more about that in the next chapters.

Summary

This chapter was a small introduction into reactive programming and it scratched the surface on Spring WebFlux so that you are more familiar with the code covered in the next two chapters.

Here are a few things you should keep in mind.

- A stream can be viewed as *data on the move.*

- A reactive stream is a non-blocking stream that supports backpressure. The consumer regulates the rate of elements being emitted by the producer.

---

[22]https://reactjs.org/
[23]https://www.typescriptlang.org/
[24]https://tools.ietf.org/html/rfc6455

- Pure functions are functions that do not mutate the input, always return a value and the returned value is based solely on the input (they have no side effects).

- Functional reactive programming is programming with Reactive Streams and pure functions.

- The key characteristics of reactive components should be composability and readability.

- Using reactive programming and writing your code according to this paradigm, does not always result in a reactive system as described by the Reactive Manifesto.

- All components of a reactive application must be reactive; otherwise, there is a risk of blocking.

- Reactive code is fully declarative and nothing happens until a subscriber is attached to a publisher.

- Spring WebFlux applications can be deployed on Servlet 3.1 containers.

- Spring WebFlux is the reactive alternative to Spring MVC.

- Spring WebFlux applications support request mapping via annotated methods and functional endpoints.

- Spring WebFlux provides a functional approach to map incoming requests to handler functions.

- Functional reactive programming is most suitable for implementing microservices applications. Spring Boot WebFlux is the perfect building block for microservices applications.

## CHAPTER 10

Building Reactive Applications with Spring WebFlux

In the previous chapter, functional reactive programming was introduced out of necessity. Spring WebFlux is a functional reactive framework for writing Spring reactive applications, and the code written for the applications in this chapter is functional and uses Reactive Streams.

Spring WebFlux is a good fit for building applications that require easy streaming. The examples introduced in the previous chapter sent data to the client over an HTTP connection using Reactive Streams. But the client only received data, and nothing was done to control the rate of emission. This chapter explores Spring WebFlux capabilities by migrating parts of the Bookstore application from MVC to Spring WebFlux, introducing a `web client` that provides information about new book releases, and adding a chat capability to the application.

From Spring Web MVC to Spring WebFlux

When migrating application logic from classic to reactive, the types handled by your methods change. The statements change too; they are no longer imperative but declarative, and their code is executed only when signals are emitted. For a multi-tier application the transformation can be done from the lower tier (data access) to the upper tier (the presentation), or from the upper tier to the lower. To get you warmed up, let's start from the bottom tier.

© Marten Deinum and Iuliana Cosmina 2021
M. Deinum and I. Cosmina, *Pro Spring MVC with WebFlux*, https://doi.org/10.1007/978-1-4842-5666-4_10

Migrating the Data Access Layer

Up until a while ago, relational databases did not support reactive access. The classic database JDBC drivers are not reactive, so in a reactive application, they represent a blocking I/O component that affects the whole application's behavior. Last year though, the R2DBC[1] project was introduced that brings reactive programming APIs to relational databases. Currently, R2DBC implementations for most used relational databases exist. But, even after three official releases, the project is still unstable.

This leaves a single option: give up the relational database and switch to a NoSQL database that supports reactive access. You will probably use Spring WebFlux to write microservices applications. Relational databases with their strong typing and rigid relationships between column tables are not compatible with the requirements of horizontal scalability and clustering of microservice architecture. There are a few modern NoSQL databases supported by Spring—Couchbase, Redis, and Cassandra, but the Spring favorite is MongoDB.[2] The Reactive BookStore application used as a case study for this chapter uses MongoDB. (The project for this chapter contains a README. adoc file with instructions for installing MongoDB locally.)

In a Spring Boot application, the `application.yml` configuration file is populated with properties that allow integration with a MongoDB database. But, they are not important for a web context, so they won't be covered here.

Using the MongoDB database in a Spring Boot application requires the `spring-boot-starter-data-mongodb-reactive` dependency on the project classpath and a few changes to the code. These changes are listed next.

- Entity classes become domain classes, and this means ID type is limited to `String` or `BigDecimal`. If you try using any other type an exception of type `org.springframework.dao.InvalidDataAccessApiUsageException` is thrown.

- Since NoSQL databases are not relational databases, the database structure changes to keep strongly linked data.

- Database tables become database collections.

---

[1]`https://r2dbc.io/`

[2]`https://www.mongodb.com/`

- JPA/hibernate annotations are replaced with Spring Data MongoDB Annotations.

- JpaRepository<T, ID> extensions are replaced with ReactiveMongoRepository<T, ID> or ReactiveCrudRepository<T, ID>.

The Book class changes to the implementation are shown in Listing 10-1. Other classes in the application are changed similarly.

Listing 10-1. The Book MongoDB Document Class

```
package com.apress.prospringmvc.bookstore.document;

import org.springframework.data.annotation.Id;
import org.springframework.data.mongodb.core.index.Indexed;
import org.springframework.data.mongodb.core.mapping.Document;
import java.math.BigDecimal;
// other imports omitted

@Document(collection="book")
public class Book {
    @Id
    private String id;

    private String title;
    private String description;
    private BigDecimal price;
    private Integer year;
    private String author;

    @Indexed(unique = true)
    private String isbn;
    private String category;

    // getters and setters omitted
}
```

The ReactiveCrudRepository<T, ID> interface is part of the org.springframework.data.repository.reactive package and contains methods declarations returning Publisher<T> implementations, for Spring, this means Flux<T> and Mono<T>. The ReactiveSortingRepository<T, ID> is part of the org.springframework.data.repository.reactive package that extends ReactiveCrudRepository<T, ID> to offer a few extra method templates optimized for MongoDB. The BookRepository interface for reactive data access uses MongoDB queries to select data from the database and is depicted in Listing 10-2.

Listing 10-2. The BookRepository Reactive Interface for Accessing the MongoDB Book Collection

```
package com.apress.prospringmvc.bookstore.repository;

import com.apress.prospringmvc.bookstore.document.Book;
import org.springframework.data.mongodb.repository.Query;
import org.springframework.data.mongodb.repository.ReactiveMongoRepository;
import reactor.core.publisher.Flux;

/**
 * Created by Iuliana Cosmina on 28/06/2020
 */
public interface BookRepository extends ReactiveMongoRepository<Book,
String>{

    @Query("{'category': { '$regex' : ?0 } }")
    Flux<Book> findByCategory(String category);

    @Query(value= "{}", fields ="{'id': 1, 'isbn' : 1, 'category'  :1 }")
    Flux<Book> findAllLight();
}
```

The arguments in the @Query annotations are used to declare finder queries directly on repository methods.

Migrating the Service Layer

If the application requires a service layer, its components must be modified to become reactive too. Besides that, the implementation must change to adapt to the new database structure too. In Listing 10-3 a few methods of BookstoreServiceImpl are depicted. findBooksByCategory(String) is modified to support an argument of type String instead of Category, and that is because there is no Category table. The results are returned as Flux<Book>.

findBooks(BookSearchCriteria) is modified to create a MongoDB query and pass that to the BookRepository to filter the results. The results are returned as Flux<Book>.

findOrdersForAccountId(String accountId) is modified to get the orders for an account instance from the account collection, since there is no order collection.

Listing 10-3. The BookRepository Reactive Interface for Accessing the MongoDB Book Collection

```java
package com.apress.prospringmvc.bookstore.service;

import org.springframework.data.mongodb.core.query.Criteria;
import org.springframework.data.mongodb.core.query.Query;
import org.springframework.transaction.annotation.Transactional;
import reactor.core.publisher.Flux;
import reactor.core.publisher.Mono;
// other imports omitted

/**
 * Created by Iuliana Cosmina on 28/06/2020
 */
@Service
@Transactional(readOnly = true)
public class BookstoreServiceImpl implements  BookstoreService {

    @Override
    public Mono<Book> findBook(String id) {
        return this.bookRepository.findById(id);
    }
```

```java
@Override
public Flux<Book> findBooksByCategory(String category) {
    return this.bookRepository.findByCategory(category);
}

@Override
public Flux<Book> findBooks(BookSearchCriteria bookSearchCriteria) {
    Query query = new Query();
    if (bookSearchCriteria.getTitle() != null) {
        query.addCriteria(Criteria.where("title")
            .is(bookSearchCriteria.getTitle()));
    }
    if (bookSearchCriteria.getCategory() != null) {
        query.addCriteria(Criteria.where("category")
            .is(bookSearchCriteria.getTitle()));
    }
    return bookRepository.findAll(query);
}

@Override
public Mono<List<Order>> findOrdersForAccountId(String accountId) {
    return this.accountRepository
        .findById(accountId).map(Account::getOrders);
}

//other code omitted
}
```

Migrating the data access and service layer is easy once you use a reactive database and present little difficulty. Just make sure you are always returning Publisher<T> instances, and you are done.

Migrating the Web Layer

Migrating the web layer requires a few changes, because rendering a view is difficult when you do not know how much data is rendered. In the past AJAX (Asynchronous JavaScript and XML) resolved this problem, but AJAX enables us to update pages only in response to user action on the page. It does not solve the problem of updates coming from the server. And since reactive communication involves data flowing in both directions, new web libraries were needed. There is more than one way to do it, so let's dig in, shall we?

Configuration of a Reactive Templating Engine

Let's take a very simple example used in previous chapters: the index page of the Bookstore application can display the list of beans in the application context. In previous chapters, IndexController contained a single method that populated the model with a List<String> containing all the names of the beans in the application context.

To make this controller reactive, the list must be replaced by a Flux<String>, and the view must be reactive too. Fortunately, Thymeleaf can be configured to support reactive views. The templates' syntax does not change; only the view resolver and the template engine must be replaced with their reactive correspondent.

In Listing 10-4, a Spring configuration class for Reactive Thymeleaf views support is depicted. The class is a little verbose. Most property values set in it are already declared as defaults, but the class is written like this to make it obvious what is customizable from a development point of view.

Listing 10-4. Spring Configuration Class for Reactive Thymeleaf Views Support

```
package com.apress.prospringmvc.bookstore.config;

import org.springframework.web.reactive.config.EnableWebFlux;
import org.springframework.web.reactive.config.ViewResolverRegistry;
import org.springframework.web.reactive.config.WebFluxConfigurer;
import org.thymeleaf.spring5.ISpringWebFluxTemplateEngine;
import org.thymeleaf.spring5.SpringWebFluxTemplateEngine;
import org.thymeleaf.spring5.templateresolver.
SpringResourceTemplateResolver;
import org.thymeleaf.spring5.view.reactive.ThymeleafReactiveViewResolver;
```

```java
import org.thymeleaf.templateresolver.ITemplateResolver;
// other imports omitted

@Configuration
public class ReactiveThymeleafWebConfig implements
            ApplicationContextAware, WebFluxConfigurer {

    ApplicationContext context;

    @Override
    public void setApplicationContext(ApplicationContext context) {
        this.context = context;
    }

    @Bean
    public ITemplateResolver thymeleafTemplateResolver() {
        var resolver = new SpringResourceTemplateResolver();
        resolver.setApplicationContext(this.context);
        resolver.setPrefix("classpath:templates/");
        resolver.setSuffix(".html");
        resolver.setTemplateMode(TemplateMode.HTML);
        resolver.setCacheable(false);
        resolver.setCheckExistence(false);
        return resolver;

    }


    @Bean
    public ISpringWebFluxTemplateEngine thymeleafTemplateEngine() {
        var templateEngine = new SpringWebFluxTemplateEngine();
        templateEngine.setTemplateResolver(thymeleafTemplateResolver());
        return templateEngine;
    }

    @Bean
    public ThymeleafReactiveViewResolver thymeleafReactiveViewResolver() {
        var viewResolver = new ThymeleafReactiveViewResolver();
        viewResolver.setTemplateEngine(thymeleafTemplateEngine());
        viewResolver.setOrder(1);
```

```
        viewResolver.setResponseMaxChunkSizeBytes(8192);
        return viewResolver;
    }

    @Override
    public void configureViewResolvers(ViewResolverRegistry registry) {
        registry.viewResolver(thymeleafReactiveViewResolver());
    }

}
```

The template resolver bean that is responsible for resolving templates does not need to be reactive. Since the template resolver bean contains data coming from application configuration, it can be dropped altogether when using Spring Boot and replaced by annotating the configuration class with @EnableConfigurationProperties(ThymeleafP roperties.class).

The template engine that uses the template resolver is reactive and is an implementation of ISpringWebFluxTemplateEngine. SpringTemplateEngine, designed for integration with a Spring MVC type, must be replaced with SpringWebFluxTemplateEngine, an implementation of the ISpringWebFluxTemplateEngine interface, designed for integration with Spring WebFlux and execution of templates in a reactive-friendly way. Since the template engine requires a template resolver and nothing else, we can skip this bean declaration as well and allow Spring Boot to configure it. The configuration class for reactive views support can be simplified as depicted in Listing 10-5.

Listing 10-5. Simplified Spring Configuration Class for Reactive Thymeleaf Views Support

```
package com.apress.prospringmvc.bookstore.config;

import org.springframework.boot.autoconfigure.thymeleaf.
ThymeleafProperties;
import org.springframework.boot.context.properties.
EnableConfigurationProperties;
// other imports omitted

@Configuration
@EnableConfigurationProperties(ThymeleafProperties.class)
```

```java
public class ReactiveThymeleafWebConfig implements
        WebFluxConfigurer {

    private final ISpringWebFluxTemplateEngine thymeleafTemplateEngine;

    public ReactiveThymeleafWebConfig(ISpringWebFluxTemplateEngine
templateEngine) {
        this.thymeleafTemplateEngine = templateEngine;
    }

    @Bean
    public ThymeleafReactiveViewResolver thymeleafReactiveViewResolver() {
        var viewResolver = new ThymeleafReactiveViewResolver();
        viewResolver.setTemplateEngine(thymeleafTemplateEngine);
        viewResolver.setOrder(1);
        return viewResolver;
    }
    //other code omitted
}
```

The @EnableConfigurationProperties annotation enables support for
Thymeleaf configuration properties. The ThymeleafProperties class is annotated
with @ConfigurationProperties(prefix = "spring.thymeleaf"), making it a
configuration bean for Thymeleaf properties. This means you can use application.
properties or application.yml to configure Thymeleaf. The properties are prefixed
with spring.thymeleaf and allow you to configure the template resolver bean without
writing additional code. Listing 10-6 is the YML configuration equivalent to the Java
configuration in Listing 10-4.

Listing 10-6. Simplified Spring Configuration Class for Reactive Thymeleaf
Views Support (snippet from the application.yml file)

```yaml
spring:
  thymeleaf:
    prefix: classpath:templates/
    suffix: .html
    mode: HTML
    cache: false
    check-template: false
    reactive:
        max-chunk-size: 8192
```

Some Thymeleaf properties have default values assigned to them in the `ThymeleafProperties` class, so this means if your application uses the defaults, the Thymeleaf YML configuration section can be skipped altogether and the configuration in Listing 10-5 still works.

The `ThymeleafReactiveViewResolver` is an implementation of the `org.springframework.web.reactive.result.view.ViewResolver` interface, the Spring WebFlux view resolver interface. The `responseMaxChunkSizeBytes` is the property you should be interested in because it defines the maximum size for the output `org.springframework.core.io.buffer.DataBuffer` instances produced by the Thymeleaf engine and passed to the server as output. This is important because if you have a lot of data sent through `Flux<T>`, you might want to render the view in chunks, bit by bit, instead of keeping a web page in a loading state until the response is complete. Especially since this is one of the main ideas of reactive communication.

Thymeleaf has three modes of operation.

- **FULL:** When there is no max chunk size configured, and there is no data-driver context variable, the template output is generated in memory as a single chunk and then sent as a response. This is very similar to the non-reactive behavior.

- **CHUNKED:** The limit for max chunk size configured is established but no data-driver context variable has been specified. The template is generated in chunks with a size roughly equal to the one configured and sent to the client. After sending a chunk the Thymeleaf engine stops and waits for the server to request more chunks; yes, this is an implementation of backpressure.

- **DATA-DRIVEN:** A `data-driver` variable wraps asynchronous objects in the form of reactive data streams, which are meant to drive the reactive-friendly execution of a template. When this kind of variable is declared in a handler method that returns the logical name of a view, the Thymeleaf engine is set to the `DATA-DRIVEN` mode, which means the resolved views are sent to the client as a data stream. Templates that support a data-driver variable must contain an iteration (`th:each`) on that variable.

The approach to rewrite the `IndexController` to make it reactive uses a `data-driver` variable. This means, instead of adding a `List<String>` to the model, an instance of `org.thymeleaf.spring5.context.webflux.IReactiveDataDriverContextVariable` is required. This variable is wrapped around a `Flux<String>` instance emitting application context bean names. Context variables implementing this interface wrap `Publisher<T>` instances in the form reactive data streams meant to drive the reactive-friendly execution of a template.[3]

To make this approach's results clear, the emitting of the values is slowed down to once every 200 milliseconds. This means when opening the `http://localhost:8080/` URL, you should see the gradual loading of the page section listing the bean names.

The implementation of the reactive `IndexController` is depicted in Listing 10-7.

Listing 10-7. Reactive `IndexController` with `Data-Driver` Variable

```
package com.apress.prospringmvc.bookstore.controller;

import org.thymeleaf.spring5.context.webflux.
IReactiveDataDriverContextVariable;
import org.thymeleaf.spring5.context.webflux.
ReactiveDataDriverContextVariable;
import reactor.core.publisher.Flux;
// other imports omitted

@Controller
public class IndexController implements ApplicationContextAware {

    private ApplicationContext ctx;

    @Override
    public void setApplicationContext(ApplicationContext
applicationContext)
                    throws BeansException {
        ctx = applicationContext;
    }
```

---

[3]https://www.thymeleaf.org/apidocs/thymeleaf-spring5/3.0.11.RELEASE/org/thymeleaf/spring5/context/webflux/IReactiveDataDriverContextVariable.html

```java
@GetMapping("/")
public String index(final Model model) {
    List<String> beans = Arrays.stream(ctx.getBeanDefinitionNames())
        .sorted()
        .collect(Collectors.toList());
    Flux<String> flux = Flux.fromIterable(beans)
        .delayElements(Duration.ofMillis(200));
    IReactiveDataDriverContextVariable dataDriver =
            new ReactiveDataDriverContextVariable( flux,10);

    model.addAttribute("beans", dataDriver);
    return "index";
}
}
```

ReactiveDataDriverContextVariable is a basic implementation of the IReactive
DataDriverContextVariable interface. Using IReactiveDataDriverContextVariable,
we set Thymeleaf in data-driven mode, which means HTML items are produced in a
reactive-friendly way.

The index.html template doesn't require any change. Thymeleaf uses the same
HTML constructs to iterate over collections and reactive sets of data. The values emitted
by the stream are added as they are emitted to a <ul> list nested inside a scrollable <div>
to keep the page size equal to the screen size. The ${beans} variable is a reference to the
reactive stream exposed by the Thymeleaf data-driver variable.

Listing 10-8. The Thymeleaf Template Snippet to Render the Bean Names
(snippet from the index.html file)

```html
<!-- other HTML parts omitted -->
<div class="scrollable">
    <ul th:each="bean : ${beans}">
        <li th:text="${bean}"> </li>
    </ul>
</div>
```

Still, loading a page gradually is not the best choice, since there are parts of the page design that are not rendered until the reactive communication is finished. This makes users feel as if they are viewing this page via an ADSL connection. Let's look at another approach that uses a reactive handler method and JavaScript function to load those bean names gradually in an HTML div, after the page was fully loaded.

Using Server-Sent Events (SSEs)

In the previous chapter, reactive controllers were mentioned. Most reactive controllers are annotated with @RestController, a composed annotation marking the controller having handler methods that return data instead of logical view names. IndexController cannot be annotated because we still need it to resolve the index. html view template. But, we can extract the bean flux into a reactive handler method annotated with @ResponseBody. This leads to the implementation in Listing 10-9.

Listing 10-9. Reactive IndexController with a Method Handler Returning a Flux<T> of Data

```
package com.apress.prospringmvc.bookstore.controller;

import org.springframework.web.bind.annotation.ResponseBody;
import reactor.core.publisher.Flux;
// other imports omitted

@Controller
public class IndexController implements ApplicationContextAware {

    private ApplicationContext ctx;

    @Override
    public void setApplicationContext(ApplicationContext
applicationContext)
        throws BeansException {
        ctx = applicationContext;
    }

    @GetMapping(path = {"/", "index.htm"})
    public String index() {
```

```
        return "index";
    }

    @ResponseBody
    @GetMapping(value = "/beans", produces = MediaType.TEXT_EVENT_STREAM_
VALUE)
    public Flux<String> getBeanNames() {
        List<String> beans = Arrays.stream(ctx.getBeanDefinitionNames())
            .sorted().collect(Collectors.toList());
        return Flux.fromIterable(beans).delayElements(Duration.
ofMillis(200));
    }
}
```

If you start the application, you can test that the method returns a flux of bean names by running the following command.

```
curl -H "Accept:text/event-stream" http://localhost:8080/beans
```

Every bean name is emitted as a server-sent event by Spring WebFlux, and now, the index.html requires a few changes to process them and display them on the page. Since the new data has to be added to the page as it arrives, JavaScript is required to write a function that modifies the least of beans.

Thus, the index.html template snippet required to display the bean names changes as depicted in Listing 10-10.

Listing 10-10. Thymeleaf template snippet used to display the bean names received as Server-Sent Events (snippet from the index.html file)

```
<!-- other HTML/JavaScript parts omitted -->
<script type="text/javascript" th:inline="javascript">
/*<![CDATA[*/
    var renderBeans = {
        source: new EventSource([[@{|/beans|}]]) ,
        start: function () {
            this.source.addEventListener("message", function (event) {
                //console.log(event);
                $("#beans").append('<li>'+ event.data +'</li>')
```

```
        });
        this.source.onerror = function () {
            this.source.close();
        };
    },
    stop: function() {
        this.source.close();
    }
};

$( window ).on( "load", function() {
    renderBeans.start();
});

$( window ).on( "onbeforeunload", function() {
    renderBeans.stop();
});
/*]]>*/
</script>
<div class="scrollable">
    <ul id="beans">
    </ul>
</div>
```

[[@{|/beans|}]] is a Thymeleaf link expression to generate a URL relative to the
application context.

In Listing 10-10, the jQuery library is used to write the JavaScript code required
to handle server-sent events, a server push technology enabling a client to receive
automatic updates from a server via HTTP connection. Which means the page gets
rendered, but the connection is kept open, so the server can send more data to the client.
The EventSource API is standardized as part of HTML5 and except Internet Explorer, all
other browsers support it.

Thymeleaf generates three types of SSEs.

- **Header**: The data is prefixed by head: or {prefix}_head: where the
  prefix value is set via the ReactiveDataDriverContextVariable
  constructor. The prefix is used for a single event during the
  communication containing all the markup before the iterated data

(if any). For example, when you are reading a Facebook thread, the moment you open the page, all the comments that exist in the database, previous to the timestamp when you opened that page, should already be rendered in the page. There is no point to render them one by one. Thymeleaf supports this type of initializing events.

- **Data message**: The data is prefixed by **message:** or **{prefix}_message:** where the `prefix` is set via the `ReactiveDataDriverContextVariable` constructor. The prefix is used for a series of events, one for each value produced by the data driver. For example, when you read a Facebook thread, comments from other users that post while you are viewing the page appear in the comments section, one by one. Data from the comment is sent to the client through an SSE of type message.

- **Tail**: The data is prefixed by `tail:` or `{prefix}_tail` where the `prefix` value is set via the `ReactiveDataDriverContextVariable` constructor. The prefix is used for a single event during the communication containing all the markup following to the iterated data (if any). For example, assuming Facebook had an option through which the user could choose to stop seeing new comments, an event of this type could be used to send all existing comments in the database with a timestamp value between the last displayed comment and the timestamp when the user chose to stop seeing new comments.[4]

In the previous snippet, the `/beans` URL was used as a source for a stream of SSEs. An `EventSource`[5] instance is created using the URL and it opens a persistent connection through which the server sends events in `text/event-stream` format. The connection remains open until closed by calling `EventSource.close()`. Those events are marked as `message` events by Spring WebFlux, and an `EventListener`[6] instance is set on the `EventSource` instance to intercept those events, extract the data, and add it to a HTML page.

---

[4]MongoDB has tailable cursors which can be combined with the Spring Data MongoDB `@Tailable` annotation to access data as a reactive stream of events with head and tail `https://docs.mongodb.com/manual/core/tailable-cursors/`

[5]`https://developer.mozilla.org/en-US/docs/Web/API/EventSource`

[6]`https://developer.mozilla.org/en-US/docs/Web/API/EventListener`

The bean names stream was intentionally slowed down to show the continuous communication. If you use Chrome or Firefox, you can see the events sent by the server in the developer console when loading the page. Remove the comment from the `console.log(event)` statement from the body of the `EventListener` instance. In Figure 10-1, the main page of the Bookstore application is opened in Firefox, and you can see the stream of data sent from the server in the developer console.

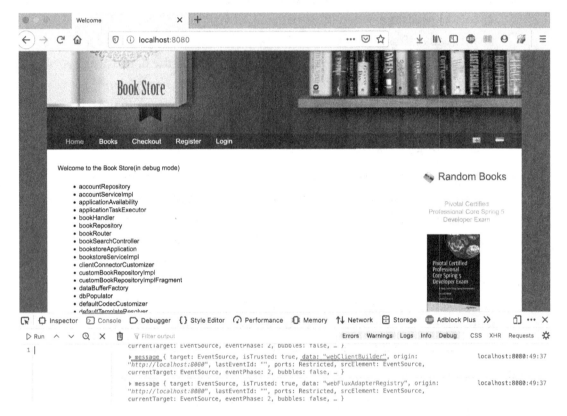

Figure 10-1. *Server-sent events displayed in Firefox's developer console*

The other way to use server-sent events to display reactive data into a Thymeleaf template is to use an `IReactiveSSEDataDriverContextVariable` context variable. Context variables implementing this interface wrap `Publisher<T>` instances in the form reactive data streams that are meant to drive the reactive-friendly execution of a template in an SSE (server-sent event) mode.[7] This means that Spring WebFlux does not wrap the data as SSEs; instead, it sends them to the Thymeleaf engine to do so.

---

[7]`https://www.thymeleaf.org/apidocs/thymeleaf-spring5/3.0.11.RELEASE/org/thymeleaf/spring5/context/webflux/IReactiveSSEDataDriverContextVariable.html`

In the context of a Spring WebFlux application using the Thymeleaf engine for its view generation, this means that each value emitted is *mapped* to a Thymeleaf template fragment, a piece of a Thymeleaf view. When a value is emitted, the Thymeleaf engine takes the data and wraps it in the HTML element the fragment describes and emits that as an SSE of type `message`. The event data is then injected into the HTML page using a JavaScript function. Listing 10-11 is a snippet of a Thymeleaf template. It shows an `<div/>` element named `newBooks.` Nested inside it is a table with a single line containing details of a book to be released.

Listing 10-11. Thymeleaf Template Snipped to Display the Bean Names Received As Server-Sent Events (snippet from the `search.html` file)

```html
<!-- other HTML parts omitted -->
<div class="releases_box">
    <div class="title">
        <span class="title_icon">
            <img th:src="@{/static/images/release.ico}" alt="" title="" />
        </span>
        <th:block th:text="#{main.title.newbooks}">New Books</th:block>
    </div>
    <div id="newBooks">
    <!-- /start/ the targeted fragment -->
        <table th:each="book : ${newBooks}" class="releases_table">
            <tr>
                <td
        th:text="${book.year} + ', ' + ${book.title} + ', by ' +  ${book.
author}">
                </td>
            </tr>
        </table>
    <!-- /end/ the targeted fragment -->
    </div>
</div>
```

The table definition represents the fragment that is rewritten by Thymeleaf engine every time a value is emitted. This is done using a JavaScript function similar with the one depicted in Listing 10-10, only this function overrides the HTML content of the newBooks div with the event data. The renderBooks variable containing the functions to implement the desired reactive behavior is depicted in Listing 10-12.

Listing 10-12. The JavaScript Function That Provides the View Reactive Behavior (snippet from the search.html file)

```
// other HTML/JavaScript parts omitted
var renderBooks = {
    source: new EventSource([[@{|/book/new|}]]) ,
    start: function () {
        renderBooks.source.addEventListener("message", function (event) {
            //console.log(event);
            $("#newBooks").html(event.data);
        });
        renderBooks.source.onerror = function () {
            this.close();
        };
    },
    stop: function() {
        this.source.close();
    }
};
```

The handler method mapped to the /book/new URL is part of the BookSearchController and is not that different from the method used to provide a stream of beans names in the IndexController. There are two main differences. The first difference is that IReactiveSSEDataDriverContextVariable is used as a reference type for the data-driver context variable. This is how Thymeleaf is told that we want the template to be executed in SSE (Server-Sent Event) mode.

The second difference is the logical view name returned by the method that must contain the identifier of the Thymeleaf template fragment that should be applied to each element emitted by the stream before sending it as an SSE. The logical view name must respect the following syntax: templateName :: #fragmentIdentifier. The context variable in Listing 10-13 does not declare an explicit prefix, which means the events are marked as having the message type.

Listing 10-13. Handler Method in BookSearchController Declaring a IReactiveSSEDataDriverContextVariable

```
package com.apress.prospringmvc.bookstore.controller;

import org.thymeleaf.spring5.context.webflux.
IReactiveSSEDataDriverContextVariable;
import org.thymeleaf.spring5.context.webflux.
ReactiveDataDriverContextVariable;
//other imports omitted

@Controller
public class BookSearchController {
  // Generates random books to be displayed
    @GetMapping( value = "/book/new", produces = MediaType.TEXT_EVENT_
STREAM_VALUE)
    public String newBooks(final Model model){
        Flux<Book> newReleases = Flux.interval(Duration.ofSeconds(3))
          .map(delay -> BookNewReleasesUtil.randomRelease());

        final IReactiveSSEDataDriverContextVariable dataDriver =
                new ReactiveDataDriverContextVariable(newReleases, 1);

        model.addAttribute("newBooks", dataDriver);
        return "book/search :: #newBooks";
    }
}
// other code omitted
```

Putting all those components together, you get a page that displays a newly released book every 3 seconds. If you use Chrome or Firefox, you can see the events sent by the server in the developer console when loading the page. Remove the comment from the `console.log(event)` statement from the body of the `EventListener` instance. In Figure 10-2, the `search` page of the Bookstore application is opened in Firefox, and you can see the stream of data sent from the server in the developer console. Notice the data is an HTML snippet matching the template fragment named `newBooks,` where the Thymeleaf variables were replaced with the emitted values.

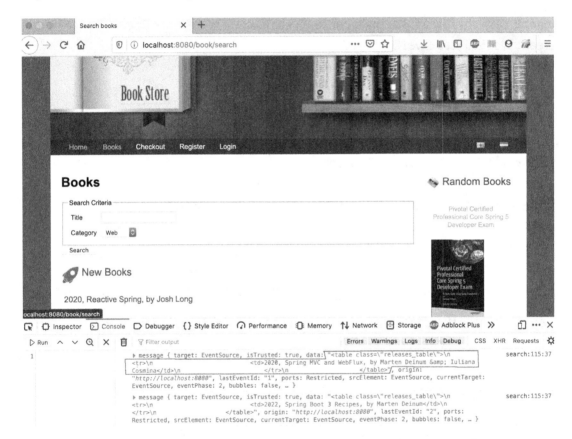

Figure 10-2. *Server-sent events displayed in Firefox's developer console*

We mentioned that prefixes are supported for SSEs. Prefixes are useful when you need more than one reactive snippet on the same page. In this case, prefixes map SSEs to different fragments in the same template. This is required because, even if two publishers are on the same server emitting events, they are doing it through the same HTTP connection. Two event listeners are needed to intercept different types of events and process them accordingly.

In the `search.html` template, if we add a new section displaying tech news, we must add prefixes to both context data-driver variables to be filtered based on them and directed to the appropriate template fragment. `newBooks` is used as a prefix for server events directed to the `newBooks` div, and `techNews` is used as a prefix for a div named `techNews` that display tech news. The HTML and JavaScript for both div elements are pretty much the same. If you want to see how the SSEs sent to the client look like, take a look at Figure 10-3.

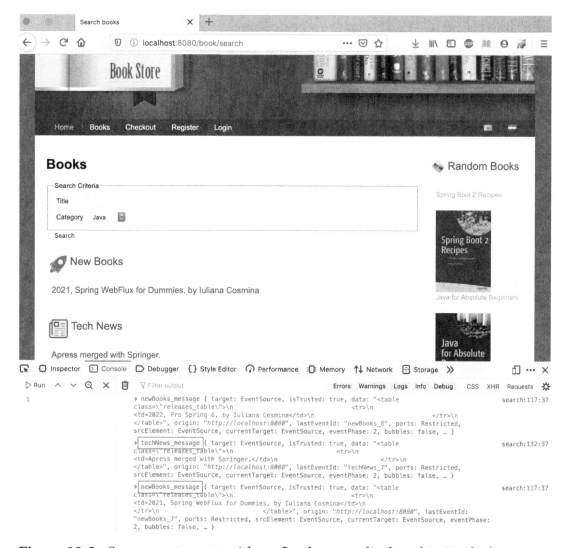

Figure 10-3. *Server-sent events with prefixed names displayed in Firefox's developer console*

In the previous examples, the books and tech news were provided by a stream that emits a random item from a fixed collection. Still, it was mentioned that reactive applications are a good choice when data from multiple services is aggregated. For a situation closer to reality, the data for the newBooks div could be provided by a reactive service external to the Bookstore application, or maybe more of them belonging to a book publisher (such as Apress). Data for the techNews div could be provided by a reactive service belonging to some public tech aggregator application. The implementation for handler methods for data emitted from those streams looks a lot like the code in Listing 10-13, so it won't be repeated here.

Spring WebFlux introduces something to integrate with other reactive services without much struggle, which is discussed in the next section.

Introducing WebClient and WebTestClient

Before Spring WebFlux, making HTTP requests was possible using org. springframework.web.client.RestTemplate. This client is synchronous and offers templates for common scenarios by HTTP method. The now deprecated AsyncRestTemplate was introduced later in the same package to support making asynchronous HTTP requests only to be replaced by WebClient. For tests, org. springframework.boot.test.web.client.TestRestTemplate can still be used for synchronous HTTP requests.

Spring WebFlux provides a reactive, non-blocking HTTP client that exposes a very practical API through the org.springframework.web.reactive.function.client. WebClient interface. A single implementation is provided, org.springframework.web. reactive.function.client.DefaultWebClient. Under the covers, it uses the HTTP client found on the classpath, such as Reactor Netty. It's a practical tool to access other reactive services from your reactive application. The WebClient interface provides two static methods for creating a WebClient instance—both named *create*. One of them receives the base URL of an application as an argument, and all subsequent calls can be simplified since their URLs are considered relative to the base URL.

Listing 10-14 shows a web client created using the static create() method. The instance then makes a GET REST call to a reactive service exposed at http:// localhost:8080/randomBookNews. This service is nothing more than a functional endpoint within the same application that returns an infinite stream of Book instances.

Listing 10-14. Using WebClient Without a Base URL Within the
BookSearchController

```java
package com.apress.prospringmvc.bookstore.controller;

import org.springframework.web.reactive.function.client.WebClient;
//other imports omitted

@Controller
public class BookSearchController {

    @GetMapping( value = "/book/new",
                produces = MediaType.TEXT_EVENT_STREAM_VALUE)
    public String newBooks(final Model model){
        // previous implementation
        //Flux<Book> newReleases = Flux.interval(Duration.ofSeconds(5))
        //        .map(delay -> BookNewReleasesUtil.randomRelease());
        WebClient webClient = WebClient.create();
        Flux<Book> newReleases = webClient
                .get().uri("http://localhost:8080/randomBookNews")
                .retrieve()
                .bodyToFlux(Book.class);

        final IReactiveSSEDataDriverContextVariable dataDriver =
                new ReactiveDataDriverContextVariable(newReleases, 1,
"newBooks");

        model.addAttribute("newBooks", dataDriver);
        return "book/search :: #newBooks";
    }
    //other code omitted
}
```

The other way uses the full URL to create the WebClient instance. All HTTP
requests using the instance can then use only a part of the URL that is relative to the
baseURL. Listing 10-15 shows a WebClient created using the static create(String)
method.

Listing 10-15. Using WebClient with a Base URL

```
WebClient webClient = WebClient.create("http://localhost:8080/
randomBookNews");

Flux<Book> newReleases = webClient.get().uri("/")
        .retrieve()
        .bodyToFlux(Book.class);
```

Another method to create a WebClient is by using the builder instance returned by calling the WebClient.builder() method. This allows a more granular configuration of the WebClient instance. When using the builder, you can set headers, cookies, additional operators to customize the returned values, and even a different client connector. (ReactorClientHttpConnector[8] is used by default. It is provided by Spring WebFlux, but you can also use a reactive Apache CloseableHttpAsyncClient,[9] for example). This means the WebClient declaration in Listing 10-15 can be written as depicted in Listing 10-16.

Listing 10-16. Creating WebClient Using a Builder

```
WebClient webClient = WebClient.builder()
        .baseUrl("http://localhost:8080/randomBookNews")
        .defaultHeader(HttpHeaders.CONTENT_TYPE, MediaType.TEXT_EVENT_
        STREAM_VALUE)
        .defaultCookie("InternalCookie", "all")
        .build();
```

Regardless of the way it was created, the WebClient instance is immutable; however, it does support a clone() method that returns a builder that can create a new instance based on the original.

---

[8]https://docs.spring.io/spring-framework/docs/current/javadoc-api/org/
 springframework/http/client/reactive/ReactorClientHttpConnector.html
[9]https://hc.apache.org/httpcomponents-client-5.0.x/httpclient5/apidocs/org/apache/
 hc/client5/http/impl/async/CloseableHttpAsyncClient.html

WebClient is flexible and allows complex constructs to be created that support making HTTP requests using URLs with path variables and request parameters. URL builders and URL encoding are supported too. We go over a few important methods quickly. For a full description of the available API, feel free to consult the official documentation, which is very good.[10]

The retrieve() method obtains an HTTP response. In the previous examples, this method was followed by calls to bodyToMono(Class) or bodyToFlux(Class). Both receive as argument the type of values emitted. But, this method can also be followed by a call to onStatus(..), and exceptions can be emitted, which are wrapped into WebClientResponseException objects, depending on the HTTP status code. Listing 10-17 depicts such an example.

Listing 10-17. Using WebClient with Customized Error Behavior, Using the onStatus(..) Method

```
Flux<Book> newReleases = webClient.get()
    .uri("/")
    .retrieve()
    .onStatus(HttpStatus::is4xxClientError, response ->
        Mono.error( response.statusCode() == HttpStatus.UNAUTHORIZED
            ? new ServiceDeniedException("You shall not pass!")
            : new ServiceDeniedException("Well.. this is unfortunate!"))
    )
    .onStatus(HttpStatus::is5xxServerError, response ->
        Mono.error(response.statusCode() == HttpStatus.INTERNAL_SERVER_ERROR
            ? new ServiceDownException("This is SpartAAA!!")
            : new ServiceDownException("Well.. this is a mystery!"))
    )
    .bodyToFlux(Book.class);
```

If the response is expected to have content, it should be consumed by the function matching the status code predicate; otherwise, its content is discarded to release resources.

---

[10]https://docs.spring.io/spring/docs/current/spring-framework-reference/web-reactive.html#webflux-client

The retrieve() method can be used with get(), post(), put(), delete() and so on. There is also an exchange() method, which provides more granular control. For example, the exchange() method provides access to the response, which allows you to inspect the response headers, cookies, or change it in any way necessary. The disadvantage is that it does not support customized behavior based on HTTP status codes.

A cool thing about WebClient is that it can be used with services developed using any other technology if its output can be deserialized correctly. To prove that this can be done, the service providing the tech news was implemented using Node.js.[11] Listing 10-18 depicts the implementation of this service.

Listing 10-18. The tech-news.js Service That Generates an Infinite Stream of Random Tech News

```
const http = require('http');
const sys = require('util');
const fs = require('fs');

const hostname = 'localhost';
const port = 3000;

const news = [
    'Apress merged with Springer.',
    // other values omitted
];

const server = http.createServer((req, res) => {
    res.setHeader('Content-Type', 'text/event-stream;charset=UTF-8');
    res.setHeader('Cache-Control', 'no-cache');
    // only if you want anyone to access this endpoint
    res.setHeader('Access-Control-Allow-Origin', '*');
    res.flushHeaders();

    // Sends a SSE every 2 seconds on a single connection.
    setInterval(function() {
```

---

[11]https://nodejs.org/en/

```
      res.write('data:'+news[Math.floor(Math.random() * news.length)] +
'\n\n');
    }, 2000);
});

server.listen(port, hostname, () => {
    console.log(`Event stream available at http://${hostname}:${port}/
techNews`);
});
```

The HTTP Node.js library is a collection of JavaScript functions that can be used to create a web server in a few lines of code. The function provided as a parameter to the `http.createServer` emits a random text every 2 seconds.

When writing reactive services with any technology, you can check the output with the `curl` command. Use the `-v` option to get a verbose representation of what the service is sending. This reveals important information necessary for writing a client, such as the media type and encoding and the format of the information being sent.

Listing 10-19 features the curl command and arguments used to inspect the response from the Node.js tech news service and its output in a terminal.

Listing 10-19. Node.js Service Output Returned by the `curl` Command

```
$  curl http://localhost:3000/techNews  -v
* Connection failed
* connect to ::1 port 3000 failed: Connection refused
*   Trying 127.0.0.1...
* TCP_NODELAY set
* Connected to localhost (127.0.0.1) port 3000 (#0)
> GET /techNews HTTP/1.1
> Host: localhost:3000
> User-Agent: curl/7.64.1
> Accept: */*
>
< HTTP/1.1 200 OK
< Content-Type: text/event-stream;charset=UTF-8
< Cache-Control: no-cache
< Access-Control-Allow-Origin: *
```

```
< Date: Thu, 30 Jul 2020 11:12:54 GMT
< Connection: keep-alive
< Transfer-Encoding: chunked
<
data:Amazon launches reactive API for DynamoDB.

data:Java 17 will be released in September 2021.
...
```

WebClient is practical for retrieving data produced by other services, but even more practical is its version for writing integration tests: WebTestClient. org. springframework.test.web.reactive.server.WebTestClient is the reactive equivalent of org.springframework.boot.test.web.client.TestRestTemplate. It can test controller and functional endpoints, and it essentially wraps around WebClient and provides a test context for it. WebTestClient provides the same API as WebClient but also supports testing assumptions on the returned response.

Listing 10-20 depicts the test method to check the POST request implementation for searching books matching criteria.

Listing 10-20. WebTestClient to Test a POST Request with Consumers

```
package com.apress.prospringmvc.bookstore.web;


import org.springframework.boot.test.context.SpringBootTest;
import org.springframework.test.web.reactive.server.WebTestClient;
import static org.junit.jupiter.api.Assertions.assertEquals;
// other imports omitted

@SpringBootTest(webEnvironment = SpringBootTest.WebEnvironment.RANDOM_PORT)
public class BookstoreWebTest {
    private static Logger logger = LoggerFactory.
getLogger(BookstoreWebTest.class);

    @Autowired
    private  WebTestClient testClient;

    @Test
    public void shouldReturnTwoBooks(){
        BookSearchCriteria criteria = new BookSearchCriteria();
        criteria.setCategory(Book.Category.JAVA);
```

```
    testClient.post()
        .uri("/book/search")
        .accept(MediaType.APPLICATION_JSON)
        .body(Mono.just(criteria), BookSearchCriteria.class)
        .exchange()
        .expectStatus().isOk() /* test */
        .expectHeader().contentType(MediaType.APPLICATION_JSON)
        .expectBodyList(Book.class)
        .consumeWith(
            result -> {
                assertEquals(2, result.getResponseBody().size());
                result.getResponseBody().forEach(p ->
                    logger.info("Response: {}",p));
            });
    }
}
```

The test runs in a test application context, and the /book/search request is made against a mock server available at http://localhost:{mockPort}. Notice the chaining of methods that could have just as well used WebClient. The WebTestClient part starts after the exchange() call. All three methods after that test assumptions on the request.

- expectStatus().isOk() checks that the HTTP status code is 200.

- expectHeader().contentType(MediaType.APPLICATION_JSON) checks that the media type of the response is JSON.

- expectBodyList(Book.class) checks that the body of the response contains a collection of Book instances.

- consumeWith(..) is provided as an argument a consumer function that checks that the size of the collection is 2 and prints each member of the collection.

The WebTestClient.consumeWith(..) method allows developers to specify consumers to test request bodies using any testing library they feel comfortable with. The implementation in Listing 10-20 might be considered verbose. A test method does not need to print the results body, which makes checking the collection size the only verification needed. In this case, consumeWith(..) can be dropped and replaced with hasSize(2).

Another way of using this instance is worth mentioning. WebTestClient supports making body assertions using JsonPath[12] expressions. This is practical for responses that contain JSON contents that we are not interested in deserializing into a Java object or do not have a corresponding class in the application. In Listing 10-21, the response body is checked for expected properties with expected values without deserializing the body to a Book instance.

Listing 10-21. WebTestClient to Test a GET Request Using JsonPath Expressions

```
package com.apress.prospringmvc.bookstore.web;
// imports omitted

@SpringBootTest(webEnvironment = SpringBootTest.WebEnvironment.RANDOM_PORT)
public class BookstoreWebTest {
    private static Logger logger = LoggerFactory.
getLogger(BookstoreWebTest.class);

    @Autowired
    private  WebTestClient testClient;

    @Test
    public void shouldReturnBook(){
        testClient.get()
            .uri(uriBuilder -> uriBuilder.path("/book/isbn/{isbn}")
                        .build("9781484237779"))
            .accept(MediaType.APPLICATION_JSON)
            .exchange()
            .expectStatus().isOk()
            .expectHeader().contentType(MediaType.APPLICATION_JSON)
            .expectBody()
            .jsonPath("$.title").isNotEmpty()
            .jsonPath("$.author").isEqualTo("Iuliana Cosmina");
    }
}
```

---

[12]https://github.com/jayway/JsonPath

WebTestClient can test a real server using the bindToServer() method. And this is great because, it can test services developed using other technologies.

Listing 10-22 depicts the creation of WebTestClient, which can run the previous test method on a real application running at http://localhost:8080.

Listing 10-22. WebTestClient Suitable to Test a GET Request on a Real Server

```
private final WebTestClient testClient = WebTestClient
        .bindToServer()
        .baseUrl("http://localhost:8080")
        .build();
```

WebTestClient testing API is rich, and official documentation should be consulted when writing tests[13] because this book cannot cover them all.

Internationalization

A hot topic when using reactive applications is internationalization. Spring MVC provides a very simple way to configure internationalization.

1. Create a configuration class that implements WebMvcConfigurer.

2. Annotate the configuration class with @EnableWebMvc (or don't if you are using Spring Boot).

3. Create translation property files.

4. Declare a MessageSource bean and configure it with their locations.

5. Declare a LocaleChangeInterceptor bean to configure the switch to a new locale based on the value of the lang parameter appended to a request.

6. Declare a LocaleResolver bean to configure a locale resolution strategy.

---

[13]https://docs.spring.io/spring/docs/current/spring-framework-reference/testing.html#webtestclient

There might be many steps, but not all of them are always needed, especially in Spring Boot applications when sticking to conventions.

Configuring internationalization support is easier because of the `WebHandler` API. First, let's discuss the default way, that relies on the `Accept-Language` header.

Internationalization Support Using the Accept-Language Header

Annotating a configuration class with `@EnableWebFlux` imports the Spring WebFlux configuration from `org.springframework.web.reactive.config.DelegatingWebFluxConfiguration`. If customization of the application context is necessary, such as internationalization support, this class can be extended, and some methods are overridden. The Spring WebFlux application context is used by `org.springframework.web.server.adapter.WebHttpHandlerBuilder` to assemble a processing chain that consists of a `WebHandler` instance, decorated with a set of `WebFilter` instances and `WebExceptionHandler` instances. By default, `WebHttpHandlerBuilder` configures `org.springframework.web.server.i18n.AcceptHeaderLocaleContextResolver` to support locale context resolution. The name of the class (`AcceptHeaderLocaleContextResolver`) gives a big hint about the locale context resolution strategy described by it: the locale is identified from the `Accept-Language` header of the HTTP request.

The `Accept-Language` request HTTP header advertises which languages the client can understand and which locale variant is preferred. Browsers set this header according to their user interface language, and users rarely change the default setting. When making REST requests, this parameter can be changed easily. Each response is translated to the language set as a value for this header in the request.

In a Spring WebFlux Boot application, adding language resource files, declaring a `MessageSource` bean, and configuring it with their location is enough to support internationalization using the Accept header.

Internationalization Support Using a Request Parameter and a Custom Implementation of LocaleContextResolver

Most web applications support internationalization using request parameters. To provide internationalization support using request parameters in a Spring WebFlux application, a custom `LocaleContextResolver` implementation must be added to the configuration to replace the default `AcceptHeaderLocaleContextResolver` (that implements the same interface). This is done by extending the `DelegatingWebFluxConfiguration` and overriding the `createLocaleContextResolver()` method to return an instance of the custom `LocaleContextResolver`.

The proposed implementation to support internationalization using a request parameter is depicted in Listing 10-23.

Listing 10-23. Custom `LocaleContextResolver` Resolving `Locale` Using a Request Parameter

```
package com.apress.prospringmvc.bookstore.config.i18n;

import org.springframework.context.i18n.LocaleContext;
import org.springframework.context.i18n.SimpleLocaleContext;
import org.springframework.util.CollectionUtils;
import org.springframework.web.server.ServerWebExchange;
import org.springframework.web.server.i18n.LocaleContextResolver;

import java.util.List;
import java.util.Locale;

public class RequestParamLocaleResolver implements LocaleContextResolver {

    private String languageParameterName;

    public RequestParamLocaleResolver(final String languageParameterName) {
        this.languageParameterName = languageParameterName;
    }

    @Override
    public LocaleContext resolveLocaleContext(final ServerWebExchange
exchange) {
        Locale defaultLocale = Locale.getDefault();
        List<String> referLang = exchange.getRequest().getQueryParams().
get(languageParameterName);
        if (!CollectionUtils.isEmpty(referLang) ) {
            String lang = referLang.get(0);
            defaultLocale = Locale.forLanguageTag(lang);
        }
        return new SimpleLocaleContext(defaultLocale);
    }
}
```

To configure Spring WebFlux to use this implementation, we need to add the configuration class extending DelegatingWebFluxConfiguration. The implementation is simple and depicted in Listing 10-24.

Listing 10-24. Custom LocaleContextResolver Resolving Locale Using a Request Parameter

```
package com.apress.prospringmvc.bookstore.config;

import com.apress.prospringmvc.bookstore.config.i18n.
RequestParamLocaleResolver;
import org.springframework.context.annotation.Configuration;
import org.springframework.web.reactive.config.
DelegatingWebFluxConfiguration;
import org.springframework.web.server.i18n.LocaleContextResolver;

@Configuration
public class LocaleSupportConfig extends DelegatingWebFluxConfiguration {

    @Override
    protected LocaleContextResolver createLocaleContextResolver() {
        return new RequestParamLocaleResolver("lang");
    }
}
```

The language parameter name should be configurable, but remember that URLs for locale changes in your views need to match. The disadvantage of the previous implementation is that the desired locale is applied to a request only if suffixed with ?lang=XX. The reason for this is because the locale is not saved anywhere. In Spring MVC applications, we used CookieLocaleResolver to create a locale cookie and read it to identify the locale the user configured. This allowed for the application to use a different locale than the one configured in the browser. CookieLocaleResolver is part of the org. springframework.web.servlet.i18n package, and there is no such resolver for Spring WebFlux.

It is easy to modify the previous RequestParamLocaleResolver to add cookie support since it has access to both request and response through ServerWebExchange. Listing 10-25 depicts an implementation of LocaleContextResolver that stores the desired locale in a cookie with a lifespan of five minutes.

Listing 10-25. Custom `LocaleContextResolver` Resolving Locale Using a Request Parameter

```
package com.apress.prospringmvc.bookstore.config.i18n;


import org.springframework.http.HttpCookie;
import org.springframework.http.ResponseCookie;
// other imports omitted

public class CookieParamLocaleResolver implements LocaleContextResolver {

    public static final String LOCALE_REQUEST_ATTRIBUTE_NAME = "Bookstore.
    Cookie.LOCALE";

    private String languageParameterName;

    public CookieParamLocaleResolver(final String languageParameterName) {
        this.languageParameterName = languageParameterName;
    }

    @Override
    public LocaleContext resolveLocaleContext(final ServerWebExchange
    exchange) {
        List<String> referLang = exchange.getRequest().getQueryParams().
        get(languageParameterName);
        Locale defaultLocale = getLocaleFromCookie(exchange);
        if (!CollectionUtils.isEmpty(referLang) ) {
            String lang = referLang.get(0);
            defaultLocale = Locale.forLanguageTag(lang);
            setLocaleToCookie(lang, exchange);
        }
        return new SimpleLocaleContext(defaultLocale);
    }

    private void setLocaleToCookie(final String lang, final
    ServerWebExchange exchange) {
```

```
    MultiValueMap<String, HttpCookie> cookies =  exchange.getRequest().
    getCookies();
    HttpCookie langCookie = cookies.getFirst(LOCALE_REQUEST_ATTRIBUTE_
    NAME);
    if(langCookie == null || !lang.equals(langCookie.getValue())) {
        ResponseCookie cookie = ResponseCookie.from(LOCALE_REQUEST_
        ATTRIBUTE_NAME, lang)
          .maxAge(Duration.ofMinutes(5)).build();
        exchange.getResponse().addCookie(cookie);
    }
}

private Locale getLocaleFromCookie(final ServerWebExchange exchange){
    MultiValueMap<String, HttpCookie> cookies =  exchange.getRequest().
    getCookies();
    HttpCookie langCookie = cookies.getFirst(LOCALE_REQUEST_ATTRIBUTE_
    NAME);
    return langCookie != null ? Locale.forLanguageTag(langCookie.
getValue()) : Locale.getDefault();
    }
}
```

Internationalization Support Using a Request Parameter and a Custom Implementation WebFilter

Implementing internationalization support using a custom web filter is a very elegant solution because it does not require any explicit modification to the WebFlux configuration. The custom WebFilter can be simply declared as a bean. As part of the WebHttpHandlerBuilder application context, the internationalization filter is picked up and added to its collection of web filters applied to every request.

The disadvantage of this implementation is that the locale is not saved anywhere, so if we want to save the locale to a cookie, or user session, extra code must be written. It's not so difficult since WebFilter also has access to both request and response through ServerWebExchange.

The implementation in Listing 10-26 is not fully mine. A developer name Jonathan Mendoza posted it on StackOverflow, and except adding cookies support, there is nothing else I can do to it to improve it.[14] We previously called this implementation the most elegant because it uses the default `AcceptHeaderLocaleContextResolver` and it does nothing more than intercept the request and decorate it with the `Accept-Language` header. The value is taken from a request parameter. If the locale cookie is not present, it is created. If there is no language request parameter, then the value is taken from the cookie or the application's default if the cookie does not exist.

To reduce the size of the book, Listing 10-26 only depicts the core methods in `LanguageQueryParameterWebFilter`. The full implementation is in the repository containing the code for this book.

Listing 10-26. Custom `WebFilter` Resolving `Locale` Using a Request Parameter

```
package com.apress.prospringmvc.bookstore.util;
import org.springframework.web.server.WebFilter;
import org.springframework.web.server.WebFilterChain;
import org.springframework.web.server.adapter.DefaultServerWebExchange;
import org.springframework.web.server.adapter.HttpWebHandlerAdapter;
// other imports omitted

@Component
public class LanguageQueryParameterWebFilter implements WebFilter {
    // other code omitted
    @Override
    public Mono<Void> filter(final ServerWebExchange exchange, final
    WebFilterChain chain) {
        final ServerHttpRequest request = exchange.getRequest();
        final MultiValueMap<String, String> queryParams = request.
        getQueryParams();
        final String languageValue = queryParams.getFirst("lang");

        final ServerWebExchange localizedExchange =
                getServerWebExchange(languageValue, exchange);
        return chain.filter(localizedExchange);
    }
}
```

---

[14]https://stackoverflow.com/questions/47527504/
 how-to-configure-i18n-in-spring-boot-2-webflux-thymeleaf/50055399#50055399

```
    private ServerWebExchange getServerWebExchange(final String
    languageValue,
        final ServerWebExchange exchange) {
      return isEmpty(languageValue)
              ? getLocaleFromCookie(exchange)
              : getLocalizedServerWebExchange(languageValue, exchange);
    }

    private ServerWebExchange getLocalizedServerWebExchange(final String
    languageValue,
        final ServerWebExchange exchange) {
      setLocaleToCookie(languageValue, exchange);
      final ServerHttpRequest httpRequest = exchange.getRequest()
              .mutate()
              .headers(httpHeaders -> httpHeaders.set("Accept-Language",
               languageValue))
              .build();

      return new DefaultServerWebExchange(httpRequest, exchange.
      getResponse(),
              httpWebHandlerAdapter.getSessionManager(),
         httpWebHandlerAdapter.getCodecConfigurer(),
              httpWebHandlerAdapter.getLocaleContextResolver());
    }
    // setLocaleToCookie & getLocaleFromCookie are pretty similar to
Listing 10-25.
}
```

Validation, Type Conversion, and Error Handling

Since Spring WebFlux application can be built using reactive controllers, validation, type conversion, and error handling are supported in the same way as in a Spring MVC application.

Validations like @Valid (from the javax.validation package) and its Spring equivalent @Validated (from the org.springframework.validation. annotation package) are supported on controller arguments. To configure a global

Validator, a bean of type org.springframework.validation.beanvalidation.
LocalValidatorFactoryBean has to be configured. If such a bean is missing,
then a bean of type org.springframework.validation.beanvalidation.
OptionalValidatorFactoryBean named webFluxValidator is declared by default.
OptionalValidatorFactoryBean is a subclass of LocalValidatorFactoryBean and is
a pseudo-validator. It does not declare any validations to be performed. To notify that
validation is not supported when booting up a Spring WebFlux application, the debug
messages in Listing 10-27 are printed in the log file.

Listing 10-27. Debug Messages Printed in the Log File When Validation for a
Spring WebFlux Application Is Not Supported

```
DEBUG o.s.b.f.s.DefaultListableBeanFactory - Creating shared instance of
singleton bean 'webFluxValidator'
DEBUG o.s.v.b.OptionalValidatorFactoryBean - Failed to set up a Bean
Validation provider
javax.validation.NoProviderFoundException: Unable to create a Configuration
because no Bean Validation provider could be found. Add a provider like
Hibernate Validator (RI) to your classpath.
at javax.validation.Validation$GenericBootstrapImpl.configure(Validation.
java:291)
```

Configuring a Validator bean is as easy as overriding the getValidator() default
method declared in the WebFluxConfigurer interface that the configuration class is
implementing. This method should return a bean of type Validator. This bean picks up
a bean validation provider from the classpath, so a library with such a provider, such as
the Hibernate Validator library, should be added to the project's dependencies.

The same goes for custom converters and formatters. The WebFluxConfigurer interface
declares default addFormatters(FormatterRegistry) that can register custom converters
and formatters. (It is the same as what the WebMvcConfigurer interface does for a Spring
MVC application.) Listing 10-28 shows a snippet from ReactiveThymeleafWebConfig that
includes a Validator bean and a Date formatter configuration.

Listing 10-28. Validator Bean and a Date Formatter Configuration for a Spring
WebFlux Application

```
package com.apress.prospringmvc.bookstore.config;

import com.apress.prospringmvc.bookstore.util.formatter.
DateFormatAnnotationFormatterFactory;
import org.springframework.web.reactive.config.WebFluxConfigurer;
import org.springframework.validation.beanvalidation.
LocalValidatorFactoryBean;
import org.springframework.format.FormatterRegistry;
// other import omitted

@Configuration
@EnableWebFlux
public class ReactiveThymeleafWebConfig implements WebFluxConfigurer {
    @Bean
    public Validator validator() {
        final var validator = new LocalValidatorFactoryBean();
        validator.setValidationMessageSource(messageSource());
        return validator;
    }

    @Override
    public Validator getValidator() {
        return validator();
    }

    @Override
    public void addFormatters(FormatterRegistry registry) {
        registry.addFormatterForFieldAnnotation(new
DateFormatAnnotationFormatterFactory());
    }
    // other code omitted
}
```

In a Spring WebFlux application, anything related to a controller is configured and works in the same way as in a Spring MVC application. The only situation that requires extra work from the developer is applying validation to functional endpoints.

Functional endpoints represent the way through which a request is mapped to a org.springframework.web.reactive.function.server.HandlerFunction<T extends ServerResponse>. A handler function takes a org.springframework.web.reactive. function.server.ServerRequest as an argument and returns a delayed response represented by the Mono<org.springframework.web.reactive.function.server. ServerResponse> return type. A handler function is equivalent to a @RequestMapping annotated method; unfortunately, it does not support arguments marked for validation with an annotation such as @Valid and @Validated, as such methods do. Because of this small disadvantage, validation must be configured by the developer within the body of the function.

For a Book object, a BookValidator class implementing org.springframework. validation.Validator should be declared to test that the title, author, ISBN, and category are not empty. This class is depicted in Listing 10-29.

Listing 10-29. BookValidator Class to Validate Book Instances

```
package com.apress.prospringmvc.bookstore.util.validation;

import com.apress.prospringmvc.bookstore.document.Book;
import org.springframework.validation.Errors;
import org.springframework.validation.ValidationUtils;
import org.springframework.validation.Validator;

public class BookValidator implements Validator {

    @Override
    public boolean supports(Class<?> clazz) {
        return (Book.class).isAssignableFrom(clazz);
    }

    @Override
    public void validate(Object target, Errors errors) {
        ValidationUtils.rejectIfEmpty
            (errors, "title", "required", new Object[] { "Title" });
```

```
ValidationUtils.rejectIfEmpty
    (errors, "author", "required", new Object[] { "Author" });
ValidationUtils.rejectIfEmpty
    (errors, "isbn", "required", new Object[] { "Isbn" });
ValidationUtils.rejectIfEmpty(
    errors, "category", "required", new Object[] { "Category" });
    }
}
```

A handler function that handles a PUT/POST request that sends a Book object to the database should first validate the Book instance and throw ServerWebInputException if the validation fails. This type of exception should be thrown for any request that contains unacceptable data because it automatically sets the HTTP status code to 400 (Bad Request) and returns the Errors object, letting the user know what the problem is. Listing 10-30 depicts a BookHandler class that contains all code required to handle the POST request for creating a Book instance.

Listing 10-30. BookHandler Class to Validate Book Instances

```
package com.apress.prospringmvc.bookstore.handler;
import com.apress.prospringmvc.bookstore.util.validation.BookValidator;
import org.springframework.validation.BeanPropertyBindingResult;
import org.springframework.validation.Errors;
import org.springframework.validation.Validator;
import org.springframework.web.server.ServerWebInputException;
import static org.springframework.web.reactive.function.server.
ServerResponse.*;
import javax.validation.ValidationException;
// other imports omitted

@Component
public class BookHandler {

    private BookstoreService bookstoreService;
    private final Validator validator = new BookValidator();

    public BookHandler(BookstoreService bookstoreService) {
        this.bookstoreService = bookstoreService;
    }
```

```java
public Mono<ServerResponse> create(ServerRequest serverRequest) {
    return serverRequest.bodyToMono(Book.class)
        .flatMap(this::validate)
            .flatMap(book -> bookstoreService.addBook(book))
            .flatMap(book -> ServerResponse.created(URI.create("/book/
isbn/" + book.getIsbn()))
                .contentType(MediaType.APPLICATION_JSON).
                bodyValue(book))
        .onErrorResume(error -> ServerResponse.badRequest().
        bodyValue(error));
}

private Mono<Book> validate(Book book) {
    Errors errors = new BeanPropertyBindingResult(book, "book");
    validator.validate(book, errors);
    if (errors.hasErrors()) {
        throw new ValidationException(errors.toString());
    }
    return Mono.just(book);
}
// other handler functions emitted
}
```

This approach is a little bit unpolished since ValidationException has the message set to the full text resulted in converting the Errors object to String. ValidationException is intercepted by the onErrorResume(..) function, which allows further configuration of the response. Without onErrorResume(..), the default error handler bean autoconfigured by Spring Boot catches the exception and generates a default response. This bean is named errorWebExceptionHandler, and its type is DefaultErrorWebExceptionHandler, the default implementation provided by Spring Boot. Figure 10-4 depicts the WebExceptionHandler hierarchy.

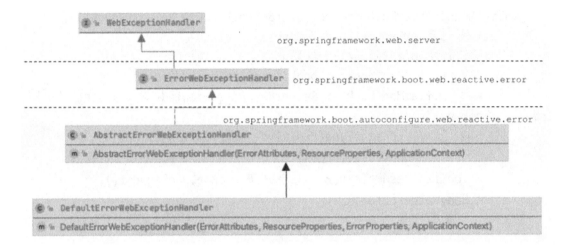

Figure 10-4. *WebExceptionHandler hierarchy*

The response returned by this bean is a generic JSON representation object that contains the HTTP status code 400 (Bad Request), the URI path, and an alfa-numeric request identifier. The easiest way to test that validation is applied is to write a negative test using WebTestClient. Listing 10-31 depicts a test that assumes creating a Book instance fails, and a response with an HTTP status code returned. And because it is interesting to see the response details, a consumer is added to print it.

Listing 10-31. Test Method Overing a Validation Failure When a Request Is Made for Creating a Book Instance

```
package com.apress.prospringmvc.bookstore.api;

import org.junit.jupiter.api.Test;
import org.springframework.test.web.reactive.server.WebTestClient;
//other imports omitted

@SpringBootTest(webEnvironment = SpringBootTest.WebEnvironment.RANDOM_PORT)
public class BookApiTest {
    private static Logger logger = LoggerFactory.getLogger(BookApiTest.
class);

    @Autowired
    private WebTestClient testClient;

    @Test
    void shouldFailCreatingABook() {
```

```
// no isbn, no category
Book book = new Book();
book.setTitle("TDD for dummies");
book.setAuthor("Test User");

testClient.post().uri("/book/isbn")
        .body(Mono.just(book), Book.class).exchange()
        .expectStatus().isBadRequest() // 400
        .expectBody()
        .consumeWith(responseEntity ->
            logger.debug("Response: {}", responseEntity)
        );
    }

}
```

The previous test passes, no Book instance is created since the ISBN and category are missing. The response HTTP code is 400, as proven by the response details printed in the console, which you can see in Listing 10-32. The response details include the object that failed validation. A few JSON lines were removed since the output was too verbose to make it part of the book, but the validation details were kept.

Listing 10-32. Response Details of a Failed Request to Create a Book Instance

```
DEBUG c.a.p.bookstore.api.BookApiTest - Response:
> POST http://localhost:51164/book/isbn
> WebTestClient-Request-Id: [1]
> Content-Type: [application/json]
> Content-Length: [132]

{
    "id":null,"title":"TDD for dummies",
    "description":null,
    "price":null,
    "year":null,
    "author":"Test User",
    "isbn":null
}
```

```
< 400 BAD_REQUEST Bad Request
< Vary: [Origin, Access-Control-Request-Method, Access-Control-Request-
Headers]
< Content-Type: [application/json]
< Content-Length: [10831]

#response body starts here
{
# other JSON code omitted
"message": "[
    Field error in object 'book' on field 'isbn':
        rejected value [null];
    codes [required.book.isbn,required.isbn,
        required.java.lang.String,required];
    arguments [Isbn];
    Field error in object 'book' on field 'category':
        rejected value [null];
    codes [required.book.category,required.category,
        required.java.lang.String,required];
    arguments [Category];
}
```

In the previous listing, you see the explicit output pointing you to the required fields that are missing values. The output is somewhat verbose since it is a String representation of the Error instance created by the BookValidator instance. The response returned in case of failure can be customized by replacing the Error instance with something else.

Validation handling for functional endpoints is straightforward and relies on adding the validation operator to pipelines that handle objects retrieved from a ServerRequest instance. Error handling can be done the same way—by adding an operator to handle errors emitted in the pipeline processing objects right before returning them using ServerResponse. From a development point of view, the easiest way is to declare a custom error object or a custom exception type and rely on the default error handler as much as possible.

For more granular customization of the error handling behavior in a Spring
Boot WebFlux application, an implementation of WebExceptionHandler or
ErrorWebExceptionHandler could be provided. Being so low-level, however, you
must directly deal with the request/response exchange, which can be a pain. The
customized error handling bean must be configured and annotated with @Order(-2)
to have precedence over WebFluxResponseStatusExceptionHandler and Spring Boot's
ErrorWebExceptionHandler. Existing implementation can be reused by extending
AbstractErrorWebExceptionHandler or DefaultErrorWebExceptionHandler.
Listing 10-33 depicts a naive implementation of a global error handler that implements
WebExceptionHandler. The handle(ServerWebExchange, Throwable) method must
be provided with a concrete implementation that customizes the returned response
message.

Listing 10-33. Custom Global Error Handler Implementation

```java
package com.apress.prospringmvc.bookstore.util;

import org.springframework.core.io.buffer.DataBuffer;
import org.springframework.web.server.ServerWebExchange;
import org.springframework.web.server.WebExceptionHandler;
import com.apress.prospringmvc.bookstore.util.MissingValueException;
// other imports omitted

@Component
@Order(-2)
public class MissingValuesExceptionHandler implements WebExceptionHandler {

    @Override
    public Mono<Void> handle(ServerWebExchange exchange, Throwable ex) {
        DataBuffer buffer;
        if (ex instanceof MissingValueException) {
            exchange.getResponse().setStatusCode(HttpStatus.BAD_REQUEST);
            exchange.getResponse().getHeaders().add("Content-Type",
"application/json");
            final String message = " {\"missing_value_for\": \""+
                ((MissingValueException)ex).getFieldNames() +"\"}";
```

```
        buffer = exchange.getResponse().bufferFactory().wrap(message.
        getBytes());
    } else {
        exchange.getResponse().setStatusCode(HttpStatus.INTERNAL_
        SERVER_ERROR);
        exchange.getResponse().getHeaders().add("Content-Type",
        "application/json");
        buffer = exchange.getResponse().bufferFactory().wrap("Ooops!".
        getBytes());
    }
    return exchange.getResponse().writeWith(Flux.just(buffer));
    }
}
```

The MissingValueException class is a custom exception class that encapsulates
the names of the fields that failed. For the previous exception handler to do its job, the
BookHandler handler functions must be changed to throw MissingValueException
exceptions when validation fails and remove the onErrorResume(..) call from the
request/response exchange pipeline. Listing 10-34 shows these changes.

Listing 10-34. Handler Function That Throws a MissingValueException When
Validation Fails

```
package com.apress.prospringmvc.bookstore.handler;

import com.apress.prospringmvc.bookstore.util.MissingValueException;
// other imports omitted

@Component
public class BookHandler {

    private BookstoreService bookstoreService;
    private final Validator validator = new BookValidator();

    public BookHandler(BookstoreService bookstoreService) {
        this.bookstoreService = bookstoreService;
    }
```

```java
    public Mono<ServerResponse> create(ServerRequest serverRequest) {
        return serverRequest.bodyToMono(Book.class)
            .flatMap(this::validate)
                .flatMap(book -> bookstoreService.addBook(book))
                .flatMap(book -> ServerResponse.created(URI.create("/book/
                isbn/" + book.getIsbn()))
                    .contentType(MediaType.APPLICATION_JSON).
bodyValue(book));
        // no 'onErrorResume()' here
    }

    private Mono<Book> validate(Book book) {
        Errors errors = new BeanPropertyBindingResult(book, "book");
        validator.validate(book, errors);
        if (errors.hasErrors()) {
            throw MissingValueException.of(errors.getAllErrors());
        }
        return Mono.just(book);
    }
    // other handler functions emitted
}
```

If you run the test in Listing 10-31 now, it won't fail because the HTTP response code is the same, but you do notice that the response body is reduced to {"missing_value_ for": "[Isbn, Category]"}.

Easy peasy, right? In a real application, you might need both: because the implementation of WebExceptionHandler is suitable for global exceptions, and validation error handling could be implemented in the place where the validation is performed, in the handler function for a specific type of object. Whatever approach you may take, make sure you let people consuming your services Know what are they doing wrong.

Summary

This chapter gave you an insight into what is important when building a reactive Spring WebFlux application. A few details of migrating multilayered applications were covered to underline the fact that a reactive application is fully reactive only if all its components are reactive. To help you make the change from Spring Web MVC to WebFlux, comparisons between configurations for the two technologies were made.

We looked at using reactive controllers to render Thymeleaf dynamic views in multiple ways: loading the view in a reactive-friendly way using a data-driver context variable, using JavaScript to consume `Flux<T>` and regenerate part of a rendered HTML template, and rewriting a fragment of a Thymeleaf view by sending SSEs.

We looked at consuming other reactive services using `WebClient` and testing a reactive application using `WebTestClient` and the `curl` command.

Internationalization, validation, and error handling for functional endpoints were also covered since they are important when building a web application.

There are a few things to take away from this chapter. Spring WebFlux comes with a few advantages, like cleaner and more concise code. Spring Boot provides many out-of-the-box components that allow more time for development and less time for configuration. Error handling is easier to implement, and code is easier to read. But not all components must be reactive. When all you have is a simple page to render to the user, there is no need to render it using a reactive component.

The most important things: never, ever call `block()`, and avoid `subscribe()` as much as possible!

## CHAPTER 11

Securing Spring WebFlux Applications

After two chapters on reactive programming, we barely scratched the surface on reactive applications. Reactive code won't make your code simpler and easier to read, but it makes it more robust and easier to extend. Complex applications exchanging a large amount of information are most suitable for implementations using reactive frameworks. By using reactive programming, data can be streamed, and operations can be executed to transform it and combine it simply and effectively without needing to write code dealing with the complexity of synchronizing threads.

Reactive web applications written with Spring WebFlux can also expose reactive views, making the user interface more responsive. Reactive views can display data sent by a reactive service without freezing the page. These topics have already been discussed, and code to implement them was covered in the two previous chapters.

This chapter covers two more important topics related to Spring WebFlux applications: how to apply backpressure and secure a Spring WebFlux application.

Backpressure

Backpressure was mentioned in the first two chapters. It was hinted that backpressure represents the subscriber's action of controlling the rate of values being emitted by a publisher it subscribed to. It did not make sense to tackle backpressure without a two-way communication protocol such as WebSocket.

A subscriber can request a specific number of items from a publisher in a configured way. The previous chapter used slowed-down publishers that emitted items at configured intervals using the `zip` operator.

© Marten Deinum and Iuliana Cosmina 2021
M. Deinum and I. Cosmina, *Pro Spring MVC with WebFlux*, https://doi.org/10.1007/978-1-4842-5666-4_11

Let's start by introducing the technology that allows backpressure to happen: the WebSocket protocol.

The WebSocket Protocol

One of the core recommendations for working with data streams is to never block. A client consuming data emitted by a stream does not own that thread, so it should never block it. To avoid other items being emitted is to store them in a buffer. But, buffers are limited, they can be filled up and overflow, and data can be lost. So that leaves the only possible option: the client should be allowed to control the rate the stream emits items. For this to happen, though, we need a two-way communication channel.

First, let's do a quick recap by looking at Figure 11-1.

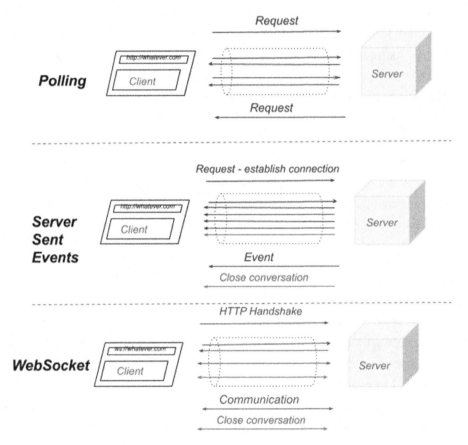

Figure 11-1. *Communication technologies on top of TCP*

The normal communication between a browser and a server is done through a TCP connection. The HTTP protocol[1] is a communication protocol on top of TCP that contains specific instructions on reading and processing this data once it arrives. A client makes an HTTP request to a server, and a server answers with an HTTP response. Multiple exchanges of requests and responses between a client and a server can be made across an HTTP persistent connection (keep-alive). This way of communicating between a client and a server is known as **polling** because they regularly request new data from the server over the HTTP connection. The applications written for Chapters 1 through 8 were designed for this type of communication.

The server-sent events (SSE)[2] introduced in Chapter 10 is a server *push* technology enabling a client to receive automatic updates from a server via HTTP connection. It is a unidirectional communication similar to the publish/subscribe model in JMS.

WebSocket[3] is a computer communications protocol, providing full-duplex communication channels over a single TCP connection. WebSocket is an alternative to HTTP that allows opening a two-way interactive communication between a browser (the client) and a server. It enables streams of messages on top of TCP, and its API messages can be sent to a server, and event-driven responses can be received without the need for polling. WebSocket is designed to be HTTP-compatible. HTTP is used only for the handshake. This is where the connection between the two protocols ends. Under the hood, they are very different. WebSocket is a low-level transport protocol, the first URL request establishes a connection, and after that, all application messages flow through the same TCP connection. Communication using WebSocket between a client and a server is roughly depicted in Figure 11-2.

---

[1]https://tools.ietf.org/html/rfc2616
[2]https://www.w3.org/TR/eventsource/
[3]https://tools.ietf.org/html/rfc6455

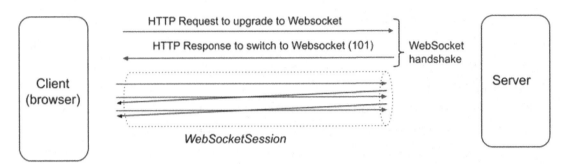

Figure 11-2. *Communication using WebSocket*

The communication over WebSocket begins with an HTTP request asking for the WebSocket protocol to be used. The request should have a header named `Upgrade` populated with the value `WebSocket`, and a header named `Connection` with the value of `Upgrade`. A few base-64 encoded random bytes headers prevent the same message from being sent twice. An example of the content of this initial HTTP request and response is depicted in Listing 11-1.

Listing 11-1. WebSocket HTTP Request and Response Handshake Example

```
--- HTTP  Request ---
GET /chat HTTP/1.1
Host: localhost
Upgrade: websocket
Connection: Upgrade
Sec-WebSocket-Version: 13
Origin: http://localhost:8080

--- HTTP  Response ---
HTTP/1.1 101 Switching Protocols
Upgrade: websocket
Connection: Upgrade
```

The response should be HTTP status code 101, which signals WebSocket's acceptance for communication. After this initial handshake, the client (browser) and the server communicate through a WebSocket session that can be ended by any of the parties.

WebSocket is the appropriate solution for applications that need a frequent exchange of small chunks of data at high speed (e.g., social feeds, trading, video games, betting sites, etc.). If the volume of information exchange is relatively low, a classic HTTP polling solution might provide an effective solution. During the data transfer portion of the communication, both the client and server can send messages to each other simultaneously, which opens the door to adding more robust, real-time communication functionality to your applications.

Most modern browsers support WebSocket.

The WebSocket protocol defines a `ws://` prefix to indicate a WebSocket connection. The `wss://` prefix indicates a secure, encrypted WebSocket connection is used for communication. WebSocket is unaware of proxy servers and firewalls, but it is compatible with HTTP and uses the HTTP 80 and 443 ports for communication. Unencrypted WebSocket traffic flows through an explicit or a transparent proxy server on its way to the WebSocket server. If the proxy server is not configured to support unencrypted WebSocket traffic, the connection is most likely to fail. Encrypted WebSocket traffic is done over a connection that uses Transport Layer Security (TLS). An HTTP CONNECT command is issued when the browser is configured to use an explicit proxy server. This sets up a tunnel, which provides low-level end-to-end TCP communication through the HTTP proxy between the Web Sockets Secure client and the WebSocket server.

As of version 4.0, the Spring Framework supports WebSocket-style messaging and STOMP as an application-level subprotocol. Within the framework, support for WebSocket is in the `spring-websocket` module, which is compatible with the Java WebSocket API standard (JSR-356).[4] For a servlet environment, there is also a Spring Boot starter dependency: `spring-boot-starter-websocket`. Before discussing communication using WebSocket in a reactive application, let's cover how WebSocket is used in a non-reactive application.

Using the WebSocket API with a Non-Reactive Application

When working with Spring's WebSocket API, you typically implement the `org.springframework.web.socket.WebSocketHandler` interface, or use convenience subclasses such as `org.springframework.web.socket.handler.BinaryWebSocketHandler` for handling binary messages, `org.springframework.web.socket.sockjs.transport.handler.SockJsWebSocketHandler` for SockJS messages, or

---

[4]`http://www.oracle.com/technetwork/articles/java/jsr356-1937161.html`

org.springframework.web.socket.handler.TextWebSocketHandler for working with
String-based messages. In our example, for simplicity, we use a TextWebSocketHandler
to pass String messages via WebSocket. You can find the JavaScript code to connect
and send messages to the server in this book's source code. This section focuses on the
Spring code necessary to implement a handler for a very basic chat functionality and
configure it. As mentioned, the handler receives and sends text messages, so the handler
class must extend TextWebSocketHandler. The code is depicted in Listing 11-2.

Listing 11-2. The ChatHandler Class That Extends TextWebSocketHandler

```java
package com.apress.prospringmvc.bookstore;

import org.springframework.web.socket.TextMessage;
import org.springframework.web.socket.WebSocketSession;
import org.springframework.web.socket.handler.TextWebSocketHandler;

import java.io.IOException;
import java.util.List;
import java.util.Random;

public class ChatHandler extends TextWebSocketHandler {

    @Override
    public void handleTextMessage(WebSocketSession session, TextMessage
    textMessage) throws IOException {
        if(textMessage.getPayload().toLowerCase().contains("hello")||
            textMessage.getPayload().toLowerCase().contains("hi")) {
            session.sendMessage(new TextMessage(BOT_ANSWERS.get(0)));
            session.sendMessage(new TextMessage(BOT_ANSWERS.get(1)));
        } else {
            session.sendMessage(new TextMessage(randomMessages()));
        }
    }

    private static final Random RANDOM = new Random(System.
    currentTimeMillis());

    private static final List<String> BOT_ANSWERS = List.of(
```

```
            "Hello!",
            "How can I help?"
            // ... more messages omitted
    );

    private static String randomMessages() {
        return BOT_ANSWERS.get(RANDOM.nextInt(BOT_ANSWERS.size() - 2) + 2);
    }
}
```

The ChatHandler implements a very basic chatbot that replies to messages received, with a random message from a fixed set. This implementation handles requests received from the client that were sent using JavaScript functions specific to the WebSocket official API.[5] Now that we have a handler for WebSocket communication, let's map it to a URL path and tell Spring that we are using WebSocket to communicate with the client. There is a special annotation for this named @EnableWebSocket.

Listing 11-3 depicts the Spring configuration class necessary for the application to support WebSocket.

Listing 11-3. The Spring WebSocket Configuration Class

```
package com.apress.prospringmvc.bookstore.web.config;

import com.apress.prospringmvc.bookstore.ChatHandler;
import org.springframework.context.annotation.Bean;
import org.springframework.context.annotation.Configuration;
import org.springframework.scheduling.annotation.EnableAsync;
import org.springframework.web.socket.config.annotation.EnableWebSocket;
import org.springframework.web.socket.config.annotation.
WebSocketConfigurer;
import org.springframework.web.socket.config.annotation.
WebSocketHandlerRegistry;

@Configuration
@EnableWebSocket
@EnableAsync
```

---

[5]https://developer.mozilla.org/en-US/docs/Web/API/WebSockets_API

```
public class WebSocketConfig implements WebSocketConfigurer {

    @Override
    public void registerWebSocketHandlers(WebSocketHandlerRegistry
registry) {
        registry.addHandler(chatHandler(), "/chatHandler").
setAllowedOrigins("*");
    }

    @Bean
    public ChatHandler chatHandler() {
        return new ChatHandler();
    }
}
```

The previous configuration class contains a few elements that need a more detailed explanation.

- **@EnableWebSocket**: When placed on a Spring configuration class, it enables WebSocket request processing.

- **WebSocketConfigurer**: This interface must be implemented to access to the WebSocketHandlerRegistry. The single method re gisterWebSocketHandlers(WebSocketHandlerRegistry) should be implemented to map WebSocket URL paths to the appropriate handlers.

- **setAllowedOrigins("*")**: This method is set to allow calls to our application from any origin. If you are familiar with CORS (cross-origin resource sharing), you know that for security reasons, browsers restrict cross-origin HTTP requests initiated from scripts. By default, only calls from the same origin are allowed. Calling that method on the resulted WebSocketHandlerRegistration ensured that you wouldn't have issues locally, especially when opening the application in the browser on 127.0.0.1 and trying to send the WebSocket messages using localhost. It happened to me when writing the code, which is why I decided it deserves mention. On production, you shouldn't do this though, at most, you should configure the list of allowed origins.

- **@EnableSync**: A very useful annotation because it enables asynchronous messaging. This means that once the connection opens, the client and server can send messages in parallel.

In this simple case, the client is represented by JavaScript code executed in the browser that is part of the chat.html view. The implementation is simple. It declares listeners using jQuery for JavaScript events to connect to the server, send/receive messages, or close the connection. The implementation and the HTML elements it applies to are depicted in Listing 11-4.

Listing 11-4. JavaScript Functions for Establishing a WebSocket Connection and Sending/Receiving Messages Over It

```
<script th:inline="javascript">
    var ping;
    var websocket;

    jQuery(function ($) {
        function writeMessage(message) {
            $('#messageOutput').append(message + '\n')
        }

        $('#connect')
            .click(function doConnect() {
                var handlerURL = 'ws://localhost:8080/chapter11-1/
                chatHandler';
                websocket = new WebSocket(handlerURL);
                websocket.addEventListener('message', function (evt) {
                    writeMessage('STAFF: ' + evt.data);
                });

                websocket.addEventListener('open', function(evt) {
                    writeMessage("CONNECTED");
                });

                websocket.addEventListener('close', function (evt) {
                    writeMessage(`DISCONNECTED.
                        Reason: code=${evt.code}, reason=${evt.reason}`);
                });

                websocket.onerror = function (evt) {
```

```
                    writeMessage('ERROR:' + evt.data);
                };
            });

        $('#disconnect')
            .click(function () {
                if(typeof websocket != 'undefined') {
                    websocket.close();
                } else {
                    alert("Not connected.");
                }
            });

        $('#send')
            .click(function () {
                if(typeof websocket != 'undefined') {
                    websocket.send($('#message').val());
                    writeMessage('USER:' + $('#message').val());
                } else {
                    alert("Not connected.");
                }
            });
    });
</script>
<div class="left_content" id="left_content"
     th:fragment="~{template/layout :: left_content}" >
    <fieldset>
        <legend th:text="#{chat.title}">CONTACT STAFF</legend>
        <table>
            <tr>
                <td colspan="2"><button id="connect"
                    th:text="#{button.connect}">CONNECT</button></td>
            </tr>
            <tr>
                <td><input id="message" value=""/></td>
                <td><button id="send"
                    th:text="#{button.send}">SEND</button></td>
            </tr>
            <tr>
```

```
            <td colspan="2" align="center">
                <textarea readonly id="messageOutput"
                    rows="10" cols="50"></textarea></td>
        </tr>
        <tr>
            <td colspan="2"><button id="disconnect"
                th:text="#{button.disconnect}">Disconnect
                </button></td>
        </tr>
    </table>
  </fieldset>
</div>
<!-- other HTML code omitted -->
```

The HTML page generated using the chat.html template is depicted in Figure 11-3.

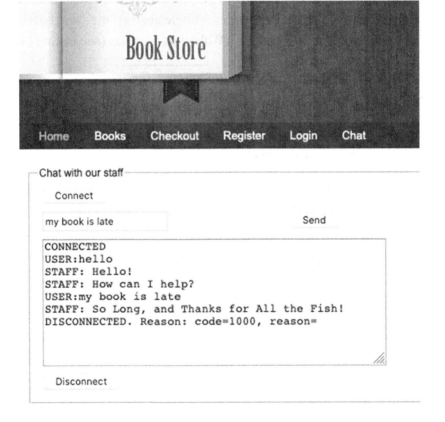

Figure 11-3. *The Chat page*

This type of implementation works very well for chats with a real person providing support, for example. Now, let's go back to the reactive world.

Using the WebSocket API with a Reactive Application

In the previous chapters, a stream of news produced by a Node.js service was consumed by the Spring WebFlux Bookstore application. A WebClient was used to consume that stream and produce a Flux<String> injected into a Thymeleaf template using a data-driver variable. Using WebSocket, we could avoid using a reactive view and use JavaScript code to communicate over a WebSocket connection directly with the server providing the data. Removing a node from the communication might speed up the transmission and remove the necessity of writing some Java code.

For this section, we move away from the Node.js service and implement the same functionality using a WebSocketHandler. The Spring Framework provides a reactive WebSocket API that you can use to write client and server-side applications that handle WebSocket messages. The reactive org.springframework.web.reactive. socket.WebSocketHandler interface declares a single abstract method that should be implemented by a developer for handling a WebSocket session (see Listing 11-5).

Listing 11-5. WebSocketHandler Method Skeleton for handle(WebSocketSession)

```
package org.springframework.web.reactive.socket;
// imports and default method omitted

public interface WebSocketHandler {
    Mono<Void> handle(WebSocketSession session);
}
```

The org.springframework.web.reactive.socket.WebSocketSession interface represents a WebSocket session that declares a set of methods to exchange information between two parties. The most important are send(Publisher<WebSocketMessage>) and receive() (see Listing 11-6).

Listing 11-6. WebSocketSession Method Skeleton for send(..) and receive()

```
package org.springframework.web.reactive.socket;
// imports and other methods omitted
```

```
public interface WebSocketSession {
    WebSocketMessage textMessage(String payload);

    Mono<Void> send(Publisher<WebSocketMessage> messages);
    Flux<WebSocketMessage> receive();

    Mono<Void> close(CloseStatus status);
}
```

Spring offers the very useful `org.springframework.web.reactive.socket.adapter.AbstractWebSocketSession<T>` implementation for this interface. It provides basic implementations for all methods in the `WebSocketSession` interface. Before sending data to a client, it must be converted to a format that the WebSocket protocol recognizes. A string representation of an object of any type can be converted to a `org.springframework.web.reactive.socket.WebSocketMessage` by using the utility method `textMessage(String)`. If the client is a browser, and the data is rendered into a browser using JavaScript, the most suitable text representation is JSON. The reverse functionality to transform `WebSocketMessage` instances into `String` is provided by the `getPayloadAsText()` method declared in the `WebSocketMessage` class.

A `WebSocketHandler` implementation must compose inbound (messages from the client) and outbound (messages being sent to the client) streams into a unified flow and return a `Mono<Void>`. It was mentioned previously that WebSocket communication could be closed by either party. This means that depending on application requirements, the unified flow completes when the following occurs.

- Either the inbound or outbound message streams complete.

- The inbound stream completes, the connection is closed, while the outbound stream is infinite.

- At a chosen point (server timeout) through calling the `close(CloseStatus)` method of the `WebSocketSession`. (The `org.springframework.web.reactive.socket.CloseStatus` class contains a set of constant values representing the most common WebSockets status codes. 1000 is the code used for a graceful communication closing.)[6]

---

[6]https://developer.mozilla.org/en-US/docs/Web/API/CloseEvent

In the context of the Bookstore application, an implementation of WebSocketHandler should receive messages from a client but also send tech news to the application at the same time. Listing 11-7 depicts such an implementation.

Listing 11-7. TechNewsHandler Implementation

```
package com.apress.prospringmvc.bookstore.handler;

import org.springframework.web.reactive.socket.WebSocketHandler;
import org.springframework.web.reactive.socket.WebSocketMessage;
import org.springframework.web.reactive.socket.WebSocketSession;
// other imports omitted

public class TechNewsHandler implements WebSocketHandler {
    private final Logger logger = LoggerFactory.
getLogger(NewsWebSocketHandler.class);

    private final AtomicLong rate = new AtomicLong(2000);

    @Override
    public Mono<Void> handle(WebSocketSession session) {
        Flux<String> newsFlux = Flux.fromStream(
                Stream.generate(BookNewReleasesUtil::randomNews))
        .delayElements(Duration.ofMillis(rate.get()));
        return session.send(newsFlux.map(session::textMessage))
                .and(session.receive()
                    .map(WebSocketMessage::getPayloadAsText)
                    .doOnNext(message -> logger.debug("Client says: {}",
message))
                );
    }
}
```

It might not be obvious in Listing 11-7 that the inbound and outbound streams are combined into a unified flow. This is the danger of declarative programming and lambdas. The two distinct streams are made clear by the implementation in Listing 11-8.

Listing 11-8. TechNewsHandler Implementation Making the Two Streams
Obvious

```
package com.apress.prospringmvc.bookstore.handler;
// other imports omitted

public class TechNewsHandler implements WebSocketHandler {
    private final Logger logger = LoggerFactory.getLogger(TechNewsHandler.
class);

    @Override
    public Mono<Void> handle(WebSocketSession session) {
        var inbound = session.receive()
                .map(WebSocketMessage::getPayloadAsText)
                .doOnNext(message -> logger.debug("Client says: {}",
message))
                .then();

        var source = Flux.generate(
            (SynchronousSink<String> synchronousSink) ->
             synchronousSink.next(BookNewReleasesUtil.randomNews())
        );

        var outbound = session.send(source.map(session::textMessage)
            .delayElements(Duration.ofSeconds(2L))); // artificial delay

        return Mono.zip(inbound, outbound).then();
    }
}
```

The send(..) method takes the source of messages being sent to the client; in this
case, the infinite Flux<String> emits random tech news. The receive() method returns
a stream emitting WebSocketMessage instances representing messages received from the
client. Those messages are converted to String using the getPayloadAsText() method
and printed in the console.

Now that we have a WebSocketHandler, we must map it to a URL. In a Spring Boot
application that declares spring-boot-starter-webflux as a dependency, this is done
by declaring a HandlerMapping bean containing the correspondence between the URL
path and the TechNewsHandler bean and by declaring a WebSocketHandlerAdapter.

The WebSocketHandlerAdapter delegates to a WebSocketService. By default, this is an instance of type HandshakeWebSocketService. Its responsibility is to perform basic checks on WebSocket-related HTTP requests and extract attributes from the WebSession to insert them into the WebSocketSession (this is useful when authentication is required).

There are no special annotations needed. Simply declare three beans in a class annotated with @Configuration, and they are picked up and used by Spring. All interfaces and classes necessary for the configuration are part of the org. springframework.web.reactive package and its subpackages. Listing 11-9 depicts this very simple configuration.

Listing 11-9. Spring Necessary Beans to Configure WebSocket Communication

```
package com.apress.prospringmvc.bookstore.config;

import org.springframework.web.reactive.socket.WebSocketHandler;
import org.springframework.web.reactive.socket.server.support.
WebSocketHandlerAdapter;
// other imports omitted

@Configuration
public class WebSocketConfig {

    @Bean
    WebSocketHandler techNewsHandler(){
        return new TechNewsHandler();
    }

    @Bean
    HandlerMapping handlerMapping(WebSocketHandler techNewsHandler) {
        return new SimpleUrlHandlerMapping() {
            {
                setUrlMap(Collections.singletonMap("/ws/tech/news",
techNewsHandler));
                setOrder(-1);
            }
        };
    }
```

```
@Bean
public WebSocketHandlerAdapter handlerAdapter() {
    return new WebSocketHandlerAdapter();
}
}
```

This is all you need to configure support for WebSocket communication in a Spring application. The mapping order set for this handler is –1 to make sure the WebSocket requests are handled before annotated controllers. The JavaScript code used to make WebSocket requests is pretty simple; it is depicted in Listing 11-10.

Listing 11-10. JavaScript Code Written Using Official WebSocket API in(part of the search.html template file)

```
<script th:inline="javascript">
    $( window ).on( "load", function() {
        renderNews.start();
    });
    $( window ).on( "onbeforeunload", function() {
        renderNews.start();
    });

    var renderNews = {
        socket : new WebSocket('ws://localhost:8080/ws/tech/news'),
        fromServer: [],
        start: function () {
            this.socket.addEventListener('message', function (event) {
                let message = event.data

                $("#techNews").html(message);
                renderNews.fromServer.push(event.data);
                if(renderNews.fromServer.length % 10 === 0) {
                    renderNews.socket.send('Slow down mate!');
                } else if(renderNews.fromServer.length % 15 === 0) {
                    renderNews.socket.send('Faster mate!');
                }
            });
```

```javascript
        this.socket.addEventListener('open', function(event) {
            console.log('Opening connection...');
            renderNews.socket.send('Give me your best shot');
        });
        this.socket.addEventListener('close', function(event) {
            if (event.wasClean) {
                console.log(`Clean closing...
                    code=${event.code} reason=${event.reason}`);
            } else {
                // event.code is usually 1006 in this case
                console.log('Server closed the connection.');
            }
        });

        this.socket.addEventListener('error', function(event) {
            console.log(`Well bummer... ${error.message}`);
        });
    },
    stop: function() {
        this.socket.close();
    }
};
</script>
```

The JavaScript code is similar to Listing 11-4 because it uses the same WebSocket API to handle connect, close and message events.

Unfortunately, there is no Java client to test WebSocket reactive communication. And curl doesn't do a good job at it either. The only way to test it is to run the project and add console.log statements to debug it. Or try the Simple WebSocket Client Chrome plugin.[7]

Now that we have a client and a server communicating using WebSocket, it is time to approach the subject of backpressure.

---

[7]https://chrome.google.com/webstore/detail/simple-websocket-client/pfdhobln gboilpfeibdedpjgfnlcodoo?hl=en

Handling Backpressure

Backpressure is the unicorn of reactive programming. Nearly every software engineer knows how to define it and must deal with it sooner than later. The term **backpressure** is borrowed from fluid dynamics, but in software it represents the force opposing the desired flow of data through software. If you have two applications exchanging data and one of them cannot process what it is receiving fast enough, it is *resisting the flow of data*. Backpressure can lead to blockages and data loss, so handling backpressure is writing code to regulate the data flow on the server side and implement some data saving mechanism on the client side.

Nowadays, server and client applications are separated through a network, and communication is done over TCP. To understand how backpressure can be handled over a network, an understanding of how TCP works is necessary. Establishing communication over the Internet can be done through various protocols and network protocols is a vast subject, and more than one book has been written about them. But, in the context of this book, I try to keep it simple. The Transmission Control Protocol (TCP) is the core protocol of the Internet Protocol suite. Applications communicating over HTTP, WebSocket, and other protocols on top of TCP are usually not sensitive about delivering each bit of information(package), but rather to the total duration of all the information delivered. That is why every time a package reaches its destination, an acknowledgment signal is emitted, and this ensures successful *end-to-end* communication.

Where does handling backpressure fit in? Some mechanism should be implemented to control the number of logical elements sent/received to/from the network. TCP has its own flow control,[8] but it applies to packages. TCP has no idea about the overall shape of what you are sending using a protocol on top of it. Thus, applications using protocols on top of TCP must convert logical elements to bytes. But they have no control over how those elements are transmitted after they were converted into packages. Backpressure is regulated by the TCP flow control. Of course, logic can be added inside the application to control the rate of the elements being emitted, but can the client have anything to say about it?

Spring Framework 5 has modernized WebSockets support in the framework, adding reactive capabilities to this communication channel. Once the WebSocket communication is established, the client and server can independently send messages to each other emitted on a dedicated stream. In a non-reactive application, the client sends one or more messages, and the server reacts by sending one or more messages as well. In a reactive application, the client and server can send streams of messages to each other over a WebSocket connection.

---

[8]http://www-sop.inria.fr/mistral/personnel/Thomas.Bonald/tcp_eng.html

In the previous example, we have seen messages being sent to the client at a certain rate. The messages sent by the client at the same time were only printed, and they did not interrupt or affect the behavior of the server in any way. The visual representation of the interaction between the browser running the code described in Listing 11-10 and the server running the code in Listing 11-8 is depicted in Figure 11-4.

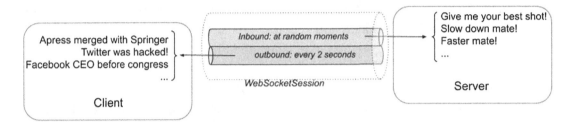

Figure 11-4. *The JavaScript client and the Spring WebFlux application communication over WebSocket*

Messages sent from the client are received by the server via the inbound stream, and messages are sent by the server to the client using the outbound stream. The client renders the messages in the HTML page in the browser, and the server prints the ones it receives in the console. Not useful, is it? It doesn't do much. Neither are other basic examples found on the Internet, which implement an echo communication where the server responds with the message the client is sending. Examples of backpressure control at the application level are as simple as regulating the flow using a customized subscriber that processes emitted elements in chunks. This assumes that the client application is written using Reactive Streams API implementation.

Listing 11-11 is a simple example of handling backpressure using an implementation of Project Reactor's BaseSubscriber<T>. The message source is the same stream used to send messages using WebSocket in the previous section, but it was limited to 20 elements to keep the execution finite.

Listing 11-11. Backpressure Handling Example Using Customized BaseSubscriber<T>

```
@Test
void testBackpressureHandlingOne() {
    var techNews = Flux.fromStream(
            Stream.generate(BookNewReleasesUtil::randomNews))
```

```
    .take(20).log(); // server outbound stream

// client
techNews.subscribe(new BaseSubscriber<>() {
    int processed;
    final int limit = 5;

    @Override
    protected void hookOnSubscribe(Subscription subscription) {
        subscription.request(limit);
    }

    @Override
    protected void hookOnNext(String news) {
        //client logic here
        if (++processed >= limit) {
            processed = 0;
            request(limit);
        }
    }
});
}
```

The hookOnSubscribe(Subscription) implementation in Project Reactor's
BaseSubscriber<T> is considered unbounded, which means it requests as many
elements as the upper limit of the type of the declared argument of the subscription.
request(..) method, which is long, so by default, it requests Long.MAX_VALUE elements
from the stream. You can check that by looking at the BaseSubscriber<T> Java code.[9]

This is not always good since the consumer can be slow to process the received values.

Making another analogy to fluid dynamics, it is normal for the client to control the
faucet lever to decide the water pressure, right? The following code is equivalent to using
the limitRate(int) method, which, when called on a Flux<T> instance, it limits the
request of the subsequent subscriber to the number provided as argument (thus acting
like a flux lever). The code equivalent to Listing 11-11 is depicted in Listing 11-12.

---

[9]https://github.com/reactor/reactor-core/blob/master/reactor-core/src/main/java/
reactor/core/publisher/BaseSubscriber.java

Listing 11-12. Backpressure Handling Example Using `Flux.limitRate(int)`

```
@Test
void testBackpressureHandlingTwo() {
    var techNews = Flux.fromStream(
            Stream.generate(BookNewReleasesUtil::randomNews))
        .take(20).log();
    consume(techNews.limitRate(5));
}

private void consume(Flux<String> input) {
    input.subscribe(/*s -> clientLogicHere(s)*/);
}
```

When you run any of the previous tests, you see log messages making it clear data is emitted in chunks of five messages, allowing the client to breathe. But, most people expect that the client tells the server the preferred emitting rate, right? Well, I did because I was promised Reactive Streams and a bidirectional connection, and I wanted to use them together. I tried to modify `TechNewsHandler` so that when a message is received from the client, the server responds with a stream emitting values at different rates depending on the message. The message *Slow down, mate!* causes the rate to drop to one value being emitted every 5 seconds and *Faster, mate!* causes the rate to increase to one value being emitted every 2 seconds. A solution might look like the one depicted in Listing 11-13.

Listing 11-13. `ServerController` Modified to Support Different Emission Rates for Messages

```
package com.apress.prospringmvc.bookstore.handler;
// other imports omitted

public class TechNewsHandler implements WebSocketHandler {
    private final Logger logger = LoggerFactory.getLogger(TechNewsHandler.
class);

    private Flux<String> getRandomNews(String message){
        long rate = "Slow down mate!".equals(message) ? 5000:2000L;
        return Flux.fromStream(Stream.generate(BookNewReleasesUtil::random
News))
```

```
        .delayElements(Duration.ofMillis(rate));
    }

    @Override
    public Mono<Void> handle(WebSocketSession session) {
        return session.send(session.receive()
                .map(WebSocketMessage::getPayloadAsText)
                .log()
                .flatMap(this::getRandomNews)
                .map(session::textMessage)).then();
    }
}
```

That looks like a very elegant solution, nice and clean, but does it work as expected? The long answer is: not really.

The short answer is: NO.

The declarative style of reactive programming and misunderstanding of it sometimes leads to monsters like these. The previous implementation of the handle(..) method can be summarized like this: send a stream of infinite messages returned by the getRandomNews() invocation every time a message is received on this session. The communication can be summarized as follows.

- The client sends, *Give me your best shot.*

- A stream on the server starts sending random tech news every 2 seconds.

- The client sends *Slow down, mate!*

- Another stream on the server starts sending random tech news every 5 seconds.

- The client sends, *Faster, mate!*

- Yet another stream on the server starts sending random tech news every 2 seconds.

And so on.

Without anyone canceling the subscription to these streams, what is the result here? All streams continue emitting elements until the user closes the web page or the server runs out of memory. All these streams send their messages to the same client on the same WebSocketSession, so the result overwhelms the browser. Backpressure control is not implemented correctly because controlling streams is not possible since the state is not shared between handling subsequent messages.

In the sources attached to this book, you find a Node.js server implementation (file tech-news-server.js) that allows the client to control the emitting rates. This is possible because of using the setInterval and clearInterval methods. The reference to the function generating messages is shared between handling subsequent messages in the same session. No JavaScript Reactive Stream Library is used, so reactivity is somewhat simulated. But, it gets the job of taking the client's wishes into account.

An equivalent version cannot be written using Spring WebFlux. A ConcurrentHash Map<String, Flux<WebSocketMessage>> could store references to outbound streams mapped to each WebSocketSession. When a message is received, the reference to the outbound stream is retrieved from the connection map, just call .subscribe(). dispose() on the existing stream and replace it with another with a different value emitting rate. The main problem is the declarative style of reactive programming prevents you from replacing the existing stream. This is because of immutability.

The presented case of random news being displayed on a web page does not require much communication with the client. The client has to open the page, which opens the WebSocket connection through which the data is delivered, an operation which also implies subscribing to the tech news stream on the server and then closes the page, which cancels the subscription since the WebSocket connection is closed too. That is all. Regulation of messages emitting rates in this context, according to the client preference, makes no sense. When was the last time a site was designed to slow down the rate of its ads to avoid freezing the browser? Nobody cares about that, which is why ad blockers were invented. The server is designed to send messages to the client with a frequency that keeps the information visible and useful.

The only way messages from the client influence what the server sends back on its stream would be to save them in a database that the stream sending messages to the client uses as a source. Add a reactive process that uses client messages as commands controlling what needs to be produced and sent to the client, and you have a decent interaction between the two. This situation is depicted in Figure 11-5, and keep this in mind: you can influence *what* is send on the outbound stream, *not the frequency* the messages are sent.

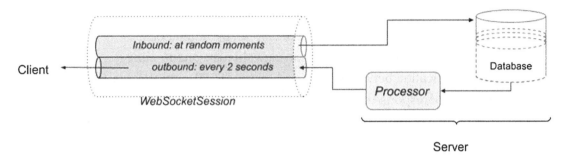

Figure 11-5. *Reactive application in which the client has control over what messages the server sends using a shared database*

Project Reactor is a Reactive Streams implementation, and thus all its operators support non-blocking backpressure. However, this applies only to the server-side Java application. The inability to properly handle backpressure is limited by the communication protocols, whether HTTP or WebSocket. The most detailed explanation about how backpressure is handled between two Spring WebFlux applications can be found on StackOverflow[10] and is a masterful contribution of Oleh Dokuka, a known contributor to Project Reactor. The conclusion that can be drawn is we can declare several prefetched elements and split the data emitted by the server into chunks to throttle the demand (like it was done in the previous examples). But there is no way for the client to influence that after the data started flowing.

Oleh Dokuka says that to achieve logical-elements backpressure through the network boundaries, we need an appropriate protocol. That protocol is RSocket, which is covered in the next section.

The RSocket Protocol

RSocket[11] is a binary application protocol providing Reactive Streams semantics that can be used on top of byte stream transports such as TCP, WebSockets, and Aeron.[12] It was created by engineers at Netflix, the most popular streaming platform nowadays. It enables the asynchronous exchange of messages over a single connection with the following flavors.

---

[10]https://stackoverflow.com/questions/52244808/
backpressure-mechanism-in-spring-web-flux
[11]https://rsocket.io/
[12]https://github.com/real-logic/aeron

- **fire-and-forget (no response)**: For example, the handler method returns Mono<Void> and declares a parameter of type *RequestMessageType*; you can view this as a *one-to-none* communication between client and server. HTTP supports this, but the lack of response confuses some browsers.

- **request/response (stream of 1)**: For example, the handler method returns Mono< *ResponseMessageType* > and declares a parameter of type *RequestMessageType* or Mono< *RequestMessageType* >; you can view this as a *one-to-one* communication between client and server. HTTP supports this.

- **request/stream (finite stream of many)**: For example, handler method returns Flux< *ResponseMessageType* > and declares a parameter of type *RequestMessageType* or Mono< *RequestMessageType* >; you can view this as a *one-to-many* communication between client and server. WebSocket supports this.

- **channel (bidirectional streams)**: For example, handler method returns Flux< *ResponseMessageType* > and declares a parameter of type Flux< *RequestMessageType* >; you can view this as a *many-to-many* communication between client and server.

ⓘ   *RequestMessageType* and *RequestMessageType* are placeholder types, replacing real types used in the communication between a client and a server to create a generic pattern.

The best thing about RSocket is that there are drivers for Java, JavaScript, Kotlin, .NET, Python, Go, and C++. In theory, this means an application developed in JavaScript can exchange messages with a Java application using this protocol, which means backpressure can be applied at the logical-elements level. RSocket is not widely used yet, but it does have a lot of potential. Unfortunately, including RSocket support in the Bookstore application would involve a lot of hassle since the rsocket-js API is provided as a set of Node.js modules. So instead, since this book is focused on Spring, we write a Spring WebFlux RSocket server and client.

The Java implementation for RSocket is built on Project Reactor. As you probably expected, there is a Spring Boot starter dependency for RSocket named `org.springframework.boot:spring-boot-starter-rsocket` that is easy to use. When this library is present on the classpath, an `org.springframework.boot.rsocket.netty.NettyRSocketServer` bean is autoconfigured and customized using properties in your `application.properties` or `application.yaml` file. Two properties are required to be set in the application configuration file: the server port and the transport protocol over which the RSocket communication takes place. Without them, the application will not start.

Listing 11-14, you see sample configuration files that configure the server to start on port 8081 to send and receive messages over WebSocket.

Listing 11-14. Spring Boot RSocket Server Application Configuration File

```
spring:
  rsocket:
    server:
      transport: websocket
      port: 8081
      mapping-path: /rsocket
```

The other option for the `spring.rsocket.server.transport` property is TCP, which is also the default one that assumes the RSocket protocol is used on top of HTTP. The `spring.rsocket.server.mapping-path` is optional and can be used to set a root context path for the RSocket application. If not specified, no context path is set.

Now that we have a server, we need a controller or a handler class to handle the RSocket requests. Only controllers are currently supported. You can have handler methods in a `@Controller` annotated class by annotating them with `@MessageMapping(path)`, from package `org.springframework.messaging.handler.annotation`. Custom handler classes and functional routing of RSocket requests is not provided yet. My technical reviewer wanted a GitHub issue link for this, but there is none. The API is not there, and nobody has requested it yet.

The four flavors of communication over RSocket were introduced previously. `ServerController` in Listing 11-15 contains four methods, each of them handling one type of communication. When the client and server exchange objects that are more complicated than simple text values, serialization and deserialization must be supported using message converters. By default, JSON is used, but if you are customizing

447

the communication and using other message converters, you might need to annotate the arguments of your RSocket handler methods with @Payload. In Listing 11-15, the annotation is used, even if not necessary, since the handled objects can be serialized and deserialized to/from JSON by default.

Listing 11-15. RSocket Requests Handler Methods in a @Controller

```
package com.apress.prospringmvc.bookstore.controller;


import org.springframework.messaging.handler.annotation.MessageMapping;
import org.springframework.messaging.handler.annotation.Payload;
import org.springframework.stereotype.Controller;
// other imports omitted

@Controller
public class ServerController {
    private final Logger logger = LoggerFactory.getLogger(ServerController.
class);

    // fire-and-forget
    @MessageMapping("introduction")
    public Mono<Void> introduction(@Payload ClientMessage clientMessage){
        logger.debug("{}:  We have a new client -->  {}" , Instant.now(),
clientMessage.getName());
        return Mono.empty();
    }

    // request/response
    @MessageMapping("check-service")
    public Mono<String> checkService(@Payload ClientMessage clientMessage){
        logger.debug("{}:  Ping request from client --> {}" , Instant.
now(), clientMessage.getName());
        return Mono.just(Instant.now() + ": Service online. Send
command.");
    }

    // request/stream
    @MessageMapping("show-books")
```

```java
    public Flux<Book> showBooks(@Payload ClientMessage clientMessage) {
        logger.debug("{}:  Random releases requested by client --> {}" ,
Instant.now(), clientMessage.getName());
        return Flux.fromStream(
                Stream.generate(BookNewReleasesUtil::randomRelease))
                .delayElements(Duration.ofSeconds(1L));
    }

    //channel (bi-directional streams)
    @MessageMapping("books-channel")
    public Flux<Book> useChannel(@Payload Flux<ClientMessage> messages) {
        return messages
                .map(message-> BookNewReleasesUtil.randomForAuthor(message.
getAuthor()))
                .delayElements(Duration.ofSeconds(1L));
    }
}
```

Each method receives as an argument a ClientMessage instance, which is a simple class containing the name of the client making the requests. The useChannel(Flux<Cl ientMessage>) method handles a bidirectional stream of communication between the client and the server. It receives a stream of messages from the client, processes each one, and responds using a stream with data emitted based on the data received from the client. In this case, the ClientMessage instance contains an author name that is used as criteria when generating a random book. It is a very simple class that is not relevant here.

If you start the application, you see that the server is started on the 8081 port, but how do we test it? Well, remember how I said this protocol has a lot of potential? I am not the only one thinking so. And that is why one of the developers working for Pivotal/ VMWare has created a command-line utility to help test RSocket servers.[13] It is called **RSocket Client CLI** (RSC) or **rsc** for short. It can test the first three methods. Testing a bidirectional is a difficult task since it's cumbersome to provide a stream as an argument using the command line. In the code for this chapter, you find commands to test all three methods. In Listing 11-16, you can see the rsc command used to test the showBooks()

---

[13]https://github.com/making/rsc

method. The --debug option gets a verbose result, showing the payload data as text and in binary format.

Listing 11-16. Output of rsc Command

```
$ rsc ws://localhost:8081/rsocket --stream --route show-books --log --debug -d
"{\"name\": \"Gigi\"}"
2020-08-17 21:44:17.425  INFO --- [ctor-http-nio-1] rsc              :
onSubscribe(FluxMap.MapSubscriber)
2020-08-17 21:44:17.425  INFO --- [ctor-http-nio-1] rsc              :
request(unbounded)
2020-08-17 21:44:17.433 DEBUG --- [ctor-http-nio-1] i.r.FrameLogger :
sending ->
Frame => Stream ID: 1 Type: REQUEST_STREAM Flags: 0b100000000 Length: 40
InitialRequestN: 9223372036854775807
Metadata:
          +--------------------------------------------------+
          | 0  1  2  3  4  5  6  7  8  9  a  b  c  d  e  f |
+--------+--------------------------------------------------+----------------+
|00000000| 0a 73 68 6f 77 2d 62 6f 6f 6b 73                |.show-books     |
+--------+--------------------------------------------------+----------------+
Data:
          +--------------------------------------------------+
          | 0  1  2  3  4  5  6  7  8  9  a  b  c  d  e  f |
+--------+--------------------------------------------------+----------------+
|00000000| 7b 22 6e 61 6d 65 22 3a 20 22 47 69 67 69 22 7d |{"name": "Gigi"}|
+--------+--------------------------------------------------+----------------+
2020-08-17 21:44:18.439 DEBUG --- [ctor-http-nio-1] i.r.FrameLogger : receiving ->
Frame => Stream ID: 1 Type: NEXT Flags: 0b100000 Length: 123
Data:
          +--------------------------------------------------+
          | 0  1  2  3  4  5  6  7  8  9  a  b  c  d  e  f |
+--------+--------------------------------------------------+----------------+
|00000000| 7b 22 74 69 74 6c 65 22 3a 22 52 65 61 63 74 69 |{"title":"Reacti|
|00000010| 76 65 20 53 70 72 69 6e 67 22 2c 22 70 72 69 63 |ve Spring","pric|
|00000020| 65 22 3a 32 35 2e 34 34 2c 22 79 65 61 72 22 3a |e":25.44,"year":|
```

```
|00000030| 32 30 32 30 2c 22 61 75 74 68 6f 72 22 3a 22 4a |2020,"author":"J|
|00000040| 6f 73 68 20 4c 6f 6e 67 22 2c 22 69 73 62 6e 22 |osh Long","isbn"|
|00000050| 3a 22 39 37 38 31 34 38 34 32 32 37 31 31 31 22 |:"9781484227111"|
|00000060| 2c 22 63 61 74 65 67 6f 72 79 22 3a 22 53 70 72 |,"category":"Spr|
|00000070| 69 6e 67 22                                     |ing"}            |
7d                                              |ing"}           |
+--------+-------------------------------------------------+----------------+
```

```
2020-08-17 21:44:18.439  INFO --- [ctor-http-nio-1] rsc:
onNext({"title":"Reactive Spring","price":25.44,"year":2020,"author":"Josh
Long","isbn":"9781484227111","category":"Spring"})
```

```
# more elements here since this stream is infinite
```

🛈 You might have noticed that the *request/response* and the *request/stream*
method do not declare a Mono<ClientMessage> as a parameter. This was
intentional because it would have made them unsuitable for testing with RSC.

To make the *request/response* and the *request/stream* abide by the reactive rules,
their parameters should be declared as having the Mono<ClientMessage>. This changes
the method's body since the argument has to be added at the front of the processing
pipeline. The changes are depicted in Listing 11-17.

Listing 11-17. The ServerController Fully Reactive Request/Response and the
Request/Stream Implementations

```
package com.apress.prospringmvc.bookstore.controller;
// other imports omitted

@Controller
public class ServerController {
    private final Logger logger = LoggerFactory.getLogger(ServerController.
    class);

    // request/response
    // no longer testable with rsc
    @MessageMapping("check-service")
```

```java
    public Mono<String> checkService(@Payload Mono<ClientMessage>
clientMessage){
        return clientMessage
                .doOnNext(message -> logger.debug("{}:  Ping request from
client --> {}" ,
                        Instant.now(), message.getName()))
                .map( message -> Instant.now() + ": Service online. Send
command.");
    }

    // request/stream
    // no longer testable with rsc
    @MessageMapping("show-books")
    public Flux<Book> showBooks(@Payload Mono<ClientMessage> clientMessage)
{
        return clientMessage
                .doOnNext(message -> logger.debug("{}:  " +
                        "Random releases requested by client --> {}" ,
Instant.now(), message.getName()))
                .thenMany(Flux.fromStream(
                        Stream.generate(BookNewReleasesUtil::randomRelea
se))
                        .delayElements(Duration.ofSeconds(1L)));
    }

    // rest of the code omitted
}
```

Once the server is up and running as expected, as confirmed by rsc, you can start writing your client. The same Spring Boot dependency provides the classes needed to write a client, but since we are connecting to a RSocket server, the application configuration file is not populated with the RSocket-specific properties. Without any properties in the application configuration file and spring-boot-starter-webflux on the classpath org.springframework.boot.web.embedded.netty.NettyWebServer starts on the default port: 8080.

Our client is a simple @RestController annotated class that contains four methods, each making an RSocket call to one of the four corresponding methods on the RSocket Server application. This includes the method that is not testable with rsc. To achieve this, an instance of org.springframework.messaging.rsocket.RSocketRequester is needed. This bean is being configured with the WebSocket URL that makes requests to the RSocket message handling methods exposed by the server. The bean is created using RSocketRequester.Builder. It is reactive and returns a Mono<RSocketRequester>, so a block() call (yes, the one I told you to avoid at the end of Chapter 10) is needed to extract the RSocketRequester instance.

Listing 11-18 depicts the declaration of this bean. Since we are using RSocket over WebSocket for communication, the connectWebSocket(..) was called on the server with a typical WebSocket URL prefixed with ws://.

If we were using HTTP, the connectTcp(..) with an HTTP URL would have been called instead.

Listing 11-18. The RSocketRequester Bean Declaration in the Spring Boot Application Main Class

```
package com.apress.prospringmvc.bookstore;
import org.springframework.messaging.rsocket.RSocketRequester;
//other imports omitted

@SpringBootApplication
public class RSocketClientBookstoreApplication {

    public static void main(String... args) {
        new SpringApplication(RSocketClientBookstoreApplication.class).
run(args);
    }

    @Bean
    RSocketRequester rSocketRequester(RSocketRequester.Builder builder) {
        return builder.connectWebSocket(URI.create("ws://localhost:8081/
rsocket")).block();
    }
}
```

The controller is nothing special, but the invocations of the RSocketRequester bean methods calls are. Listing 11-19 depicts ClientController, and each handler method in it can be considered an RSocket client making a request to the RSocket server using the same RSocketRequester bean.

Listing 11-19. The ClientController Containing Handler Methods Making RSocket Requests

```
package com.apress.prospringmvc.bookstore;
import org.springframework.messaging.rsocket.RSocketRequester;
//other imports omitted

@RestController
public class ClientController {

    private final RSocketRequester requester;

    public ClientController(RSocketRequester requester) {
        this.requester = requester;
    }

    @GetMapping("introduction")
    public Mono<String> introduction(){
        ClientMessage clientMessage = new ClientMessage().name("gigi");
        requester.route("introduction").data(clientMessage).send();
        return Mono.just("Introduction data was sent.");
    }

    @GetMapping("check-service")
    public Mono<String> checkService(){
        ClientMessage clientMessage = new ClientMessage().name("gigi");
        return requester.route("check-service").data(clientMessage).
        retrieveMono(String.class);
    }

    @GetMapping(path = "show-books", produces = MediaType.TEXT_EVENT_
    STREAM_VALUE)
    public Flux<Book> showBooks(){
        ClientMessage clientMessage = new ClientMessage().name("gigi");
```

```
    return requester.route("show-books").data(clientMessage).
        retrieveFlux(Book.class).limitRate(20);
    }

    @GetMapping(value = "books-channel", produces = MediaType.TEXT_EVENT_
STREAM_VALUE)
    Flux<Book> booksChannel() {
        return this.requester.route("books-channel")
                .data(Flux.range(0, 10).map(i -> new ClientMessage().
name("gigi").author(RandomUtil.randomAuthor()))))
                .retrieveFlux(Book.class).limitRate(5).log();
    }
}
```

The `introduction()` and `checkService()` methods do not need a `produces` attribute because they return a `Mono<String>` which Spring is smart enough to deserialize on its own without special instructions. Being a single value, there is no need to send it to the client as a SSE. It is also practical since these methods can be tested using a browser.

The `RSocketRequester` routes every client request to the appropriate server method. The method is identified on the server side by the attribute specified using the `@MessageMapping` annotation. The `introduction()` handler method was designed to make a server call and then return a `Mono<String>`, so the method can be executed by opening the `http://localhost:8080/introduction` in the browser. If left to return nothing, accessing this URL confuses most browsers. For example, Firefox complains about the inability to read the response because it cannot convert it to text, while Chrome says nothing. But, in the context of reactive services talking to each other directly (without a browser being involved), it makes sometimes sense to be able just to send a message without expecting a response. For example, let's take Internet ads. Do you think the server sending them to the page expects a response from you?

The `checkService()` method can be tested in the browser, and the response received from the server is displayed as a web page. The last two methods return streams of events; to test them, you need to use the `curl` command[14].

---

[14]https://curl.se/

RSocket is currently the poster child of Pivotal in the context of more and more interest being shown to writing microservices applications using Spring Boot. It is easy to set up, and it integrates perfectly in the Spring ecosystem. If you want to learn more about RSocket in the context of Spring Reactive applications, there is a series of articles on the spring.io official blog.[15]

WebFlux Security

WebFlux security is the last reactive applications topic in this book. Any application meant to be exposed publicly needs to support multiple users and control access to sensitive resources. To configure in a Spring WebFlux application is easier than doing so for a non-reactive Spring web application.

The Spring Security library was modified, starting with version 5 to include reactive components to set up security in a Spring WebFlux reactive application. Spring Security has a dedicated chapter in the book. If you are not familiar with securing Spring applications, we recommend you read about that first. Everything we said about Spring Security in a servlet environment applies to reactive applications too. The only differences are represented by a few classes and annotations that allow configuring security in a reactive application by using Reactive Streams and declarative programming.

Table 11-1 contains the annotations and classes involved in configuring security for a Spring WebFlux application and a Spring MVC application side by side.

---

[15]https://spring.io/blog/2020/03/02/getting-started-with-rsocket-spring-boot-server

Table 11-1. *Spring MVC and WebFlux Security Components Comparison*

Spring WebFlux	Spring Web MVC	Description
`org.springframework. security. config. annotation .web. reactive`	`org.springframework.security. config.annotation.web. configuration`	Root package where most components are located.
`@EnableWeb FluxSecurity`	`@EnableWebSecurity / @ EnableWebMvcSecurity`	Annotation used on a configuration class to enable Spring Security. (`@EnableWebMvcSecurity` is deprecated and will probably be removed in Spring 6. All its functionality is already part of the `@ EnableWebSecurity`.)
`@EnableRSocketSecurity`	–	`@EnableRSocket Security` is part of the `org.springframework. security.config. annotation.rsocket` package and adds Spring Security added in applications communicating over the RSocket protocol.
`@EnableReactive MethodSecurity`	`@EnableGlobalMethodSecurity`	Annotation used on a configuration class to enable Spring Security at the method level.
–	`SecurityConfigurer`	Interface to implement by the security config class.

(*continued*)

Table 11-1. (*continued*)

Spring WebFlux	Spring Web MVC	Description
ServerHttpSecurity (class)	HttpSecurity (final class)	Allows configuring web-based security for specific HTTP requests.
ReactiveUser DetailsService	UserDetailsService	Instances of classes implementing these interfaces store user information, which is later encapsulated into Authentication objects. ReactiveUserDetails Service is a reactive wrapper around UserDetailsService.
ServerHttpRequest	HttpServletRequest	ServerHttpRequest is part of the Spring Web library, while HttpServletRequest is part of the Java Servlet library.
ServerHttpResponse	HttpServletResponse	ServerHttpResponse is part of the Spring Web library, while HttpServletResponse is part of the Java Servlet library.

(*continued*)

Table 11-1. (*continued*)

Spring WebFlux	Spring Web MVC	Description
ServerWebExchange	–	ServerWebExchange represents a contract for an HTTP request-response interaction. It provides access to ServerHttpRequest and ServerHttpResponse.
SecurityWeb FilterChain	SecurityFilterChain	Interfaces representing a filter chain being matched against a ServerWebExchange/ HttpServletRequest to decide whether it applies to that request.
WebFilter ChainProxy	DelegatingFilterProxy	Delegate the job of filtering requests to a list of SecurityWebFilterChain/SecurityFilterChain instances.
WebSessionServer CsrfTokenRepository	HttpSessionCsrfToken Repository	A CSRF token repository implementation that stores the CsrfToken in the HttpSession.

When using Spring Boot to write a secured web reactive application, the presence of the `spring-boot-starter-security` dependency on the project classpath autoconfigures security for you based on a few internal classes. The application still starts, but any URL redirects to a default login form.

To customize the security configuration in a Spring Boot WebFlux application, you can declare a bean of type `org.springframework.security.web.server.SecurityWebFilterChain` in any configuration class. When the application starts, it picks it up and enables all the access rules configured by it. If Spring Boot is not used, the configuration class needs to be annotated with `@EnableWebFluxSecurity`. This annotation is declared in the `org.springframework.security.config.annotation.web.reactive` package, and although not necessary in a Spring Boot application, most developers tend to gather all security-related beans in a configuration class that is annotated with this annotation, thus using it as a marker.

The method to create the SecurityWebFilterChain bean takes as argument an `org.springframework.security.config.web.server.ServerHttpSecurity` object that is injected by Spring. The `ServerHttpSecurity` class exposes almost the same methods as its non-reactive equivalent, `HttpSecurity`, allowing a developer to specify access rules for URLs, authentication providers, a login form, a logout form, CSRF implementation, and so on. Chapter 12 provides a detailed explanation of how to configure Spring Security.

In a Spring WebFlux application, the quickest way to configure authentication is to declare a `MapReactiveUserDetailsService` bean initialized with one or more `UserDetails` instances. This bean provides the data for in-memory authentication. Listing 11-20 is an example of a `MapReactiveUserDetailsService` bean being configured to provide authentication data for two users. You can see the `PasswordEncoder` bean, which sets up password hashing for better security. A configuration for a development environment can be set up using the `NoOpPasswordEncoder`, which does not change the passwords in any way. This approach is frowned upon because of security concerns.

Listing 11-20. The MapReactiveUserDetailsService Bean

```
package com.apress.prospringmvc.bookstore.config.security;

import org.springframework.security.config.annotation.web.reactive.
EnableWebFluxSecurity;
import org.springframework.security.config.web.server.ServerHttpSecurity;
import org.springframework.security.core.userdetails.
MapReactiveUserDetailsService;
import org.springframework.security.core.userdetails.User;
import org.springframework.security.core.userdetails.UserDetails;
```

```java
import org.springframework.security.crypto.bcrypt.BCryptPasswordEncoder;
import org.springframework.security.crypto.password.PasswordEncoder;

//other import omitted

@Configuration
@EnableWebFluxSecurity
public class SecurityConfig  {
    //other code omitted
    @Bean
    public MapReactiveUserDetailsService userDetailsService() {
        UserDetails john = User.withUsername("john")
                .password(passwordEncoder().encode("doe")).roles("USER")
                .build();
        UserDetails admin = User.withUsername("admin")
                .password(passwordEncoder().encode("admin")).roles("ADMIN")
                .build();
        return new MapReactiveUserDetailsService(john, admin);
    }

    @Bean
    public PasswordEncoder passwordEncoder() {
        return new BCryptPasswordEncoder();
    }
}
```

The MapReactiveUserDetailsService class implements org.springframework. security.core.userdetails.ReactiveUserDetailsService to declare a simple API for retrieving a Mono<UserDetails> based on the username. If authentication data is provided by a database or any external system (e.g., a single sign-on provider like Google or Okta), the simplest way to use the existing data is to implement this interface and provide a customized way to retrieve the authentication data. Declare a bean of your type, and it is picked up automatically. Since the authentication data for the Bookstore application is saved in a MongoDB table, the implementation is simple since the reactive MongoDB repository returns data using Reactive Streams. Listing 11-21 depicts the implementation of the ReactiveUserDetailsService used in the Bookstore application.

Listing 11-21. The ReactiveAuthenticationService Bean Used in the
Bookstore Application

```
package com.apress.prospringmvc.bookstore.config.security;
import com.apress.prospringmvc.bookstore.repository.AccountRepository;
import org.springframework.security.core.userdetails.
ReactiveUserDetailsService;
import org.springframework.security.core.userdetails.
UsernameNotFoundException;
// other imports omitted

@Service
public class ReactiveAuthenticationService implements
ReactiveUserDetailsService {

    private final AccountRepository accountRepository;

    public ReactiveAuthenticationService(AccountRepository
accountRepository) {
        this.accountRepository = accountRepository;
    }

    @Override
    public Mono<UserDetails> findByUsername(String username) {
        return accountRepository.findByUsername(username).switchIfEmpty(
                Mono.defer(() -> Mono.error
                (new UsernameNotFoundException("User Not Found"))
        )).map(this::toUserDetails);
    }

    private UserDetails toUserDetails(Account account) {
        String[] authorities = new String[account.getRoles().size()];
        authorities = account.getRoles().toArray(authorities);
        return User.withUsername(account.getUsername())
                .password(account.getPassword())
                .authorities(authorities)
                .build();
    }
}
```

The data returned by ReactiveAuthenticationService is used to authenticate the user. Its role is used to decide which resources the user is allowed to access, and the actions is allowed to perform within the application. Now that we have the authentication provider data set up, the next step is to configure the SecurityWebFilterChain. Listing 11-22 depicts the configuration used in the Bookstore application.

Listing 11-22. The SecurityWebFilterChain Bean

```
package com.apress.prospringmvc.bookstore.config.security;

import org.thymeleaf.extras.springsecurity5.dialect.SpringSecurityDialect;
import org.springframework.security.web.server.util.matcher.
ServerWebExchangeMatchers;
// other imports omitted

@Configuration
@EnableWebFluxSecurity
@EnableReactiveMethodSecurity
public class SecurityConfig  {

    @Bean
    SecurityWebFilterChain authorization(ServerHttpSecurity http) {
        final RedirectServerLogoutSuccessHandler logoutSuccessHandler =
            new RedirectServerLogoutSuccessHandler();
        logoutSuccessHandler.setLogoutSuccessUrl(URI.create("/"));

        return http
                .formLogin(formLogin -> formLogin.loginPage("/login"))
                .logout(logoutSpec -> logoutSpec.logoutUrl("/signout")
                    .logoutSuccessHandler(logoutSuccessHandler))
                .authorizeExchange(authorize -> authorize
                        .matchers(PathRequest.toStaticResources().
atCommonLocations()).permitAll()
                        .pathMatchers("/book/edit/*", "/book/create").
hasRole("ADMIN")
                        .pathMatchers("/customer/edit/*").hasRole("ADMIN")
```

```
                          .matchers(ServerWebExchangeMatchers.
pathMatchers(HttpMethod.DELETE,
                              "/book/delete/*", "/customer/delete/*", "/
                              account/delete/*")).hasRole("ADMIN")
                      .anyExchange().permitAll()
            )
            .csrf(csrf ->  csrf.csrfTokenRepository(repo()))
            .build();
    }

    @Bean
    public ServerCsrfTokenRepository repo() {
        WebSessionServerCsrfTokenRepository repo = new
        WebSessionServerCsrfTokenRepository();
        repo.setParameterName("_csrf");
        repo.setHeaderName("X-CSRF-TOKEN"); // default header name
        return repo;
    }

    @Bean
    public SpringSecurityDialect securityDialect() {
        return new SpringSecurityDialect();
    }

}
```

The configuration describes the following.

- `.formLogin(formLogin → formLogin.loginPage("/login"))` configures the form declared in the view returned by the /login URL to be used for logging a user in. To use the default, generated form you can use `.formLogin(Customizer.withDefaults())`.

- `.logout(logoutSpec → logoutSpec.logoutUrl("/signout"))` is a POST request to the URL /signout triggers a logout action. The default is /logout.

- `.authorizeExchange(..)` uses the `Customizer<T>` instance to configure authorization.

- The line .matchers(PathRequest.toStaticResources().
  atCommonLocations()) builds a ServerWebExchangeMatcher that
  matches the Spring Boot default locations where static sources
  reside(/resources/static directory) and the .permitall()
  invocation excludes them from security.

- The pathMatchers(String...) method uses Ant Style patterns for
  URLs and returns ServerWebExchangeMatcher instances that map
  URLs to handler methods.

- The ServerWebExchangeMatchers contains a few utility methods for
  creating ServerWebExchangeMatcher instances. The example shown
  in the previous listing uses an HTML method and a list of URLs to
  create a ServerWebExchangeMatcher instance the security rule is
  applied to.

- .csrf(csrf → csrf.csrfTokenRepository(repo())) secures
  the application by introducing a CSRF Token generated by the
  ServerCsrfTokenRepository configured in the same code sample.

- RedirectServerLogoutSuccessHandler redirects the user to the root
  page ("/") after logging out.

All exchanges between clients and servers are secured with this configuration,
regardless of whether they were set up using a controller handler method or a functional
endpoint.

Testing security configuration can be done very easily by using the @WithMockUser
annotation on methods testing endpoints. This annotation is part of the spring-
security-test library and is located in the org.springframework.security.test.
context.support package. It was introduced in Spring 4 and in Spring 5 was extended to
cover reactive endpoints too.

Listing 11-23 depicts four test methods. Each endpoint is covered by the
configuration in Listing 11-22.

Listing 11-23. Class Testing Secured Endpoints Access

```
package com.apress.prospringmvc.bookstore.api;
import org.springframework.security.test.context.support.WithMockUser;
//other imports
```

```java
@SpringBootTest(webEnvironment = SpringBootTest.WebEnvironment.RANDOM_PORT)
public class BookSecuredApiTest {
    private static Logger logger = LoggerFactory.
getLogger(BookSecuredApiTest.class);

    @Autowired
    private WebTestClient testClient;

    @WithMockUser(roles = "USER")
    @Test
    void shouldFindByIsbn(){
        testClient.get()
            .uri(uriBuilder -> uriBuilder.path("/book/by/{isbn}").
             build("9781484230042"))
            .accept(MediaType.APPLICATION_JSON)
            .exchange()
            .expectStatus().isOk()
            .expectHeader().contentType(MediaType.APPLICATION_JSON)
            .expectBody(Book.class)
            .consumeWith(responseEntity -> {
                logger.debug("Response: {}", responseEntity);
                Book book = responseEntity.getResponseBody();
                assertAll("book", () ->
                {
                    assertNotNull(book);
                    assertAll("book",
                            () -> assertNotNull(book.getTitle()),
                            () -> assertEquals("Iuliana Cosmina", book.
                            getAuthor()));
                });
            });
    }

    @Test
    @WithMockUser(roles = "ADMIN")
    void shouldCreateABook() {
        Book book = new Book();
```

```
        book.setTitle("TDD for dummies");
        book.setAuthor("Test User");
        book.setPrice(BigDecimal.valueOf(40.99));
        book.setIsbn("12232434324");
        book.setCategory("test");
        testClient.post().uri("/book/create")
            .body(Mono.just(book), Book.class)
            .exchange()
            .expectStatus().isCreated()
            .expectHeader().contentType(MediaType.APPLICATION_JSON)
            .expectHeader().exists("Location")
            .expectBody(Book.class)
            .consumeWith(responseEntity -> {
                logger.debug("Response: {}", responseEntity);
                assertAll("book", () ->
                {
                    assertNotNull(book);
                    assertAll("book",
                            () -> assertNotNull(book.getIsbn()),
                            () -> assertEquals("test", book.
getCategory())));
                });
            });
    }

    @WithMockUser(roles = "ADMIN")
    @Test
    void shouldDeleteByIsbn(){
        testClient.delete()
            .uri(uriBuilder -> uriBuilder.path("/book/delete/{isbn}")
                .build("9781484230042"))
            .accept(MediaType.APPLICATION_JSON)
            .exchange()
            .expectStatus().isNoContent();
    }
```

```java
@Test
public void shouldReturnTwoBooks(){
    BookSearchCriteria criteria = new BookSearchCriteria();
    criteria.setCategory(Book.Category.JAVA);

    testClient.post()
        .uri("/book/search")
        .accept(MediaType.APPLICATION_JSON)
        .body(Mono.just(criteria), BookSearchCriteria.class)
        .exchange()
        .expectStatus().isOk()
        .expectHeader().contentType(MediaType.APPLICATION_JSON)
        .expectBodyList(Book.class)
        .hasSize(2);
    }
}
```

When @WithMockUser is placed on a test method in a Spring Secured Boot Test context, the call to the endpoint being tested is made using an emulated security context specific to a mock user. The user can be specified using a name @WithMockUser("john"), but since in Listing 11-21, the security rules are declared using roles, the annotation form using roles is more suitable.

The Bookstore application uses Thymeleaf as a template engine. To support security Thymeleaf elements in the views, a bean of type SpringSecurityDialect must be added to the configuration.

If the security section seems slim, this is because Chapter 12 is dedicated fully to Spring Security. Consider reading that and then coming back to this section.

Summary

At the end of our trio of reactive chapters, there are a few things that should stay with you. To build reactive applications, you need a reactive mindset and to write your code declaratively. Spring WebFlux is an excelled candidate for writing reactive applications that run on a robust JVM platform. Spring WebFlux simplifies threaded work by making it unnecessary to interact with the underlying components parallelizing the work. It provides a lot of operators that simplify transformations of data streams. The resulted code is cleaner, more readable, and more robust.

Server-sent events and the WebSocket protocol are supported. RSocket (another brainchild of Netflix developers) is a new messaging protocol designed to solve common microservice communication challenges, such as handling backpressure at logical elements level over TCP. You get modern controls like multiplexing, backpressure, resumption, and routing, and you get multiple messaging modes, including fire-and-forget, request-response, and streaming.

Securing WebFlux applications is also easy.

Reactive applications improve user experience, and most web and mobile applications nowadays are reactive applications. So, if you think you might postpone learning reactive programming a little more, maybe don't. :)

There are drawbacks as well. The learning curve can be steep, and it is easy to manage subscriptions incorrectly and end up with memory leaks that affect users' experience. The general approach is to ease into it and only make reactive the components that need to be.

When building high-load or multi-user applications, you need to go reactive. A social network application is a good case for a reactive application. An online chat application is another. You want to stream music or videos? Going reactive is the proper choice as well. Do you want to build an online game with highly interactive UI elements? Yup, you need to build it as a reactive application.

Reactive programming is here to stay, and using it well is a must-have skill for any accomplished developer.

CHAPTER 12

Spring Security

It is said that information is power. That is even more true nowadays when all web applications are hosted in the cloud and deployed in containers somebody else designed and hopefully secured and audited. The least that developers can do is keep passwords safe. Most web applications have public pages meant to be seen by anyone and private pages reserved for verified users. For example, the Bookstore application should have pages for adding, editing, and deleting book entries that are available only to users with an administrative role. Spring MVC was used to build a Spring web application in previous chapters. Spring Security is the best framework for securing a Spring web application.

Spring Security is a highly customizable authentication and access-control framework. This framework is based on Acegi security,[1] which was written when Spring was in infancy. It provides a powerful and flexible security solution for Java enterprise applications built using the Spring Framework. Spring Security provides comprehensive support for authentication, authorization, and protection against common exploits. It also provides integration with other libraries to simplify its usage.

This chapter takes a closer look at different ways to secure a Spring web application. Let's start with a few key security terms and principles.

---

[1]https://spring.io/blog/2007/01/25/why-the-name-acegi

© Marten Deinum and Iuliana Cosmina 2021
M. Deinum and I. Cosmina, *Pro Spring MVC with WebFlux*, https://doi.org/10.1007/978-1-4842-5666-4_12

Security Basics

An entity that accesses a web application and can perform actions is called a **principal**. The principal identifies itself using identification keys that are referred to as **credentials**. When accessing a web application, a small package of information is created and stored on your system by your computer's browser. This is called a **cookie***.[2] A cookie can store personalized information (e.g., language and theme) in order to customize your next visit. Search the projects for the book for CookieResolver. This is a typical Spring bean type designed to create a cookie named org.springframework.web.servlet. i18n.CookieLocaleResolver.LOCALE that stores your preferred locale. The cookie name mentioned here is the default one set by Spring, but it can be customized when configuring the for CookieResolver bean. These cookies are called **persistent**, and they remain in operation even when you have closed the browser. They are stored as files in one of your browser's subfolders until you delete them manually, or your browser deletes them based on the expiration period contained within the persistent cookie's file. Some web applications use this type of cookies to store your credentials, so you don't have to type them in every time you use the site.

Cookies that are not permanent are called **session cookies**, and their lifespan is determined by that of an HTTP user session. An HTTP user session starts when you log into a web application and ends when you log out. Some applications also end the user's session when the page is closed. Information stored in a session cookie is shared between the pages of the site. This type of cookies is used by shopping sites to store the product you added to your virtual cart.

When the user logs in, the server sets a temporary cookie in your browser to remember that you are currently logged in, and your identity was confirmed. Session cookies are suitable for storing credentials, too, since their reduced lifespan also reduces the interval when they can be hijacked.[3]

---

[2]https://www.allaboutcookies.org/
[3]https://owasp.org/www-community/attacks/Session_hijacking_attack

The process of confirming your identity is called **authentication** and consists of checking the user-provided credentials against the server database. The most basic type of authentication requires a user id and password, and it relies on a single authentication factor. It is a type of **single-factor authentication**. After a user is authenticated, it usually goes through a process of **authorization**. This process is needed to determine the parts of the application the user should be able to access. For example, a normal user of the Bookstore application should not be allowed to edit or delete books. The parts of the application that a user can access are usually described by **roles**.

The Spring Security framework offers the possibility to configure authentication and authorization independently. Being loosely coupled, one or both can be replaced with external providers of those services. Spring Framework also supports authorization at the web request level, on service methods, and on individual domain objects. With such a myriad of possibilities, no wonder Spring Security is almost the default go-to for securing Spring applications.

Minimal Spring Web Security

Spring MVC is a very powerful and versatile framework, and minimal restrictions can be implemented by implementing `org.springframework.web.servlet. HandlerInterceptor` and storing credentials in the HTTP user session.

Custom implementations of `org.springframework.web.servlet. HandlerInterceptor` can be registered in the Spring MVC configuration to execute code before and after `org.springframework.web.servlet.HandlerAdapter` invokes the handler. This means the code in the `HandlerInterceptor` can prevent the normal execution of the handler. Thus, implementing minimal security using a `HandlerInterceptor` is possible. When a user logs in, its information and credentials are stored in the HTTP session. An implementation of `HandlerInterceptor` very similar to the one in Listing 12-1 could be written to look for this attribute.

Listing 12-1. SecurityHandlerInterceptor to Control Access to Pages Requiring Authentication

```
package com.apress.prospringmvc.bookstore.web.interceptor;

import org.springframework.web.servlet.HandlerInterceptor;
// Other imports omitted

public class SecurityHandlerInterceptor implements HandlerInterceptor {
```

```
    @Override
    public boolean preHandle(HttpServletRequest request,
HttpServletResponse response, Object handler) throws Exception {
        var account = (Account) WebUtils.getSessionAttribute(request,
"ACCOUNT_ATTRIBUTE");
        if (account == null) {
            //Retrieve and store the original URL.
            var url = request.getRequestURL().toString();
            WebUtils.setSessionAttribute(request, "REQUESTED_URL", url);
            throw new AuthenticationException("Authentication required.",
"authentication.required");
        }
        return true;
    }
}
```

The REQUESTED_URL attribute is set by the SecurityHandlerInterceptor when a user tries to access a page that requires authentication. This ensures that upon successful authentication, the user is redirected to the page he was trying to access before authentication. This configuration is important for the login process because the login page must be excluded from this behavior, and that is what the last if statement in Listing 12-2 in the handleLogin(..) method takes care of.

Listing 12-2. The LoginController Code Snippet That Ensure No Endless Loop Is Caused When User Logs In

```
package com.apress.prospringmvc.bookstore.web.controller;
// Other imports omitted
@Controller
@RequestMapping(value = "/login")
public class LoginController {

    public static final String ACCOUNT_ATTRIBUTE = "account";
    public static final String REQUESTED_URL = "REQUESTED_URL";

    @Autowired
    private AccountService accountService;
```

```
@RequestMapping(method = RequestMethod.GET)
public void login() {
}
@RequestMapping(method = RequestMethod.POST)
public String handleLogin(@RequestParam String username, @RequestParam
String password, HttpSession session)
        throws AuthenticationException {
    var account = this.accountService.login(username, password);
    session.setAttribute(ACCOUNT_ATTRIBUTE, account);
    var url = (String) session.getAttribute(REQUESTED_URL);
    // Remove the attribute
    session.removeAttribute(REQUESTED_URL);
    // Prevent loops for the login page.
    if (StringUtils.hasText(url) && !url.contains("login")) {
        return "redirect:" + url;
    } else {
        return "redirect:/index.htm";
    }
  }
}
```

Since handler methods have versatile signatures, when accessing any of those URLs, a HttpSession object can be used as an argument, and the Account instance can be extracted from it and used.

A SecurityHandlerInterceptor instance must be added to the registry of interceptors configured for the Spring application. This is done by making sure the overridden addInterceptors(..) method in the web configuration class includes a reference to it. Listing 12-3 depicts this snippet of configuration.

Listing 12-3. Adding a SecurityHandlerInterceptor Instance to the List of Interceptors

```
package com.apress.prospringmvc.bookstore.web.config;

import org.springframework.web.servlet.config.annotation.
InterceptorRegistry;
// Other imports omitted
```

```
@Configuration
@EnableWebMvc
@ComponentScan(basePackages = { "com.apress.prospringmvc.bookstore" })
public class WebMvcContextConfiguration implements WebMvcConfigurer {

    // code omitted

    @Override
    public void addInterceptors(InterceptorRegistry registry) {
        // other interceptors omitted
        registry.addInterceptor(new SecurityHandlerInterceptor())
                .addPathPatterns("/customer/account", "/cart/checkout");
    }

}
```

This is the simplest way to secure access to a few pages in a Spring application. For simple applications built for teaching purposes, this works fine since it makes it clear just how powerful Spring is, but you rarely use an implementation like this in a real production application. Also, a lot more code needs to be written to support the process of authentication. Supporting authorization requires even more code to be written, which is why Spring Security exists.

Using Spring Security

One of the biggest advantages of Spring Security is its portability. It does not need a special container to run in. Spring Security can be set up by adding the required dependencies to your application and configuring a few beans. Another big advantage is its extensibility: a developer can decide how a principal is defined, where the credentials are stored, in what format, how the authorization decision is made, and so on. Also, since securing resources is done using proxying mechanisms, Spring Security makes it easy to detach security logic from the application logic, avoiding code tangling and scattering.

When Spring Security is configured for a Spring web application, before reaching DispatcherServlet, requests are filtered through a security filter chain. These filters are all implementations of the javax.servlet.Filter interface. The order of the filters is important, and any filter can modify the request and then invoke the next filter in the chain. Spring's ApplicationContext integrates with the Servlet container's life cycle through its core implementation of Filter: org.springframework.web.filter. DelegatingFilterProxy.

By registering it via standard servlet container mechanisms, all the work can be delegated to a Spring bean that implements `Filter`.

When Spring Security is configured in an application, `DelegatingFilterProxy` delegates the job of filtering requests to a special bean of type `org.springframework.security.web.FilterChainProxy` named `springSecurityFilterChain`. This bean allows delegating to many `Filter` instances using its list of `org.springframework.security.web.SecurityFilterChain` instances. Each `SecurityFilterChain` matches a part of the application configured by an URL slice. A full list of all the Spring Security `Filter` implementations and their exact order can be found in the official reference documentation.[4]

Thus, overall, this chain of filters set in place provide support for authentication, ensure authorization, maintain `org.springframework.security.core.context.SecurityContext` in the HTTP session and manage an efficient end of the user session at logout. If you recall, `ApplicationContext` is the central interface providing configuration for an application. Likewise, `SecurityContext` is the central interface providing security configuration for an application.

Table 12-1 lists the most important web filters in the order they appear in the chain and with a simple explanation of their responsibilities.

Table 12-1. *The Most Important Security Filters* `springSecurityFilterChain` *Delegates To*

Filter	Description
`org.springframework.security.web.access.channel.ChannelProcessingFilter`	Provides support for delivering requests using the appropriate channel. Secured requests are delivered using a secured channel.
`org.springframework.security.web.context.request.async.WebAsyncManagerIntegrationFilter`	Provides support asynchronous secured requests processing.

(*continued*)

---

[4]https://docs.spring.io/spring-security/site/docs/current/reference/html5/#servlet-security-filters

Table 12-1. (*continued*)

Filter	Description
`org.springframework.security.web.header.HeaderWriterFilter`	Provides support to add security headers like `X-Frame-Options`, `X-XSS-Protection`, and `X-Content-Type-Options` to the response.
`org.springframework.security.web.context.SecurityContextPersistenceFilter`	Populates SecurityContextHolder with information specific to the user session and maintains SecurityContext between requests.
`org.springframework.security.web.csrf.CsrfFilter`	Provides support for requests containing a CSRF token.[5]
`org.springframework.security.web.authentication.logout.Logout Filter`	Ends a user session by calling a set of handlers to clean the Authentication object from the security context. At the end of its execution, the user is no longer authenticated; thus it has no access to secured pages.
`org.springframework.security.web.authentication.UsernamePassword AuthenticationFilter`	Processes an authentication form submission. Login forms provide the two parameters for this filter: a username and a password.
`org.springframework.security.web.authentication.ui.DefaultLogin PageGeneratingFilter`	If the application doesn't need a login page, this filter can generate one for you.
`org.springframework.security.web.authentication.ui.DefaultLogout PageGeneratingFilter`	If the application doesn't need a logout page, this filter can generate one for you. Most applications do not really need a logout page anyway.

(*continued*)

---

[5]https://www.owasp.org/index.php/Cross-Site_Request_Forgery_(CSRF)

Table 12-1. (*continued*)

Filter	Description
org.springframework.security.web.authentication.www.BasicAuthenticationFilter	Provides support for basic authentication.[6] This type of authentication involves requests having an Authorization header with a Base-64 encoded value of username:password. Since an authentication token is transmitted in clear text, use digest authentication instead of basic authentication.
org.springframework.security.web.authentication.www.DigestAuthenticationFilter	Provides support for digest authentication.[7] View the previous table row.
org.springframework.security.web.servletapi.SecurityContextHolderAwareRequestFilter	SecurityContextHolder is the core component of Spring Security. This filter provides a request wrapper which implements the Security API methods. Calling these methods is what populates SecurityContextHolder with configuration, authentication and authorities information, thus configuring the security context of the application.
org.springframework.security.web.authentication.AnonymousAuthenticationFilter	Provides support for anonymous users.
org.springframework.security.web.session.SessionManagementFilter	Provides support for various HTTP session related functionalities, such as session-fixation protection attack prevention.[8]

(*continued*)

---

[6]https://tools.ietf.org/html/rfc2617
[7]https://tools.ietf.org/html/rfc2617
[8]https://owasp.org/www-community/attacks/Session_fixation

Table 12-1. *(continued)*

Filter	Description
org.springframework.security.web. access.ExceptionTranslationFilter	Provides support for security exceptions being thrown in the chain. It represents a link between Java exceptions and HTTP status codes that are needed to maintain the user interface and show the appropriate message to the user.
org.springframework.security. web.access.intercept. FilterSecurityInterceptor	Provides support for authorizing HTTP requests and raises AccessDeniedExceptions.
org.springframework.security. web.authentication.switchuser. SwitchUserFilter	Provides support for user context switching. A user with higher authority can switch to a lower authority user.

A high-level overview of the request processing workflow when Spring Security is configured within a web application is illustrated in Figure 12-1.

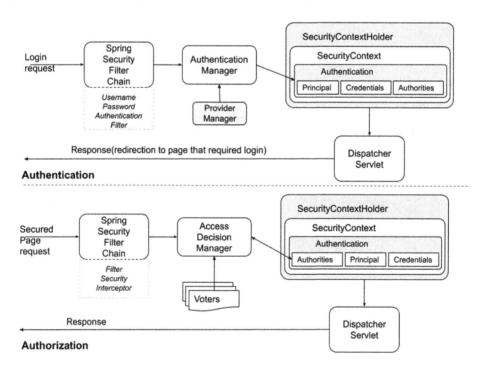

Figure 12-1. *The authentication and authorization processes with Spring Security*

Figure 12-1 depicts how requests are handled by a Spring web application secured with Spring Security.

The user tries to access a secured page of the application. Since the page is secured, the application redirects the user to the login page. The user provides its username and password and submits the login request.

The login request is filtered, and `springSecurityFilterChain` and a suitable filter to handle the authentication are identified. In this case, it is the `UsernamePasswordAuthenticationFilter`. This filter uses `AuthenticationManager` to verify the credentials. The most used implementation of `AuthenticationManager` is `ProviderManager,` which declares a list of configured `AuthenticationProvider` instances that can be used to support the authentication process.

If the credentials are verified, an `Authentication` instance is created and stored in the `security context` of the application. `SecurityContext` is contained inside the `SecurityContextHolder,` which is the nucleus of Spring Security.

Configuring Authentication

The `Authentication` instance contains the following information.

- The **principal** used to identify the user. In basic user/password authentication, it is often a `UserDetails` instance.

- The **credentials** contain the password. To avoid it being leaked, the password is usually cleared after the user is authenticated.

- The **authorities** represent application permissions granted to the user, also known as **roles** or **scopes**.

Once the user is authenticated, the response being returned is either the default page configured for the login process or the page the user was trying to access before being authenticated, if the user is authorized to access that page. The authorities contained in the `Authentication` object are analyzed by `AccessDecisionManager` using a list of voters to decide whether the user can access the requested resource.

Spring Security provides a way to configure and customize most of the processes in a very practical manner. **In a Spring MVC application, three things are required to configure Spring Security configuration:**

- Integrate the `springSecurityFilterChain` with the container servlet environment.

- Provide the security configuration for authentication and authorization, which defines the application's `securityContext`.

- Integrate the security context with the web application context.

To integrate the `springSecurityFilterChain` with the container servlet environment a class extending `org.springframework.security.web.context.AbstractSecurityWebApplicationInitializer` must be added to the configuration. Listing 12-4 depicts such a class. Subclasses of `AbstractSecurityWebApplicationInitializer` register `DelegatingFilterProxy` to use `springSecurityFilterChain` before any other registered `filter`. This is necessary because every request made on the application must be intercepted and analyzed for permissions.

Listing 12-4. Subclass of AbstractSecurityWebApplicationInitializer

```
package com.apress.prospringmvc.bookstore.web.config.sec;

import org.springframework.security.web.context.
 AbstractSecurityWebApplicationInitializer;

class SecurityInitializer extends AbstractSecurityWebApplicationInitializer
{
}
```

A configuration class annotated with `@EnableWebSecurity` must be provided to configure `securityContext`. To help the developer easily create this class, Spring Security provides the `org.springframework.security.config.annotation.SecurityConfigurer` interface and multiple implementations that already contain default implementations that work out of the box, so the customization needed is minimal.

The easiest way to configure Spring Security for web applications is to extend the `WebSecurityConfigurerAdapter` and provide an implementation for the `configure(AuthenticationManagerBuilder auth)` method to configure the `AuthenticationManagerBuilder`. Spring Security uses this builder to create an `org.springframework.security.authentication.AuthenticationManager` that authenticates the user.

Spring supports multiple authentication mechanisms:[9] Basic, Form, OAuth, X.509, SAML, but for this chapter, the focus is in setting up form authentication using username and password.

For simple, small-sized applications, an in-memory database is enough to store usernames and credentials. Even if the database is in memory, passwords should not be stored in clear text, which is why one of the Spring Security `PasswordEncoder` implementations should apply a hash function on the password. In Listing 12-5, `org.springframework.security.crypto.bcrypt.BCryptPasswordEncoder` is applying the BCrypt strong hashing function on the password text before storing it into the database.

For testing purposes, Spring Security still supports `org.springframework.security.crypto.password.NoOpPasswordEncoder`, an implementation that does nothing and saves passwords in clear text. The class is, however, marked deprecated, so it might be removed in the future.

Listing 12-5. Configuration of an AuthenticationManager by Extending WebSecurityConfigurerAdapter

```
package com.apress.prospringmvc.bookstore.web.config.sec;

import org.springframework.security.config.annotation.web.configuration.
 EnableWebSecurity;
import org.springframework.security.config.annotation.web.configuration.
 WebSecurityConfigurerAdapter;
import org.springframework.security.config.annotation.authentication.
 builders.AuthenticationManagerBuilder;
```

---

[9]https://docs.spring.io/spring-security/site/docs/current/reference/
html5/#servlet-authentication

```
import org.springframework.security.crypto.bcrypt.BCryptPasswordEncoder;
import org.springframework.security.crypto.password.PasswordEncoder;
import com.apress.prospringmvc.bookstore.util.ConfigurationException;
// Other imports omitted

@Configuration
@EnableWebSecurity
public class SecurityConfiguration extends WebSecurityConfigurerAdapter {

    @Autowired
    public void configureGlobal(AuthenticationManagerBuilder auth) {
        try {
            PasswordEncoder passwordEncoder = new BCryptPasswordEncoder();
            auth.inMemoryAuthentication()
                .passwordEncoder(passwordEncoder)
                .withUser("john")
                    .password(passwordEncoder.encode("doe"))
                    .roles("USER")
                .and().withUser("jane")
                    .password(passwordEncoder.encode("doe"))
                    .roles("USER", "ADMIN")
                .and().withUser("admin")
                    .password(passwordEncoder.encode("admin"))
                    .roles("ADMIN");
        } catch (Exception e) {
            throw new ConfigurationException(
                    "In-Memory authentication was not configured.", e);
        }
    }

    // code omitted
}
```

Each user is assigned a role within the application. The role encapsulates the actions the user can perform within an application. Most applications have at least two roles. For the Bookstore application, the ADMIN role is assigned to users that can add, edit, and delete book entries. Users that can view and order books have the USER role.

A GrantedAuthority instance represents an authority granted to an Authentication object. There is no significant difference between roles and authorities, except semantics, and how they are used. Roles are stored in a secured location configured with Spring Security, most commonly a database. When declaring for an in-memory database, as shown in Listing 12-5, the roles(..) method can be used. This method is provided by a builder class named UserDetailsManagerConfigurer(located in a package with a very long name that is not relevant here) provided by Spring Security to create the UserDetails instances encapsulating the authentication data of the users allowed to access the application. Roles cannot be null, and their name **must not** start with ROLE_, because the roles(..) method is a shortcut for the authorities(..) method declared in the UserDetailsManagerConfigurer class prefixes the role name with ROLE_. Thus, the code in Listing 12-5 can also be written the way it is in Listing 12-6. It has the same effect.

Listing 12-6. Configuration of an AuthenticationManager by Setting Up Authorities

```
package com.apress.prospringmvc.bookstore.web.config.sec;

// Imports omitted (view Listing 12-3)

@Configuration
@EnableWebSecurity
public class SecurityConfiguration extends WebSecurityConfigurerAdapter {

    @Autowired
    public void configureGlobal(AuthenticationManagerBuilder auth) {
        try {
            PasswordEncoder passwordEncoder = new BCryptPasswordEncoder();
            auth.inMemoryAuthentication()
                .passwordEncoder(passwordEncoder)
                    .withUser("john")
                        .password(passwordEncoder.encode("doe"))
                        .authorities("ROLE_USER")
                    .and().withUser("jane")
                        .password(passwordEncoder.encode("doe"))
                        .authorities("ROLE_USER", "ROLE_ADMIN")
```

```
                        .and().withUser("admin")
                            .password(passwordEncoder.encode("admin"))
                            .authorities("ROLE_ADMIN");
        } catch (Exception e) {
            throw new ConfigurationException(
                    "In-Memory authentication was not configured.", e);
        }
    }
}

    // code omitted
}
```

Roles or authorities are used in the authorization process that is explained later in the chapter.

When an H2 in-memory database is used for storing credentials, its content can be inspected by accessing the H2 web client for the database. To add this web client to your application, you must add `org.h2.server.web.WebServlet` to the application and map it to a secured URL. Even if the passwords are encrypted, securing access to your database is still a mandatory thing to do. This is explained later in the chapter.

The `auth.inMemoryAuthentication()` line adds in-memory authentication to the `AuthenticationManagerBuilder`. The `withUser(String username)` method builds an `org.springframework.security.core.userdetails.UserDetails` instance containing user core information. These instances are not used by Spring Security for security purposes. They hold information that is loaded into `Authentication` objects. `UserDetails` instances are managed by `UserDetailsService`. Developers can provide their own implementation to declare a different way to store and retrieve authentication information.

Spring Security provides `org.springframework.security.provisioning.JdbcUserDetailsManager` which is a JDBC(database)-based `UserDetailsService`. The restriction for this approach is the database must have the structure required by Spring Security,[10] and it must be an SQL database. But since the Bookstore application has its own database table where the users' information is saved—the ACCOUNT table,

---

[10]https://docs.spring.io/spring-security/site/docs/current/reference/
  html5/#appendix-schema

it would be more appropriate to use that table for authentication too. There are two ways to do this. The first one is to implement a customized UserDetailsService that loads the user details from the ACCOUNT table. The other way is to implement a customized AuthenticationProvider.

ℹ   This method is preferred for most applications because the authentication provider can be implemented to retrieve authentication information from external providers, too (e.g., an external system like a single sign-on provider like Google). This allows the externalization of the authentication process.

Listing 12-7 depicts the changes needed in the SecurityConfiguration class to set up authentication with a custom authentication provider.

Listing 12-7. Custom Implementation of AuthenticationManagerBuilder Using a Database Table

```
package com.apress.prospringmvc.bookstore.web.config.sec;

import org.springframework.security.authentication.AuthenticationProvider;
// Other imports omitted

@Configuration
@EnableWebSecurity
public class SecurityConfiguration extends WebSecurityConfigurerAdapter {

    @Autowired
    public void configure(AuthenticationManagerBuilder auth) {
        auth.authenticationProvider(bookstoreAuthenticationProvider());
    }

    @Bean
    public AuthenticationProvider bookstoreAuthenticationProvider(){
        return new BookstoreAuthenticationProvider();
    }

    // code omitted
}
```

The bookstoreAuthenticationProvider bean type is
BookstoreAuthenticationProvider, which implements AuthenticationProvider.
AuthenticationProvider is a simple interface with two methods. Listing 12-8 depicts
the code of this interface.[11]

Listing 12-8. AuthenticationProvider Interface Code

```
package org.springframework.security.authentication;

import org.springframework.security.core.Authentication;
import org.springframework.security.core.AuthenticationException;

// some comments omitted
public interface AuthenticationProvider {
    /**
     * @param authentication the authentication request object.
     * @return a fully authenticated object including credentials.
     * @throws AuthenticationException if authentication fails.
     */
    Authentication authenticate(Authentication authentication)
            throws AuthenticationException;

    /**
     * @param authentication
     * @return <code>true</code> if the implementation can more closely
evaluate the
     * <code>Authentication</code> class presented
     */
    boolean supports(Class<?> authentication);
}
```

The authenticate(..) method handles authentication requests. The
BookstoreAuthenticationProvider implementation is where the code extracting
the user from the ACCOUNT table, the password verification, and the creation of the
Authentication object takes place.

---

[11]https://github.com/spring-projects/spring-security/blob/master/core/src/main/
java/org/springframework/security/authentication/AuthenticationProvider.java

The supports(..) method declares the type of Authentication implementation supported. Since simple authentication using a username and password is used, the type declared to be supported is UsernamePasswordAuthenticationToken.

Listing 12-9 depicts the full code for BookstoreAuthenticationProvider.

Listing 12-9. BookstoreAuthenticationProvider Code

```
package com.apress.prospringmvc.bookstore.web.config.sec;


import com.apress.prospringmvc.bookstore.domain.Account;
import com.apress.prospringmvc.bookstore.service.AccountService;
import org.springframework.beans.factory.annotation.Autowired;
import org.springframework.security.authentication.AuthenticationProvider;
import org.springframework.security.authentication.BadCredentialsException;
import org.springframework.security.authentication.
UsernamePasswordAuthenticationToken;
import org.springframework.security.core.Authentication;
import org.springframework.security.core.AuthenticationException;
import org.springframework.security.core.GrantedAuthority;
import org.springframework.security.core.authority.SimpleGrantedAuthority;

// Other imports omitted

public class BookstoreAuthenticationProvider implements
AuthenticationProvider {

  private PasswordEncoder passwordEncoder = new BCryptPasswordEncoder();

  @Autowired
  private AccountService accountService;
  @Override
  public Authentication authenticate(Authentication authentication)
throws AuthenticationException {
        String username = authentication.getName();
        String password = authentication.getCredentials().toString();

        Account account = accountService.getAccount(username);
```

```java
        if(account == null) {
            throw new BadCredentialsException(
                    "Authentication failed for " + username);
        }
        if(!passwordEncoder.matches(password, account.getPassword())) {
            throw new BadCredentialsException(
                    "Authentication failed for " + username);
        }
        List<GrantedAuthority> grantedAuthorities = new ArrayList<>();
        account.getRoles().forEach(role ->
            grantedAuthorities.add(new SimpleGrantedAuthority(role.
getRole())));
        return new
                UsernamePasswordAuthenticationToken(
                        username, password, grantedAuthorities);
    }

    @Override
    public boolean supports(Class<?> authentication) {
        return authentication.equals(
                UsernamePasswordAuthenticationToken.class);
    }
}
```

Configuring Authorization

The other important method that needs to be implemented in the security configuration class is the configure(HttpSecurity security). This method customizes the org. springframework.security.config.annotation.web.builders.HttpSecurity instance that is used by Spring Security to enable web security for HTTP requests.

The HttpSecurity security object is versatile and can configure rules to intercept certain URLs, configure login and logout form generation, redirection after a successful or failed authentication request, CSRF protection, and so on. Deciding which requests a user can make is based on its authorities, which is what authorization is all about.

By default, Spring Security requires all requests to be authenticated. But Spring Security can be configured to have different rules by adding more rules in the order of their precedence. The order of the listed intercepted URLs is important. Patterns are evaluated in the order they are defined. This means, more specific patterns are defined higher in the list than less specific patterns. You can define the patterns for the URLs that require some degree of security and end the list with a pattern allowing access to anything that doesn't match the previous entries in the list. Or you can define patterns for URLs that require public access first and end the list with a pattern prohibiting access to anything that doesn't match the previous entries in the list. It depends on the purpose of the application.

Listing 12-10 depicts a simple Spring Security authorization that allows unauthenticated users access to all the pages of the Bookstore application except for the pages that are to be accessible to authenticated users with an `ADMIN` role.

There is also an additional `configure(WebSecurity web)` method. This method takes a parameter of type `WebSecurity` and tells Spring Security to ignore static web requests(such as *.css, *js, images, etc.). There is no reason to pass these requests through the security filters, as it would only slow down the process of rendering views.

Listing 12-10. Spring Security Authorization Configuration for Intercepting URLs Using AntPathRequestMatchers

```
package com.apress.prospringmvc.bookstore.web.config.sec;

import org.springframework.security.web.util.matcher.RequestMatcher;
import org.springframework.security.web.util.matcher.AntPathRequestMatcher;
import org.springframework.security.config.annotation.web.builders.
WebSecurity;

// Other imports omitted

@Configuration
@EnableWebSecurity
public class SecurityConfiguration extends WebSecurityConfigurerAdapter {

    @Override
    protected void configure(HttpSecurity http) throws Exception {
        http
                .authorizeRequests()
```

```
                .antMatchers("/customer/account", "/cart/checkout").
                authenticated()
                .antMatchers("/book/edit", "/book/delete").hasRole("ADMIN")
                .antMatchers("/customer/delete").hasRole("ADMIN")
                .antMatchers("/**").permitAll();
        }

    @Override
    public void configure(WebSecurity web) throws Exception {
        web.ignoring().antMatchers("/resources/**", "/images/**", "/
        styles/**");
    }

    // some code omitted
}
```

With the configuration snippet in Listing 12-10, a non-authenticated user sees the Bookstore application view depicted in Figure 12-2.

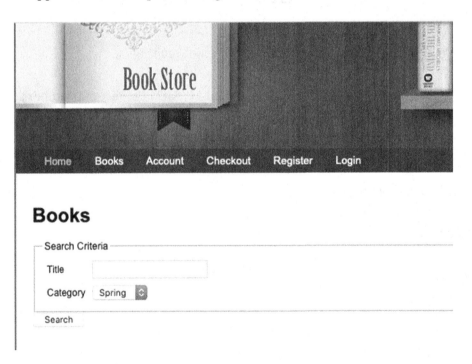

***Figure 12-2.** Bookstore application view for non-authenticated users*

`authorizeRequests()` returns an instance of `HttpSecurity` that is configured to allow restricting access for requests using `RequestMatcher` implementations. Listing 12-10 depicts the usage of `AntPathRequestMatcher` instances to declare a URL template that request URLs should be matched against. The name of this class makes it clear that the ant-style pattern is supported. For each request URL matching a pattern declared with an `antMatchers(..)` method, the restriction associated with the returned matcher instance is applied.

Only authenticated users should have access to their own Account and Checkout pages, so the next line

```
.antMatchers("/customer/account", "/cart/checkout").authenticated()
```

restricts access to those resources based on their URLs only to authenticated users.

The following line declares that requests with /book/edit and /book/delete URLs should be handled only if the authenticated user has an ADMIN role.

```
.antMatchers("/book/edit", "/book/delete").hasRole("ADMIN")
```

If a user without that role tries to access one of those URLs, an exception is thrown, and the user is redirected to an error page.

The order of the matchers is important. The first declared template that matches a URL decides the access rule applied to the request.

That is why this configuration line `.antMatchers("/**").permitAll()` comes last. This declares that all remaining requests are to be resolved, regardless if a user is authenticated or not. These are also called **public resources**.

This is not usually done in production applications, where `.antMatchers("/**").denyAll()` is preferred to avoid exposing anything than shouldn't be.

In Security 4.1.1, the `MvcRequestMatcher` implementation was introduced. It extends the support for ant-style patterns by supporting extensions of the declared template and adding support for variables.

`.antMatchers("/customer/account")` declares an exact match of the request URL to the "/customer/account" string.

`.mvcMatchers("/customer/account")` declares a more extensive match. The URLs "/customer/account/", "/customer/account.pdf", and "/customer/account.html" are considered a match to this template.

Also, as you might have noticed, wildcards are supported when declaring a URL template in both `antMatchers` and `mvcMatchers`.

When ending a URL pattern with a '*' the pattern matches the prefix plus one single term (e.g., `/h2-console/*` matches `/h2-console/a` and `/h2-console/20`).

When ending a URL pattern with **, the pattern matches the prefix, with any number of terms, the whole directory tree. So, `/h2-console/**` matches `/h2-console/a`, `/h2-console/20`, `/h2-console/a/20`, `/h2-console/1/2/3/4`, and many more.

It could be said that `MvcRequestMatchers` provide more security because they include a wider set of URLs using the same template and avoid keeping things public by mistake.

There is also a parametrized version of `authorizeRequests`(Cutomizer<T>) that can configure authentication. Using lambda, we can create and configure in place an instance of `org.springframework.security.config.Customizer<T>` dedicated to declaring URL intercepting rules, which is used as an argument for it. This offers a more readable configuration. The previous configuration can be simplified even more because all URLs containing *edit* and *delete* are reserved for users with the `ADMIN` role, so we can use a more general configuration for that.

The configuration in Listing 12-10 can thus be upgraded to the one depicted in Listing 12-11.

Listing 12-11. Spring Security authorization Configuration for Intercepting URLs Using MvcRequestMatchers

```java
package com.apress.prospringmvc.bookstore.web.config.sec;
import org.springframework.security.web.util.matcher.RequestMatcher;
import org.springframework.security.web.util.matcher.MvcRequestMatcher;

// Other imports omitted

@Configuration
@EnableWebSecurity
public class SecurityConfiguration extends WebSecurityConfigurerAdapter {
    @Override
    protected void configure(HttpSecurity http) throws Exception {
        http
                .authorizeRequests(
                        authorize -> authorize.mvcMatchers("/*/edit/*",
"/*/delete/*").hasRole("ADMIN")
                                .mvcMatchers("/customer/account", "/cart/
checkout").authenticated()
                                .anyRequest().permitAll()
                );
    }
  // some code omitted
}
```

The rules associated with matchers are versatile as well. Starting with Spring Security version 3.0 Spring EL expressions can be used as an authorization mechanism. A construct like the following is correct and restricts access to the /h2-console URL to users with ADMIN and DBADMIN roles.

```java
.mvcMatchers("/h2-console").access("hasRole('ADMIN') and
hasRole('DBADMIN')")
```

The previous configuration is not equivalent to the next one, which restricts access to the /h2-console URL to users either ADMIN or DBADMIN roles.

```
.mvcMatchers("/h2-console").hasAnyRole("ADMIN", "DBADMIN")
```

Limiting to a single role can be done using the hasRole(..) method.

```
.mvcMatchers("/h2-console").hasAnyRole("DBADMIN")
```

Security expressions are supported in Spring Security tags[12] and they are useful in dynamically reshaping a view returned to a user based on its role. Using Spring Security tags in JSP templates requires declaring the following taglib in the JSP page.

```
<%@ taglib prefix="sec" uri="http://www.springframework.org/security/tags"
%>
```

For example, the Logout menu item should not be part of a view unless a user is authenticated. The logout form should not be a part of the view, either. Both of them can be conditioned by encapsulating them into a <sec:authorize access="isAuthenticated()"> .. </sec:authorize> element.

There are also menu items like Register and Login that should only be rendered if there is no authenticated user. This can be done by encapsulating the specific HTML elements in a similar construct but using a negation of the expression.

This can easily be done using a construct like the one depicted in Listing 12-12.

Listing 12-12. header.jsp Navigation Menu with Security Configurations

```
<!-- other taglibs declarations omitted -->
<%@ taglib prefix="sec" uri="http://www.springframework.org/security/tags"
%>
<div class="header">
    <!-- other JSP elements omitted -->
    <div class="nav">
        <ul style="float: left;">
            <li class="selected">
```

---

[12]https://docs.spring.io/spring-security/site/docs/3.0.x/reference/taglibs.html

```jsp
    <a href="${homeUrl}">
    <spring:message code="nav.home"/>
    </a>
 </li>
<!-- other unsecured JSP elements omitted -->
<sec:authorize access="!isAuthenticated()">
  <li>
      <a href="<c:url value="/customer/register"/>">
      <spring:message code="nav.register"/>
      </a>
  </li>
  <li>
      <a href="<c:url value="/login"/>">
      <spring:message code="nav.login"/>
      </a>
  </li>
</sec:authorize>
<sec:authorize access="hasRole('ADMIN')">
  <li>
      <a href="<c:url value="/customer/list"/>">
      <spring:message code="nav.admin"/>
      </a>
  </li>
</sec:authorize>
<sec:authorize access="isAuthenticated()">
  <li>
      <a href="#" onclick="document.getElementById('logout').
      submit();">
      <spring:message code="nav.logout"/>
      </a>
  </li>
 <spring:url value="/logout" var="logoutUrl"/>
   <form action="${logoutUrl}" id="logout" method="post">
      <input type="hidden" name="${_csrf.parameterName}"
          value="${_csrf.token}"/>
```

```
            </form>
          </sec:authorize>
      </ul>
      <ul style="float: right;">
          <sec:authorize access="isAuthenticated()">
          <li>(<em><sec:authentication property="principal" /></em>)</li>
          </sec:authorize>
          <!-- other unsecured JSP elements omitted -->
      </ul>
    </div>
</div>
```

The Spring Security tag library also offers the possibility to access authentication data. In Listing 12-12 the last element is populated with the authenticated username.

And there is even more, if you do not like using Security expressions in your view template, configure the rule for the URL in your security configuration and use a reference to the URL instead. Rather than writing the following,

```
<sec:authorize access="hasRole('ADMIN')">
  <a href="<c:url value="/book/edit/${book.id}"/>">
<spring:message code="label.edit"/>
```

you can write this.

```
<sec:authorize url="/*/edit/*">
  <a href="<c:url value="/book/edit/${book.id}"/>">
<spring:message code="label.edit"/>
```

At the beginning of this chapter, you learned that Spring Security provides means to secure individual objects. This can be easily implemented since security expressions are powerful and can access beans and path variables. So, assuming our Bookstore has a special book that is reserved to users with VIP status, a bean can be configured to restrict access to that book only to them.

```
http
    .authorizeRequests(
        authorize -> authorize.mvcMatchers("/book/{bookId}")
            .access("bookSecurity.checkVIP(authentication,#bookId)")
        ...
);
```

The access(String) method takes as a parameter a text representing
a SpEL expression that customizes the Security infrastructure bean of type
ExpressionUrlAuthorizationConfigurer, which adds URL-based authorization based
upon SpEL expressions to an application.

Spring Security provides multiple ways to secure access to resources, but some
attention to detail is advised because it is very easy to expose too much or too little.

Listing 12-12 shows how the Spring Security tag library can dynamically generate
views taking security settings into account using Apache Tiles. This tag library can be
used with other JSP based templating engines.

Being designed for full integration with Spring, Thymeleaf comes with an extensive
library that includes a Spring Security dialect. The Spring Security integration module
works as a replacement for the Spring Security tag library. And it does have advantages—
one of them is that no CSRF hidden elements can be explicitly added to the forms. CSRF
is discussed later in the chapter, but for now, look at Listing 12-13, which is a Thymeleaf
version of Listing 12-12.

Listing 12-13. Thymeleaf layout.html Navigation Menu with Security
Configurations

```
<html xmlns:th="http://www.thymeleaf.org"
    xmlns:sec="http://www.thymeleaf.org/thymeleaf-extras-springsecurity5">
<!-- other HTML elements omitted -->
<div class="header">
    <!-- other unsecured HTML elements omitted -->
    <div class="nav">
        <ul style="float: left;">
        <!-- other HTML elements omitted -->
        <li sec:authorize="! isAuthenticated()">
            <a th:href="@{/customer/register}"
                th:text="#{nav.register}">REGISTER</a>
        </li>
        <li sec:authorize="! isAuthenticated()">
            <a th:href="@{/login}"
                th:text="#{nav.login}">LOGIN</a>
        </li>
        <li sec:authorize="isAuthenticated()">
```

```
        <a th:href="@{/logout}"
            th:text="#{nav.logout}">LOGOUT</a>
      </li>
    </ul>
    <ul style="float: right;">
      <li sec:authorize="isAuthenticated()">
          (<em sec:authentication="name"></em>)
      </li>
      <!-- other unsecured  HTML elements omitted -->
    </ul>
  </div>
</div>
```

The syntax is a little bit better, isn't it?

Configure Login and Logout

To support easy development, Spring Security comes out of the box with a default login form and logout support. This is useful when a backend developer doesn't want to waste time setting up an HTML page to test his security settings. Most methods in an HttpSecurity object return a reference to themselves. This provides the opportunity to configure security by chaining methods together. Similar to authorizeRequests(..), login form, and logout support can be configured using Customizer instances specific for each purpose. A very simple example of default form generation and logout support being configured is seen in Listing 12-14.

Listing 12-14. Default Form Generation and Logout Support Configuration Using Spring Security

```
package com.apress.prospringmvc.bookstore.web.config.sec;

import org.springframework.security.config.Customizer;
// Other imports omitted

@Configuration
@EnableWebSecurity
```

```
public class SecurityConfiguration extends WebSecurityConfigurerAdapter {
    @Override
    protected void configure(HttpSecurity http) throws Exception {
        http
            .authorizeRequests(
                authorize -> authorize.mvcMatchers("/*/
edit/*",                                    "/*/delete/*")
                    .hasRole("ADMIN")
                    .anyRequest().permitAll()
            ).formLogin(Customizer.withDefaults())
            .logout(Customizer.withDefaults());
    }
    // other code omitted
}
```

When the Bookstore application starts with this configuration, clicking the Login menu item opens a page with a very simple login form. Figure 12-3 is a screenshot of the HTML-generated login page.

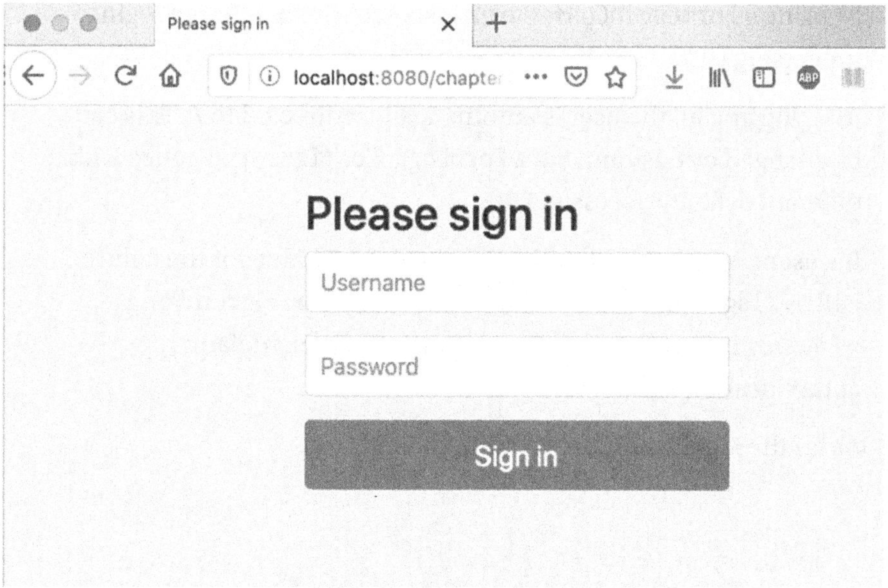

Figure 12-3. *Spring Security–generated logout page*

If you use the "View page source" browser option, you can also peek at the HTML code. The following is a list of things that you should know/notice about this page.

- The generated login view is mapped to /login. This can be changed by calling the formLogin(..) with a custom implementation Customizer to build a FormLoginConfigurer instance with a different login page mapping.

- The generated form has two fields named username and password. These are the default values. They can be changed by calling the formLogin(..) method with a custom implementation Customizer to build a FormLoginConfigurer instance with a different name for the username and password fields.

- The form contains a hidden field named CSRF. In Spring Security 4.3, CSRF protection configuration became a default option to prevent cross-site request forgery attacks.[13] It can be disabled for testing scenarios.

- The POST request to submit the username and password values is sent to /login, also a default value. This one can be customized by using a FormLoginConfigurer instance with a different login processing URL.

- After logging in, the user is automatically redirected to /. This can be changed by customizing a FormLoginConfigurer instance with a different default successful URL.

- If a user cannot be authenticated, the default value for the failure URL is /login?error, which can be changed by customizing a FormLoginConfigurer instance with a different default authentication failure URL.

- As for the logout support, it has its defaults too.

---

[13]https://owasp.org/www-community/attacks/csrf

- The POST request to log a user out is mapped to /logout. This default value can be changed by calling the logout(..) method with a custom implementation Customizer to build a LogoutConfigurer with a different logout URL.

- When a user is logged out successfully, it is redirected to /login? logout. This value can be changed by customizing a LogoutConfigurer instance with a different successful logout URL.

There are more methods on the two configurer types (FormLoginConfigurer and LogoutConfigurer), allowing configuration of failure or success authentication handlers for login and logout, special options of invalidating session, clearing cache for logout, and many more that you will probably read about when you need them. Until then, look at the code sample in Listing 12-15. The Spring Security configuration has been modified to customize all the properties mentioned and add support for CSRF protection.

Listing 12-15. Customized Login Form and Logout Support Configuration Using Spring Security

```
package com.apress.prospringmvc.bookstore.web.config.sec;

import org.springframework.security.config.Customizer;
import org.springframework.security.web.csrf.CsrfTokenRepository;
import org.springframework.security.web.csrf.
HttpSessionCsrfTokenRepository;
import org.springframework.security.config.annotation.web.configurers.
    FormLoginConfigurer;
import org.springframework.security.config.annotation.web.configurers.
    LogoutConfigurer;
// Other imports omitted

@Configuration
@EnableWebSecurity
public class SecurityConfiguration extends WebSecurityConfigurerAdapter {
    @Override
    protected void configure(HttpSecurity http) throws Exception {
        http
```

```
        .authorizeRequests(
            authorize -> authorize.mvcMatchers("/*/edit/*", "/*/
            delete/*")
                .hasRole("ADMIN")
              .anyRequest().permitAll()
        ).formLogin(
            formLogin -> formLogin.loginPage("/auth")
                .usernameParameter("user")
                .passwordParameter("secret")
                .loginProcessingUrl("/auth")
                .failureUrl("/auth?auth_error=1")
                .defaultSuccessUrl("/home")
        )
        .logout(
            logout -> logout.logoutUrl("/custom-logout")
                .logoutSuccessUrl("/home")
                .invalidateHttpSession(true)
                .clearAuthentication(true)
        ).csrf().csrfTokenRepository(repo());
    }

    @Bean
    public CsrfTokenRepository repo() {
        HttpSessionCsrfTokenRepository
            repo = new HttpSessionCsrfTokenRepository();
        repo.setParameterName("_csrf");
        repo.setHeaderName("X-CSRF-TOKEN");
        return repo;
    }
    // other code omitted
}
```

> ℹ️ In Spring Security, it is practical to name your components in a way that uses the defaults. Any customization needs components to support it—views, controllers, exception handlers, and so on.

Listing 12-16 shows the full configuration of the HttpSecurity object for the Bookstore application. Its simplicity is proof that it was designed to use Spring default configurations while still being able to use a custom login form that matched the overall theme of the application.

Listing 12-16. Customized Login Form and Logout Support Configuration Using Spring Security

```java
package com.apress.prospringmvc.bookstore.web.config.sec;

import org.springframework.security.config.Customizer;
import org.springframework.security.web.csrf.CsrfTokenRepository;
import org.springframework.security.web.csrf.
HttpSessionCsrfTokenRepository;
import org.springframework.security.config.annotation.web.configurers.
    FormLoginConfigurer;
import org.springframework.security.config.annotation.web.configurers.
    LogoutConfigurer;
// Other imports omitted

@Configuration
@EnableWebSecurity
public class SecurityConfiguration extends WebSecurityConfigurerAdapter {

        @Override
    protected void configure(HttpSecurity http) throws Exception {
        http
            .authorizeRequests(
                authorize -> authorize.mvcMatchers("/*/edit/*", "/*/
                delete/*")
                        .hasRole("ADMIN")
                    .anyRequest().permitAll()
            ).formLogin(
                formLogin -> formLogin.loginPage("/login")
                        .failureUrl("/login?auth_error=1")
            ).logout(Customizer.withDefaults())
```

```
            .csrf().csrfTokenRepository(repo());
    }

    // other code omitted
}
```

ℹ️   Even if the login page is mapped to the default URL, the login page was explicitly configured here to tell Spring Security that the login page is provided. If it were left unspecified, Spring Security would generate the default page and use it.

Also, the login form that is part of the custom login page *must* have a hidden CSRF field declared; otherwise, the request won't make it past the Spring Security filter chain and an error page with HTTP status code 403 (forbidden) is returned instead.

The advantage of having a custom login form is that it looks like it is part of the site (can include the company logo), but it can also be internationalized. For example, the Bookstore login custom form code is depicted in Listing 12-17.

Listing 12-17. `login.jsp` Custom Login Form

```
<form action="<c:url value="/login"/>" method="post">
  <input type="hidden"
      name="${_csrf.parameterName}"
      value="${_csrf.token}"/>
  <fieldset>
    <legend>
      <spring:message code="login.title" />
    </legend>
    <table>
    <tr>
      <td>
        <spring:message code="account.username"/>
      </td>
      <td>
        <input type="text" id="username"
          name="username"
```

```
            placeholder="<spring:message code="account.username"/>"/>
      </td>
    </tr>
    <tr>
      <td>
        <spring:message code="account.password"/>
      </td>
      <td>
        <input type="password" id="password"
          name="password"
          placeholder="<spring:message code="account.password"/>"/>
      </td>
    </tr>
    <tr>
      <td colspan="2" align="center">
       <button id="login">
          <spring:message code="button.login"/>
       </button>
      </td>
    </tr>
    </table>
  </fieldset>
</form>
```

When Thymeleaf is used as a templating engine, there is no need to declare the hidden CSRF field for the login form, the Thymeleaf integration module takes care of injecting that field in every form declared with the th:action attribute. For this we only need to configure the templating engine to recognize and support the elements declared with a sec: prefix. This is done by configuring support for the Spring Security Dialect by calling templateEngine.addDialect(new SpringSecurityDialect()).

The default names for the CSRF parameter and header name are declared in the org.springframework.security.web.csrf.HttpSessionCsrfTokenRepository class. A bean of this type can be configured to support different CSRF parameter and header name. The names configured in the Spring Security configuration class created for this chapter are the default ones: _csrf and X-CSRF-TOKEN. The following example uses a different header name.

If you are using JavaScript, then it is not possible to submit the CSRF token within an HTTP parameter. Since Thymeleaf does not have a form to add the hidden field to the header of the page must be enriched with two meta entries that are populated with the CSRF header name and the CSRF token. These two meta entries declare the CSRF parameter and header names, and they must match the ones declared in the Spring Security configuration class. These values are then extracted in the JavaScript code and added to the JSON body of the request being submitted. In previous chapters, the "Search books" request was sent using JavaScript. Therefore, the "search.html" page content must be modified as depicted in Listing 12-18 to work in a secured web application.

Listing 12-18. search.html with CSRF Protection

```
<!DOCTYPE HTML>
<html xmlns:th="http://www.thymeleaf.org"
 th:with="lang=${#locale.language}"
 th:lang="${lang}"
 xmlns:sec="http://www.thymeleaf.org/thymeleaf-extras-springsecurity5">
<head th:fragment="~{template/layout :: head('Search books')}">
  <meta id="_csrf" name="_csrf" th:content="${_csrf.token}"/>
  <meta id="_csrf_header" name="_csrf_header" th:content="${_csrf.
  headerName}"/>
</head>

<!-- most of HTML and Javascript code omitted-->
 <script th:inline="javascript">
 /*<![CDATA[*/
 $('#bookSearchForm').submit(function(evt){
     evt.preventDefault();
     var title = $('#title').val();
     var category = $('#category').val();
     var json = { "title" : title, "category" : { "id" : category}};
     var token = $('#_csrf').attr('content');
     var header = $('#_csrf_header').attr('content');

     $.ajax({
         url: $('#bookSearchForm').action,
```

```
        beforeSend: function(xhr) {
            xhr.setRequestHeader(header, token);
        },
        type: 'POST',
        dataType: 'json',
        contentType: 'application/json',
        data: JSON.stringify(json),
        success: function(responseData) {
          console.log(responseData); // debugging purposes
          renderBooks(responseData);
        }
    });
  });
  /*]]>*/
</script>
```

Until now in the chapter, the Spring Security context was configured and integrated with the container servlet environment, but the security context is not properly integrated with the application context. Spring is smart and picks up all files annotated with @Configuration in the packages configured to be scanned. But if you have a multi-layered application, where should the Spring Security beans be placed? In the root web application context or in the dispatcher servlet context?

The answer to this question depends on the application requests and architecture.

– If an application context hierarchy is not required, no special configuration is needed; but make sure the package where the security configuration class is declared is scanned.

– If an application context hierarchy is required, there are two cases.

- Assuming there is a service layer, can it be accessed directly? Does it need to be secured? Then the security configuration class should be a component of the root application context so that service components can be secured as well.

- If the security configuration can only be accessed through the web application, the security configuration class should be set as a component of the servlet application context.

Let's assume we need a configuration for the last scenario in the previous list. This is done by adding the security configuration class to the WebApplicationInitializer implementation. For complex applications that do not receive requests through the web layer exclusively, the security configuration class can be added as a root context class, but for our simple Bookstore application, adding it as a servlet context class is justified. Listing 12-19 depicts the configuration snippet that integrates security into the servlet application context.

Listing 12-19. WebApplicationInitializer Implementation Class with Spring Security

```
package com.apress.prospringmvc.bookstore.web.config;


import org.springframework.security.config.Customizer;
import org.springframework.security.web.csrf.CsrfTokenRepository;
import org.springframework.security.web.csrf.
HttpSessionCsrfTokenRepository;
import org.springframework.security.config.annotation.web.configurers.
   FormLoginConfigurer;
import org.springframework.security.config.annotation.web.configurers.
   LogoutConfigurer;
// Other imports omitted

public class BookstoreWebApplicationInitializer
    extends AbstractAnnotationConfigDispatcherServletInitializer {

    @Override
    protected Class<?>[] getRootConfigClasses() {
        return new Class<?>[]{
                DbConfiguration.class,
                JpaConfiguration.class};
    }

    @Override
    protected Class<?>[] getServletConfigClasses() {
        return new Class<?>[]{
                WebMvcContextConfiguration.class,
                SecurityConfiguration.class};
    }
```

```
    @Override
    protected String[] getServletMappings() {
        return new String[]{"/"};
    }

    @Override
    protected Filter[] getServletFilters() {
        CharacterEncodingFilter cef = new CharacterEncodingFilter();
        cef.setEncoding("UTF-8");
        cef.setForceEncoding(true);
        return new Filter[]{new HiddenHttpMethodFilter(), cef};
    }

@Override
    public void onStartup(ServletContext servletContext) throws
ServletException {
        super.onStartup(servletContext);
        ServletRegistration.Dynamic servlet = servletContext
                .addServlet("h2-console", new WebServlet());
        servlet.setLoadOnStartup(2);
        servlet.addMapping("/h2-console/*");
    }
}
```

In Listing 12-19, there is one extra method that needs an explanation.
onStartup(ServletContext) adds org.h2.server.web.WebServlet to the Spring
application context and maps it to the /h2-console/* URL. This servlet is part of the
H2 library and provides a web client for the in-memory database used within the
application. This servlet was mentioned first in the "Configure Authentication" section
of this chapter. You can use this web client to query the information in all the tables of
the application, but especially the ACCOUNT table, if you are curious to see what encrypted
password values look like.

The servlet.setLoadOnStartup(2); method sets the priority of loading this servlet.
Any value greater than or equal to zero means that this servlet must be initialized after
the container has invoked all the ServletContextListener objects configured for
ServletContext at their ServletContextListener.contextInitialized(…) method.
Which means this servlet is loaded after the full Spring application context was loaded.

Since it provides access to sensitive user data, this servlet's URL should be secured; preferably, only ADMIN users should be able to access it. Another thing to mention here is that this servlet uses forms to send and retrieve data and is not part of the application. This means there is no CSRF token in those forms and no way to modify them. This means that CSRF protection must be disabled for all URLs starting with / h2-console/. This is done by calling another method of the CsrFConfigurer in the configure(HttpSecurity) method.

```
protected void configure(HttpSecurity http) throws Exception {
  http
      .authorizeRequests(..)
      .formLogin(..).logout(Customizer.withDefaults())
      .csrf()
          .csrfTokenRepository(repo())
          //don't apply CSRF protection to /h2-console
          .ignoringAntMatchers("/h2-console/**");
}
```

You might have noticed in Listing 12-16 that URLs "/customer/account" is not among the specific URL patterns configured to be secured even though it is supposed to be available only to authenticated users. This was intentional to show how security can be applied at the method level using Spring Security.

Securing Methods

URL security rules are applied to endpoints, and thus they apply to all controller methods matching the endpoint without the need to add any extra configuration in the controllers. Securing methods requires annotating controller methods with special security annotations. Having all security declared in a single place (the security configuration class) has some appeal since it is decoupled from the rest of the code, but it is suitable for small, simple applications. When an application grows, it might make more sense to keep authorization rules close to the code being protected. In the past, an extra advantage of securing methods was the possibility of using SpEL, but since SpEL can now be used with MvcMatchers, only the advantage of being close to the secured code remains.

Securing methods is done under the hood by using an AOP proxy. Marking the methods that need to be called by a secured proxy is done by a few annotations.

- **@Secured** (from the `org.springframework.security.access. annotation` package) is a Spring Security annotation that defines a list of security configuration attributes for methods, such as roles. This annotation is picked up when the security configuration class is annotated with `@EnableGlobalMethodSecurity(secured = true)`. This annotation does not support SpEL expressions, so it is rarely used nowadays.

- **@RolesAllowed** (from `javax.annotation.security`) is the JSR-250[14] equivalent of the @Secured annotation. This annotation is picked up when the security configuration class is annotated with `@EnableGlob alMethodSecurity(jsr250Enabled = true)` and the JSR-250 library in on the project classpath.

- **@PreAuthorize** (from the `org.springframework.security. access.prepost` package) specifies a method access-control SpEL expression, which is evaluated to decide if the method is to be executed or not. This annotation is picked up when the security configuration class is annotated with `@EnableGlobalMethodSecurity (prePostEnabled = true)`.

- **@PostAuthorize** (from the `org.springframework.security. access.prepost` package) specifies a method access-control SpEL expression, which is evaluated after the method is executed. This annotation is picked up when the security configuration class is annotated with `@EnableGlobalMethodSecurity(prePostEnabled = true)`. This is useful when domain-level security is implemented. Ownership of the returned object is tested using the @PostAuthorize declared rule, and the object is not returned if the check fails to pass.

---

[14]`https://jcp.org/en/jsr/detail?id=250`

- **@PostFilter** (from the org.springframework.security.access.
  prepost package) specifies a method access-control SpEL expression,
  which is evaluated after the method is executed, and the result is
  a collection. The SpEL expression can modify the collection and
  remove the objects the user doesn't have access to before returning it.
  This annotation is picked up when the security configuration class is
  annotated with @EnableGlobalMethodSecurity(prePostEnabled =
  true). (There is also a @PreFilter annotation that filters a collection
  based on an authorization expression before the annotated method
  manipulates it.)

Security annotations can be placed at class and method level, and the expressions on method level override the ones in the class. Using security at the class level is useful when you have all admin functionality declared in a single controller.

The JSR-250 library contains a small set of security annotations (e.g., @DenyAll, @ PermitAll) that have no correspondent in Spring Security because the same effect can be obtained by using Spring Security expressions. The JSR-250 annotations were mentioned because you might find them in projects that use a mix of JEE and Spring, so you should know that Spring Security can be configured to support them as well, but the focus of this chapter is on Spring Security annotations.

The contents of the Account page are retrieved using an HTTP GET request with URL "/customer/account". The method that handles this request is depicted in Listing 12-20.

Listing 12-20. Handler Method for "/customer/account"

```
package com.apress.prospringmvc.bookstore.web.controller;

import org.springframework.security.access.prepost.PreAuthorize;
import java.security.Principal;

// other imports omitted

@PreAuthorize("isAuthenticated()")
@Controller
@RequestMapping("/customer/account")
public class AccountController {

    @GetMapping
    public String index(Model model, Principal activeUser) {
```

```
        Account account = accountRepository.findByUsername(activeUser.
getName());
        model.addAttribute("account", account);
        model.addAttribute("orders", this.orderRepository.
findByAccount(account));
        model.addAttribute("fileOrders", getAsWebFiles());
        return "customer/account";
    }

    // other code omitted
}
```

The method declares a parameter of type Principal that Spring injects with the currently authenticated user principal. This is needed because the username is needed to extract the account details from the database. Ironically, this method is not made to be executed for an unauthenticated user. If this request is made by an unauthenticated user, Spring cannot find a principal; so the parameter is null, and a NullPointerException is thrown. Still, making internal exceptions public is not a good practice, so securing that method is a must.

And now the fun part, this method can be secured in many ways. For the next examples, assume the security configuration class is configured to support the annotations mentioned.

- @PreAuthorize("isAuthenticated()") accesses to the method is reserved for authenticated users. If an unauthenticated user tries to access the Account page, the request is made, but because of this annotation, it is intercepted by a secured proxy that checks if there is an authenticated user, and if there is not, it throws AccessDeniedException. The common way of configuring handling of this type of exception is to declare SimpleMappingExceptionResolver, which maps AccessDeniedException to the login view and a user-friendly error message, preferably an internationalized one. This bean adds the exception to the model of the view, and a combination of JSP taglib elements can display the messages in the current locale. In Listing 12-21, a code snippet depicting the declaration of this bean within the Spring web configuration class is shown. Listing 12-22, you can see the JSP snipped that shows the error message in the HTML login page.

Listing 12-21. SimpleMappingExceptionResolver to Handle
AccessDeniedException

```
package com.apress.prospringmvc.bookstore.web.config;
import
  org.springframework.web.servlet.handler.SimpleMappingExceptionResolver;
// other imports omitted
@Configuration
@EnableWebMvc
public class WebMvcContextConfiguration implements WebMvcConfigurer {

    Bean
    public SimpleMappingExceptionResolver simpleMappingExceptionResolver()
{
        SimpleMappingExceptionResolver exceptionResolver = new
SimpleMappingExceptionResolver();
        Properties mappings = new Properties();
        mappings.setProperty("AccessDeniedException", "login");

        Properties statusCodes = new Properties();
        mappings.setProperty("login", String.valueOf(HttpServletResponse.
SC_UNAUTHORIZED));

        exceptionResolver.setExceptionMappings(mappings);
        exceptionResolver.setStatusCodes(statusCodes);
        return exceptionResolver;
    }

        // other code omitted
}
```

Listing 12-22. JSP Code to Show an Error Requiring User Authentication in the
login.jsp Page

```
<%@taglib prefix="c" uri="http://java.sun.com/jsp/jstl/core"%>
<%@taglib prefix="spring" uri="http://www.springframework.org/tags" %>

<c:if test="${exception ne null}">
    <div class="error">
```

```
<spring:message code="authentication.required"
    text="${e.getMessage}" htmlEscape="true"/>
  </div>
</c:if>
<!-- rest of this template omitted -->
```

- @Secured({ "ROLE_USER", "ROLE_ADMIN" }) Since we know that all users in the Account table have one of these roles, this expression works too. Fun fact: the equivalent with JSR-250 is @RolesAllowed({"USER", "ADMIN"}).

- @PreAuthorize("hasRole('USER') or hasRole('ADMIN')")

- @PreAuthorize("hasAnyRole('USER','ADMIN')")

@Secured is the initial security annotation and has no support for SpEL expressions. @PreAuthorize was added in Spring Security 3 and is powerful. @PreAuthorize supports declaring access rules using SpEL, so you can get as creative as you want.

The "/customer/list" is not secured either. This page displays all the users in the ACCOUNT table, and it should be accessible only to users with the ADMIN role. This can be easily set up by annotating the method with @Secured({"ROLE_ADMIN" }) or @PreAuthorize("hasRole('ADMIN')").

But let's assume that we want to make sure only the admin user named "admin" can access that page. The only annotation suitable for the job is @PreAuthorize because it can interpret an expression like this.

```
@PreAuthorize("hasRole('ADMIN') and principal == 'admin'").
```

Securing methods adds an extra layer of security to a web application. Because of support for expressing security rules using SpEL, access can be controlled in very specific and granular ways.

So, have fun securing things!

Securing Spring Boot Web Applications

Securing a Spring Boot web application is not that different from securing a Spring MVC application. But there are a few things to keep in mind. Once the security starter library is added as a dependency, public access to your application is off the table, any URL redirects to the default Spring Security login generated form. If you want to allow access to anything, you must provide a configuration.

There is no need to integrate `springSecurityFilterChain` with the container servlet environment since you are using one of the embedded servers that Spring Boot supports. Thus, there is no need for the class extending `AbstractSecurityWebApplicationInitializer`.

There is no need to integrate your configuration class with the web application context explicitly.

That is all there is. Configuring Spring Security in a Spring Boot Web application resumes to the following.

- Add the `spring-boot-starter-security` dependency to your configuration

- Write a Spring Security configuration class that extends `WebSecurityConfigurerAdapter` (in the same way as a Spring MVC application with a classic setup; add annotations for enabling web security, method security, configure matches for the URLs, etc.)

- Add your custom `AuthenticationProvider` implementation (if you have one)

- Modify your views to secure sensitive content

And, if you use Thymeleaf, do not forget to register the Spring Security dialect with the template engine.

Summary

This chapter covered the essential parts of Spring Security in the context of a Spring web application. We looked at how Spring Security could be integrated with a classic Spring MVC application. Core concepts like cookies, sessions, authentication, authorization, principal, and authorities were introduced, and their roles in securing a web application were explained.

We showed how Apache Tiles and Thymeleaf view templates could be modified to take security settings into account. This means that the shape of what the users are served depends on their roles within the application.

The surface was scratched about common type attacks such as session hijacking and CSRF and the means Spring Security provides to prevent them.

Spring Security in the context of a Spring Boot web application was covered too, and the minimum set of actions a developer is required to provide to secure the application were made clear.

We used an in-memory database with password hashing to hold authentication data and then showed how a custom authentication provider could be implemented to use an existing table within the application.

## CHAPTER 13

Spring Applications in the Cloud

Few technical universities touch the subject of the cloud when teaching development. Unless the university is a big one and has a cloud provider like Amazon, Microsoft, or Google, as a partner, as a student, you will probably graduate without writing an application for the cloud or deploying it in the cloud. This chapter scratches the surface of development for the cloud and shows how Spring can develop microservices.

Nowadays, most applications are hosted in the cloud, and any newly written application is probably designed to be hosted in the cloud, so it is important to know how that affects an application's architecture.

Let's step back to before the word *cloud* was ever mentioned in software development and go over application architecture.

Application Architecture

Application architecture refers to the process of deciding which parts an application should have and how they should connect to each other.

Introducing the Monolith

Imagine you want to start a business selling books online (very creative, I know!). You either hire a company to create your site or if you are already interested in software development, you can build it yourself. You need a database to store information about books, orders, and users. You need an application that manages that information. The application is made of more parts or layers.

© Marten Deinum and Iuliana Cosmina 2021
M. Deinum and I. Cosmina, *Pro Spring MVC with WebFlux*, https://doi.org/10.1007/978-1-4842-5666-4_13

- The **user interface** (also known as the **presentation layer**): For this, you need HTML, CSS, JavaScript, and so on. If the application is meant to be accessed from multiple devices (computers, tablets, mobiles), you might need a specific technology for each device (e.g., Android SDK for Android devices).

- The **frontend** (also known as the **application layer**): The part that receives the requests from your user interface and transforms the data into something the next layer in the chain can process. For a Spring web application, this is represented by controllers and functional endpoints.

- The **service** (also known as the **business layer**): Receives the data from the front end and processes it, getting it ready to be stored in the database.

- The **data access layer** (also known as the **persistence layer**): It retrieves data from the database and transforms it into data that can be processed by the service layer. It also takes data from the service layer and saves it to the database. Contains DAOs (Data Access Objects) and special classes managing the entities. For a Spring application, this is represented by entities/documents, classes, and repositories.

Designing your application like this means you are building a **multilayered** or **multi-tier architecture** or a **monolithic architecture**.

During development, all layers are located on a single computer. But, when the application must go to production, the database is usually separated on a different computer that is backed up more often than the others since it contains the data that it is most important to the application. If you are using Java, the rest of the layers are packed into a single WAR or EAR deployed on an application server, like Apache Tomcat.

If that sounds familiar, it is because it was done in this book. Spring Boot applications do not even need an application server since it is embedded in them. Even in the reactive chapters, we often mentioned that they are suitable for building microservices, but the architecture was still monolithic. In Figure 13-1, you can see how such an application could be deployed for public use.

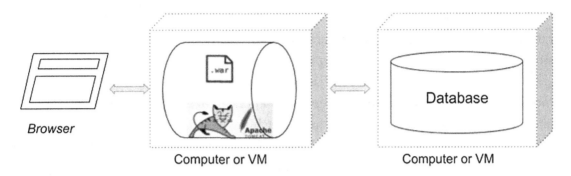

Figure 13-1. *A multi-tier application deployed for public use*

Monolithic applications are easy to develop, test, deploy, and scale—at least initially, because as more users access your application, the drawbacks become apparent.

- If the database size increases, you replace the hard drive with a bigger one, and the problem is solved—*at least for a while.*

- If there are too many users accessing your application, increase your computer's or VM's memory and the number of threads on your Apache server. This should solve the problem—*for a while.*

- But, maintaining a monolithic codebase is difficult. As the codebase grows, the knowledge must be split between developers since it is rare for a single developer to know all the pieces well; this is how knowledge is lost when people leave the company.

- When the codebase is big, changing, and upgrading technologies becomes very risky, which is how technology debt creeps in.

- Continuous deployment is impossible.

- Scaling is limited and costly.

If you have your own datacenter, upgrading the hardware is possible but costs a lot and imagine the cost of maintaining a datacenter! This is where Amazon, Google, and others saw the potential for a great business—providing an infrastructure where applications could be deployed and managed with less hassle and costs for those developing them. This how the cloud was born. The cloud is a lot of computers all over the world and the software running on them. Deploying your application and managing it on a remote computer that is part of a cloud is called **cloud computing**. By using cloud computing, users and companies don't have to manage physical servers themselves or run software applications on their own machines.

There are a few cloud providers in the world right now. Most of them offer a wide range of services, such as automatic backups, autoscaling, load balancing, and data storage, with Amazon probably leading in the number of services.

Resizing the resources (CPU, RAM) used by computers in the way it is needed for a monolith is called **vertical scaling**. Even if your application is deployed on the cloud, and the computers are replaced with virtual machines, resizing their resources (CPU, RAM) in the way it is needed for a monolith is cumbersome and limited. There is another type of scaling that involves adding more machines into your pool of resources that is called **horizontal scaling**. Unfortunately, a monolith architecture is not fully suitable for horizontal scaling, but microservice architecture is.

Introducing Microservices

Microservice architecture, also called **microservices**,[1] is a specialization and implementation approach for service-oriented architectures (SOA). It builds flexible, independently deployable services. Microservice architecture is different from monolith architecture because it defines an application not by using layers but as a collection of services.

Microservices is a paradigm that requires services to be broken down into highly specialized instances as functionality and interconnected through agnostic communication protocols (like REST, for example) that work together to accomplish a common business goal. Each microservice is a tiny unit of stateless functionality, a process that does not care where the input is coming from and does not know where its output is going; it has no idea what the big picture is. Being this specialized and decoupled, each problem can be identified, the cause localized and fixed, and the implementation redeployed without affecting other microservices. This means that microservices systems have high cohesion of responsibilities and low coupling. These qualities allow the architecture of an individual service to evolve through continuous refactoring, reduce the necessity of a big up-front design, and allow the software to be released earlier and continuously. Splitting up a large complex application into smaller detached applications allows rapid, frequent, and reliable delivery of features and facilitates the evolution of a company's technology stack.

---

[1]https://microservices.io/

Microservices have grown in popularity in recent years due to low granularity and lightweight communication protocols. They have become the preferred way to build enterprise applications. Microservices modular architectural style seems particularly well suited to cloud-based environments. This architectural method is scalable and considered ideal when multiple platforms and devices must be supported. Consider the biggest players on the Web right now: Facebook, Twitter, Netflix, Amazon, PayPal, SoundCloud, and others. They have large-scale websites and applications that have evolved from a monolithic architecture to microservices so that they can be accessed from any device. Amazon and Google are currently the biggest in the business by providing a suite of cloud computing services, ideal for building complex applications made up of numerous microservices working together. Businesses that provide software and services for banks, retailers, restaurants, small businesses, and telecom and technology have no choice but to rely on AWS or GCP to keep their services available at all times. This is done by building their microservices using Apigee[2] or the Amazon API Gateway.[3] Amazon and Google provide the infrastructure for microservices to communicate and a myriad of tools to build them. Eventually, writing the code for those services is still the developers' responsibility.

Spring Boot is a good tool for building a small, niched application representing a microservice in a more complex application. And reactive services can do more with less, lowering the costs of cloud infrastructure.

What are the main advantages of using microservices? The following is praised in the IT industry.

- Increased granularity

- Increased scalability

- Easy-to-automate deployment and testing (sure depends on the context, because if transactions are involved, things start to become difficult), since microservices are characterized by well-defined interfaces that facilitate communication (JSON/ WSDL/JMS/AMQP)

- Increased decoupling, since microservices do not share the state of the service

- Enhanced cohesion

---

[2]https://cloud.google.com/apigee/
[3]https://aws.amazon.com/api-gateway/

- Suitable for continuous refactoring, integration, and delivery

- Increased module independence

- Specialized—organized around capabilities; each microservice is designed for one specific capability

- Improved agility and velocity, because when a system is correctly decomposed into microservices, each service can be developed and deployed independently and in parallel with the others.

- Each service is elastic, resilient, composable, minimal, and complete

- Improvement of fault isolation

- Elimination of long-term commitment to a single technology stack, because microservices can be written in different programming languages

- Easier knowledge sharing because new developers can work on a few microservices without the need to understand the whole system

Since there is no perfection in this world, especially in software development, there are a few disadvantages.

- Microservices introduce additional complexity and the necessity of carefully handling of requests between services.

- Handling shared resources like entity classes can cause problems.

- Handling multiple databases and transactions (distributed transactions) can be painful.

- Testing microservices can be cumbersome because each microservice dependency must be confirmed as valid before the service can be tested.

- Deployment can become complex, requiring coordination among services.

Moving to the Cloud: Yea or Nay?

In this chapter, we convert the Bookstore into its microservice equivalent that is more suitable for deployment to the cloud. But, before doing that, we should list a few advantages of moving to the cloud.

- A clear advantage—lowers infrastructure costs

- Since developers learn to configure cloud services, there might be lower costs with personnel because you no longer need a big infrastructure department

- Flexibility—configure cloud services like load balancers and autoscaling groups to make sure that your application is always up and self-heals

- Cloud infrastructure is automatically maintained, so no need to worry about software updates

- Everything is in the cloud, so you can work from anywhere

- And many others

Are there disadvantages of moving to the cloud? Sure.

- The **main disadvantage** is that you are fully dependent on your cloud provider.

- Vendor lock-in—switching your cloud providers is a pain; control over services is provided through custom APIs, and there is no bridge between them.

- If your cloud provider experiences technical issues because of natural disasters, you might be cut out of the system.

- If the software to manage your resources happens to malfunction, the autoscaling and self-healing might be affected. Even if you configure your cloud infrastructure right and take everything into account, the services that are supposed to scale it and keep it up are still hosted within the same cloud. Downtime remains a possibility.

- Although cloud service providers implement the best security standards and industry certifications, storing data and important files on external service providers still comes with a degree of risk. Hacking is especially dangerous for a cloud provider; for example, if Amazon were to be hacked, all its clients' data would be at risk.

- Limited control—most cloud providers let you manage your infrastructure using web consoles and SSH connections, but the control is ultimately minimal.

- Costs—although using cloud computing reduces your costs compared to setting up and managing your own datacenter, there are situations when the cost of cloud services might increase. Most cloud providers advertise pay-as-you-go models that give you flexibility and lower hardware costs, but they are still unsuitable for small-scale, short-term projects. Also, misconfigurations of cloud resources could raise your bill.

Although there are disadvantages, many organizations benefit from the agility, scale, and pay-as-you-go models that cloud services offer. However, as with any infrastructure service, cloud computing's suitability for your specific use case should be assessed in a risk-based evaluation. Amazon, for example, encourages companies to plan wisely and use only what they need. They have a few partner companies that provide consultancy in designing and maintaining cloud infrastructure with minimal costs. Because for a business to have a long lifespan and profit, their clients must do so too.

Still, when you are a developer at the start of your career and want to learn about the cloud, you might not be in the position to pay for cloud access. No need to worry; most cloud providers offer free limited access account to their users. Amazon offers 12 months of Free Tier Access[4] for new users to learn to use their services. GCP offers a three-month free trial[5] with $300 credit to use with any Google Cloud services. But, if you are still reluctant to give any of them a try, no worries, Spring has you covered. The Spring Cloud project collection is a treasure trove of tools to build microservices according to the most common patterns in distributed systems, and you can run those services locally as they would run in a cloud.

---

[4]https://aws.amazon.com/free
[5]https://cloud.google.com/free

Introducing Spring Cloud

To develop an application consisting of a set of microservices with Spring components, good knowledge of the following Spring technologies is needed.

- Service registration and discovery technology like Netflix's OSS Eureka

- Spring Cloud projects like Eureka or Consul

- REST concepts (since the communication between microservices is done using REST)

Spring Boot is designed for developers heightened productivity by making common concepts—like RESTful HTTP and embedded web application runtimes—easy to wire up and use. It is flexible and allows developers to pick only modules they want to use, removing the overwhelming or bulky configurations and runtime dependencies.

Spring Cloud[6] is a collection of projects designed to ease the development of distributed applications.

- Configuration management (Spring Cloud Config provides centralized external configuration backed by a Git repository)

- Service discovery (Eureka is a service registry for resilient mid-tier load balancing and failover and is supported by Spring Cloud)

- Circuit breakers (Spring Cloud supports Netflix's Hystrix that is a library that provides components that stop calling services when a response is not received in a predefined threshold)

- Intelligent routing (Zuul forwards and distributes calls to services)

- Micro-proxy (client-side proxies to mid-tier services)

- Control bus (a messaging system can be used for monitoring and managing the components within the framework as is used for application-level messaging)

- One-time tokens (used for data access only once with Spring Vault[7])

---

[6]https://spring.io/projects/spring-cloud
[7]https://spring.io/projects/spring-vault

- Global locks (coordinates, prioritizes, or restricts access to resources)

- Leadership election (the process of designating a single process as the organizer of some task distributed among several nodes)

- Distributed messaging (Spring Cloud Bus can be used links nodes of a distributed system with a lightweight message broker)

- Cluster state (cluster state request is routed to the master node to ensure that the latest cluster state is returned)

- Client-side load balancing

In case you are interested in building microservices applications with Spring Cloud, the official Spring documentation covers all the bases. Coordinating distributed systems is not easy and can lead to boilerplate code. Spring Cloud makes it easier for developers to write this type of management code. The results work in any distributed environment, including a development station, data centers, or managed platforms as Cloud Foundry.

Spring Cloud builds on Spring Boot, and it comes with the typical Spring Boot advantages: out of the box preconfigured infrastructure beans that can be further configured or extended to create a custom solution. It follows the same Spring declarative approach, relying on annotations and property (YAML) files.

Spring Cloud Netflix provides integration with Netflix OSS (Netflix Open Source Software). The official GitHub page is at `https://netflix.github.io/`. It is a collection of open source libraries that their developers wrote to solve distributed-systems problems at scale. Written in Java, it became pretty much the most used software when writing microservices applications in Java.

Redesigning for the Cloud

The Bookstore application we've been writing throughout this book is a monolith. Its layers, although separated in different modules, are all being combined into a single war deployed on an Apache Tomcat or a single Spring Boot application packed as an executable jar. Even when making it reactive, the monolith architecture was kept because this was a small application, and there was no reason to change it yet. Deploying it to a cloud as a monolith is possible but inefficient for all the reasons listed in the previous sections. It needs a redesign.

In previous chapters, every module of the application contained (more or less) functionality specific to a monolith layer for all the objects handled by the application. For example, all repository classes for Book, Account, and Orders were responsible for database operations, thus belonged in the DAO layer.

Microservices require that the separation is based on business functionality, so each service should have a single role related to a single type of object. So, we might need a microservice that handles all operations for Book objects, one for Account objects, and so on. The tech news service can be made into a microservice since it is independent of the application.

The same goes for the service providing random book releases. A proposal of how the Bookstore application could be redesigned for the cloud is depicted in Figure 13-2.

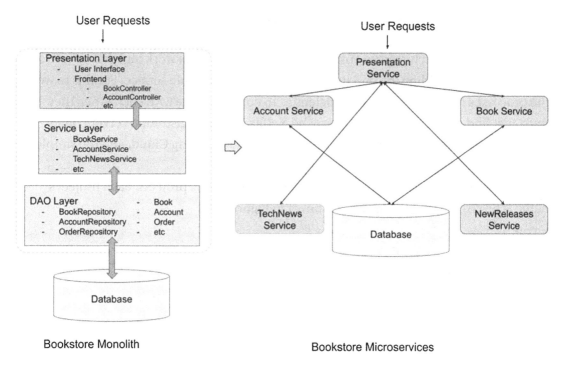

Figure 13-2. *Comparison of Bookstore monolith and microservices architectures*

Figure 13-2 has a database that is shared between all microservices, but this is not a requirement. Anything that provides a service can become a microservice. You can have security as a separate service that relies on the cloud provider's authentication service. You could decide to have a separate database for accounts. You could decide to have a separate database for orders too. When it comes to databases, there are three models.

- **Private-tables-per-service**: Each service owns a set of tables that must only be accessed by that service.

- **Schema-per-service**: Each service has a database schema that is private to that service.

- **Database-server-per-service**: Each service has its own database server.

It all depends on the requirements of your design. In the rest of the chapter, you learn how to write your services and ensure their communication using Spring Cloud.

Registration and Discovery Server

The microservices architecture ensures that a set of processes work together toward a common goal: providing the end user a competent and reliable service. For this to work, the processes must communicate efficiently. To communicate with each other, they must first find each other. This is where the Netflix Eureka registration server comes in. And because it is open source, it was incorporated in Spring Cloud, and the simple principles of Spring now apply.

In this chapter, the Bookstore application is split into six projects; each project's name is prefixed with chapter13, as shown in Figure 13-3.

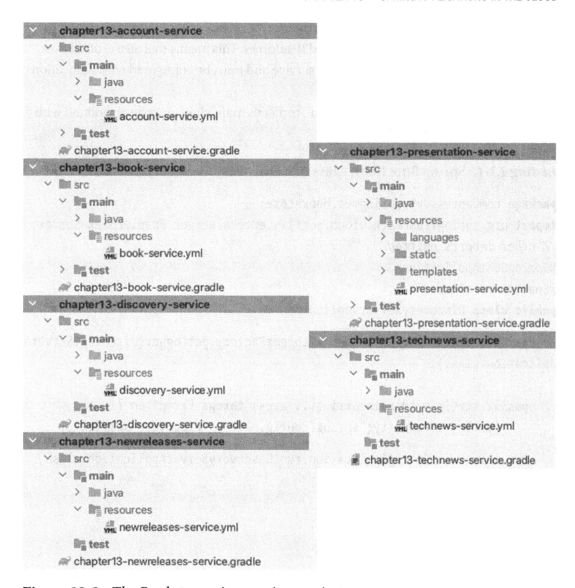

Figure 13-3. *The Bookstore microservices projects*

The **discovery-service** is a core component. It is the hub of the project used by all other microservices to register and discover each other.

The configuration of the project is nothing special. It is a simple Spring Boot Web application with a single Spring Cloud starter project on its classpath: the `spring-cloud-starter-netflix-eureka-server` starter. This dependency adds to the project all necessary dependencies to build a Netflix Eureka service registry. This is a special type of service that catalogs other existing services and enables client-side communication and load-balancing. Every other microservice registers itself so that Eureka knows all the applications running on each port and IP address. This means that all the other five microservices are clients of the discovery service and must be configured with its location to know where to register themselves.

To create a Eureka Service registry, the project's main class must be annotated with @ EnableEurekaServer (see Listing 13-1).

Listing 13-1. Spring Boot Main Class of a Discovery Microservice

```
package com.apress.prospringmvc.bookstore;
import org.springframework.cloud.netflix.eureka.server.EnableEurekaServer;
// other imports omitted
@SpringBootApplication
@EnableEurekaServer
public class DiscoveryServerApplication {

    private static Logger logger = LoggerFactory.getLogger(DiscoveryServerA
pplication.class);

    public static void main(String... args) throws Exception {
        System.setProperty("spring.config.name", "discovery-service");

        var ctx = SpringApplication.run(DiscoveryServerApplication.class,
args);
        assert (ctx != null);
        logger.info("Started ...");
        System.in.read();
        ctx.close();
    }
}
```

ⓘ   The System.in.read(); call is used, so you can stop the application gracefully by pressing the <ENTER> key. To avoid confusion during development, the Spring Boot configuration file has been renamed to discovery-service. yml and the spring.config.name environment variable was set to let Spring Boot know the name of the file to take its configuration from.

The @EnableEurekaServer annotation is very important since it activates Eureka server-related configuration. This annotation is responsible for providing a Eureka server instance for the project. The server comes with a very nice web interface where the registered microservices can be monitored. The main page is accessible at http://[ip]:[port]/. Where the IP is your computer's IP or any of localhost, 127.0.0.1, 0.0.0.0, or all of them if you configured it so in the Spring Boot configuration file. The port is taken from the Spring Boot configuration file too.

The discovery-service.yml contains settings for this server, and its contents are depicted in Listing 13-2.

Listing 13-2. The Eureka Discovery Server Configuration (discovery-service. yml)

```
spring:
  application:
    name: discovery-service

# Configure the Server
eureka:
  client:
    registerWithEureka: false # do not auto-register as client
    fetchRegistry: false
    server:
        waitTimeInMsWhenSyncEmpty: 0

server:
  port: 3000    # where this discovery server is accessible
  address: 0.0.0.0
```

The previous configuration starts the server on port 3000, and if you access the web interface, you can see that no microservices are registered at the moment, as seen in Figure 13-4.

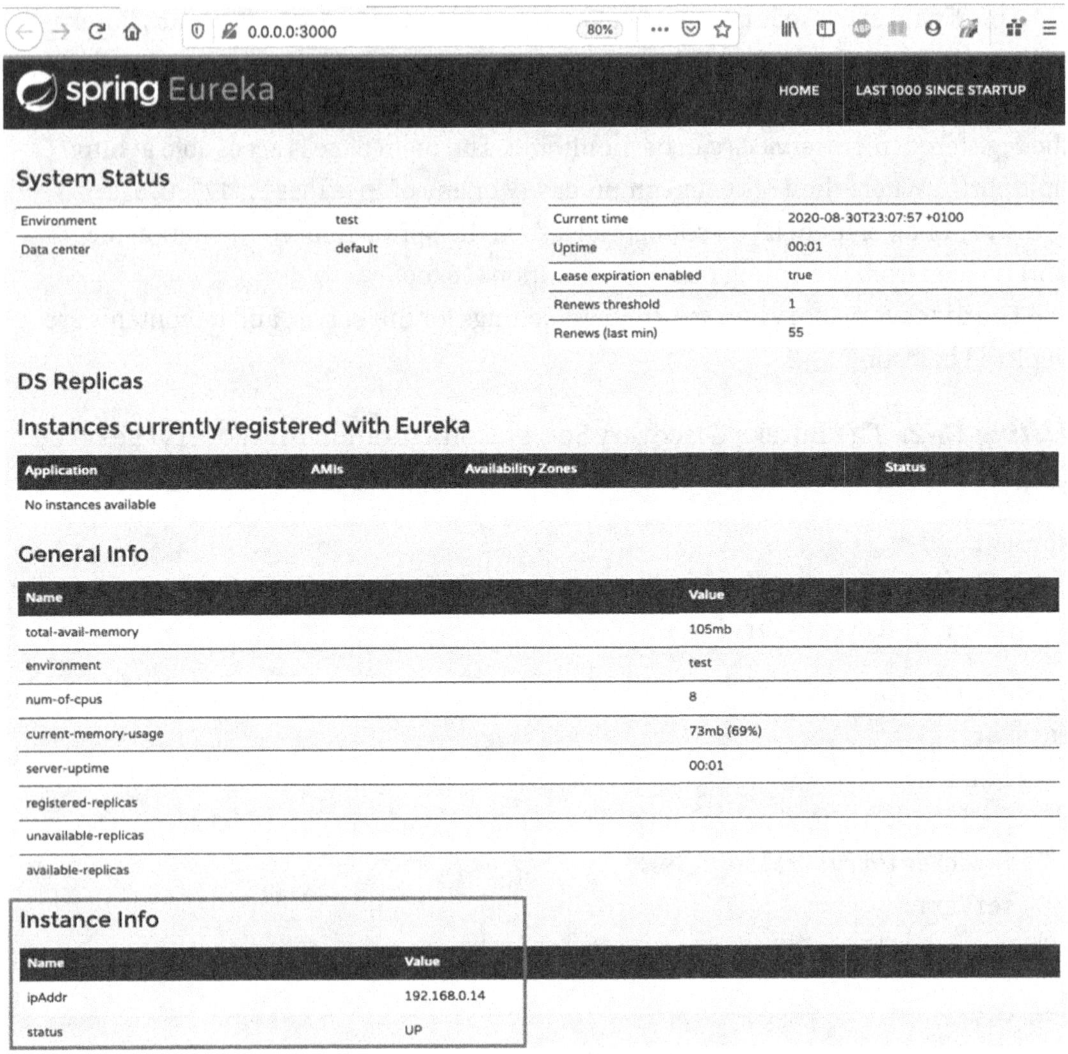

Figure 13-4.   *The Eureka Discovery Server web interface*

The main page shows a few metrics about the discovery server instance. Netflix's original version of the Eureka server avoids answering clients for a configurable time if it starts with an empty registry. The `eureka.server.waitTimeInMsWhenSyncEmpty` property controls this behavior, and it was designed so clients would not get partial/ empty registry information until the server has had enough time to build the registry. This is useful when some microservices must start only after their dependencies are up and ready. In Listing 13-2, the values are set to zero to start answering clients as soon as possible. This configuration is suitable for a development environment as it speeds things up.

> **ℹ** If not set, the default value for `eureka.server.waitTimeInMsWhenSyncEmpty` is 5 minutes.

The `eureka.client.registerWithEureka` property is used to register Eureka clients and is usually set to `false` on a Eureka discovery server. It tells this instance not to register itself with the Eureka server it finds since it's itself.

If the discovery server exposes any endpoint with functionality not related to registration and discovery of services (such as exposing metrics for a monitoring microservice), it must register itself as a client.

And now that we have a server, we can start writing our microservices.

Developing a Microservice

Creating a microservice using Spring Boot is very easy. You have to pick the functionality, write the code necessary to implement the behavior, expose the endpoints that can be accessed by other microservices, and configure it to register as a Eureka client.

A microservice is a stand-alone process that handles a well-defined requirement. When creating a distributed application based on microservices, each microservice component should be wrapped in packages based on its purpose. The overall implementation should be very loosely coupled but very cohesive. Let's start with the smallest and most simple microservice we could write for the Bookstore application: the tech news service. This service should expose a single endpoint where an infinite stream of tech news can be accessed.

Since it is a reactive service with no web interface, the only dependencies of this project are `spring-boot-starter-webflux` and `spring-cloud-starter-netflix-eureka-client`.

The `spring-cloud-starter-netflix-eureka-client` adds to the project all necessary dependencies that allow you to build a Netflix Eureka client.

Aside from these two, it is practical to add `spring-boot-starter-actuator`.[8] This dependency adds Spring Actuator to your project, which adds production-ready features to our application. Through several endpoints, it exposes operational information about the running application.

---

[8]https://docs.spring.io/spring-boot/docs/current/reference/html/production-ready-features.html

537

The Tech News service is very simple. It has a Spring Boot main configuration class which is annotated with @EnableEurekaClient. This is the key component that transforms this application into a microservice because it enables Eureka client discovery configuration.

Within this class, a router bean is declared to configure the mapping between endpoints and handler functions.

Listing 13-3 depicts the contents of the TechNewsApplication.

Listing 13-3. Spring Boot Tech News Microservice Configuration Class

```
package com.apress.prospringmvc.technews;
import org.springframework.cloud.netflix.eureka.EnableEurekaClient;
// other imports omitted

@SpringBootApplication
@EnableEurekaClient
public class TechNewsApplication {

    public static void main(String... args) {
        System.setProperty("spring.config.name", "technews-service");
        SpringApplication springApplication = new SpringApplication(TechNew
sApplication.class);
        springApplication.run(args);
    }

    @Bean
    public RouterFunction<ServerResponse> router(TechNewsHandler handler){
        return RouterFunctions
                .route(GET("/"), handler.main)
                .andRoute(GET("/index.htm"), handler.main)
                .andRoute(GET("/tech/news"), handler.data);
    }
}
```

The TechNewsHandler class contains the two handler functions implementations. Its contents are listed in Listing 13-4.

Listing 13-4. TechNewsHandler Handler Functions

```java
package com.apress.prospringmvc.technews;
// other imports omitted
@Component
class TechNewsHandler {
    private static final Random RANDOM = new Random(System.
currentTimeMillis());

    public static final List<String> TECH_NEWS = List.of(
            "Apress merged with Springer."
            // other values omitted
    );

    public static String randomNews() {
        return TECH_NEWS.get(RANDOM.nextInt(TECH_NEWS.size()));
    }
    final HandlerFunction<ServerResponse> main = serverRequest -> ok()
            .contentType(MediaType.TEXT_HTML)
            .bodyValue("Tech News service up and running!");

    final HandlerFunction<ServerResponse> data = serverRequest -> ok()
        .contentType(MediaType.TEXT_EVENT_STREAM)
        .body(Flux.interval(Duration.ofSeconds(5))
            .map(delay -> randomNews()), String.class);
}
```

The Spring Boot configuration file for this application is named `technews-service. yml` and is depicted in Listing 13-5.

Listing 13-5. Spring Boot Configuration File for the Tech News Microservice

```yaml
# Spring Properties
spring:
  application:
    name: technews-service # Service registers under this name

# HTTP Server
server:
```

```
  port: 4000    # HTTP (Netty) port
  address: 0.0.0.0

# Discovery Server Access
eureka:
  client:
    registerWithEureka: true
    fetchRegistry: false
    serviceUrl:
      defaultZone: http://localhost:3000/eureka/
    healthcheck:
      enabled: true

  instance:
    leaseRenewalIntervalInSeconds: 5
    preferIpAddress: false

# Actuator endpoint configuration
info:
  app:
    name: technews-service
    description: Spring Cloud Random Tech News Generator
    version: 2.0.0-SNAPSHOT
```

The previous configuration contains three sections.

- The **Spring section** defines the application name as technews-service. The microservice registers with the Eureka server using this name.

- The **Server section** defines the port to listen on for requests. In this case, it was set to 4000. Being a reactive application using an embedded Netty instance, if left unspecified, it tries to use 8080. Since only one process can listen on a port at one time, each microservice has a different port assigned via configuration. The server.address is set to 0.0.0.0 for this microservice, which means its endpoints are accessible on all addresses of the computer it is installed on.

- The **Eureka section** defines the URI where the server to register is located using the `eureka.client.serviceUrl.defaultZone` property.

  `eureka.client.registerWithEureka` is `true` by default; it is used to configure registration of Eureka clients. It is explicitly set in this configuration to avoid confusion regarding the type of this microservice.

  Eureka clients fetch the registry information from the server and cache it locally. After that, the clients use that information to find other services. As the `technews-service` does not depend on another microservice being already registered, there is no need to fetch the registry information. The `eureka.client.fetchRegistry` is set to `false` to prevent it from doing that.

  After successful registration, the Eureka server always reports a client application as UP. This behavior can be altered by enabling Eureka health checks, which results in propagating application status to Eureka. This is done by setting the `eureka.client.healthcheck.enabled` property to `true`.

  Eureka clients need to tell the server they are still active by sending a signal called **heartbeat**. By default, the interval is 30 seconds. It can be set to smaller intervals by customizing the value of the `eureka.instance.leaseRenewalIntervalInSeconds` property. During development, it can be set to a smaller value, which speeds up registration, but on production, this generates extra communication with the server that might cause service lag. For production, the default value should not be modified.

  `eureka.instance.preferIpAddress` tells the Eureka server if it should use the domain name or an IP of the registered clients. In our case, because everything is working on the same machine, the value of this property is irrelevant.

- In the **Actuator section**, the information displayed when the `/actuator/info` is accessed in the browser is customized by the `information` block of properties. The health information is accessed by the `/actuator/health` URI.

This information and more is available on the Netflix GitHub page.[9] Only the sections relevant to our implementation were explained here.

Now that we have a microservice that is a Eureka client, the next step is to start it and check if it registers with the discovery server. The registration should be completed when you see the following output in the log of the discovery-service application.

```
DEBUG o.s.c.n.e.server.InstanceRegistry - register TECHNEWS-SERVICE, vip
technews-service, leaseDuration 90, isReplication false
INFO  c.n.e.r.AbstractInstanceRegistry - Registered instance
TECHNEWS-SERVICE/192.168.0.14:technews-service:4000 with status UP
(replication=false)
```

After registration, when accessing the web interface for the Eureka server at http://localhost:3000/, you should see that in the `Instances currently registered with Eureka` section, an entry specific to the `technews-service` microservice was added, as depicted in Figure 13-5.

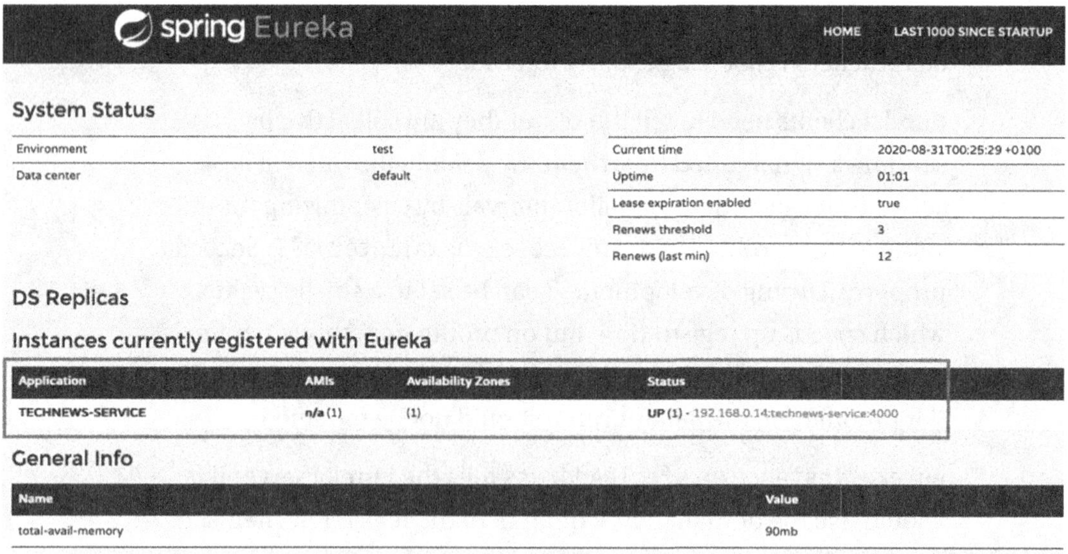
spring Eureka
HOME
LAST 1000 SINCE STARTUP
System Status
Environment
test
Data center
default
Current time
2020-08-31T00:25:29 +0100
Uptime
01:01
Lease expiration enabled
true
Renews threshold
3
Renews (last min)
12
DS Replicas
Instances currently registered with Eureka
Application
AMIs
Availability Zones
Status
TECHNEWS-SERVICE
n/a (1)
(1)
UP (1) - 192.168.0.14:technews-service:4000
General Info
Name
Value
total-avail-memory
90mb

Figure 13-5. *The Eureka Discovery Server web interface*

[9] `https://github.com/Netflix/eureka/wiki/Understanding-eureka-client-server-communication`

If you click the link in the Status column, you notice that it takes you to the /actuator/info in the Tech News application, where you should see the information in the Actuation section (see Figure 13-6).

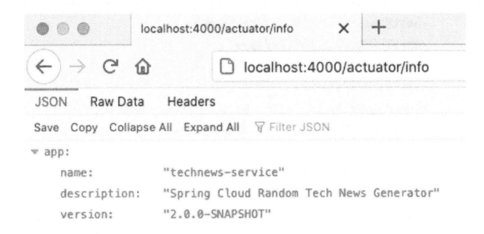

Figure 13-6. *TechNews Actuator info*

The newreleases-service is a very simple service too, it is almost identical to the technews-service, but it returns an infinite stream of Book instances. It is a Spring Boot application that can be started by executing its main class just like the tech news microservice, so there is no need to add more code or any text here about it since it adds no real value to this chapter. These two microservices provide the data depicted in the Book page's news section in the Bookstore application.

Once you have the technews-service and the newreleases-service microservices started, you can open the following URL http://localhost:3000/eureka/apps in your browser. This endpoint exposes registry metadata for all registered microservices, such as when they registered, health checks, the time they sent their heartbeat, and more—all standard information for a microservice. This information is published in the service registry, and it is available to all clients. The purpose of your Eureka server is to generate and manage information and share it with all microservices that need it. The format of the data is XML. A short snippet is depicted in Listing 13-6.

Listing 13-6. Eureka Server Registered Microservices Information

```
<applications>
    <versions__delta>1</versions__delta>
    <apps__hashcode>UP_2_</apps__hashcode>
```

```
<application>
    <name>TECHNEWS-SERVICE</name>
    <instance>
        <instanceId>192.168.0.14:technews-service:4000</instanceId>
        <hostName>192.168.0.14</hostName>
        <app>TECHNEWS-SERVICE</app>
        <ipAddr>192.168.0.14</ipAddr>
        <status>UP</status>
        <homePageUrl>http://192.168.0.14:4000/</homePageUrl>
        <statusPageUrl>http://192.168.0.14:4000/actuator/info</
statusPageUrl>
        <healthCheckUrl>http://192.168.0.14:4000/actuator/health</
healthCheckUrl>
        <lastUpdatedTimestamp>1598830791842</lastUpdatedTimestamp>
        <lastDirtyTimestamp>1598830791711</lastDirtyTimestamp>
        <actionType>ADDED</actionType>
    </instance>
</application>
<!-- other output omitted -->
</applications>
```

If you want to view only the metadata information for a certain service, add the service name to the previously mentioned URI. Thus, to view only the information about technews-microservice, you must access http://localhost:3000/eureka/apps/ TECHNEWS-SERVICE.

Additional metadata can be added to an instance registration by customization of the eureka.instance.metadataMap metadata. Usually, adding additional metadata does not modify remote client behavior in any way unless the client was designed to be aware of its meaning. For more information, check the official Spring Eureka documentation.[10]

At registration time, each microservice gets a unique registration identifier from the server, which you can see in the <instanceId> element in the previous output snippet. If another process registers with the same ID, the server treats it as a restart, so the first process is discarded.

---

[10]https://cloud.spring.io/spring-cloud-netflix/multi/multi__service_discovery_ eureka_clients.html#_eureka_metadata_for_instances_and_clients

To run multiple instances of the same process, for reasons of load balancing and resilience, we must make sure the server generates a different registration ID. Locally, this can be achieved by using a different port for the microservice. This is the easiest way to get it done without invasive changes in the codebase or configuration.

The registration ID with the configuration used so far—the one in the `<instanceId>` element—is constructed using the following default pattern.

```
${ipAddress}:${spring.application.name:${server.port}}
```

The registration ID for the `technews-service` microservice instance is

```
192.168.0.14:technews-service:4000
```

The microservice name and port are coupled together in the format pattern because they provide a unique way to identify the microservice and the port it listens to for requests.

The registration ID template can be modified by adding a different value for the Eureka `eureka.instance.metadataMap.instanceId` property in the Spring Boot configuration file. Listing 13-7 depicts a configuration sample that modifies the registration ID template.

Listing 13-7. Registration ID Is Configured to Use a Different Naming Template

```
eureka:
  instance:
    metadataMap:
      instanceId: ${spring.application.name}:${spring.application.instance_
id:${server.port}}
```

If `spring.application.instance_id` is not defined, it falls back to this default template (if there are any doubts about which one it is).

```
${ipAddress}:${spring.application.name:${server.port}}
```

When running a microservices application locally (as I imagine you are while going through this book), a microservice's main method can be parametrized to take the port as an argument. This allows you to start as many instances of that service as you wish by supplying a different port as an argument. In Listing 13-8, the port value is read and injected in the Spring Boot `server.port` environment variable.

Listing 13-8. NewReleasesApplication That Takes Port As an Argument

```
package com.apress.prospringmvc.newreleases;
// other imports omitted

@SpringBootApplication
@EnableEurekaClient
public class NewReleasesApplication {

    public static void main(String... args) {
    if (args.length == 1) {
        System.setProperty("server.port", args[0]);
    }
    System.setProperty("spring.config.name", "newreleases-service");
    SpringApplication springApplication = new SpringApplication(NewRele
asesApplication.class);
    springApplication.run(args);
  }

}
```

In Figure 13-7, you can see that three newreleases-service instances were started: the default on port 5000 and two more on ports 5001 and 5002.

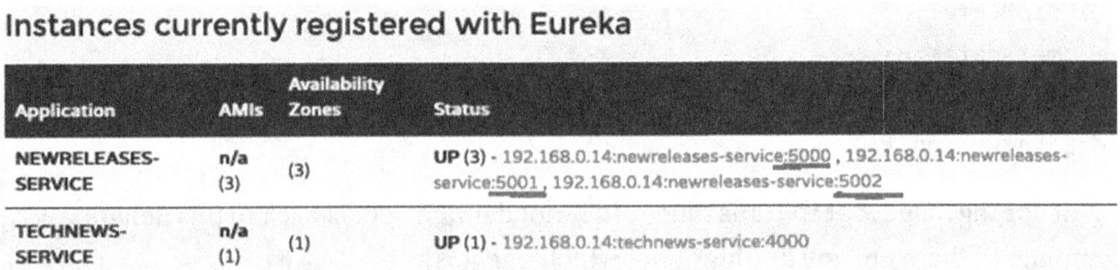

Instances currently registered with Eureka

Application	AMIs	Availability Zones	Status
NEWRELEASES-SERVICE	n/a (3)	(3)	**UP** (3) - 192.168.0.14:newreleases-service:5000 , 192.168.0.14:newreleases-service:5001 , 192.168.0.14:newreleases-service:5002
TECHNEWS-SERVICE	n/a (1)	(1)	**UP** (1) - 192.168.0.14:technews-service:4000

Figure 13-7. *Multiple NewReleases microservice instances registered*

Each instance was started by creating a new IntelliJ IDEA launcher and configuring the port as a program argument, as depicted in Figure 13-8.

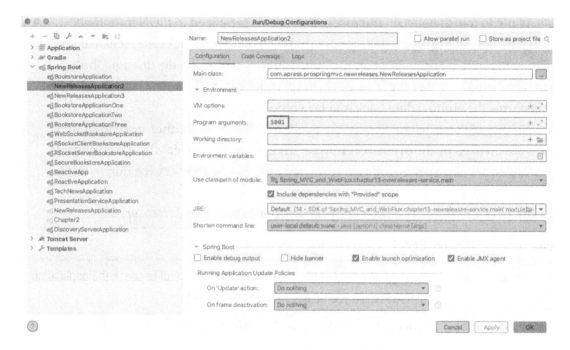

Figure 13-8. *IntelliJ IDEA launcher for the* `newreleases-service` *application with the port provided as a program argument*

The Tech News and New Releases microservices are basic, they do not require using a database, and there is no communication between them. The next step is to develop a microservice that uses a database.

Microservice Using a Database

Considering that our services are reactive, the database of choice is MongoDB. Since the document mapping classes `Book` and `Account` introduced in the previous chapters are detached from each other, `book-service` and `account-service` are independent. Each uses its own MongoDB collection.

The `book-service` microservice exposes a REST API for various book operations: list, create, update, delete, search, get Random book. The implementation of this service has been described in the reactive chapters.

The `account-service` microservice exposes a REST API for various account operations: list, create, delete, update. The implementation of this service has been described in the reactive chapters.

While in transit between microservices, data is serialized to JSON by default, using the default `org.springframework.http.codec.json.Jackson2JsonEncoder<T>` autoconfigured in Spring Boot application. When reaching the destination, the autoconfigured `org.springframework.http.codec.json.Jackson2JsonDecoder<T>` transforms the emitted data back into Java objects.

Neither of these two microservices needs a web interface either since their REST APIs are invoked by the `presentation-service`, the only service with a web console.

Table 13-1 lists all the endpoints exposed by the `account-service` microservice.

Table 13-1. *Endpoints Exposed by the* `account-service` *Microservice*

URI	Method	Effect
`/`,`/index.htm`	GET	Returns "Account service up and running!". Useful to check the application status in case you do not want to use Actuator.
`/account`	GET	Returns a response containing a reference to a `Flux<Account>`.
`/account/{username}`	GET	Returns a response with a body representing a reference to a `Mono<Account>` corresponding to the username provided as a path variable.
`/account/{username}`	PUT	Updates the `Account` instance corresponding to the username provided as a path variable and returns a response with a body representing `Mono<Account>` that emits the updated instance.
`/account`	POST	Creates the `Account` instance using the data from the request body and returns a response with a body representing `Mono<Account>` that emits the created instance. The response has the location header populated with the URI to access the new instance.
`/account`	DELETE	Deletes the `Account` instance corresponding to the username provided as a path variable and returns an empty response.

Table 13-2 lists all the endpoints exposed by the `book-service` microservice.

Table 13-2. *Endpoints Exposed by the* book-service *Microservice*

URI	Method	Effect
/, /index. htm	GET	Returns "Book service up and running!".
/book/ random	GET	Returns a response with a body representing a reference to a Flux<Book> containing two books.
/book/ search	GET	Returns a response with a body representing a reference to a Flux<Book> that emits Book instances matching the BookCriteria details provided in the request body.
/book/ by/ {isbn}	GET	Returns a response with a body representing a reference to a Mono<Book> corresponding to the ISBN provided as a path variable.
/book/ {isbn}	PUT	Updates the Book instance corresponding to the ISBN provided as a path variable and returns a response with a body representing Mono<Book> that emits the updated instance.
/book/ create	POST	Creates the Book instance using the data from the request body and returns a response with a body representing Mono<Book> that emits the created instance. The response has the location header populated with the URI to access the new instance.
/book/ delete/ {isbn}	DELETE	Deletes the Book instance corresponding to the ISBN provided as a path variable and returns an empty response.

ⓘ   We are using /book/by/{isbn} as URI to retrieve a book instance by ISBN because the type of the ISBN is String. If we were to declare a GET handler method with URI template /book/{isbn} for retrieving books by ISBN, this template would match GET requests on /book/random and /book/search, and the handler methods for the two URI templates are never called. The other solution would be to declare a regex for the {isbn} path variable, but the easiest way out was taken.

The configuration file for each of these services must be modified to add a MongoDB section since each of them needs access to its own collection. But the implementation is no different overall than any reactive service built in the book. Thus, they can also be tested using WebTestClient to make sure they work as expected. They can also be tested using curl to make sure they emit elements rendered by the presentation service.

Microservice with a Web Console

It has already been said that microservices communicate using agnostic protocols such as REST. The account-service, book-service, technews-service, and newreleases-service expose RESTful APIs over HTTP (although different communication channels can be used, such as JMS or AMQP).

The presentation-service is more interesting because it uses the data emitted by the other four(see Figure 13-2) and is getting it using REST API calls. This service exposes a web interface where an end user can access the data. To consume data produced by reactive services, Spring provides the WebClient interface that we have already used in previous chapters. WebClient sends HTTP requests and fetches data in several formats such as XML or JSON, or data streams.

The presentation-service microservice client uses a balanced WebClient to connect and request data from the other registered microservices. The balanced WebClient is agnostic of their location and the exact URI since Spring Cloud takes care of this under the hood.

The implementation of presentation-service is a little different as a web interface is configured for it. The Eureka server uses FreeMarker templates by default, so if a different implementation is desired, these have to be ignored via configuration by setting the spring.application.freemarker.enabled property to false. The configuration file is named presentation-service.yml, and its contents are depicted in Listing 13-9.

Listing 13-9. presentation-service.yml Configuration File

```
spring:
  application:
    name: presentation-service # Service registers under this name
  freemarker:
    enabled: false      # Ignore Eureka dashboard FreeMarker templates
  thymeleaf:
```

```
    cache: false
    prefix: classpath:/templates/

# HTTP Server
server:
  port: 7000    # HTTP (Netty) port
  address: 0.0.0.0
  context-path: /
  compression:
    enabled: true

# Discovery Server Access
eureka:
  client:
    registerWithEureka: true
    fetchRegistry: true
    serviceUrl:
      defaultZone: http://localhost:3000/eureka/

  instance:
    leaseRenewalIntervalInSeconds: 10
    preferIpAddress: false
info:
  app:
    name: presentation-service
    description: Spring Cloud Bookstore Service accessing data from all
other services
    version: 2.0.0-SNAPSHOT
```

Since presentation-service is a Spring Boot WebFlux application with
internationalized Thymeleaf templates, extra configuration must be added, as explained
in previous reactive chapters. The project is configured using a configuration class
annotated with @EnableWebFlux and the main Spring Boot class annotated with @
EnableEurekaClient to make this application a Eureka client.

Aside from the freemarker.enabled property is set to false to allow our application
to use Thymeleaf templates; the most important property in the previous configuration
is eureka.client.fetchRegistry that is set to true for this service. This property is

set to `false` for the other services because they do not care what other microservices are registered with the Eureka server. They were designed to be independent and stand-alone. They do not need data provided by other microservices to do their job. There is no need for them to register themselves with the Eureka server to ask about other registered services. The `presentation-service` microservice needs these microservices to do its job. After registering itself with the Eureka server, it needs to know if those are registered as well, and setting this property to `true` makes this happen.

Communication with the other microservices is facilitated by a load balancer named Ribbon.[11] The default Netflix Ribbon–backed load balancing strategy has been in place since Spring Cloud debuted in 2015. Ribbon is a client-side load balancer that provides control over the behavior of HTTP and TCP clients. Ribbon's Client component offers a good set of configuration options such as connection timeouts, retries, retry algorithm (exponential, bounded back off), and so on. Ribbon comes built-in with a pluggable and customizable Load Balancing component. Of course, because we are using Spring Boot, there is no need to tweak the default configurations too much. Ribbon is added by default as a dependency to the project when `spring-cloud-starter-netflix-eureka-client` is on the classpath, and is part of the `spring-cloud-netflix-ribbon` module. Ribbon is used under the hood by a balanced `WebClient` instance annotated with `@LoadBalanced` to identify existing microservices and direct calls.

In 2019, Spring Cloud switched to its own load balancer solution, and the Spring Cloud Netflix OSS projects were moved to the maintenance mode. To avoid Ribbon being used by default, the `spring.cloud.loadbalancer.ribbon.enabled` property must be set to `false`

Since `presentation-service` needs to access data from four other microservices, and `WebClient` is immutable once created, we need to create a `WebClient` bean for each microservice. We could do that and have four singleton `WebClient` beans injected everywhere, or we could use a builder bean. The builder bean creates balanced `WebClient` instances whenever needed and then discard them and let the garbage collector do its job.

`@LoadBalanced` can be placed on `WebClient.Builder` as well. In Listing 13-10, you can see the main Spring Boot configuration class, where the `WebClient.Builder` balanced bean is declared, and the routing function for this project.

---

[11]https://cloud.spring.io/spring-cloud-netflix/multi/multi_spring-cloud-ribbon.html

Listing 13-10. PresentationServiceApplication Configuration File

```
package com.apress.prospringmvc.presentation;

import org.springframework.cloud.client.loadbalancer.LoadBalanced;
import org.springframework.cloud.netflix.eureka.EnableEurekaClient;
import org.springframework.web.reactive.function.client.WebClient;
// other imports omitted

@EnableEurekaClient
@SpringBootApplication
public class PresentationServiceApplication {

    private static Logger logger = LoggerFactory
        .getLogger(PresentationServiceApplication.class);

    public static void main(String... args) throws IOException {
        System.setProperty("spring.config.name", "presentation-service");
        var ctx = SpringApplication.run(PresentationServiceApplication.
class, args);
        assert (ctx != null);
        logger.info("Started ...");
        System.in.read();
        ctx.close();
    }

    @LoadBalanced @Bean
    WebClient.Builder webClientBuilder() {
        return WebClient.builder();
    }

    @Bean
    public RouterFunction<ServerResponse> router(PresentationHandler
handler){
        return RouterFunctions
                .route(GET("/"), handler.main)
                .andRoute(GET("/index.htm"), handler.main)
                .andRoute(GET("/book/search"), handler.searchPage)
```

```
            .andRoute(POST("/book/search"), handler::retrieveResults)
            .andRoute(GET("/cart/checkout"), handler.checkoutPage)
            .andRoute(GET("/customer/register"), handler::registerPage)
            .andRoute(GET("/customer/login"), handler.loginPage)
            .andRoute(GET("/book/random"), handler::randomFragment)
            .andRoute(GET("/tech/news"), handler::newsFragment)
            .andRoute(GET("/book/releases"),
handler::releasesFragment);
    }
}
```

The `PresentationHandler` class is a simple custom class containing a lot of `Handler Function<ServerResponse>` to handle application requests. It uses `WebClient.Builder` to forward requests to the other microservices. Spring Cloud intercepts the requests and uses a custom `org.springframework.http.client.reactive.ClientHttpRequest` implementation that uses `org.springframework.cloud.client.loadbalancer. reactive.ReactiveLoadBalancer<ServiceInstance>` for microservice lookup and to facilitate interprocess communication in the cloud (or on a single machine as in this scenario).

> ℹ️   When writing code, if you need to reference the `ClientHttpRequest` directly, be careful not to mix it up with its non-reactive counterpart from the `org. springframework.http.client` package.

Out of the box, Spring Cloud provides an implementation for the `ReactiveLoadBalancer<T>` interface: the `org.springframework.cloud.loadbalancer. core.RoundRobinLoadBalancer` class that configures round-robin load balancing. Requests are randomly distributed across any number of configured instances. If you want to plug in your own load balancer, you can do so by providing your own class implementing `ReactiveLoadBalancer<T>`.

Now that we've covered how microservices are identified, let's check if it works by printing the microservices URIs where data for the `presentation-service` comes from in the console. Since we have four microservices, we need four `ReactiveLoadB alancer<ServiceInstance>`, since you know—immutability. The solution is to use `ReactiveLoadBalancer.Factory<ServiceInstance>` to create these reactive load balancer instances. For this purpose, we create a bean that has an init method that for each of our services uses the factory instance to create a load balancer, obtain the URI, and print it in the console. The code for the ServiceUriBuilder class is depicted in Listing 13-11.

Listing 13-11. ServiceUriBuilder Class

```
package com.apress.prospringmvc.presentation;
import org.springframework.cloud.client.ServiceInstance;
import org.springframework.cloud.client.loadbalancer.Response;
import org.springframework.cloud.client.loadbalancer.reactive.
ReactiveLoadBalancer;
//other imports committed

@Component
public class ServiceUriBuilder {
    private static Logger logger = LoggerFactory.
getLogger(ServiceUriBuilder.class);
    final ReactiveLoadBalancer.
Factory<ServiceInstance>  loadBalancerfactory;
    public ServiceUriBuilder(ReactiveLoadBalancer.Factory<ServiceInstance>
loadBalancerfactory) {
        this.loadBalancerfactory = loadBalancerfactory;
    }

    @PostConstruct
    public void getServiceURIs(){
        Flux.just("technews-service","newreleases-service","book-
service","account-service")
            .map(serviceId -> {
                ReactiveLoadBalancer<ServiceInstance> loadBalancer =
loadBalancerfactory.getInstance(serviceId);
                Flux<Response<ServiceInstance>> chosen = Flux.
from(loadBalancer.choose());
                chosen.map(responseServiceInstance -> {
                    ServiceInstance server = responseServiceInstance.
getServer();
```

```
                    var url = "http://" + server.getHost() + ':' + server.
                    getPort();
                    logger.debug("--->> {} : {}", serviceId, url);
                    return url;
                }).subscribe();
                return serviceId;
            }).subscribe();
    }
}
```

As you can see, the names given to the services using the Spring Boot configuration using the `spring.application.name` property are used as arguments for the `loadBalancerfactory.getInstance(String)` method that returns a `ReactiveLoad Balancer<ServiceInstance>` instance. Because it is a reactive component, calling `loadBalancer.choose()` returns a `Publisher<Response<ServiceInstance>>` (that is converted to a `Flux<T>` by wrapping it in `Flux.from(..)`) that emits the chosen server based on the load balancing algorithm. The `ServiceInstance` is extracted from the `Response<T>` object, and only now the microservice URI can be put together using its metadata.

If all works well, when starting the `presentation-service` application by running the Spring Boot executable class as you probably did hundreds of times by now, you should see some URIs printed in the console similar to the ones shown in Listing 13-12.

Listing 13-12. Output Generated by the `ServiceUriBuilder` Bean Containing the Microservices URIs

```
DEBUG c.a.p.presentation.ServiceUriBuilder - --->> technews-service :
http://192.168.0.14:4000
DEBUG c.a.p.presentation.ServiceUriBuilder - --->> newreleases-service :
http://192.168.0.14:5000
DEBUG c.a.p.presentation.ServiceUriBuilder - --->> newreleases-service :
http://192.168.0.14:5001
DEBUG c.a.p.presentation.ServiceUriBuilder - --->> newreleases-service :
http://192.168.0.14:5002
DEBUG c.a.p.presentation.ServiceUriBuilder - --->> book-service :
http://192.168.0.14:6001
DEBUG c.a.p.presentation.ServiceUriBuilder - --->> account-service :
http://192.168.0.14:6002
```

Do not expect all the URLs to be printed together or in the same order as in the previous listing. The results are obtained by invoking reactive functions, so the URIs might be scattered between other log statements.

Now that we've confirmed that the `presentation-service` application knows the location of the other microservices, let's see how a `WebClient` can access their data. The `PresentationHandler` class contains all handler functions of the project, and some of its content is depicted in Listing 13-13.

Listing 13-13. The `PresentationHandler` Class

```
package com.apress.prospringmvc.presentation;

import org.apache.commons.lang3.tuple.Pair;
// other imports omitted

@Component
public class PresentationHandler {
    private final PresentationService presentationService;

    public PresentationHandler(PresentationService presentationService) {
        this.presentationService = presentationService;
    }

    final HandlerFunction<ServerResponse> main = serverRequest -> ok()
        .contentType(MediaType.TEXT_HTML)
        .render("index");

    final HandlerFunction<ServerResponse> searchPage = serverRequest -> ok()
        .contentType(MediaType.TEXT_HTML)
        .render("book/search", Map.of(
                "categories", List.of(WEB, SPRING, JAVA),
                "bookSearchCriteria", new BookSearchCriteria()));

    public Mono<ServerResponse>  newsFragment(ServerRequest request) {
        final IReactiveSSEDataDriverContextVariable dataDriver =
                new ReactiveDataDriverContextVariable(presentationService.
                techNews(),
```

```
                              1, "techNews");

        return ok().contentType(MediaType.TEXT_EVENT_STREAM)
                .render("book/search :: #techNews",  Map.of("techNews",
dataDriver));
    }
        // other code omitted
}
```

The main handler function, when invoked, returns the realization of the index.html view template.

The searchPage handler function, when invoked, returns the realization of the search.html view template that requires two model attributes: categories and a BookSearchCriteria instance.

The newsFragment method returns a reactive view fragment populated with data emitted by the Flux<String> returned by the presentationService.techNews() call.

The PresentationService bean is the one using the balanced WebClient.Builder to make calls to the microservices presentation-service. Listing 13-14 shows the code of the techNews() method that returns Flux<String> emitting random tech news that is displayed on the search.html page.

In the same listing, the newReleases() method retrieves new books releases returned by newreleases-service as Flux<Book>.

Listing 13-14. The PresentationService Class

```
package com.apress.prospringmvc.presentation;
import org.springframework.web.reactive.function.client.WebClient;
// other imports omitted

@Service
public class PresentationService {
    private static final String TECHNEWS_SERVICE_URI = "http://technews-
service";
    private static final String NEWRELEASES_SERVICE_URI = "http://
newreleases-service";

    private WebClient.Builder webClientBuilder;
```

```java
public PresentationService(WebClient.Builder webClientBuilder) {
    this.webClientBuilder = webClientBuilder;
}

public Flux<Book> newReleases() {
return webClientBuilder.baseUrl(NEWRELEASES_SERVICE_URI).build()
        .get().uri("/book/releases")
        .retrieve()
        .bodyToFlux(Book.class).map(book -> {
            logger.debug("Retrieved book: {}", book);
            return book;
        });
}

public Flux<String> techNews() {
    return webClientBuilder.baseUrl(TECHNEWS_SERVICE_URI).build()
        .get().uri("/tech/news")
        .retrieve()
        .bodyToFlux(String.class).map(val -> {
            logger.debug("Retrieved val : {}", val);
            return val;
        });
}
// other code omitted
}
```

The WebClient.Builder is injected by Spring using the constructor.

Most methods in this class look similar, and as long as the microservices are up, the load balancer knows where to send the requests.

You've probably noticed the TECHNEWS_SERVICE_URI and NEWRELEASES_SERVICE_URI are not real URIs and have no ports. They are created by prefixing the service name with "http://". The load balancer intercepts WebClient requests to these URLs, and the URI to send the request to is reconstructed using the reconstructURI() method from the `org.springframework.cloud.client.loadbalancer.LoadBalancerUriTools` class.[12]

Sharing Classes

The `presentation-service` handles Book and Account objects, provided via Reactive Streams by `newreleases-service`, `books-service,` and `account-service`.

The `books-service` project contains a MongoDB document class named Book to represent book objects.

The `account-service` project contains a MongoDB document class named Account to represent account objects.

The `newreleases-service` project contains a very simple Book class, with three properties, those important for an upcoming book: title, author, and year. Random Book instances are created and emitted using an infinite reactive stream. The `presentation-service` makes a GET request to "/book/releases". These Book instances are sent to it using a reactive stream.

The `presentation-service` project contains a Book and an Account class, two simple POJOs dedicated to holding data displayed in the web interface.

This is a redundant, maybe lazy approach to keep the projects as decoupled as possible. There could be a project containing all common classes added to the classpath of all of them. But with the magic of JSON, having different classes in different projects is possible, and serialization and deserialization still work.

After all the microservices are up, you should be able to see them all in the Eureka web app and access the Bookstore application's web interface (see Figure 13-9).

---

[12]https://javadoc.io/doc/org.springframework.cloud/spring-cloud-commons/2.1.4.RELEASE/org/springframework/cloud/client/loadbalancer/LoadBalancerUriTools.html

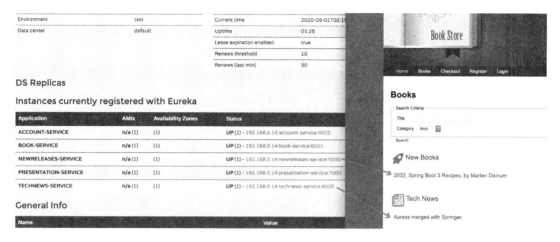

Figure 13-9. *Multiple microservices registered in Eureka and the Bookstore microservice application displaying data received from* `technews-service` *and* `newreleases-service`

Summary

This chapter offered a short introduction to the world of cloud development.

We showed you the difference between monolithic and microservices architecture and explained why applications made of multiple microservices are better for a cloud environment.

Spring Cloud makes it easy to practice development for the cloud in a local environment. Spring Boot applications can be easily converted to microservices by adding the Spring Eureka libs to the project.

You learned how to split a monolith into multiple independent microservices and use a discovery server to register them and ensure they can communicate with each other. Each Spring Boot microservice can be deployed onto its own VM in a private cloud or container in a Kubernetes cluster. As long as the discovery server is reachable, the services can still find each other.

Index

A

AcceptHeaderLocaleResolver, 113
Annotation-based controllers, 126, 127
    book search page
        BookSearchController, 157
        data binding, 159
        HttpServletRequest, 158
        results, 158
        search page form, 155
    detail page
        BookDetailController, 161
        detail.html page, 162
        details page, 163
        search page, 160
    login page, 149
        directory structure, 149
        login button page, 151
        LoginController, 151
        login.html, 150
        modification, 152, 153
        RedirectAttributes, 154
        RequestParam, 153
Apache Tomcat, 5, 7, 9, 13–16, 329
ApplicationContext implementations
    ant-style regular expressions, 38
    AOP concepts, 46, 47
    ApplicationContext hierarchy, 37
    component scanning, 38, 39
    configuration file, 34
    enabling features, 44–46

load resources, 37, 38
MoneyTransferSpring class, 35
profiles, 40–43
resource loading location, 33
scopes, 39
singleton, 39
specialized version, 32
Aspect-oriented programming (AOP), 21,
    46, 47, 222, 257
Asynchronous JavaScript and XML (AJAX)
    book search page, 267, 272
    FormContentFilter, 273, 274
    graceful degradation, 274
    HTML code, 266–268
    JSON producing method, 268–270
    progressive enhancement, 274
    RequestBody annotation, 271
    REST combination, 273, 274
    sending/receiving JSON, 270–273
    technologies, 264
    template.jsp header, 265
    web layer, 375
Authentication
    AbstractSecurityWeb
        ApplicationInitializer, 482
    AuthenticationProvider interface
        code, 488
    BookstoreAuthenticationProvider
        code, 489, 490
    configuration, 482, 485, 486

© Marten Deinum and Iuliana Cosmina 2021
M. Deinum and I. Cosmina, *Pro Spring MVC with WebFlux*, https://doi.org/10.1007/978-1-4842-5666-4

D

S

X, Y, Z

Printed in the United States
By Bookmasters